THE
REY CHOW
READER

EDITED BY **PAUL BOWMAN**

THE
REY CHOW
READER

COLUMBIA UNIVERSITY PRESS / NEW YORK

Columbia University Press
Publishers Since 1893
New York   Chichester, West Sussex

Library of Congress Cataloging-in-Publication Data
Chow, Rey.
The Rey Chow reader / edited by Paul Bowman.
p. cm.
Includes bibliographical references and index.
ISBN 978-0-231-14994-5 (cloth : alk. paper) — ISBN 978-0-231-14995-2 (pbk. :
alk. paper) — ISBN 978-0-231-52078-2 (e-book)
1. Culture. 2. Politics and culture. 3. Social change. 4. Poststructuralism.
5. Motion pictures—China. 6. Motion pictures and transnationalism. 7. Motion
pictures and globalization. 8. Culture in motion pictures.   I. Bowman, Paul,
1971– II. Title.

CB430.C4975   2010
306.2—dc22   2009052179

Columbia University Press books are printed on permanent and durable acid-free
paper.
This book is printed on paper with recycled content.
Printed in the United States of America

c 10 9 8 7 6 5 4 3 2 1
p 10 9 8 7 6 5 4 3 2 1

CONTENTS

CONTENTS

vii

Editor's Introduction

Cultural studies is an umbrella term covering a multitude of possibilities: studies of popular culture, national culture, regional culture, cross-cultural or intercultural encounters; studies of subculture and marginal or "subaltern" culture; studies focusing on questions and issues of class, gender, ethnicity, and identity; studies focusing on the significance and effects of different aspects and elements of technology, globalization, "mediatization," and virtualization; studies of the historical, cultural, and economic contexts of the production and consumption of literature, film, TV, and news media; studies elaborating on the cultural implications of government policy, law, legislation, educational paradigms, and so on; as well as studies concentrating on the myriad details of everyday life, approached in terms of anything from power to pleasure to politics. This diversity and heterogeneity can have a dizzying effect. On the one hand, it may seem that these different cultural studies are not connected or related and that the term *cultural studies* does not refer to anything in particular or designate a specific field.

On the other hand, many of these diffuse things and terms do seem to be interconnected, interimplicated, and interrelated. Despite being divergent and dislocated, these heterogeneous phenomena often seem to converge. Local practices of everyday life cannot be extricated from larger economic and political forces. Cultural activities and issues involve dimensions and decisions that are ethical and political. Phenomena that are often felt to be most intimate, private, and personal may be ensnared in or even produced by larger technologies. For instance, the printing press, the airplane, and the film camera have been instrumental in producing public and private sensibilities and passions and, hence, both collective and "individual" (or individuated) identities. The techniques of representation used in literature, newspapers, radio, TV, and film throughout their histories have been implicated in the production, amplification, or magnification of such structures of feeling as nationalism and racism and the emergence, manipulation, or management of personal, private, and group affects, sentiments, and investments.

Given the complexity of culture as a "field" of relations, connections, and separations, where should we begin? How are we to select, organize, and orient our scholarly, analytical, and interpretive efforts? What is to be deemed important, and on what grounds? As Stuart Hall once put it, because of the irreducible complexity of culture,

> it has always been impossible in the theoretical field of cultural studies—whether it is conceived either in terms of texts and contexts, of intertextuality, or of the historical formations in which cultural practices are lodged—to get anything like an adequate theoretical account of culture's relations and its effects.[1]

Given this complexity and uncertainty, the question is how might intervention be established? How does "motivated" work—whether scholarly, cultural, or political— fit in, connect with, affect, or alter anything else? In what relations do our efforts exist, and with what effects? In Hall's words,

> The question is what happens when a field, which I've been trying to describe . . . as constantly changing directions, and which is defined as a political project, tries to develop itself as some kind of coherent theoretical intervention? Or, to put the same question in reverse, what happens when an academic and theoretical enterprise tries to engage in pedagogies which enlist the active engagement of individuals and groups, tries to make a difference in the institutional world in which it is located? These are extremely difficult issues to resolve, because what is asked of us is to say "yes" and "no" at one and the same time. It asks us to assume that culture will always work through its textualities—and at the same time that textuality is never enough. But never enough of what? Never enough for what?[2]

In the wake of both poststructuralist and postcolonialist thinkers, including Louis Althusser, Michel Foucault, Edward Said, Jacques Derrida, Gayatri Spivak, and, indeed, Stuart Hall, as well as feminist theorists of film and culture like Laura Mulvey and Teresa de Lauretis, Rey Chow's work starts out from a number of what now may appear to be methodological and empirical "givens." Culture is regarded as always in some sense biased, and knowledge production or knowledge establishment as always in some sense contingent and conventional. In addition, these biases, contingencies, and conventions have ethical and political consequences. These postulates or propositions may seem uncontroversial or even commonplace today. But they owe their "givenness," intelligibility, and acceptability to some immensely significant and still contentious disciplinary innovations associated particularly with cultural studies, feminism, poststructuralism, and postcolonialism. At the same time, much of what is specific to Chow's interventions doubtlessly relates to the way she uses features of the contingencies of her own cross-cultural and cross-disciplinary intellectual history. (Chow's own account of the relations between her cultural and intellectual experiences in British Hong Kong and the United States is found in chapter 2, "The Postcolonial Difference: Lessons in Cultural Legitimation.") But Chow's own cross-cultural experience is never allowed to remain unquestioned in her work or to present itself as if her biography endowed her voice with an aura of cross-cultural legitimacy or postcolonial authenticity. Rather, Chow uses personal experience as a point from which to stage and illustrate investigations that interrogate the familiar by exposing it to very rigorous questioning and analysis.

Among assumptions often made is the idea that an ethnic subject owns or equals some kind of essential authenticity or truth or that the opinions of a traveler from "there" have the status of profound insights into the truth of "here." Rather than assuming anything like this, Chow's interrogations of the familiar do not proceed according to romantic or orientalist notions of the value of defamiliarizing the familiar by viewing it as if through foreign eyes, whether naïve (like, say, Mick "Crocodile" Dundee or Forrest Gump) or alienated through the excesses of hard experience (like Gulliver). Rather, Chow approaches the personal and familiar by attending to both the deeply felt problematics of postcolonialism and cultural studies and—perhaps surprisingly and certainly controversially—the rubrics and rigors of poststructuralist theory, as well as film theory, particularly feminist film theory.

In other words, Chow's work consistently executes the precise but difficult maneuver implied in Hall's famous injunction that responsible intellectual work must "say 'yes' and 'no' at one and the same time."[3] Chow consistently says (or "performs" a) "yes" to poststructuralist theory but "no" to some of its own biases and contingencies (what the vernacular of poststructuralism would call its own "founding violences," "enabling violations," inaugural "blind spots," and "constitutive outsides"), as she does, for instance, when she follows Spivak in identifying and analyzing poststructuralism's "Chinese prejudice."[4]

Chow also says "yes" to the fraught, felt, lived, and very real political stakes, exigencies, and urgencies that congregate, condense, and flare up around aspects and issues of race, ethnicity, and cultural identity. But this "yes" is accompanied by a clear "no" to any essentialist thinking or any thinking that would help notions of race, ethnicity, and nationalism to persist in ways that are *violent*—physically, institutionally, legislatively, or intellectually—toward other ethnicities, peoples, identities, or thoughts of self and other. In all Chow's studies, but especially in her work that develops Fredric Jameson's claim that stereotypes are inevitable in cross-cultural representations and encounters (see chapter 4), her interest is in working out how to ensure that the potentially violent antagonisms that always threaten to arise at the borders of cultures might be transformed—to use the vocabulary of Chantal Mouffe—from warlike *antagonistic* relations into productive/political *agonistic* interactions.[5] At the same time, however, Chow focuses on the problematic ways that even the most radical, subversive, or leftist Western thought is often indifferent to non-Western lives, cultural productions, and histories. This indifference is often the outcome of simple ignorance. But as Chow asks, how has such ignorance been historically sanctioned, and why is it all right to continue to "practice" it?

Chow's double-pronged methodological decision exemplifies the injunctions of both poststructuralism (particularly Derridean deconstruction) and cultural studies (particularly in such versions as the account given by Stuart Hall to which I have been referring).[6] Accordingly, it is not surprising that her work is not immediately understood by all readers. The decision to "say 'yes' and 'no' at the same time" without merely accepting or rejecting alternatives and also without simply sitting on the fence, is neither easy to execute nor easy for the reader to follow. Nevertheless, Chow's steps and conclusions are always remarkably concise and clear, even though her method proceeds according to the often declared need to think and analyze as fully, attentively, and rigorously as possible before making any interpretive decisions or declarations.

In this regard, Chow's work is reminiscent of that of Jacques Derrida. Indeed, it is important to note that even though Chow is now well known for her work in film studies, cultural studies, and so on, her writing has always involved the study of language, literature, and narrative. Even though her shift across disciplines may not always foreground her investment in the literary, questions of the literary, the figural, and the way in which language works are always present in her analyses. This investment is testified to by the fact that Chow has always held appointments in comparative literature and arguably owes her skills as a reader to the literary and theoretical training that is perceptible even in her analyses of film, media, and technology.

Chow's prose and arguments nonetheless differ in crucial ways from those of most deconstructionists and poststructuralists. This is not least because she has picked up the gauntlet thrown down by Gayatri Spivak, who, in her translator's preface to Derrida's *Of Grammatology*, points out that "although something of the Chinese prejudice of the West is discussed in Part I [of *Of Grammatology*], the *East* is never seriously studied or deconstructed in the Derridean text." This, Spivak explains, means that the enigmatic term "the *East*" exists in Derridean deconstruction "as the name of the limits of the text's knowledge."[7] Whereas poststructuralism has tended to ab/use the idea of "the East" by figuring it as the Other of Western metaphysics in long, circuitous, and discursive readings of aspects of "the West," Chow (like Spivak) states the problem directly.

This observation is not meant to reject or disdain deconstruction. As is well known, Derrida repeatedly argued that deconstruction was not, as his critics often claimed, either gratuitously complex or "irrational" or unjustifiably "excessive" but was, rather, a "hyperanalyticism."[8] That is, for Derrida, by being deliberately and hyperbolically inquisitive, deconstruction constituted an approach that was actually attempting to be responsible to the Enlightenment idea of reason, analysis, and argument. Chow subscribes to this poststructuralist, deconstructive argument, although she does not simply accept poststructuralism's belief in the necessity and value of "always making things more complicated." She even explores this trait of poststructuralism, historicizing it and exposing it to a Foucauldian-inspired "genealogical" analysis. Thus, rather than "being" poststructuralist or deconstructionist, Chow "does" deconstruction in such a way as to transform not only "external" cultural and political questions and topics but also many of the assumptions of poststructuralist and deconstructionist theory, philosophy, and analysis itself. She has been greatly influenced by Derrida but has also been receptive to thinkers like Lacan (as seen, for example, in chapter 9, "The Dream of a Butterfly") and increasingly to the legacies of Foucault. This range entails a shift from the more explicitly literary focus on the workings of language to other types of significations, problematizing poststructuralism while never abandoning the Derridean investments in language, alterity, supplementarity, and so on. In other words, Chow's double-pronged methodological decision produces an analytical machine that "holds theoretical and political questions in an ever irresolvable but permanent tension" and that "constantly allows the one to irritate, bother, and disturb the other, without insisting on some final theoretical closure."[9]

Many of the topics, themes, and problematics that concern Chow are familiar: the varieties and persistence of orientalism, racism, xenophobia, and sexism; the complexity of identity formation and its vicissitudes; the possibilities of cultural transformation and the policing of boundaries; the unequal lines of force structuring intercultural encounters; the ways that ideas such as "resistance," "revolution," and "change" have been approached, both academically and culturally (particularly in feminist and postcolonialist thought) and the ways in which these might be rethought. But if these themes are "familiar" at first glance, at least two things transform them when they arise in Rey Chow's work. The first is the remarkable revelatory effect that her double-pronged analytical approach has on the study of questions, texts, and debates. The second is the way that Chow treats what I call *empirical givens*, namely, those facts of cultural life whose importance is undeniable and yet whose significance is often overlooked, forgotten, or even foreclosed. These empirical givens include such putatively distinct events as the continued presence of the history of imperialism and colonialism, the dropping of atomic bombs on Nagasaki and Hiroshima in 1945, the globalization of academic languages and paradigms, and the emergence of the cinematic apparatus and its intervention in everyday life. Such givens may seem heterogeneous, discrete, and un- or underrelated, but in essays like "The Age of the World Target: Atomic Bombs, Alterity, Area Studies" (chapter 1), Chow amplifies the startling (and, again, all too easily overlooked) connections that can be made among all these phenomena, and more. As

xiii

the subtitle of "The Age of the World Target: Atomic Bombs, Alterity, Area Studies" indicates, there is a significant connection between the instruments and the instrumental decision making behind the military activity and their relation to academic knowledge production, specifically the construction of others, or "alterity," in the discipline of area studies.

The common link that Chow foregrounds and magnifies in these and other essays is the notion of *visuality*. Here she builds on thinkers and theorists like Benjamin and Heidegger, who regarded modernity as characterized not only by technologization, dislocation, massification, and the shocks and jolts of alienation but also by the technologies and techniques of visualization. Foucault came to regard methods of visualization such as mapping, measuring, diagramming, filming, registering, recording, revealing, demonstrating and "showing" (in all senses of the word) as part and parcel of "biopolitics." Chow follows Foucault's line of inquiry here. But following another line, she also takes up Heidegger's assertion that in modernity the world becomes a picture. Combining these arguments and adding elements from thinkers like Virilio, Chow adds that that if in modernity the world becomes a picture, it also becomes a target. For instance, crucial to American military domination was both the atomic technology itself and the cartographic and ballistic connections between "seeing" and "destroying."

Visuality is multiply inscribed in Chow's thinking. It has the status of a primary problematic in her thinking, and she pursues it in several senses: the importance of making visible in biopolitical administration; the impact of the cinematic apparatus as an epochal modern field in its own right and as a new cultural realm that sent shock waves through other cultural fields (such as literature), challenging them, altering their cultural status and their forms; the ethical and political implications of different "ways of seeing" in academic disciplines and cultural discourses; the implications of feminist film studies' assertion of "the primacy of to-be-looked-at-ness"; the significance of the resemblance of ethnography and anthropology to looking at animals in the zoo; and as we have seen, the way in which the shock of the atomic age entered the world primarily as an *image*: on the one hand, as the cinematic image of the mushroom cloud and, on the other, as the famous equation $E=mc^2$, which functioned primarily not as meaningful scientific algebra but as the other way of signifying the mushroom cloud, the unimaginably, unintelligibly terrible power of modern science.

Along with visuality, Chow focuses on *visibility*, two terms that are distinct but intimately related. Again, visibility has several senses. Chow considers it to involve more than mere literal vision (as in "I see it! There it is") or even metaphorical seeing (as in "Aha! I see! I understand!"). Instead, she directs us to the sense of "visibility as the structuration of knowability,"[10] in which she takes her inspiration broadly from Foucault and occasionally from Gilles Deleuze (especially in his explicitly Foucauldian moments).[11] But one might equally evoke Jacques Rancière's notion of the "partition of the perceptible" here, or Derrida's (or Attali's) focus on "hearing" and "audibility." That is, as Chow puts it, "becoming visible is no longer simply a matter of becoming visible in the visual sense (as an image or object)."[12] Besides visible images and objects, there is also a sense in which visibility should refer us to "the condition of possibility for what becomes visible." Whatever objects and images are visible, and the way in which they are visible, depends on what she calls "this other, epistemic sense of visibility."[13] Visibility and "making visible," then, are a more complex problematic than a simply empirical orientation could comprehend (or "see"). The political issues of visibility involve more than empirical considerations, such as the selection and makeup of who or what is represented where and when and how. They are, rather, "a matter of participating in a discursive politics of (re)configuring the relation between center and margins."[14] Translated from a visual to a phonic "image," Chow's argument is similar to Jacques Derrida's observation that "being-heard is structurally phenomenal and belongs to an order radically dissimilar to that of the real sound in the world."[15] In a political sense, "being-heard" is not a matter of shouting louder and louder but depends first on the establishment of a shared field of intelligibility as the condition of possibility for understanding ("hearing"/"seeing") and being understood (or "heard"/"seen").[16] The condition of possibility for any "shared meaning" (figured through visual or aural concept metaphors), and hence "intelligibility" or "visibility" per se, is already a complex "achievement," "construction," "outcome," or "stabilization."

Chow's work is supplemented by, and also can be said to supplement and clarify further, such theoretical and philosophical perspectives as those of Lacan, Derrida, Deleuze, and Rancière. Yet it does so not by giving further philosophical expositions or explications but by producing concrete analyses, demonstrations, and verifications through analyses of literature, film, cinema, identity, culture, and technology within the circuits of global capital and with specific reference to postcolonial contexts and scenes. By *visuality*, Chow refers us to the specific epistemological implications and cultural consequences of the cinematic apparatus. The technologies involved with and encapsulated in the film camera are cortical to contemporary cultural life and signal an epistemic "tectonic shift" in cultural logics the world over. As she argues in "The Political Economy of Vision in *Happy Times* and *Not One Less*; or, A Different Type of Migration" (chapter 13), "the ever-expanding capacities for seeing and, with them, the infinite transmigrations and transmutations of cultures—national, ethnic, rural, illiterate—into commodified electronic images are part and parcel of a dominant global regime of value making that is as utterly ruthless as it is utterly creative."[17]

The immense range and scope of the significances of the near-absolute hegemony of the regime of visuality have become more and more prominent and fundamental to Chow's orientation. Her concerns with visuality extend from its involvement in the most intimate aspects of subjective and intersubjective identity and cultural relationships to dimensions that are, in Heidegger's terms, the most "gigantic." In this sense, visuality refers to the epistemological rupture caused by filmic modernity. But it should be reiterated that this rupture is not simply filmic or relegated solely to a particular realm or context. Rather, it permeates what Foucault would term the entire *episteme*.

Within academia, Chow directs us to the emergence of visuality in the paradigm of *visualism*, a term that she appropriated from Johannes Fabian[18] and that she initially takes to refer to "a deeply ingrained ideological tendency in anthropology, which relies for its scientific, 'observational' objectivity on the use of maps, charts, tables, etc."[19] As we have seen, this tendency is attuned to the needs of both the instrumentalist approaches of militaristic or xenophobic interests in "the other" (conceived as a threat or target) and the needs of biopolitical governmentality. The paradigm of visualism also bears directly on the other signature theme that permeates almost all of Chow's work: ethnicity. Ethnicity organizes her first book, *Woman and Chinese Modernity* (1991), but does not emerge explicitly, directly, and forcefully until *Writing Diaspora* (1993).

Writing Diaspora opens with the question of the formulation and treatment of ethnicity, by Chinese and non-Chinese scholars alike, beginning with a reading of an essay by a Western academic who "attacks 'third world' poets for pandering to the tastes of Western audiences seeking 'a cozy ethnicity.'"[20] By considering the formulation of ethnicity implied in the reviewer's critique, Chow problematizes the various ways of handling the "fact" of ethnicity. It is necessary to problematize the givenness or naturalness of ethnicity because of the simple fact that—to borrow a phrase from Laclau and Mouffe—ethnicity "is not a datum but a construction."[21] That is, "having" or "being" this or that ethnicity is not an inevitability, and ethnicity is not a natural or spontaneous property of the world. Rather, notions, categories, and conceptual universes of ethnicity are discursive constructions. One is not *born* ethnic; one *becomes* ethnic. One's ethnic identity and cultural "place" and "status" are determined in contingent and variable ways.

Although this sort of argument will be familiar to many readers, this familiarity does not, of course, diminish its significance. Yet debates about ethnicity have attained a peculiarly banal predictability, so it is precisely the problem of this banal, stabilized, regularized dimension of debates about ethnicity that Chow isolates and interrogates. As she proposes, "Ethnicity is fast acquiring the kind of significance and signifying value that Foucault attributes to sexuality in the period since the seventeenth century."[22] That is, the issue of ethnicity involves a "discursive ferment" that is extremely regularized and predictable. As Chow argues, like the discourse of sexuality before it, the discourses "and mechanisms that surround 'ethnicity' in our time share many similar features with the 'repressive hypothesis' that Foucault attributes to the discourse of sexuality."[23] That is, she writes,

> one of the most well-known of Foucault's arguments is that sexuality is not natural but constructed, and that in the multiple processes of discursive constructions, sexuality has, however, always been produced as the hidden, truthful secret—that intimate something people take turns to discover and confess about themselves. The discursive, narrative character of the productions of sexuality means that even though our institutions, our media, and our cultural environment are saturated with sex and sexuality, we continue to believe that it is something which has been repressed and which must somehow be liberated. Foucault calls this "the repressive hypothesis," by which he refers to the restrictive economy that is incorporated into the politics of language and speech, and that accompanies the social redistributions of sex.[24]

This different form of this distinctive problematization of ethnicity is a consistent feature of Chow's work. In *Writing Diaspora*, Chow asserts, "Part of the goal of 'writing diaspora' is to *unlearn* . . . submission to one's ethnicity."[25] Such an apparently "theoretical" problematization of ethnicity is neither willful nor gratuitous. As she points out, for instance, one familiar aspect of the discourse of ethnicity is the element of autobiographical confession: the championing of speaking up; the regarding of speaking out as being a significant act of, first, "resistance" and, second, "emancipation." Without diminishing the historical importance of political movements that have involved this sense of consciousness raising and speaking out, Chow adds the supplementary point that because such discourses have now become regular and familiar, perhaps their political efficacy has not only waned but actually switched polarities. If we emphasize a Foucauldian approach, then it can clearly be seen that the belief that to speak out about oneself somehow amounts to an act of "resistance" or "emancipation" actually operates according to a "repressive hypothesis." Thus, cautions Chow,

> when minority individuals think that, by referring to themselves, they are liberating themselves from the powers that subordinate them, they may actually be allowing such powers to work in the most intimate fashion—from within their hearts and souls, in a kind of voluntary surrender that is, in the end, fully complicit with the guilty verdict that has been declared on them socially long before they speak.[26]

Moreover, Chow points out, "ethnicity can be used as a means of attacking others, of shaming, belittling, and reducing them to the condition of inauthenticity, disloyalty, and deceit."[27] Ironically, such attacks are "frequently issued by ethnics themselves against fellow ethnics, that is, the people who are closest to, who are most *like* them ethnically," in what she calls a "fraught trajectory of coercive mimeticism."[28]

Coercive mimeticism designates the way in which the forces of all different kinds of discourses and institutions *call* us into place, *tell* us our place, and work to *keep* us in our place.[29] These forces include (Althusserian) interpellation and (Foucauldian) discipline. According to Chow, coercive mimeticism ultimately works as "an institutionalized mechanism of knowledge production and dissemination, the point of which is to manage a non-Western ethnicity through the disciplinary promulgation of the supposed difference."[30] In the words of Étienne Balibar, to whom Chow frequently refers, "The problem is to keep 'in their place,' from generation to generation, those who have no fixed place; and for this, it is necessary that they have a genealogy."[31] In other words, even the work of well-meaning specialists of ethnicity, even expert scholars of ethnicity and ethnic experts in ethnicity, can reinforce ethnicized hierarchies structured in dominance, simply by insisting on (re)producing their field or object: ethnicity.

Chow proposes that it is helpful to compare and contrast nonwhite and white subjects, that is, "obvious" (nonwhite) ethnics and those who have ethnicity-without-ethnicity (whiteness). In her discussion, Chow considers the case of nonwhite ethnic critics, scholars, and academics. They, she argues, are pressured directly and indirectly to behave "properly"—to act and think and "be" the way "they" are supposed to act and think and be as nonwhite ethnic academic subjects. If they forget their ethnicity or their nationalistically or geographically—and hence essentialistically and positivistically—defined "cultures" and "heritages," such subjects will be deemed to be sellouts, traitors—*inauthentic*. But, Chow explains, if such an ethnic scholar "should . . . choose, instead, to mimic and perform her own ethnicity"—that is, to respond or perform in terms of the implicit and explicit hailing or interpellation of her as an ethnic subject as such, by playing along with the "mimetic enactment of the automatized stereotypes that are dangled out there in public, hailing the ethnic"[32]—"she would still be considered a turncoat, this time because she is too eagerly pandering to the orientalist tastes of Westerners"[33] and, this time, most likely by other nonwhite ethnic subjects. Thus, the ethnic subject seems damned if she does and damned if she doesn't "be" an ethnic subject. This damnation, of course, comes from different parties and with different implications. But Chow's point is that in contrast, "however far he chooses to go, a white person sympathetic to or identifying with a nonwhite culture does not in any way become less white."[34] Indeed, she claims,

> when it comes to nonwhite peoples doing exactly the same thing . . . —that is, becoming sympathetic to or identified with cultures other than their own—we get a drastically different kind of evaluation. If an ethnic critic should simply ignore her own

ethnic history and become immersed in white culture, she would, needless to say, be deemed a turncoat (one that forgets her origins).[35]

It is important to be aware that it is not just whites who pressure nonwhite ethnics to conform. Chow gives many examples of the ways that scholars of Chinese culture and literature, for instance, relentlessly produce an essentialist notion of China that is used to berate modern diasporic Chinese (and their cultural productions). That is, they produce an idea of an "essence" of "China" or "Chineseness" that no persons can live up to precisely because they are alive and, as such, contaminated, diluted, or corrupted by non-Chinese ("Western") influences.

Chow's focus on Chinese ethnicity, films, figures and phenomena may seem, at first glance, to be far from the concerns of those working on other aspects of film, culture, cultural politics, race, gender, and ethnicity, and the like. But appearances can be deceptive. As suggested earlier, Chow reveals the ways that "China" and "Chineseness" are figures (Derridean "specters" or "absent presences") that are inscribed (indeed, *hegemonic*) at the heart of the theoretical and political discourses of "Western" cultural studies, poststructuralism, and feminism. According to Chow, this is so in at least three ways. First, the Chinese "other" played a constitutive role in the deconstructive critique of logocentrism and phonocentrism, in ways that include, but exceed, the general "turn East" (in the search for "alternatives") characteristic of "French" theory and much else of the 1960s and 1970s. Second, Western feminism of the 1960s and 1970s admired and championed China's encouragement of women to "speak bitterness" against patriarchy. Third, the enduring interest in the "subaltern" in politicized projects in the West has always found an example in the Chinese peasantry. In these and other ways, says Chow, "'modern China' is, whether we know it or not, the foundation of contemporary cultural studies."[36]

Thus Chow recasts the investments and orientations of cultural studies, poststructuralism, and other politicized "suffix studies" according to the unacknowledged but constitutive "Chinese prejudice" that Spivak first identified. According to Chow, "China" has multiple statuses in Western discourses, including cultural studies. Besides representing the Other of capitalism, of freedom, of democracy, and so on, "China" offers to "radical thought" in the West an image of alterity, revolution, difference, alternativeness, and, hence, resistance as such. This is important because as Chow also observes, one of the most enduring metanarratives that has organized cultural studies and cultural theory (plus much more besides) is "resistance" as such. She argues:

> If there is a metanarrative that continues to thrive in these times of metanarrative bashing, it is that of "resistance": Seldom do we attend a conference or turn to an article in an academic journal of the humanities or the social sciences without encountering

some call for "resistance" to some such metanarrativized power as "global capitalism," "Western imperialism," "patriarchy," "compulsory heterosexuality," and so forth.[37]

The discourses of cultural theory and cultural studies do seem to be structured by keywords or, worse, buzzwords like *resistance, struggle, difference, hybridity,* and *multiculturalism.* Many scholars have interpreted this as evidence that such "radical" work is basically nothing more than fashionable nonsense. Rather than disregarding it, though, Chow proposes that one of the key problems with the notion of resistance resides in the consequences of its rhetorical construction. She contends that the popular rhetoric of resistance is itself implicitly organized and underwritten by a subject/object divide in which "we" speak against that which oppresses (capital, patriarchy, the West, etc.) and for (or "in the name of") the oppressed other. Thus, "we" rhetorically position ourselves as somehow "with" the oppressed and "against" the oppressors, even when "we" are more often than not at some distance from the sites and scenes of oppression.[38]

"Speaking out" and publicizing the plight of the oppressed may be regarded, of course, as *responsibility itself.* It is certainly the case that one dominant interpretation of academic-political responsibility is the idea that to be responsible we should speak out. It is equally the case, though, that unless the distances, relations, aporias, and irrelations are acknowledged and interrogated, there is a strong possibility that "our" discourse will become what Chow calls a version of Maoism. She explains:

> Although the excessive admiration of the 1970s has since been replaced by an often-times equally excessive denigration of China, the Maoist is very much alive among us, and her significance goes far beyond the China and East Asian fields. Typically, the Maoist is a cultural critic who lives in a capitalist society but who is fed up with capitalism—a cultural critic, in other words, who wants a social order opposed to the one that is supporting her own undertaking. The Maoist is thus a supreme example of the way desire works: What she wants is always located in the other, resulting in an identification with and valorization of that which she is not/does not have. Since what is valorized is often the other's deprivation—"having" poverty or "having" nothing—the Maoist's strategy becomes in the main a *rhetorical* renunciation of the material power that enables her rhetoric.[39]

In other words, such rhetoric claims a "position of powerlessness" in order to claim a particular form of "moral power":[40] a conceptual and rhetorical mix that can be seen to underpin much academic work today. Derrida regularly referred to this position as "clear-consciencism," namely, the belief that speaking out, speaking for, speaking against, and so on equals being responsible. However, Derrida also believed in the promise of the "most classical of protocols" of questioning and critical vigilance as ways to avoid the greater violence of essentialist fundamentalisms. Unfortunately, Derrida's work of questioning how to interpret "responsibility" and how to establish who "we" are, in what relations "we" exist, and what our responsibilities might be (drawing them into what he called the "ordeal of undecidability") was often regarded as an advocacy of theoretical obscurantism and irresponsibility. This charge was—and remains—the most typical type of "resistance" to deconstruction. Despite the clarity and urgency of Derrida's reasons for subjecting all presumed certainties to the ordeal of undecidability, the resistance to deconstruction surely points to a distaste for the complexity of Derrida's ensuing close readings/ rewritings of texts.[41]

Such a resistance to deconstruction is familiar. It is often couched as a resistance to theory made in the name of a resistance to "disengagement," a resistance to "theory" for the sake of "keeping it real." This rationale for rejecting deconstruction (or, indeed, "theory" as such) is widespread. But when "keeping it real" relies on refusing to interrogate the ethical and political implications of one's own rhetorical and conceptual coordinates—one's own "key terms"—the price is too high. Chow identifies some of the ways and places in which this high price is paid, and she reflects on the consequences of it. For instance, in politicized contexts such as postcolonial cultural studies, "deconstruction" and "theory" are sometimes classified (reductively) as being "Western" and therefore as being just another cog in the Western hegemonic (colonial, imperial) apparatus. As Chow states, in studies of non-Western cultural others, organized by postcolonial antiimperialism, all things putatively "Western" become suspect. Accordingly, "the general criticism of Western imperialism" can lead to the rejection of "Western" approaches at the same time as "the study of non-Western cultures easily assumes a kind of moral superiority, since such cultures are often also those that have been colonized and ideologically dominated by the West."[42] In other words, "for all its fundamental questioning of Western logocentrism," "theory" is too hastily "lumped together with everything 'Western' and facilely rejected as a non-necessity."[43] Unfortunately,

in the name of studying the West's "others," then, the *critique* of cultural politics that is an inherent part of both poststructural theory and cultural studies is pushed aside, and "culture" returns to a coherent, idealist essence that is outside language and outside mediation. Pursued in a morally complacent, antitheoretical mode, "culture" now functions as a shield that hides the positivism, essentialism, and nativism—and with them the continual acts of hierarchization, subordination, and marginalization—that have persistently accompanied the pedagogical practices of area studies; "cultural studies" now becomes a means of legitimizing continual conceptual and methodological irresponsibility in the name of cultural otherness.[44]

What is at stake here is that even the honest and principled or declared aim of studying others can amount to working for the very forces one opposes or seeks to resist. Chow clarifies this by considering the *uncanny proximity but absolute difference* between cultural studies and area studies. That is, area studies is a disciplinary field that "has long been producing 'specialists' who report to North American political and civil arenas about 'other' civilizations, 'other' regimes, 'other' ways of life, and so forth."[45] Unlike cultural studies and postcolonial studies' declared aims and affiliative interests in alterity and "other cultures," however, in area studies "others" ("defined by way of particular geographical areas and nation states, such as South Asia, the Middle East, East Asia, Latin America, and countries of Africa") are studied as if they were potential threats, challenges, and—hence—ultimately "information target fields."[46]

Thus, Chow maintains, there is "a major difference" between cultural studies and area studies—and indeed between cultural studies and "normal" academic disciplines per se.[47] This difference comes down to a paradigmatic decision, itself an act or effort of resistance. This is the resistance to "proper" disciplinarity; the resistance to becoming "normal" or "normalized," wherever it might equal allowing power inequalities, untranslatables, and heterogeneities to evaporate in the production of universalistic "objective" knowledge. This is why Chow's attitude is always that

> in the classroom, . . . students should not be told simply to reject "metadiscourses" in the belief that by turning to the "other" cultures—by turning to "culture" as the "other" of metadiscourses—they would be able to overturn existing boundaries of knowledge production that, in fact, continue to define and dictate their own discourses. Questions of authority, and with them hegemony, representation, and right, can be dealt with adequately only if we insist on the careful analyses of texts, on responsibly engaged rather than facilely dismissive judgments, and on deconstructing the ideological assumptions in discourses of "opposition" and "resistance" as well as in discourses of mainstream power. Most of all, as a form of exercise in "cultural literacy," we need to continue to train our students to read—to read arguments on their own terms rather than discarding them perfunctorily and prematurely—not in order to find out about authors' original intent but in order to ask, "Under what circumstances would such an argument—no matter how preposterous—make sense? With what assumptions does it produce meanings? In what ways and to what extent does it legitimize certain kinds of cultures while subordinating or outlawing others?" Such are the questions of power and domination as they relate, ever asymmetrically, to the dissemination of knowledge. Old-fashioned questions of pedagogy as they are, they nonetheless demand frequent reiteration in order for cultural studies to retain its critical and political impetus in the current intellectual climate.[48]

In light of the complexity and double movements of Chow's work, it simply is not possible to disentangle, separate out, and compartmentalize these diverse but interconnected themes as they run through her work. Nevertheless, it is possible to group her texts according to certain similarities and affinities and to distinguish certain of her works from others. Consequently, this book is organized according to certain tendencies and impulses in Chow's work into two nominally discrete sections. The first is entitled "Modernity and Postcolonial Ethnicity," and the second, "Filmic Visuality and Transcultural Politics." The texts in part 1 deal with issues of technologized modernity and the politics of ethnicity, in ways that are both direct and unexpected. Part 2 contains works that are obviously filmic in focus. As readers will find, these key words are umbrella terms covering a dense and rich texture of lucid and compelling analysis and argument, whose significance and implications open out into unexpected fields and exceed simple categorization or compartmentalization.

Acknowledgments

The author, editor, and publisher wish to thank the following for permission to reproduce material previously published elsewhere: Duke University Press, for chapter 1, "The Age of the World Target: Atomic Bombs, Alterity, Area Studies," first published in *The Age of the World Target: Self-Referentiality in War, Theory, and Comparative Work* (2006), 25–43; and also for chapter 11, "A Filmic Staging of Postwar Geotemporal Politics: On Akira Kurosawa's *No Regrets for Our Youth*, Sixty Years Later," in *Modern Chinese Literary and Cultural Studies in the Age of Theory: Reimagining a Field* (2000), first published in *boundary 2* 34, no. 1 (2007): 67–77. *Postcolonial Studies* for chapter 2, "The Postcolonial Difference: Lessons in Cultural Legitimation," first published in *Postcolonial Studies* 1, no. 2 (1998): 161–69. Indiana University Press for chapter 3, excerpt from "Introduction: Leading Questions," first published in *Writing Diaspora: Tactics of Intervention in Contemporary Cultural Studies* (1993), 1–22; also chapter 5, "The Politics of Admittance: Female Sexual Agency, Miscegenation, and the Formation of Community in Frantz Fanon," and chapter 9, "The Dream of a Butterfly," both first published in *Ethics After Idealism: Theory—Culture—Ethnicity—Reading* (1998), 55–73 and 74–97. Columbia University Press for chapter 4, "Brushes with the-Other-as-Face: Stereotyping and Cross-Ethnic Representation," and chapter 6, "When Whiteness Feminizes . . . : Some Consequences of a Supplementary Logic," both first published in *The Protestant Ethnic and the Spirit of Capitalism* (2002), 54–60 and 154–160; chapter 10, "Film as Ethnography; or, Translation Between Cultures in the Postcolonial World," first published in *Primitive Passions: Visuality, Sexuality, Ethnography, and Contemporary Chinese Cinema* (1995), 176–202; chapter 12, excerpt from the introduction to *Sentimental Fabulations, Contemporary Chinese Films: Attachment in the Age of Global Visibility* (2007), 1–17; and chapter 13, an excerpt from *Sentimental Fabulations*, 146–65. Oxford University Press for chapter 7, "Film and Cultural Identity," first published in *The Oxford Guide to Film Studies*, ed. J. Hill et al. (1998), 169–75; and the University of Minnesota Press for chapter 8, "Seeing Modern China: Toward a Theory of Ethnic Spectatorship," first published in *Woman and Chinese Modernity: The Politics of Reading Between West and East* (1990), 3–33.

THE REY CHOW READER

PART 1

MODERNITY AND POSTCOLONIAL ETHNICITY

The establishment of knowledge, hierarchy, structure, and order is not a neutral or natural process, as it always involves the more or less conscious taking of decisions, decisions that have consequences. Likewise, part 1 also is about contexts, orientations, starting points, and the taking of decisions and their consequences. In the first chapter, "The Age of the World Target: Atomic Bombs, Alterity, Area Studies," Chow analyzes the epochal (epistemic) significance of the instruments and rationality culminating in the decision to drop two atomic bombs on Japan in World War II, as well as the enormity and ongoing ramifications of these events. The second chapter, "The Postcolonial Difference: Lessons in Cultural Legitimation," is an autobiographically organized account of Chow's own orientations within (and vis-à-vis) the field of postcolonial studies. But this is not merely a personal narrative. Instead, Chow's account emphasizes certain "lessons in cultural legitimation," lessons about the lines of force and bias that structure and guide intellectual and cultural work. Such unacknowledged and unconsidered biases, assumptions, and prejudices are considered further in the third chapter, an excerpt from "Introduction: Leading Questions" (from *Writing Diaspora*). Here Chow tackles the persistence of orientalism and the processes by which scholars regularly "sanctify" and fetishize "the other," before considering alternative tactics of intervention in postcolonial cultural studies.

The starting point of any cultural encounter always includes "facing," in both the literal and metaphorical (catachrestic) senses; that is, individuals, groups, cultures, nations, and the like are said—at different times and in different ways—to "face" one another. They represent themselves and their others to themselves; they "look" and "contemplate" the other in ways that always entail both imaging and imagining. This relation is both inevitable and delicate. It also, of course, is highly consequential and is why Chow explores this relation in chapter 4, which faces up to what she calls "the inevitability of stereotypes." This "inevitability" is a difficult proposition for progressive thought in studies of ethnicity and culture to countenance, as it implies that we all are in some sense "violent," "reductive," "simplistic," and "unethical" in our first encounters with others. But Chow offers ways out of this impasse that do not require us to hide from the implications of the inevitability of stereotypes.

In a similar spirit, she engages with the implications of Frantz Fanon's theoretical treatment of women in his influential work on postcolonial community building, in chapter 5, "The Politics of Admittance: Female Sexual Agency, Miscegenation, and the Formation of Community in Frantz Fanon." The complex, deconstructive status of "woman" and "female agency" is explored again in chapter 6, which lays out the unstable status of "woman" in contemporary cultural criticism and clarifies some of the uncomfortable consequences of this constitutive instability for various schools of thought, from poststructuralist to Anglo-American feminism.

1

The Age of the World Target

ATOMIC BOMBS, ALTERITY, AREA STUDIES

For most people who know something about the United States' intervention in the Second World War, one image seems to predominate and preempt the rest: the dropping of the atomic bombs on Hiroshima and Nagasaki, pictorialized in the now familiar image of the mushroom cloud, with effects of radiation and devastation of human life on a scale never before imaginable.[1] Alternatively, we can also say that our knowledge about what happened to Hiroshima and Nagasaki is inseparable from the image of the mushroom cloud. As knowledge, "Hiroshima" and "Nagasaki" come to us inevitably as representation and, specifically, as a picture. Moreover, it is not a picture in the older sense of a mimetic replication of reality; rather, it has become in itself a sign of terror, a kind of gigantic demonstration with us, the spectators, as the potential target.

For someone such as myself, who grew up among survivors of Japan's invasion of China in the period of 1937–53—*banian kangzhan* or the "Eight Year War of Resistance" as it is still called among the Chinese—the image of the atomic bomb has always stood as a signifier of another kind of violence, another type of erasure. As a child, I was far more accustomed to hearing about Japanese atrocities against Chinese men and women during the war than I was to hearing about U.S. atrocities against Japan. Among the stories of the war was how the arrival of the Americans brought relief, peace, and victory for China; however hard the times were, it was said to be a moment of "liberation." As I grow older, this kind of knowledge gathered from oral narratives persists in my mind not as proof of historical accuracy but rather as a kind of emotional dissonance, a sense of something out-of-joint that becomes noticeable because it falls outside the articulations generated by the overpowering image of the mushroom cloud. It is as if the sheer magnitude of destruction unleashed by the bombs demolished not only entire populations but also the memories and histories of tragedies that had led up to that apocalyptic moment, the memories and histories of those who had been brutalized, kidnapped, raped, and slaughtered in the same war by other forces. As John W. Dower writes:

Hiroshima and Nagasaki became icons of Japanese suffering—perverse national treasures, of a sort, capable of fixating Japanese memory of the war on what had happened to Japan and simultaneously blotting out recollection of the Japanese victimization of others. Remembering Hiroshima and Nagasaki, that is, easily became a way of forgetting Nanjing, Bataan, the Burma-Siam railway, Manila, and the countless Japanese atrocities these and other place names signified to non-Japanese.[2]

Lisa Yoneyama sums up this situation succinctly: "Hiroshima memories have been predicated on the grave obfuscation of the prewar Japanese Empire, its colonial practices, and their consequences."[3] To this day many people in Japan still passionately deny the war crimes committed by the Japanese military in East and Southeast Asia, and the label "Japanese" is hardly ever as culturally stigmatized as, say, the label "German," which for many is still a straightforward synonym for "Nazi" and "fascist."[4]

But my aim in this chapter is not exactly that of reinstating historical, literary, or personal accounts of the innumerable instances of victimization during and after the war.[5] Rather, I'd like to explore the significance of the atomic bomb as an epistemic event in a global culture in which everything has become (or is mediated by) visual representation and virtual reality. What are some of the consequences in *knowledge production* that were unleashed with the blasts in the summer of 1945? To respond to this question, I turn briefly to the civil, pedagogical apparatus known as area studies: whereas it is common knowledge that area studies programs in the United States are a postwar, cold war, government-funded phenomenon, I want to ask how rethinking the most notorious U.S. action in the Second World War— the dropping of two atomic bombs—can complicate and change our conventional understanding of such programs.

SEEING IS DESTROYING

As an anonymous journalist commented in 1995, the fiftieth anniversary of the catastrophes, the bombs that fell on the two Japanese cities in August 1945 ended any pretense of equality between the United States and Japan. It was, he writes, "as if a steel battleship had appeared at Trafalgar, effortlessly and ruthlessly destroying the wooden enemy fleet. There was absolutely no contest."[6] Passages such as this rightly point to the fundamental shift of the technological scale and definition of the war, but what remains to be articulated is the political and ideological significance of this shift.

From a purely scientific perspective, the atomic bomb was, of course, the most advanced invention of the time. Like all scientific inventions, it had to be tested in order to have its effectiveness verified. It was probably no accident that the United

States chose as its laboratory, its site of experimentation, a civilian rather than military space, since the former, with a much higher population density, was far more susceptible to demonstrating the upper ranges of the bomb's spectacular potential.[7] The mundane civilian space in the early hours of the morning, with ordinary people beginning their daily routines, offered the promise of numerical satisfaction, of a destruction whose portent defied the imagination. Such civilian spaces had to have been previously untouched by U.S. weaponry so as to offer the highest possible accuracy for the postwar evaluations of the bombing experiments.[8] And, destroying one city was not enough: since the United States had two bombs, one uranium (which was simple and gunlike, and nicknamed Little Boy) and the other plutonium (which worked with the complex and uncertain means or assembly known as the implosion design, and was nicknamed Fat Man),[9] both had to be tested to see which one should continue to be produced in the future.[10] After the more "primitive" uranium bomb was dropped on Hiroshima, the more elaborate plutonium one was dropped on Nagasaki a few days later. The fact that there were Christians and U.S. prisoners-of-war in such spaces, which were therefore not purely Japanese or "enemy" territories, did not seem to matter. As Evan Thomas writes:

> If there was little debate over the moral rights and wrongs of atomizing Hiroshima, there was even less over Nagasaki; indeed, no debate at all. The operation was left to [General Leslie R.] Groves, who was eager to show that an implosion bomb, which cost $400 million to develop, could work as well as the trigger-type bomb that had destroyed Hiroshima. Exploding over the largest Roman Catholic cathedral in the Far East, the Nagasaki bomb killed an additional 70,000 people. The victims included as many Allied prisoners of war as Japanese soldiers—about 250.[11]

There are many ways in which the development of modern science, with its ever-more refined criteria for conceptualization, calculation, objectification, and experimentation, led up to these moments of explosion in what Michael S. Sherry calls "technological fanaticism."[12] Yet what was remarkable in the incident of the nuclear blast was not merely the complexity of scientific understanding but the manner in which science—in this case, the sophisticated speculations about the relationships among energy, mass, speed, and light—was itself put at the service of a kind of representation whose power resides not in its difficulty but in its brevity and ready visibility. In a flash, the formula $E = mc^2$, which summarizes Einstein's theory of relativity and from which the bomb was derived, captured the magnitude of the bomb's destructive potential: one plane plus one bomb = minus one Japanese city. Was the formula a metaphor for the blinding flash of the atomic explosion itself, or vice versa?

Precisely because the various units of measurement must be carefully selected for such a formula to be even approximately correct, and precisely because, at the same time, such exactitude is incomprehensible and irrelevant to the lay person, $E= mc^2$ exists far more as an image and a slogan than as substance, and far more as a political than as a scientific act. If the scientific accuracy and verifiability of this formula remain uncertain to this day, it was nonetheless a supremely effective weapon of persuasion and propaganda. The speed of light is supposed to be a maximum, the fastest anything could possibly travel. The speed of light *squared* is thus clearly and easily perceived as a very large multiplier. Because of its simplicity and visual representability, the formula successfully conveyed the important messages that one bomb could create great terror and that one airplane was enough to destroy an entire nation's willingness to resist. It seized the imagination, most crucially, of the non-scientist, such as the U.S. president who consented to dropping the bombs on Hiroshima and Nagasaki.[13]

With the gigantic impact of the explosion thus elegantly encapsulated—as if without effort—in a neat little formula that anyone could recall and invoke, an epochal destruction became, for the ordinary person, an instantly perceivable and graspable thing, like a control button at his or her command. In this manner, the most rarefied knowledge of science became conceptually democratized—that is, readily accessible, reproducible, and transmissible—as a weapon of attack.

I should make clear that what I am suggesting is not simply that hard science was replaced by a visual gimmick, that the "real thing" was replaced by a mere representation. Instead, it is that the dropping of the bombs marked the pivot of the progress of science, a pivot which was to continue its impact on all aspects of human life long after the Second World War was over. Science has, in modernity, reached the paradoxical point whereby it is simultaneously advanced and reduced. Having progressed far beyond the comprehension of nonspecialists and with complexities that challenge even the imagination of specialists, science is meanwhile *experienced* daily as the practically useful, in the form of minuscule, convenient, matter-of-fact operations that the lay person can manipulate at his or her fingertips. This is the situation to which Martin Heidegger refers in a passage such as this one from his well-known essay "The Age of the World Picture":

> Everywhere and in the most varied forms and disguises the gigantic is making its appearance. In so doing, it evidences itself simultaneously in the tendency toward the increasingly small. We have only to think of numbers in atomic physics. The gigantic presses forward in a form that actually seems to make it disappear—in the annihilation of great distances by the airplane, in the setting before us of foreign and remote worlds in their everydayness, which is produced at random through radio by a flick of the hand.[14]

Our daily uses of the light switch, the television, the computer, the cell phone, and other types of devices are all examples of this paradoxical situation of scientific advancement, in which the portentous—what Heidegger calls "the gigantic"—disappears into the mundane, the effortless, and the intangible. We perform these daily operations with ease, in forgetfulness of the theories and experiments that made them possible. Seldom do we need to think of the affinity between these daily operations and a disaster such as the atomic holocaust. To confront that affinity is to confront the terror that is the basis of our everyday life. For Heidegger, hence, the explosion of the atomic bomb is "the mere final emission of what has long since taken place, has already happened"[15]—a process of annihilation that began with the very arrival of modern science itself.

From a military perspective, the mushroom cloud of smoke and dust signals the summation of a history of military invention that has gone hand in hand with the development of representational technologies, in particular the technologies of seeing. As Paul Virilio asserts, "For men at war, the function of the weapon is the function of the eye."[16] Virilio argues time and again in his work that close affinities exist between war and vision. Because military fields were increasingly reconfigured as fields of visual perception, preparations for war were increasingly indistinguishable from preparations for making a film: "The Americans prepared future operations in the Pacific," Virilio writes, "by sending in film-makers who were supposed to look as though they were on a location-finding mission, taking aerial views for future film production."[17]

In the essay cited above, Heidegger argues that in the age of modern technology, the world has become a "world picture." By this, he means that the process of (visual) objectification has become so indispensable in the age of modern scientific research that understanding—"conceiving" and "grasping" the world—is now an act inseparable from the act of seeing—from a certain form of "picturing." However, he adds, "picture" in this case does not mean an imitation. As he explains:

> World picture, when understood essentially, does not mean a picture of the world but the world conceived and grasped as a picture. What is, in its entirety, is now taken in such a way that it first is in being and only is in being to the extent that it is set up by man, who represents and sets forth. Wherever we have the world picture, an essential decision takes place regarding what is, in its entirety. The Being of whatever is, is sought and found in the representedness of the latter.[18]

For Heidegger, the world becoming a picture is what distinguishes the essence of the modern age, and he emphasizes the point "that the world becomes picture is one and the same event with the event of man's becoming *subiectum* in the midst of that which is" (132). By the word *subiectum,* he is referring to "that-which-lies-before, which, as ground, gathers everything onto itself" (128). As such "ground," men struggle to conquer the world as *their own* particular pictures, bringing into play an "unlimited power for the calculating, planning, and molding of all things." As is clearly demonstrated by the case of the United States, science and research have thus become "an absolutely necessary form of this establishing of self in the world" (135).[19]

Supplementing Heidegger, we may say that in the age of bombing, the world has also been transformed into—is essentially conceived and grasped as—a target. To conceive of the world as a target is to conceive of it as an object to be destroyed. As W. J. Perry, a former United States Under Secretary of State for Defense, said: "If I had to sum up current thinking on precision missiles and saturation weaponry in a single sentence, I'd put it like this: once you can see the target, you can expect to destroy it."[20] Increasingly, war would mean the production of maximal visibility and illumination for the purpose of maximal destruction. It follows that the superior method of guaranteeing efficient destruction by visibility during the Second World War was aerial bombing, which the United States continued even after Japan had made a conditional surrender.[21]

If the dropping of the atomic bomb created "deterrence," as many continue to believe to this day, what is the nature of deterrence? (We can ask the same question about "defense," "protection," "security," and other similar concepts.) The atomic bomb did not simply stop the war; it also stopped the war by escalating and intensifying violence to a hitherto unheard of scale. What succeeded in "deterring" the war was an ultimate (am)munition; destruction was now outdone by destruction itself. The elimination of the actual physical warring activities had the effect not of bringing war to an end but instead of promoting and accelerating terrorism, and importantly, the terrorism of so-called "deterrent" weaponry. The mushroom cloud, therefore, is also the image of *this* semiotic transfer, this blurring of the boundary between war and peace. The transfer ushered in the new age of relativity and virtuality, an age in which powers of terror are indistinguishable from powers of "deterrence," and technologies of war indissociable from practices of peace. These new forces of relativity and virtuality are summarized in the following passages from Virilio:

> There is no war, then, without representation, no sophisticated weaponry without psychological mystification. Weapons are tools not just of destruction but also of perception—that is to say, stimulants that make themselves felt through chemical, neurological processes in the sense organs and the central nervous system, affecting human reactions and even the perceptual identification and differentiation of object. . . .
>
> By demonstrating that they would not recoil from a civilian holocaust, the Americans triggered in the minds of the enemy that *information explosion* which Einstein, towards the end of his life, thought to be as formidable as the atomic blast itself. . . .
>
> Even when weapons are not employed, they are active elements of ideological conquest.[22]

This fuzzing of the line between war and representation, between war technology and peacetime technology, has brought about a number of consequences.

First, the visual rules and boundaries of war altered. While battles formerly tended to be fought with a clear demarcation of battlefronts versus civilian spaces, the aerial bomb, by its positionings in the skies, its intrusion into spaces that used to be off-limits to soldiers, and its distance from the enemies (a distance which made it impossible for the enemies to fight back), destroyed once and for all those classic visual boundaries that used to define battle. Second, with the transformation of the skies into war zones from which to attack, war was no longer a matter simply of armament or of competing projectile weaponry; rather, it became redefined as a matter of the logistics of perception, with seeing as its foremost function, its foremost means of preemptive combat.

Third, in yet a different way, the preemptiveness of seeing as a means of destruction continues to operate as such even after the war. Insofar as the image of the atomic blast serves as a peacetime weapon to mobilize against war, it tends to preclude other types of representation. For a long time *nuclear* danger remained the predominant target against which peace coalitions aimed their efforts, while the equally disastrous effects caused by chemical and biological weapons (nerve gases such as sarin and bacteria such as anthrax) seldom received the same kind of extended public consideration until the Gulf War of 1991. The overwhelming effect of the continual imaging of the mushroom cloud means that the world has been responding to the nuclear blast as if by mimicry, by making the nuclear horror its point of identification and attack, and by being oblivious (until fairly recently) to other forms of damage to the ecosphere that have not attained the same level of *visibility*.

THE WORLD BECOMES VIRTUAL

The dropping of the atomic bombs effected what Michel Foucault would call a major shift in *epistemes,* a fundamental change in the organization, production, and circulation of knowledge.[23] War after the atomic bomb would no longer be the physical, mechanical struggles between combative oppositional groups, but would increasingly come to resemble collaborations in the logistics of perception between partners who occupy relative, but always mutually implicated, positions.[24] As in the case of the competition between the United States and the Soviet Union for several decades, war was more and more to be fought in virtuality, as an exchange of defensive positionings, a tacitly coordinated routine of upping the potential for war, a race for the deterrent. Warring in virtuality meant competing with the enemy for the stockpiling, rather than actual use, of preclusively horrifying weaponry. To terrorize the other, one specializes in representation, in the means of display and exhibition. As Virilio writes, "A war of pictures and sounds is replacing the war of objects (projectiles and missiles)."[25] In the name of arms reduction and limitation, the SALT and START agreements served to promote, improve, and multiply armament between the United States and the Soviet Union, which were, strictly speaking, allies rather than adversaries in the so-called "Star Wars" or SDI (Strategic Defense Initiative).[26]

Moreover, war would exist from now on as an agenda that is infinitely self-referential: war represents not other types of struggles and conflicts—what in history classes are studied as "causes"—but war itself. From its previous conventional, negative signification as a blockade, an inevitable but regretted interruption of the continuity that is "normal life," war shifts to a new level of force. It has become not the cessation of normality, but rather, the very definition of normality itself. The space and time of war are no longer segregated in the form of an other; instead, they operate from within the here and now, as the internal logic of the here and now. From being negative blockade to being normal routine, war becomes the positive mechanism, momentum, and condition of possibility of society, creating a hegemonic space of global communication through powers of visibility and control.

It is important to note that the normativization of war and war technology takes place as well among—perhaps especially among—the defeated. As Dower writes, in Japan, deficiency in science and technology was singled out as the chief reason for defeat, and the atomic bomb was seen simultaneously as "a symbol of the terror of nuclear war and the promise of science."[27] Because it was forbidden to advance in militarism, postwar Japan specialized in the promotion of science and technology for "peace" and for the consolidation of a "democratic" society. Instead of bombs and missiles, Japan became one of the world's leading producers of cars, cameras, computers, and other kinds of "high tech" equipment.[28] With Honda, Toyota, Nissan, Hitachi, Toshiba, Sony, Sanyo, Nikon, Mitsubishi, and their like becoming household names throughout the world, the defeated "victim" of the war rises again and rejoins the "victor" in a new competition, the competition in bombarding the world with a different type of implosion—information.[29]

With the preemptiveness of seeing-as-destruction and the normativization of technology-as-information, thus, comes the great epistemic shift, which has been gradually occurring with the onset of speed technologies and which finally *virtualizes* the world. As a condition that is no longer separable from civilian life, war is thoroughly absorbed into the fabric of our daily communications—our information channels, our entertainment media, our machinery for speech and expression. We participate in war's virtualization of the world as we use—without thinking—television monitors, remote controls, mobile phones, digital cameras, PalmPilots, and other electronic devices that fill the spaces of everyday life. We do not usually notice the strangeness of, say, listening to news on the radio about different calamities while preparing lunch or dinner, nor are we shocked by the juxtaposition on television of commercials with reports of rapes, tortures, or genocides. Our consumption of war, bloodshed, and violence through our communication technologies is on a par with our consumption of various forms of merchandise.

There is, furthermore, another side to the virtualization of the world which most of us do not experience but which is even more alarming: when a war does occur, such as the Gulf Wars that began in 1991 and 2003, the ubiquitous virtualization of everyday life means that war can no longer be fought without the skills of playing video games. In the aerial bombings of Iraq, the world was divided into an above and a below in accordance with the privilege of access to the virtual world. Up above in the sky, war was a matter of maneuvers across the video screen by U.S. soldiers who had been accustomed as teenagers to playing video games at home; down below, war remained tied to the body, to manual labor, to the random disasters falling from the heavens. For the U.S. men and women of combat, the elitism and aggressiveness of panoramic vision went hand in hand with distant control and the instant destruction of others; for the ordinary men, women, and children of Iraq (as for the ordinary people of Korea and Vietnam in the 1950s and 1960s), life became more and more precarious—immaterial in the sense of a readiness for total demolition at any moment.[30] Even as we speak, the Pentagon is reported to be building its own Internet for the wars of the future, with the goal "to give all American commanders and troops [including those on the ground] a moving picture of all foreign enemies and Threats—'a God's-eye view' of battle."[31]

THE ORBIT OF SELF AND OTHER

Among the most important elements in war, writes Karl von Clausewitz, are the "moral elements."[32] From the United States' point of view, this phrase does not seem at all ironic. Just as the bombings of Afghanistan and Iraq in the first few years of the twenty-first century were justified as benevolent acts to preserve the United States and the rest of the world against "the axis of evil," "weapons of mass destruction," and the like, so were the bombings of Hiroshima and Nagasaki considered pacific acts, acts that were meant to save lives and save civilization in a world threatened by German Nazism. (Though, by the time the bombs were dropped in Japan, Germany had already surrendered.) Even today, some of the most educated, scientifically knowledgeable members of U.S. society continue to believe that the atomic bomb was the best way to terminate the hostilities.[33] And, while the media in the United States are quick to join the media elsewhere in reporting the controversies over Japan's refusal to apologize for its war crimes in Asia or over France's belatedness in apologizing for the Vichy Government's persecution of the Jews, no

U.S. head of state has ever visited Hiroshima or Nagasaki, or expressed regret for the nuclear holocaust.[34] In this—its absolute conviction of its own moral superiority and legitimacy—lies perhaps the most deeply ingrained connection between the foundation myth of the United States as an exceptional nation and the dropping of the atomic bombs (as well as all the military and economic interventions the United States has made in nationalist struggles in Asia, Latin America, and the Middle East since the Second World War).[35] Even on occasions such as Pearl Harbor (December 7, 1941) and September 11, 2001, when the United States had to recognize that it was just part of the world (and hence could be attacked like any other country), its response was typically that of reasserting U.S. exceptionalism—This cannot happen to us! We are unique, we cannot be attacked!—by ferociously attacking others.

In the decades since 1945, whether in dealing with the Soviet Union, the People's Republic of China, North Korea, Vietnam, and countries in Central America, or during the Gulf Wars, the United States has been conducting war on the basis of a certain kind of knowledge production, and producing knowledge on the basis of war. War and knowledge enable and foster each other primarily through the collective fantasizing of some foreign or alien body that poses danger to the "self" and the "eye" that is the nation. Once the monstrosity of this foreign body is firmly established in the national consciousness, the decision makers of the U.S. government often talk and behave as though they had no choice but war.[36] War, then, is acted out as a moral obligation to expel an imagined dangerous alienness from the United States' self-concept as the global custodian of freedom and democracy. Put in a different way, the "moral element," insofar as it produces knowledge about the "self" and "other"—and hence the "eye" and its "target"—as such, justifies war by its very dichotomizing logic. Conversely, the violence of war, once begun, fixes the other in its attributed monstrosity and affirms the idealized image of the self.

In this regard, the pernicious stereotyping of the Japanese during the Second World War—not only by U.S. military personnel but also by social and behavioral scientists—was simply a flagrant example of an ongoing ideological mechanism that had accompanied Western treatments of non-Western "others" for centuries. In the hands of academics such as Geoffrey Gorer, writes Dower, the notion that was collectively and "objectively" formed about the Japanese was that they were "a clinically compulsive and probably collectively neurotic people, whose lives were governed by ritual and 'situational ethics,' wracked with insecurity, and swollen with deep, dark currents of repressed resentment and aggression."[37] As Dower points out, such stereotyping was by no means accidental or unprecedented:

> The Japanese, so "unique" in the rhetoric of World War Two, were actually saddled
> with racial stereotypes that Europeans and Americans had applied to nonwhites for
> centuries: during the conquest of the New World, the slave trade, the Indian wars in

the United States, the agitation against Chinese immigrants in America, the coloniza-tion of Asia and Africa, the U.S. conquest of the Philippines at the turn of the century. These were stereotypes, moreover, which had been strongly reinforced by nineteenth-century Western science.

In the final analysis, in fact, these favored idioms denoting superiority and infe-riority transcended race and represented formulaic expressions of Self and *Other* in general.[38]

The moralistic divide between "self" and "other" constitutes the production of knowledge during the U.S. Occupation of Japan after the Second World War as well. As Monica Braw writes, in the years immediately after 1945, the risk that the United States would be regarded as barbaric and inhumane was carefully monitored, in the main by cutting off Japan from the rest of the world through the ban on travel, con-trol of private mail, and censorship of research, mass media information, and other kinds of communication. The entire Occupation policy was permeated by the view that "the United States was not to be accused; guilt was only for Japan":[39]

> As the Occupation of Japan started, the atmosphere was military. Japan was a defeated
> enemy that must be subdued. The Japanese should be taught their place in the world:
> as a defeated nation, Japan had no status and was entitled to no respect. People should
> be made to realize that any catastrophe that had befallen them was of their own mak-
> ing. Until they had repented, they were suspect. If they wanted to release information
> about the atomic bombings of Hiroshima and Nagasaki, it could only be for the wrong
> reasons, such as accusing the United States of inhumanity. Thus this information
> was suppressed.[40]

As in the scenario of aerial bombing, the elitist and aggressive panoramic "vision" in which the other is beheld means that the sufferings of the other matter much less than the transcendent aspirations of the self. And, despite being the products of a particular culture's technological fanaticism, such transcendent aspirations are typically expressed in the form of selfless universalisms. As Sherry puts it, "The reality of Hiroshima and Nagasaki seemed less important than the bomb's effect on 'mankind's destiny,' on 'humanity's choice,' on 'what is happening to men's minds,' and on hopes (now often extravagantly revived) to achieve world govern-ment."[41] On Japan's side, as Yoneyama writes, such a "global narrative of the univer-sal history of humanity" has helped sustain "a national victimology and phantasm of innocence throughout most of the postwar years." Going one step further, she remarks: "The idea that Hiroshima's disaster ought to be remembered from the transcendent and anonymous position of humanity . . . might best be described as 'nuclear universalism.'"[42]

Once the relations among war, racism, and knowledge production are under-lined in these terms, it is no longer possible to assume, as some still do, that the recognizable features of modern war—its impersonality, coerciveness, and deliberate cruelty—are "divergences" from the "antipathy" to violence and to con-flict that characterize the modern world.[43] Instead, it would be incumbent on us to realize that the pursuit of war—with its use of violence—and the pursuit of peace—with its cultivation of knowledge—are the obverse and reverse of the same coin, the coin that I have been calling "the age of the world target." Rather than being irreconcilable opposites, war and peace are coexisting, collaborative func-tions in the continuum of a virtualized world. More crucially still, only the privi-leged nations of the world can afford to wage war and preach peace at one and the same time. As Sherry writes, "The United States had different resources with which to be fanatical: resources allowing it to take the lives of others more than its own, ones whose accompanying rhetoric of technique disguised the will to destroy."[44] From this it follows that, if indeed political and military acts of cruelty are not unique to the United States—a point which is easy enough to substanti-ate—what is nonetheless remarkable is the manner in which such acts are, in the United States, usually cloaked in the form of enlightenment and altruism, in the form of an aspiration simultaneously toward technological perfection and the pursuit of peace. In a country in which political leaders are held accountable for their decisions by an electorate, violence simply cannot—as it can in totalitarian countries—exist in the raw. Even the most violent acts must be adorned with a benign, rational story.

It is in the light of such interlocking relations among war, racism, and knowl-edge production that I would make the following comments about area studies, the academic establishment that crystallizes the connection between the epistemic targeting of the world and the "humane" practices of peacetime learning.

FROM ATOMIC BOMBS TO AREA STUDIES

As its name suggests, area studies as a mode of knowledge production is, strictly speaking, military in its origins. Even though the study of the history, languages, and literatures of, for instance, "Far Eastern" cultures existed well before the Second World War (in what Edward W. Said would term the old Orientalist tradition predi-cated on philology), the systematization of such study under the rubric of special geopolitical areas was largely a postwar and U.S. phenomenon. In H. D. Harootuni-an's words, "The systematic formation of area studies, principally in major universi-ties, was . . . a massive attempt to relocate the enemy in the new configuration of the Cold War."[45] As Bruce Cumings puts it:

It is now fair to say, based on the declassified evidence, that the American state and especially the intelligence elements in it shaped the entire field of postwar area studies, with the clearest and most direct impact on those regions of the world where communism was strongest: Russia, Central and Eastern Europe, and East Asia."[46]

In the decades after 1945, when the United States competed with the Soviet Union for the power to rule and/or destroy the world, these regions were the ones that required continued, specialized super-*vision*; to this list we may also add Southeast Asia, Latin America, and the Middle East. As areas to be studied, these regions took on the significance of target fields—fields of information retrieval and dissemination that were necessary for the perpetuation of the United States' political and ideological hegemony.

In the final part of his classic *Orientalism*, Said describes area studies as a continuation of the old European Orientalism with a different pedagogical emphasis:

> No longer does an Orientalist try first to master the esoteric languages of the Orient; he begins instead as a trained social scientist and "applies" his science to the Orient, or anywhere else. This is the specifically American contribution to the history of Orientalism, and it can be dated roughly from the period immediately following World War II, when the United States found itself in the position recently vacated by Britain and France.[47]

Whereas Said draws his examples mainly from Islamic and Middle Eastern area studies, Cumings provides this portrait of the East Asian target field:

> The Association for Asian Studies (AAS) was the first "area" organization in the U.S., founded in 1943 as the Far Eastern Association and reorganized as the AAS in 1956. Before 1945 there had been little attention to and not much funding for such things; but now the idea was to bring contemporary social science theory to bear on the non-Western world, rather than continue to pursue the classic themes of Oriental studies, often examined through philology. . . . In return for their sufferance, the Orientalists would get vastly enhanced academic resources (positions, libraries, language studies)— and soon, a certain degree of separation which came from the social scientists inhabiting institutes of East Asian studies, whereas the Orientalists occupied departments of East Asian languages and cultures. This implicit Faustian bargain sealed the postwar academic deal.[48]

A largely administrative enterprise, closely tied to policy, the new American Orientalism took over from the old Orientalism attitudes of cultural hostility, among which is, as Said writes, the dogma that "the Orient is at bottom something either to be feared (the Yellow Peril, the Mongol hordes, the brown dominions) or to be controlled (by pacification, research and development, outright occupation whenever possible)."[49]

Often under the modest and apparently innocuous agendas of fact gathering and documentation, the "scientific" and "objective" production of knowledge during peacetime about the various special "areas" became the institutional practice that substantiated and elaborated the militaristic conception of the world as target.[50] In other words, despite the claims about the apolitical and disinterested nature of the pursuits of higher learning, activities undertaken under the rubric of area studies, such as language training, historiography, anthropology, economics, political science, and so forth, are fully inscribed in the politics and ideology of war. To that extent, the disciplining, research, and development of so-called academic information are part and parcel of a *strategic* logic. And yet, if the production of knowledge (with its vocabulary of aims and goals, research, data analysis, experimentation, and verification) in fact shares the same scientific and military premises as war—if, for instance, the ability to translate a difficult language can be regarded as equivalent to the ability to break military codes[51]—is it a surprise that it is doomed to fail in its avowed attempts to "know" the other cultures? Can "knowledge" that is derived from the same kinds of bases as war put an end to the violence of warfare, or is such knowledge not simply warfare's accomplice, destined to destroy rather than preserve the forms of lives at which it aims its focus?

As long as knowledge is produced in this self-referential manner, as a circuit of targeting or *getting* the other that ultimately consolidates the omnipotence and omnipresence of the sovereign "self"/"eye"—the "I"—that is the United States, the other will have no choice but remain just that—a target whose existence justifies only one thing, its destruction by the bomber. As long as the focus of our study of Asia remains the United States, and as long as this focus is not accompanied by knowledge of what is happening elsewhere at other times as well as at the present, such study will ultimately confirm once again the self-referential function of virtual worlding that was unleashed by the dropping of the atomic bombs, with the United States always occupying the position of the bomber, and other cultures always viewed as the military and information target fields. In this manner, events whose historicity does not fall into the epistemically closed orbit of the atomic bomber—such as the Chinese reactions to the war from a primarily anti-Japanese point of view that I alluded to at the beginning of this chapter—will never receive the attention that is due to them. "Knowledge," however conscientiously gathered and however large in volume, will lead only to further silence and to the silencing of diverse experiences.[52] This is one reason why, as Harootunian remarks, area studies has been, since its inception, haunted by "the absence of a definable object"—and by "the problem of the vanishing object."[53]

As Harootunian goes on to argue, for all its investment in the study of other languages and other cultures, area studies missed the opportunity, so aptly provided by Said's criticism of Orientalism, to become the site where a genuinely alternative form of knowledge production might have been possible. Although, as Harootunian writes, "Said's book represented an important intellectual challenge to the mission of area studies which, if accepted, would have reshaped area studies and freed it from its own reliance on the Cold War and the necessities of the national security state" (152), the challenge was too fundamentally disruptive to the administrative and instrumentalist agendas so firmly routinized in area studies to be accepted by its practitioners. As a result, Said's attempt to link an incipient neo-colonial discourse to the history of area studies was almost immediately belittled, dismissed, and ignored, and his critique, for all its relevance to area studies' future orientation, simply "migrated to English studies to transform the study of literature into a full-scale preoccupation with identity and its construction" (152–53).

A long-term outcome of all this, Harootunian suggests, has been the consolidation of a type of postcolonial studies that, instead of fully developing the comparative, interdisciplinary, and multicultural potential that is embedded theoretically in area studies, tends to specialize in the deconstruction of the nature of language, in the amalgamation of poststructuralist theory largely with Anglo-American literary studies, and in the investigation mostly of former British colonial cultures rather than a substantial range of colonial and semicolonial histories from different parts of the world.[54] On its part, having voluntarily failed to heed Said's call, area studies can only remain "locked in its own enclaves of knowledge"[55] based on the reproduction of institutional and organizational structures with claims to normativity, while being defensively guarded against the innovations of poststructuralist theory that have radicalized North American humanistic and social scientific learning since the 1970s.

As I have already suggested, the truth of the continual targeting of the world as the fundamental form of knowledge production is xenophobia, the inability to handle the otherness of the other beyond the orbit that is the bomber's own visual path. For the xenophobe, every effort needs to be made to sustain and secure this orbit—that is, by keeping the place of the other-as-target always filled. With the end of the cold war and the disappearance of the Soviet Union, the United States must hence seek other substitutes for war. As has often been pointed out, drugs, poverty, and illegal immigrants have since become the new targets, which occupy—together with Moslems, Arabs, and communists (that is, Cuba, North Korea, and mainland China)—the status of that ultimate danger to be "deterred" at all costs.

Even so, xenophobia can backfire. When anxiety about the United States' loss of control over its target fields—and by implication its own boundaries—becomes overwhelming, bombing takes as its target the United States itself. This is so because, we remember, bombing the other has, as a rule, been held as the most effective means to end the war, the violence to stop violence, and, most important, the method to affirm moral righteousness. Why, then, when the United States is perceived to be threatened and weakened by incompetent leadership, should bombing not be the technique of choice for correcting the United States itself? And so, in spite of all the suspicions of racist conspiracy quickly raised about "foreigners" in the bombing of the federal office building in Oklahoma City on April 19, 1995, U.S. militiamen were arrested in the case. Spurred by a supremacist determination to set things right, the targeting of "others" turned into the targeting of innocent American men, women, and children, with a violence that erupted from within the heart of the country. The worst domestic terrorist incident in U.S. history,[56] the bombing in Oklahoma City took place with the force of an emblem: the vicious circle of the-world-as-target had returned to its point of origin.[57]

2

The Postcolonial Difference

LESSONS IN CULTURAL LEGITIMATION

Growing up in British Hong Kong in the 1960s and 1970s, I am probably one of few "postcolonial" intellectuals working in the North American humanities academy today who can lay claim to having been subjected to a genuinely classic colonial education. There are many possible ways to define the nature of this "classic" quality, but in my case it was distinguished by the peculiar intellectual choices I made from an early age on. Unlike many of my friends who, under family pressure or out of personal preference, had gone into medicine, law, accounting, engineering, computer science, banking or business management, I decided I was going to pursue language and literature studies. However, although I had received a fair amount of formal education in the Chinese language and its literature, my favourite subjects from secondary school (where we had to decide whether to go into the "arts" or "science" stream at around age 15) to what was known as the "Advanced Level" or matriculation were English language and literature. Because I had the fortune of having had some very good teachers, I was, by the time I entered university, sufficiently acquainted with the theoretical method of reading literature known as New Criticism. As an undergraduate at the University of Hong Kong, my curriculum included Comparative Literature (European fiction and drama of the modern period

since the seventeenth century) as well as English literature (from Chaucer to the early decades of the twentieth century); it also included an introduction to structuralism and the fundamental issues in poststructuralist theory. It was in order to further my knowledge of poststructuralist theory that I embarked upon graduate studies in the United States—even though my institution, Stanford University, was perhaps not the perfect match for my intellectual ambition at the time, and I was repeatedly told throughout my time at Stanford that I must have come from or should have gone to Yale. If I was working with a theoretical commitment in my early graduate student years, it was a commitment to the possibility of radicalising the concept of literature (and by implication, the concept of the literary "work" *per se*), a possibility that I had learned by way of poststructuralism's problematisation of the sign. Politically, this also meant the exciting possibility of historicising the methods of reading—specifically, those of New Criticism—in which I had been trained since secondary school, and of calling into question the Anglo-Americanness of such methods.

Although I had a substantial grounding in the standard Chinese language and modern Chinese literature, as well as a fair acquaintance with premodern Chinese poetry, prose and fiction, Chinese was not my chosen option of formal study during the undergraduate and graduate years. In retrospect, I would attribute this decision not to specialise in Chinese as the overdetermined outcome of the "classic" processes of cultural legitimation and subordination that are typical of the colonial experience.

As a first approximation, cultural legitimation may be defined as a procedure in which a first set of terms acquires validity and significance—becomes "viable" and "real"—through a second set of terms. Events, including the event of the production of knowledge, usually do not become "legitimate" until and unless they are being reinforced by other events that provide the grounds or terms of their validation or justification. What interests me about postcolonial studies, then, is the manner in which it addresses this recurrent but none the less historical two-part structure of cultural legitimation, in particular as such legitimation pertains to the dissemination and acquisition of knowledge.

To this extent, I have not found some of the highly visible controversies over "postcolonialism" to be very challenging. For instance, the endless debates about the infelicity of labelling (that is, why we should or should not use the term "postcolonial"), the dogmatic chastisements against "third world" intellectuals' "postcolonial aura" as something complicit with the evil forces of global capital, and the well-intentioned attempts to distinguish the ontological and philosophical status of postcolonialism as such from other ideologies such as postmodernism—such controversies appear to me to obfuscate or trivialise the historical import of the emergence of postcolonial studies, which has many genealogical affinities with the radical implications of Marxism, deconstruction and feminism. My own attention to postcolonial studies stems rather from an attempt to trace these affinities, especially in terms of the types of critical questions postcolonial theory enables us to ask.

If my multi-level educational experience in Hong Kong accounted for some of the origins of my intellectual trajectory, these origins were deeply immersed in lessons of cultural legitimation, and perhaps only those who have lived through the colonial experience on a day-by-day level would recognise the subtle mechanisms of the processes involved. In this light, it is instructive to remember how the predominant native/local "culture"—the Chinese—was handled by the British administration in comparison with the coloniser's—the British (and by extension, Western European cultures in general) in colonial Hong Kong. To say that Chinese culture had been made unavailable, or simply wiped out or disallowed, would be inaccurate. (For instance, in what comes across as a gross simplification of how colonialism, especially British colonialism, worked, many intellectuals from the People's Republic of China assume mistakenly to this day that only English was used in Hong Kong's schools.) Instead, what needs to be emphasised is that Chinese culture was never eradicated *tout court* but always accorded a special status—and that this was actually the more effective way to govern. During the era when I was in secondary school (1970s), English was the mandatory medium of instruction in Hong Kong's Anglo-Chinese schools (there were also Chinese schools where Cantonese was the medium of instruction), but Chinese language and literature, and Chinese history were also possible subjects (for public examinations). The native culture, in other words, continued to be taught (all the way to university and postgraduate levels) and allowed a role in the colonised citizens' education. Rather than being erased, its value became "specialised" and ghettoised over time, precisely through the very opportunities that were made available for its learning. Albeit not a popular one, the study of Chinese remained an "option." It was in this manner that British colonialism avoided the drastic or extremist path of cultural genocide (which would have been far too costly anyway) and created a socially stable situation based on the pragmatist hierarchisation of cultures, with the British on top and the Chinese beneath them. To study Chinese was never against the law but was simply constructed as a socially inferior phenomenon. Racism was indeed very much in operation, but it was a racism that had turned race and culture into *class* distinctions, so that, in order to head toward the upper echelons of society, one would, even (and especially) if one was a member of the colonised race, have no choice but collaborate with the racist strategies that were already built into the class stratification informing the management, distribution and consumption of knowledge.[1]

Clearly, being somewhat of an idealistic bookworm, I was not interested in the more lucrative trades and professions, but the intellectual path I had chosen (that of abandoning the option of Chinese after my "A" levels), like that of most young people in Westernised Asian countries, was still largely in conformity with the opportunities of upward social mobility that were made available and endorsed by the political system at large. (Typically, a university degree in English, History, or other humanities disciplines was the key to a respectable and prestigious job in the government bureaucracy.) To assert anything less material-value-conscious would be disingenuous. Subsequently, it was only in my period as a graduate student in the US that I became interested in using the knowledge and experience in Chinese literature that I had all along for serious scholarly purposes. But even that, I would emphasise, was by no means a straightforward development. It was simply not the case that, once in the West, I saw the light, realised the flaws of my colonial education, and rediscovered my "own" ethnic culture. It was simply not a case of a born-again conversion experience.

The path toward the study of Chinese culture, too, was mediated by the West, except this time it was mediated by my ongoing commitment to poststructuralist theory, which, at the same time that it deconstructed the logos, also brought about a heightened sensitivity to difference. During the latter part of my graduate student years, my interest was no longer simply in radicalising the methods of New Criticism. From the critique of structures, it had shifted into an interest in genres of writing that fragmented, exceeded or simply became non-confinable within accepted historical or literary paradigms. Put in an alternative manner, poststructuralist theory had led, in my case, to a concern with difference, and this concern with differ-ence quickly developed into a concern with forms of difference—generic, sexual and cultural. It was this kind of theoretical preoccupation—firmly from within a West-ern literary training—that finally directed my attention (back) to a more systematic study of modern Chinese literature and culture.

But the cross-over from English and Comparative Literature to Chinese was by no means simple: it was not a mere matter of switching from one language area into another because, as anyone working in non-Western cultures knows, the study of these cultures already has well-established and at times obstinately defended ter-ritorial boundaries. Thus, one cannot embark on the study of the literature of mod-ern China, say, without somehow running up against all the strategies that have long been in place to protect it against the invasion by "aliens"—those who do not have or are not undergoing advanced formal training in Chinese—such as myself. (Ever since my work became known, for instance, there have been claims by various sinologists that I do not actually know Chinese or have real knowledge about China and Hong Kong.)

At the time I turned to the study of modern China (in the mid-1980s), and spe-cifically to the study of a popular type of literature produced in the early twentieth century known as "Mandarin Duck and Butterfly" literature, China study in the US was still predominantly organised within the parameters of "area studies" that had been established during the Cold War years. China experts tended to be either con-servative or leftist in their politics—the former being people who identified more or less with the official ideological position of the US government; the latter often being those who had chosen their fields of specialisation during the 1960s and 1970s, when China represented that inaccessible (and hence idealised) "third world difference" to the mainstream values of materialistic America. Whether lodged in convictions of the right or the left, the terms of legitimation provided for the study of China in the US were largely in accordance with US foreign policy *vis-à-vis* com-munist countries, which required that a place such as China be subject to politi-cal, military and cultural surveillance in the form of an enemy-to-be-deciphered. In hindsight, even those whose political idealism had led them to defend the mer-its of Chinese culture were, I think, partaking of a kind of knowledge production the benefits of which accrued to themselves rather than to their objects of study, the Chinese people, an entity which was held at a distance and which remained an abstraction. This was still the time before significant numbers of ethnic Chi-nese (especially those from the PRC) burst on the scene as job seekers equipped with American PhDs; the academic enterprise of studying China—as a "foreign" culture—remained by and large in the hands of white China specialists. This enter-prise was secured along an untroubled dividing line between the "object" and "sub-ject" of study: China and the Chinese were objects to be explored and investigated, while the subjects weighing the pros and cons of these objects—that is, doing the work of evaluation—were Western.

In spite of the Maoist aspirations of some of its practitioners, China studies in those years was hardly connected with the issues of colonialism and postcolonialism. It was as if, their idealism notwithstanding, once they were confronted with the modern culture of China, even the left-leaning China specialists collaborated with their right-wing countrymen and adopted the language of cultural exceptionalism, completely obliterating the fact that modern Chinese history itself was part of the non-Western world's prolonged humiliating encounter with the West for the past 500 years. Today, with postcolonial theory becoming a trendy thing among white specialists of the non-West, including white China specialists, and with ethnic Chinese intellectuals (inside and outside China) becoming alert to the implications of colonialism and imperialism, it seems almost unthinkable that things in the past could have been so different, but it is sobering to bear in mind that, merely a decade ago, the study of China and the articulation of postcolonial issues existed in entirely unrelated intellectual universes.

So what and how exactly does postcolonial theory contribute to China study? I believe I have been providing some answers to this question, beginning with the publication of my first book, *Woman and Chinese Modernity* (1991). In the study of the non-West, what may appear to be a two-part structure in the process of cultural legitimation involves a third element, namely, the people who are carrying out such study—and the biases that accompany their perspectives. This, essentially, is the lesson from Edward Said's *Orientalism*, the foundational text for postcolonial studies. Much of the critical inquiry that follows Said's lead, then, has been produced in the spirit of questioning the legitimacy of this kind of European representation of the non-West, a representation that often reduces members of the non-Western communities that are being "studied" to silence. Once it is no longer possible to ignore representation as an act initiated by parties with definite self-interests, questions of *who can represent whom* inevitably follow, ultimately leading to the realization that perhaps the most underprivileged classes do not have the right to represent anything, not even themselves. The implications of these questions constitute the focus of Gayatri Chakravorty Spivak's essay "Can the Subaltern Speak?" Taken together, the works of Said, Spivak and other postcolonial critics account for a paradigm shift in the type of question being asked of the previously colonised world—from merely *what* is being "studied" to *who* it is who is doing this "studying." And, once the question of *who* is added, we have obviously left behind the more taxonomic categorisations of cultural difference and entered the complex realm of the *subjectivities* involved in any engagement with cultural difference. Hence, the poststructuralist specialisation in deconstructing language becomes, by necessity, supplemented by considerations of language as acts that originate from "subjects," and the more straightforward analyses of textual nuances are obliged to come to terms with what may be called identity politics.

As I now look back on my own intellectual trajectory, it is possible to say that the preoccupation with cultural difference, which made me pay attention to questions raised by postcolonial theory, provided the preliminary grounds for working out a new set of terms for the study of modern China. These new terms include—indeed foreground—what was hitherto precluded: the experience of China as part of a larger world history, in which the forces of Western imperialism and colonialism, at the same time that they mandate modernisation in non-Western countries, have left indelible, discernible ideological imprints on various forms of cultural production such as literary writing and film-making. To see China in these postcolonial theoretical terms is, ultimately, to wrest it from a long orientalist tradition, in which the fraught realities of Chinese modernity are characteristically understood as the continuations of or aberrations from a pure native tradition. To this day there remains, among China scholars of high institutional standing, an entrenched habit of writing whereby the consideration of Chinese history, even modern Chinese history, is methodologically confined within strictly "Chinese" events in such a manner as to downplay or omit entirely the coercive role played by the West. In the ostensible guise of not diverting attention to non-Chinese issues, such sinocentric historiographic and literary habits in fact collaborate in the perpetuation of a kind of imperialistic gaze at China as object, and postpone the need to confront the racial implications of such a gaze.

Despite its incessant and often unpleasant interrogations of "who is doing what to whom," then, I believe identity politics should be recognised as having made a substantial contribution to fundamentally reshaping our assumptions about knowledge. In this regard, many of the notions that have acquired great currency in the realms of cultural studies and postcolonial studies, such as "hybridity," "performativity," "migrancy," "diaspora," and their affiliates, can all be seen to have taken off from a certain kind of identity politics. Rather than understanding identity in terms of stable reference points, the theorists of these notions have collectively shifted the conceptualisation of identity to an epistemological paradigm in which it is liminality, instability, impurity, movement and fluidity that inform the formation of identities. While the merits and demerits of this new type of theorisation must be debated on a different occasion,[2] my point is simply that these notions are part and parcel of new discursive practices which are drastically transforming knowledge by stubbornly focusing our attention on what has hitherto been cast outside the boundaries of what can be known.

Michel Foucault wrote in *The Order of Things* that Man is not an eternal but a rather recent historical phenomenon, who arose with the steady fragmentation of the modern world into compartments of intelligibility known as the "disciplines"—

such as biology, archaeology, literature, economics, and so forth.[3] The most important part of Foucault's argument is that "knowledge" itself is not a given but rather an outcome of shifting historical relations of representation. Specifically, these relations involve two parallel, though seemingly paradoxical, sets of developments. The first is an increasing exactitude that accompanies the scientific *objectification* of the world. Knowledge, in other words, is a matter of a progressive detailing in methodology, of being able to capture things instrumentally in as precise and meticulous a manner as possible—as facts, data, information. Simultaneously, however, the linkages between observable phenomena and the evolving historical conditions which produced them have become increasingly elusive or hidden. As the world becomes more visible and observable, it has also become largely symptomatic. To probe its "causes," which are no longer readily understandable, more and more interpretation is needed. But the criteria for such interpretation are themselves far from being continuous or natural; instead, they are constantly being reinvented and reconceptualised. Hence, the attempt to render the world as a knowable object is paralleled by increasingly abstract, *theoretical* processes of explanation and justification—in what I have been referring to as cultural legitimation.

Postcolonial studies furthers Foucault's arguments by foregrounding a dimension he did not broach—that of race and ethnicity.[4] Once this dimension has been restored to the picture, the increasing "objectification" of the world that Foucault so eloquently elucidates can be historicised as part of the ongoing imperialist European agenda for transforming the world into observable and hence manageable units, and the intensification of abstract theoretical processes, too, must be seen as inseparable from the historical conditions that repeatedly return the material benefits of such processes to European subjectivities. The terms of postcolonial studies thus help accentuate the binarism of objectification and theorisation introduced by Foucault in the following manner: *some humans have been cast as objects, while other humans have been given the privilege to become subjects.* Once we see this, Foucault's point that Man is a recent historical invention begins to make perfect sense—but less because of the emergence of disciplinary knowledge *per se* than because the objectification-theorisation mechanism that is constitutive of disciplinary knowledge is, arguably, best exemplified in the colonial experience, whereby "Man" is epistemologically as well as practically divided into object and subject on grounds of racial and ethnic difference. If Man is a historical invention, it is because he is a Western invention, which relies for its inventiveness—its "originality" so to speak—on the debasement and exclusion of others. And it is these debased and excluded others, the "men" who were at one time considered not quite Man enough—not only because they had been banished to the European madhouses, prisons and hospitals that Foucault investigated, but also because they happened to be living as subordinates within the European colonial apparatus—who are now swarming around the disciplinary boundaries between subject and object. In the presence of these other "men," Western Man is now (to borrow Heidegger's famous verb for being) *thrown* back to his proper place in history, where he, too, must be seen as object.

Although the questions brought about by identity politics are an ineluctable part of postcolonial studies, therefore, postcolonial studies itself is not reducible to identity politics. My brief allusion to Foucault above is meant to emphasise the genealogical affinity postcolonial theory shares with the development of *abstract* theoretical thought in the modern world in general. In an age that is driven by the utilitarianism, pragmatism and anti-intellectualism of corporate interests, it is, I think, crucial to underscore this point and keep alive the theoretical edge of postcolonial studies. (In other words, I do not believe that the familiar move of pitting "concrete reality" against "abstract theory" will in the long run do postcolonial studies any good.) This is not to say, of course, that postcolonial studies should not continue to remain on the alert *vis-à-vis* the tendency toward imperialism on the part of many Western theorists as the latter claim to go "global." Indeed, it is the inextricable mutual entanglement of both kinds of practices—that of being sophisticatedly theoretical and that of being vigilant against the many guises of imperialism—that makes postcolonial studies such an intellectually exciting event. Yet precisely because of this two-pronged nature of its articulation also, postcolonial studies is potentially disturbing, and forces of subordination and delegitimation are at work even as the field gathers momentum.

I was informed recently by a white graduate student that she had been discouraged by her adviser (a white academic who advocates the need to "globalise" Western theory) from pursuing postcolonial studies because she was not a person of colour. This kind of information, being anecdotal in nature, does not really constitute any concrete source of "scholarly" evidence, but anecdotes like this do convey some sense of the reality of which they partake. What may be safely deduced from my student's report is a general (mis)perception that postcolonial studies is or should remain the exclusive domain of "peoples of colour"—perhaps specifically of those who have gone through, or whose ancestors have gone through, the experience of colonialism. What is alarming is the imperialist strategy of ghettoisation that is thus skilfully being deployed to restrict a field—in this case, in the guise of benevolent professional advice to a student who in fact has a strong and legitimate interest in postcolonial issues. If enough of this kind of advice is given and taken, then the fate of postcolonial studies would probably become, indeed, that of a self-fulfilling prophecy, with the status of something that is untouched by white people, and reproduced and circulated only among so-called "peoples of colour." Should that happen, it would, in effect, have been successfully delegitimated as a viable field of study, while the blame for its loss of credibility could, once again, be comfortably laid at the door of the "peoples of colour" and the acrimonious identity politics they bring to the study of the postcolonial world. (To the credit of my student, she had, entirely on her own initiative, already decided to change advisers by the time she reported this incident to me.)

What this little anecdote indicates is the familiar pattern of a vicious circle that haunts the emergence of an area of intellectual inquiry the point of which is precisely to query injustice—not only the injustice of the suppression of certain groups of peoples and their histories but also the injustice of established institutional processes of cultural legitimation. Emerging as a response to the massive inequities created by the historical phenomena of European and American imperialism and colonialism, postcolonial studies, even as it rigorously addresses such inequities (by drawing on identity politics, for instance, in addition to the many theoretical attempts to transform the boundaries of accumulated knowledge), may in the end be delegitimated by the very historical conditions that propelled it into being in the first place. Perhaps, like the study of things Chinese in British Hong Kong, postcolonial studies need never be eradicated entirely but could simply be channelled into a second-class or third-class "option" with a socially inferior status in the grand scheme of the "global" production of knowledge.

For these reasons, postcolonial studies cannot, to my mind at least, be regarded simply as yet another new, fashionable kind of theoretical framework (that may eventually be supplanted). Rather, I think of it as a kind of scholarship that has the capacity for keeping alive the questions of disciplined knowledge, on the one hand, and those of the continued conditions of inequity—the class implications—that accompany such knowledge as it seeks to deal with racial, ethnic and cultural difference, on the other. For me, the "postcolonial difference" remains the lesson in cultural legitimation it teaches. All knowledges are created equal—but some are more equal than others.[5]

Argument is that Other wants China to stay as singularity, different from Adorized, mirror reflection of its fantasy.

Chow questions this as a Orientalist stance.

Chinese poets are accommodating for the work for the Westerners —

ORIENTALISM AND EAST ASIA: THE PERSISTENCE OF A SCHOLARLY TRADITION

study of Chinese Tradition

The sinologist Stephen Owen wrote a controversially negative essay about "world poetry" not too long ago in the pages of *The New Republic*.[1] While ostensibly reviewing the English translation of the collection *The August Sleepwalker* by the mainland Chinese poet Bei Dao, Owen attacks "third world" poets for pandering to the tastes of Western audiences seeking "a cozy ethnicity" (29). Much of what is written by non-Western poets is, he complains, no longer distinguished by a true national identity but is instead "supremely translatable" (32):

> Most of these poems translate themselves. These could just as easily be translations from a Slovak or an Estonian or a Philippine poet. . . . We must wonder if such collections of poetry in translation become publishable only because the publisher and the readership have been assured that the poetry was lost in translation. But what if the poetry wasn't lost in translation? What if this is it? This *is* it. (31; emphasis in the original)

As a sinologist, Owen's biggest concern is that contemporary Chinese writers are sacrificing their national cultural heritage for a "translation" that commodifies experiences of victimization. He warns: "And there is always a particular danger of using one's victimization for self-interest: in this case, to sell oneself abroad by what an international audience, hungry for political virtue, which is always in short supply, finds touching" (29).

Like other "new poetries" such as new Hindi poetry and new Japanese poetry (29), the "disease of modern Chinese poetry" (30) is that it is too Westernized. For Owen, the most important question is therefore: "is this Chinese literature, or literature that began in the Chinese language?" (31)[2]

In her criticism of Owen's essay, Michelle Yeh points out the obvious contradictions that underlie what appears to be an objective and scholarly discussion:

> On the one hand, he is disappointed at the lack of history and culture that would distinguish China from other countries. On the other hand, the historical context essential to the writing and reading of contemporary Chinese poetry is not taken seriously and is used only as an occasion for chastising the poet who writes "for self-interest." . . . The cynicism is oddly out of step with the high regard in which Professor Owen holds poetry, for it not only ignores personal and literary history but also underestimates the power of poetry as a vital means of spiritual survival, of affirming individual dignity and faith when virtually all else fails.[3]

Rey Chow -> Owen's stance is simply orientalist.

For readers who know something about China, Owen's attitude is not a particularly novel one. It is typical of the disdain found in many relatively recent American scholarly reactions toward the liberalized China of the 1980s. Harry Harding has written informatively about this kind of "debilitating contempt" that succeeded the euphoric China fever of the 1960s and 1970s.[4] But more is at stake here. What kind of cultural politics is in play when a professor from Harvard University accuses the men and women from the "third world" of selling out to the West? While he criticizes poets like Bei Dao for succumbing to the commodifying tendencies of transnational culture out of "self-interest," what is absent from Owen's musings is an account of the institutional investments that shape his own enunciation. This absence constitutes a definite form of power by not drawing attention to itself and thus not subjecting itself to the harsh judgment of "self-interest" that is so useful in criticizing others. The elaboration and fortification of this kind of absence amounts to the perpetuation of a deeply ingrained Orientalism in the field of East Asian studies, of which Owen's practice is but one example. Because this is an Orientalism at which many East Asia scholars, *both* native and non-native, connive, it is of some urgency to mobilize criticism of it.

Colin MacKerras writes about Edward Said's *Orientalism:* "Although designed specifically as a critique of the Western study of West Asian civilizations, its main points are equally applicable to the study of China."[5] Precisely because of this, the arguments against Said's work in the East Asian field are often similar to their counterparts in South Asian and West Asian studies. Critics like Said, it is often said, belittle and ignore the work that is being done by specialists of these non-Western cultures and that has produced knowledge about peoples whose traditions would otherwise perish. I have indicated elsewhere that we need to acknowledge the significance of this type of work as sharing an *episteme* with primatology.[6] It is, however, not enough simply to align a field like East Asian studies with primatology and compare the salvational motives of their respective practitioners. What needs to be foregrounded is the nature and extent of the self-interestedness involved in the disapproval of the critique of Orientalism as a trans-cultural phenomenon.

Although Owen in his piece is not directly criticizing Said's work, his arguments clarify many of the current feelings in his field. Basic to Owen's disdain toward the new "world poetry" is a sense of loss and, consequently, an anxiety over his own intellectual position. This anxiety can be understood in part through Sigmund Freud's analysis of melancholia.[7] For Freud, we remember, the melancholic is a person who cannot get over the loss of a precious, loved object and who ultimately introjects this loss into his ego. What Freud emphasizes throughout his discussion as the unique feature of the melancholic, who differs from other kinds of mourners, is that he exhibits the symptoms of a delusional belittling of himself. Because the nature of the loss remains unconscious to the patient, the loss is directed inward, so that he becomes convinced of his own worthlessness as if he has been unjustly abandoned.

In his essay, Freud is concerned with the relationship between the self and the lost loved object. Freud's construction involves two parties, subject and object, and does not go on to show how the melancholic acts in regard to other subjects. Post-coloniality here offers a use of Freud that necessitates a rethinking of his theory about the melancholic disorder. In the case of the sinologist's relationship with his beloved object, "China," melancholia is complicated by the presence of a third party—the living members of the Chinese culture, who provide the sinologist with a means of *externalizing* his loss and directing his blame. What Freud sees as "self"-directed denigration now finds a concrete realization in the denigration of others.

For Owen, the inferior poetic skills of Bei Dao are, ostensibly, what he considers to be signs of the "third world" poet's inability to rise to the grandeur of his own cultural past. But this moralistic indictment of the other's infidelity masks a more fundamental anxiety. This is the anxiety that the Chinese past which he has undertaken to penetrate is evaporating and that the sinologist himself is the abandoned subject. What this means, significantly, is that a situation has been constructed in which the historical relation between the "first world" and the "third world" is reversed: writers of the "third world" like Bei Dao now appear not as the oppressed but as oppressors, who aggress against the "first world" sinologist by robbing him of his love. Concluding his essay sourly with the statement, "Welcome to the late twentieth century," Owen's real complaint is that *he* is the victim of a monstrous world order in front of which a sulking impotence like his is the only claim to truth.

Characteristic of this Orientalist melancholia are all the feelings proper to nineteenth-century Anglo-German Romanticism: the assumption that literature should be about depth and interiority, that expression of emotional truth should be modest, if not altogether wordless, and that being cultured means being hostile toward any form of reification and exhibitionism. Notably, Owen is not insensitive to oppression and suffering (he repeatedly points to the injustice caused by Western imperialism and Western cultural hegemony), but such sensitivity demands that oppression and suffering should not be announced loudly or even mentioned too often by those who are undergoing it, for that would amount to poor taste and insincerity. Reading him, one has the sense that in order to be good, poetry must be untranslatable because any translation would be suspect of *betraying* the truth. By implication, human language itself is a prime traitor to preverbal phenomenal sentiments.[8]

Confined to a discursive space that is theoretically at odds with the comparative tenets of contemporary cultural studies, the sinologist holds on to the language of the nation-state as his weapon of combat. This is one of the major reasons why "history," in the sense of a detailed, factographic documentation of the local, the particular, and the past (understood as what has already happened and been recorded), enjoys such a prioritized disciplinary status in East Asian cultural politics. The hostility toward the critique of Orientalism currently heard in some East Asian scholarly circles is a direct consequence of this language of the nation-state. But if the critique of Orientalism is rejected, as is often the argument, for its "universalizing" overtones, then the idea of China, Japan, or "East Asia" as distinct historical entities is itself the other side of Orientalism. In a discussion about how universalism and particularism reinforce and supplement each other, Naoki Sakai writes:

> Contrary to what has been advertised by both sides, universalism and particularism reinforce and supplement each other; they are never in real conflict; they need each other and have to seek to form a symmetrical, mutually supporting relationship by every means in order to avoid a dialogic encounter which would necessarily jeopardize their reputedly secure and harmonized monologic worlds. Universalism and particularism endorse each other's defect in order to conceal their own; they are intimately tied to each other in their accomplice [sic]. In this respect, *a particularism such as nationalism can never be a serious critique of universalism, for it is an accomplice thereof.*[9]

Of Japan, for instance, Sakai writes specifically:

> Japan did not stand *outside* the West. Even in its particularism, Japan was already implicated in the ubiquitous West, so that neither historically nor geopolitically could Japan be seen as the *outside* of the West. This means that, in order to criticize the West in relation to Japan, one has necessarily to begin with a critique of Japan. Likewise, the critique of Japan necessarily entails the radical critique of the West.[10]

What these passages indicate is that Orientalism and a particularism like nationalism or nativism are the obverse and reverse of the same coin, and that criticism of one cannot be made without criticism of the other. The tendency in area studies, nonetheless, is to play them off against each other with nationalism/nativism gaining the upper hand. This has led to what Gayatri Spivak calls a "new culturalist alibi,"[11] by which some seek to avoid the pitfalls of the earlier Orientalism simply by particularizing their inquiries as meticulously as possible by way of class, gender, race, nation, and geographical locale. We see this in "a title construction such as 'Funu, guojia, jiating' [Chinese women, Chinese state, Chinese family]."[12] The use of "Chinese" as a specifier signals a new kind of care and a new kind of attentiveness to the discursive imperatives—"Always contextualize! Never essentialize!"—of cultural pluralism. But *funu, guojia, jiating* are simply words in the Chinese language that mean women, state, family. Had the title been "La femme, l'état, la famille," would it be conceivable to append a phrase like "French woman, French state, French family"? In the name of investigating "cultural difference," ethnic markers

34

such as "Chinese" easily become a method of differentiation that precisely blocks criticism from its critical task by reinscribing potentially radical notions such as "the other" in the security of fastidiously documented archival detail. A scholarly nativism that functions squarely within the Orientalist dynamic and that continues to imprison "other cultures" within entirely conventional disciplinary boundaries thus remains intact.

At a conference on gender issues in twentieth-century China, my commentator, an American female anthropologist who has done pioneering work on rural Chinese women, told the audience that what I said about the relation between China studies and Western cultural imperialism made her feel politically uncomfortable. Instead, she suggested, we should focus on the "internal colonization" of Chinese women by Chinese patriarchy. This person was thus still illustrating, in 1991, the point G. Balandier made in 1951, namely that "Out of a more or less conscious fear of having to take into consideration . . . the society of the colonial power to which they themselves belong," Western anthropologists persistently neglect the "colonial situation" that lies at the origin of their "field of research" in most parts of the world.[13]

These examples of pressures to focus on the "internal" and the specifically "Chinese" problems are examples of how what many profess to be "cross-cultural" study can remain trapped within a type of discourse that is geographically deterministic *and hence* culturally essentialist. "China," "Japan," and "East Asia" become signs of "difference" that reaffirm a sense of identity as originary self-identicalness. The problems posed by women and imperialism in the East Asian field are thus often subordinated, philosophically, to a local native tradition (in which any discussion of women alone would be guilty of coloniality) and, institutionally, to "area studies," where imperialism as a transnational phenomenon is dismissed as irrelevant. What this means is that, while plenty of work is done on East Asian women, much of it is not feminist but nationalist or culturalist; while plenty of work is done on the modern history of East Asia, much of it is not about East Asia's shared history with other orientalized cultures but about East Asia as a "distinct" territory with a distinct history. What is forgotten is that these notions of East Asia are fully in keeping with U.S. foreign policy in the post-Second World War period, during which the older European Orientalism was supplanted by the emergence of the U.S. as the newest imperialist power with major military bases in countries such as Japan, Korea, Taiwan, the Philippines, and Vietnam.

What is also missed is that when we speak against Orientalism and nativism, we understand them as *languages* which can be used by natives and non-natives alike. A critique of the Orientalism in East Asian pedagogy neither implies that only "natives" of East Asian cultures are entitled to speaking about those cultures truthfully nor that "natives" themselves are automatically innocent of Orientalism as a mode of discourse.

The most crucial issue, meanwhile, remains Orientalism's general and continuing *ideological* role. Critics of Said in the East Asian field sometimes justify their criticism by saying that Said's theory does not apply to East Asia because many East Asian countries were not, territorially, colonial possessions. This kind of positivistic thinking, derived from a literal understanding of the significance of geographical captivity, is not only an instance of the ongoing anthropological tendency to deemphasize the "colonial situation" as I mention above; it also leaves intact the most important aspect of Orientalism—its legacy as everyday culture and value. The question ought, I think, to be posed in exactly the opposite way: *not* how East Asia cannot be understood within the paradigm of Orientalism because it was not everywhere militarily occupied, but how, *in spite of* and perhaps because of the fact that it remained in many cases "territorially independent," it offers even better illustrations of how imperialism works—i.e., how imperialism as ideological domination succeeds best without physical coercion, without actually capturing the body and the land.

Here, the history of China vis-à-vis the West can be instructive in a number of ways.[14] Unlike India or countries in Africa and America, most parts of China were, in the course of European imperialism, never territorially under the sovereignty of any foreign power, although China was invaded and had to grant many concessions throughout the nineteenth century to England, France, Germany, Russia, Japan, and the U.S. Major political movements in China, be they for the restoration of older forms of government (1898) or for the overthrow of the dynastic system (1911), be they led by the religious (1850–1864), the well educated (1919), the antiforeign (1900, 1937–1945), or Communists (1949), were always conducted in terms of China's relations with foreign powers, usually the West. However, my suggestion is that the ability to preserve more or less territorial integrity (while other ancient civilizations, such as the Inca, the Aztec, India, Vietnam and Indochina, Algeria, and others, were territorially captured) as well as linguistic integrity (Chinese remains the official language) means that as a "third world" country, the Chinese relation to the imperialist West, until the Communists officially propagandized "anti-imperialism," is seldom purely "oppositional" ideologically; on the contrary, the point has always been for China to become as strong as the West, to become the West's "equal." And even though the Chinese Communists once served as the anti-imperialist inspiration for other "third world" cultures and progressive Western intellectuals, that dream of a successful and consistent opposition to the West on ideological grounds has been dealt the death blow by more recent events such as the Tiananmen Massacre of 1989, in which the Chinese government itself acted as viciously as if it were one of its capitalist enemies.[15] As the champion of the unprivileged classes and nations of the world, Communist China has shown itself to be a failure, a failure which is now hanging on by empty official rhetoric while its people choose to live in ways that have obviously departed from the Communist ideal.

The point of summarizing modern Chinese history in such a schematic fashion is to underscore how the notion of "coloniality" (together with the culture criticisms that follow from it), when construed strictly in terms of the *foreignness* of race, land, and language, can *blind* us to political exploitation as easily as it can alert us to it. In the history of modern Western imperialism, the Chinese were never completely dominated by a foreign colonial power, but the apparent absence of the "enemy" as such does not make the Chinese case any *less* "third world" in terms of the exploitation suffered by the people, whose most important colonizer remains their own government. China, perhaps because it is an exception to the rule of imperialist domination by race, land, and language involving a foreign power, in fact highlights the effects of the imperialistic *transformation of value and value-production* more sharply than in other "third world" cultures. Unlike, say, India, where the British left behind insurmountable poverty, a cumbersome bureaucracy, and a language with which to function as a "nation," but where therefore the sentiment of opposition can remain legitimately alive because there is historically a clearly identifiable *foreign* colonizer, the Chinese continue to have "their own" system, "their own" language, and "their own" problems. The obsession of Chinese intellectuals remains "China" rather than the opposition to the West. The cultural production that results is therefore narcissistic, rather than simply oppositional, in structure. Whatever oppositional sentiment there exists is an oppositional sentiment directed toward itself—"China," the "Chinese heritage," the "Chinese tradition," the "Chinese government," and variants of these.

To give to Chinese and East Asian studies the critical energy they need is therefore to articulate the problems of *narcissistic value-production within*—rather than in negligence of—the larger context of the legacy of *cultural imperialism*. Neither of these alone suffices for a genuine intervention. The work that has yet to be done in the field of East Asia is not a matter of sidestepping the critique of Orientalism in order to talk about what are "authentically" East Asian historical issues. Instead, putting the myth of "authenticity" within the history of a mutually reinforcing universalism and particularism, we must demand: Why were questions of Orientalism not asked earlier, and why are they being avoided even now?

SANCTIFYING THE "SUBALTERN": THE PRODUCTIVITY OF WHITE GUILT

The Orientalist has a special sibling whom I will, in order to highlight her significance as a kind of representational agency, call the Maoist. Arif Dirlik, who has written extensively on the history of political movements in twentieth-century China, sums up the interpretation of Mao Zedong commonly found in Western Marxist analyses in terms of a "Third Worldist fantasy"—"a fantasy of Mao as a Chinese reincarnation of Marx who fulfilled the Marxist promise that had been betrayed in the West."[16] The Maoist was the phoenix which arose from the ashes of the great disillusionment with Western culture in the 1960s and which found hope in the Chinese Communist Revolution.[17] In the 1970s, when it became possible for Westerners to visit China as guided and pampered guests of the Beijing establishment, Maoists came back with reports of Chinese society's absolute, positive difference from Western society and of the Cultural Revolution as "the most important and innovative example of Mao's concern with the pursuit of egalitarian, populist, and communitarian ideals in the course of economic modernization."[18] At that time, even poverty in China was regarded as "spiritually ennobling, since it meant that [the] Chinese were not possessed by the wasteful and acquisitive consumerism of the United States" (941).

Although the excessive admiration of the 1970s has since been replaced by an oftentimes equally excessive denigration of China, the Maoist is very much alive among us, and her significance goes far beyond the China and East Asian fields. Typically, the Maoist is a cultural critic who lives in a capitalist society but who is fed up with capitalism—a cultural critic, in other words, who wants a social order opposed to the one that is supporting her own undertaking. The Maoist is thus a supreme example of the way desire works: What she wants is always located in the other, resulting in an identification with and valorization of that which she is not / does not have. Since what is valorized is often the other's deprivation—"having" poverty or "having" nothing—the Maoist's strategy becomes in the main a *rhetorical* renunciation of the material power that enables her rhetoric.

In terms of intellectual lineage, one of the Maoist's most important ancestors is Charlotte Brontë's Jane Eyre. Like Jane, the Maoist's means to moral power is a specific representational position—the position of powerlessness. In their reading of *Jane Eyre*, Nancy Armstrong and Leonard Tennenhouse argue that the novel exemplifies the paradigm of violence that expresses its *dominance through a representation of the self as powerless*:

> Until the very end of the novel, Jane is always excluded from every available form of social power. Her survival seems to depend on renouncing what power might come to her as teacher, mistress, cousin, heiress, or missionary's wife. She repeatedly flees from such forms of inclusion in the field of power, as if her status as an exemplary subject, like her authority as narrator, depends entirely on her claim to a kind of truth which can only be made from a position of powerlessness. By creating such an unlovely heroine and subjecting her to one form of harassment after another, Brontë demonstrates the power of words alone.[19]

This reading of Jane Eyre highlights her not simply as the female underdog who is often identified by feminist and Marxist critics, but as the intellectual who acquires power through a moral rectitude that was to become the flip side of West-ern imperialism's ruthlessness. Lying at the core of Anglo-American liberalism, this moral rectitude would accompany many territorial and economic conquests overseas with a firm sense of social mission. When Jane Eyre went to the colo-nies in the nineteenth century, she turned into the Christian missionary. It is this understanding—that Brontë's depiction of a socially marginalized English woman is, in terms of ideological production, fully complicit with England's empire-building ambition rather than opposed to it—that prompted Gayatri Spivak to read *Jane Eyre* as a text in the service of imperialism. Referring to Brontë's treatment of the "mad-woman" Bertha Mason, the white Jamaican Creole character, Spivak charges *Jane Eyre* for, precisely, its humanism, in which the "native subject" is not created as an animal but as "the object of what might be termed the terrorism of the categori-cal imperative." This kind of creation is imperialism's use/travesty of the Kantian metaphysical demand to "*make* the heathen into a human so that he can be treated as an end in himself."[20]

In the twentieth century, as Europe's former colonies became independent, Jane Eyre became the Maoist. Michel de Certeau describes the affinity between her two major reincarnations, one religious and the other political, this way:

> The place that was formerly occupied by the Church or Churches vis-à-vis the estab-lished powers remains recognizable, over the past two centuries, in the functioning of the opposition known as leftist. . . .
>
> [T]here is vis-à-vis the established order, a relationship between the Churches that defended an *other world* and the parties of the left which, since the nineteenth century, have promoted a *different future*. In both cases, similar functional characteristics can be discerned.[21]

The Maoist retains many of Jane's awesome features, chief of which are a protes-tant passion to turn powerlessness into "truth" and an idealist intolerance of those who may think differently from her. Whereas the great Orientalist blames the living "third world" natives for the loss of the ancient non-Western civilization, his loved object, the Maoist applauds the same natives for personifying and fulfilling her ideals. For the Maoist in the 1970s, the mainland Chinese were, in spite of their "backwardness," a puritanical alternative to the West in human form—a dream come true.

In the 1980s and 1990s, however, the Maoist is disillusioned to watch the China they sanctified crumble before their eyes. This is the period in which we hear disap-proving criticisms of contemporary Chinese people for liking Western pop music and consumer culture, or for being overly interested in sex. In a way that makes her indistinguishable from what at first seems a political enemy, the Orientalist, the Maoist now mourns the loss of her loved object—Socialist China—by pointing angrily at living "third world" natives. For many who have built their careers on the vision of Socialist China, the grief is tremendous.

In the "cultural studies" of the American academy in the 1990s, the Maoist is reproducing with prowess. We see this in the way terms such as "oppression," "victimization," and "subalternity" are now being used. Contrary to Orientalist disdain for contemporary native cultures of the non-West, the Maoist turns precisely the "disdained" other into the object of his/her study and, in some cases, identification. In a mixture of admiration and moralism, the Maoist sometimes turns all people from non-Western cultures into a generalized "subaltern" that is then used to flog an equally generalized "West."[22]

Because the representation of "the other" as such ignores (1) the class and intellectual hierarchies within these other cultures, which are usually as elaborate as those in the West, and (2) the discursive power relations structuring the Maoist's mode of inquiry and valorization, it produces a way of talking in which notions of lack, subalternity, victimization, and so forth are drawn upon indiscriminately, often with the intention of spotlighting the speaker's own sense of alterity and political righteousness. A comfortably wealthy white American intellectual I know claimed that he was a "third world intellectual," citing as one of his credentials his marriage to a Western European woman of part-Jewish heritage; a professor of English complained about being "victimized" by the structured time at an Ivy League institution, meaning that she needed to be on time for classes; a graduate student of upper-class background from one of the world's poorest countries told his American friends that he was of poor peasant stock in order to authenticate his identity as a radical "third world" representative; male and female academics across the U.S. frequently say they were "raped" when they report experiences of professional frustration and conflict. Whether sincere or delusional, such cases of self-dramatization all take the route of self-subalternization, which has increasingly become the assured means to authority and power. What these intellectuals are doing is robbing the terms of oppression of their critical and oppositional import, and thus depriving the oppressed of even the vocabulary of protest and rightful demand. The oppressed, whose voices we seldom hear, are robbed twice—the first time of their economic chances, the second time of their language, which is now no longer distinguishable from those of us who have had our consciousnesses "raised."

In their analysis of the relation between violence and representation, Armstrong and Tennenhouse write: "[The] idea of violence as representation is not an easy one for most academics to accept. It implies that whenever we speak for someone else we are inscribing her with our own (implicitly masculine) idea of order."[23] At present, this process of "inscribing" often means not only that we "represent" certain historic others because they are/were "oppressed"; it often means that *there is interest in representation only when what is represented can in some way be seen as lacking.* Even though the Maoist is usually contemptuous of Freudian psychoanalysis because it is "bourgeois," her investment in oppression and victimization fully partakes of the Freudian and Lacanian notions of "lack." By attributing "lack," the Maoist justifies the "speaking for someone else" that Armstrong and Tennenhouse call "violence as representation."

As in the case of Orientalism, which does not necessarily belong only to those who are white, the Maoist does not have to be racially "white" either. The phrase "white guilt" refers to a type of discourse which continues to position power and lack against each other, while the narrator of that discourse, like Jane Eyre, speaks with power but identifies with powerlessness. This is how even those who come from privilege more often than not speak from/of/as its "lack." What the Maoist demonstrates is a circuit of productivity that draws its capital from others' deprivation while refusing to acknowledge its own presence as endowed. With the material origins of her own discourse always concealed, the Maoist thus speaks as if her charges were a form of immaculate conception.

The difficulty facing us, it seems to me, is no longer simply the "first world" Orientalist who mourns the rusting away of his treasures, but also students from privileged backgrounds Western *and* non-Western, who conform behaviorally in every respect with the elitism of their social origins (e.g., through powerful matrimonial alliances, through pursuit of fame, or through a contemptuous arrogance toward fellow students) but who nonetheless *proclaim* dedication to "vindicating the subalterns." My point is not that they should be blamed for the accident of their birth, nor that they cannot marry rich, pursue fame, or even be arrogant. Rather, it is that they choose to see in others' powerlessness an idealized image of themselves and refuse to hear in the dissonance between the content and manner of their speech their own complicity with violence. Even though these descendents of the Maoist may be quick to point out the exploitativeness of Benjamin Disraeli's "The East is a career,"[24] they remain blind to their own exploitativeness as they make "the East" *their* career. How do we intervene in the productivity of this overdetermined circuit?

TACTICS OF INTERVENTION

Between Orientalism and nativism, between the melancholic cultural connoisseur and the militant Maoist—this is the scene of postcoloniality as many diasporic intellectuals find it in the West. "Diasporas are emblems of transnationalism because they embody the question of borders," writes Khachig Tololyan.[25] The "question of borders" should not be a teleological one. It is not so much about the transient eventually giving way to the permanent as it is about an existential condition of which "permanence" itself is an ongoing fabrication. Accordingly, if, as William Safran writes, "diasporic consciousness is an intellectualization of [the] existential condition"[26] of dispersal from the homeland, then "diasporic consciousness" is perhaps not so much a historical accident as it is an intellectual reality—the reality of being intellectual.

Central to the question of borders is the question of propriety and property. Conceivably, one possible practice of borders is to anticipate and prepare for new proprietorship by destroying, replacing, and expanding existing ones. For this notion of borders—as margins waiting to be incorporated as new properties—to work, the accompanying spatial notion of a field is essential. The notion of a "field" is analogous to the notion of "hegemony," in the sense that its formation involves the rise to dominance of a group that is able to diffuse its culture to all levels of society. In Gramsci's sense, revolution is a struggle for hegemony between opposing classes.

While the struggle for hegemony remains necessary for many reasons—especially in cases where underprivileged groups seek equality of privilege—I remain skeptical of the validity of hegemony over time, *especially if it is a hegemony formed through intellectual power*. The question for me is not how intellectuals can obtain hegemony (a question that positions them in an oppositional light against dominant power and neglects their share of that power through literacy, through the culture of words), but how they can resist, as Michel Foucault said, "the forms of power that transform [them] into its object and instrument in the sphere of 'knowledge,' 'truth,' 'consciousness,' and 'discourse.'"[27] Putting it another way, how do intellectuals struggle against a hegemony which already includes them and which can no longer be divided into the state and civil society in Gramsci's terms, nor be clearly demarcated into national and transnational spaces?

Because "borders" have so clearly meandered into so many intellectual issues that the more stable and conventional relation between borders and the "field" no longer holds, intervention cannot simply be thought of in terms of the creation of new "fields."[28] Instead, it is necessary to think *primarily* in terms of borders—of borders, that is, as *para-sites* that never take over a field in its entirety but erode it slowly and *tactically*.

The work of Michel de Certeau is helpful for a formulation of this parasitical intervention. De Certeau distinguishes between "strategy" and another practice—"tactic"—in the following terms. A strategy has the ability to "transform the uncertainties of history into readable spaces."[29] The type of knowledge derived from strategy is "one sustained and determined by the power to provide oneself with one's own place" (36). Strategy therefore belongs to "an economy of the proper place" (55) and to those who are committed to the building, growth, and fortification of a "field." A text, for instance, would become in this economy "a cultural weapon, a private hunting preserve," or "a means of social stratification" in the order of the Great Wall of China (171). A tactic, by contrast, is "a calculated action determined by the absence of a proper locus" (37). Betting on time instead of space, a tactic "concerns an operational logic whose models may go as far back as the age-old ruses of fishes and insects that disguise or transform themselves in order to survive, and which has in any case been concealed by the form of rationality currently dominant in Western culture" (xi).

Why are "tactics" useful at this moment? As discussions about "multiculturalism," "interdisciplinarity," "the third world intellectual," and other companion issues develop in the American academy and society today, and as rhetorical claims to political change and difference are being put forth, many deep-rooted, politically reactionary forces return to haunt us. Essentialist notions of culture and history; conservative notions of territorial and linguistic propriety, and the "otherness" ensuing from them; unattested claims of oppression and victimization that are used merely to guilt-trip and to control; sexist and racist reaffirmations of sexual and racial diversities that are made merely in the name of righteousness—all these forces create new "solidarities" whose ideological premises remain unquestioned. These new solidarities are often informed by a *strategic* attitude which repeats what they seek to overthrow. The weight of old ideologies being reinforced over and over again is immense.

We need to remember as intellectuals that the battles we fight are battles of words. Those who argue the oppositional standpoint are not *doing* anything different from their enemies and are most certainly not directly changing the downtrodden lives of those who seek their survival in metropolitan and non-metropolitan spaces alike. What academic intellectuals must confront is thus *not* their "victimization" by society at large (or their victimization-in-solidarity-with-the-oppressed), but the power, wealth, and privilege that ironically accumulate from their "oppositional" viewpoint, and the widening gap between the professed contents of their words and the upward mobility they gain from such words. (When Foucault said intellectuals need to struggle against becoming the object and instrument of power, he spoke precisely to this kind of situation.) The predicament we face in the West, where intellectual freedom shares a history with economic enterprise, is that "if a professor wishes to denounce aspects of big business, . . . he will be wise to locate in a school whose trustees are big businessmen."[30] Why should we believe in those who continue to speak a language of alterity-as-lack while their salaries and honoraria keep rising? How do we resist the turning-into-propriety of oppositional discourses, when the intention of such discourses has been that of displacing and disowning the proper? How do we prevent what begin as tactics—that which is "without any base where it could stockpile its winnings"[31]—from turning into a solidly fenced-off field, in the military no less than in the academic sense?

THE CHINESE LESSON

The ways in which modern Chinese history is inscribed in our current theoretical and political discourses, often without our knowing about them, are quite remarkable. I can think of at least three major instances. First, post-structuralism's dismantling of the sign, which grew out of a criticism of phonetic logocentrism from within the Western tradition and which was to activate interest in "text" and "discourse" across humanistic studies, began in an era when Western intellectuals, in particular those in France (Jacques Derrida, Julia Kristeva, Philippe Sollers, Roland Barthes, Louis Althusser, to name a few) "turned East" to China for philosophical and political alternatives. Chinese "writing" has been a source of fascination for European philosophers and philologists since the eighteenth century because its ideographic script seems (at least to those who do not actually use it as a language) a testimony of a different kind of language—a language without the mediation of sound and hence without history.[32] Second, the feminist revolutions of the 1960s and 1970s drew on the Chinese Communists' practice of encouraging peasants, especially peasant women, to "speak bitterness" (*suku*) against an oppressive patriarchal system. The various methods of "consciousness-raising" that we still practice today, inside and outside the classroom, owe their origins to the Chinese "revolution" as described in William Hinton's *Fanshen*.[33] Third, the interest invested by current culture criticism in the socially dispossessed rejoins many issues central to the founding ideology of the Chinese Communist party, which itself drew on Soviet and other Western philosophies.[34] As I indicate in the chapter "Against the Lures of Diaspora," the one figure that is represented and discussed repeatedly in modern Chinese writings since the turn of the twentieth century has been none other than the "subaltern."

To prioritize modern Chinese history this way—to say that "modern China" is, whether we know it or not, the foundation of contemporary cultural studies—is not to glorify "Chinese wisdom." Rather, my aim is to show how the "fate" of an ancient civilization turned modern epitomizes and anticipates many problems we are *now* facing in the West, which in many ways is condemned to a kind of belated consciousness of what its forces set in motion in its others, which usually experience the traumas much earlier. In this regard, the impasses long felt by modern Chinese intellectuals vis-à-vis "their" history, which not only comprises a language used by over a quarter of the world's population but also a long tradition of writing, printing, publishing, examinations, revolutions, and state bureaucracy, can serve as a model for the West's future in the negative sense, that is, a future whose disasters have already been written.

To give one example, the sanctification of victimization in the American academy and its concomitant rebuke of "theory" as intellectualist and elitist parallel, in an uncanny fashion, the treatment of intellectuals during the Cultural Revolution, when labels of "feudalist," "reactionary," "Confucianist," and the like led to murder and execution in the name of salvaging the oppressed classes. This alleged separation of intellectuals from life continues today, not so much in China, where intellectuals are poorly paid, as in places where part of the power enjoyed by intellectuals comes precisely from "bashing" themselves from an anti-intellectual position of "solidarity with the masses." Terry Eagleton's recent diatribe against "American" intellectuals—even though his own publications are bestsellers in the American intellectual market—is a good example of this kind of Cultural Revolution thinking inside capitalist society. Eagleton's attitude is consistent with the typical European intellectual disdain toward "America" and with British intellectual disdain toward "French thought." This is how he uses the Tiananmen incident to target *his own* enemies:

45

> Viewed from eight thousand miles off, [the new historicist] enthusiasm for Foucault has a good deal to do with a peculiarly American left defeatism, guilt-stricken relativism and ignorance of socialism—a syndrome which is understandable in Berkeley but, as I write, unintelligible in Beijing. The unconscious ethnocentrism of much of the U.S. appropriation of such theory is very striking, at least to *an outsider.* What seems on the surface like a glamorous theory of the Renaissance keeps turning out to be about the dilemmas of ageing 1960s radicals in the epoch of Danforth Quayle. I write this article while the Chinese students and workers are still massing outside the Great Hall of the People; and I find it rather hard to understand why the neo-Stalinist bureaucrats have not, so far anyway, moved among the people distributing copies of Derrida, Foucault and Ernesto Laclau. For the Chinese students and workers to learn that their actions are aimed at a "social totality" which is, theoretically speaking, non-existent would surely disperse them more rapidly than water cannons or bullets.[35]

The claim to being an "outsider" is a striking one, bringing to mind not only Jane Eyre's self-marginalization but also nineteenth-century Britain's "splendid isolation." Needless to say, it remains the case that the "people" of the "third world" are invoked only in the form of an indistinguishable mass, while "first world" intellectuals continue to have names.

Growing up in the 1960s and 1970s in Hong Kong, that "classic immigrant city" and "junction between diaspora and homeland,"[36] I experienced Chinese communism differently from many of my colleagues in the American academy and as a result am incapable of drawing from it the sense of revolutionary conviction that still infuses the speeches of Marxist intellectuals in the West. If Gramsci writing in prison "might have been Mao announcing the Cultural Revolution," then the problem of Mao, for many Chinese, was precisely that he "did what Gramsci thought."[37] My most vivid childhood memories of the Cultural Revolution were the daily reports in 1966 and 1967 of corpses from China floating down into the Pearl River Delta and down into the Hong Kong harbor, of local political unrest that led to disruption of school and business, and of the brutal murder of Lam Bun, an employee of Hong Kong's Commercial Radio (a pro-British institution, as were many of Hong Kong's big financial enterprises of that time) whose work during that period involved reading a daily editorial denouncing leftist activities. On his way to work with his brother one day in 1967, Lam Bun was stopped by gangsters, who barred them from getting out of his car, and burned them alive. There are also memories of people risking their lives swimming across the border into Hong Kong and of people visiting China with "the little red book" but also with supplies of food and clothing. This was a period of phenomenal starvation in China. Some people from Hong Kong were going in the hope that, if not searched by border authorities, they could leave behind the food and clothing for needy relatives. (One woman, I recall, wore seven pairs of pants on one of her trips.)

What I retain from these memories is not a history of personal or collective victimization but the sense of immediacy of a particular diasporic reality—of Hong Kong caught, as it always has been since the end of the Second World War, between two dominant cultures, British colonial and Chinese Communist, neither of which takes the welfare of Hong Kong people into account even though both would turn to Hong Kong for financial and other forms of assistance when they needed it. This marginalized position, which is not one chosen by those from Hong Kong but one constructed by history, brings with it a certain privilege of observation and an unwillingness to idealize oppression. To find myself among colleagues from the U.S., Europe, India, and Africa who speak of Chinese communism in idealized terms remains a culture shock. My point, however, is not that of denouncing communism as an error of human history.[38] With the collapse of communism in the Soviet Union and the waning of communism in China, it is easy to bash Marxists and Communists as "wrongdoers" of the past two centuries. This would be like saying that Christians and the church misrepresent the true teachings of the Bible. To the contrary, I think an understanding of what "went wrong" would be possible only if we are willing to undertake what Foucault advocates as a historical analysis of "fascism," a term which, as Foucault said, has been used as a floating signifier with which we blame the other for what goes wrong.[39] The first step in this analysis is not, for instance, to show how the Soviet Union has woken up to its error of the past seventy-four years but to acknowledge that what happened in the Soviet Union and China are necessary events of a positive present of which we, living in the other half of the globe in "capitalistic freedom," are still a functioning part. To pose the "Gulag question," Foucault said, means

[r]efusing to question the Gulag on the basis of the texts of Marx or Lenin or to ask one-self how, through what error, deviation, misunderstanding or distortion of speculation or practice, their theory could have been betrayed to such a degree. On the contrary, it means questioning all these theoretical texts, however old, from the standpoint of the reality of the Gulag. Rather than of searching in those texts for a condemnation in advance of the Gulag, it is a matter of asking what in those texts could have made the Gulag possible, what might even now continue to justify it, and what makes it [sic] intolerable truth still accepted today. The Gulag question must be posed not in terms of error (reduction of the problem to one of theory), but in terms of reality.[40]

47

The hardest lesson from Chinese communism, as with Soviet communism, is that it has *not* been an accident but a process in the history of modern global enlightenment. This is a process that strategizes on the experiences of the "sub-alterns" while never truly resolving the fundamental division between intellectual and manual labor, nor hence the issues of hierarchy, inequity, and discrimination based on *literate* power. What the Chinese Cultural Revolution accomplished in a simplistic attempt to resolve that fundamental division was a *literal* destruction of intellectuals (as bearers of the division). While actual lives were thus sacrificed *en masse*, literate power as social form and as class division lives on. If indeed the "sub-alterns" were revolutionized, then why, we must ask, are we still hearing so much about problems in China that obviously indicate the opposite, such as the sexual oppression of women, the persistent illiteracy of the peasants, the abuse of bureau-cratic power by those in charge of the welfare of the people—all in all what amounts to continued class injustice in a supposedly classless society?

4

Brushes with the-Other-as-Face

STEREOTYPING AND CROSS-ETHNIC REPRESENTATION

THE INEVITABILITY OF
STEREOTYPES IN CROSS-
ETHNIC REPRESENTATION

... Among contemporary cultural critics, Fredric Jameson is the only one I know of who has unambiguously and unapologetically affirmed the inevitability of stereotypes as something fundamental to the representation of one group by another.[1] The unique stance taken by Jameson on this controversial topic is refreshing, and it deserves a closer examination. Not surprisingly, Jameson's statements about stereotypes are situated in his long discussion of the new field of cultural studies, a field in which representations of our others are a regular and unavoidable practice.[2] He begins with an astonishing reference to Erving Goffmann's classic *Stigma* in order to remind us that what we call "culture" is really "the ensemble of stigmata one group bears in the eyes of the other group (and vice versa)" (271). In light of the fact that Goffmann's subject is, as indicated in the subtitle of his book, what he calls "spoiled identity"—namely, the inferior sense of self experienced by people such as cripples, deformed persons, criminals, or ethnic outcasts (Goffmann's specific example being Jews), who are considered deviant from normative society because of their peculiar physiological, sociological, or cultural conditions—Jameson's analogy

is, to say the least, provocative.[3] The reasons behind this analogy are compelling. Using Goffmann enables Jameson to argue that so-called deviance or "stigma" is actually constitutive of cultural identity itself and that that is how one group is usually perceived by another. In this manner, not only does Jameson make the conventional division between normativity and deviancy irrelevant; he has also turned (the perception of) stigmatization into the very condition, the very possibility, for cross-cultural recognition. It is, then, precisely in a stigmatized state that culture becomes "a vehicle or a medium whereby the relationship between groups is transacted."[4]

At the same time, Jameson writes, there is nothing natural about such transactions:

> The relationship between groups is, so to speak, unnatural: it is the chance external contact between entities which have only an interior (like a monad) and no exterior or external surface, save in this special circumstance in which it is precisely the outer edge of the group that—all the while remaining unrepresentable—brushes against that of the other. Speaking crudely then, we would have to say that the relationship between groups must always be one of struggle and violence. (272)

This little passage is remarkable because it defines cross-cultural contact in the unsentimental terms of a brushing against the other as a mere external surface and underscores the struggle and violence inherent to this process. One finds here not the liberalist, progressivist view that different cultures together form one big multicultural family but a reminder of the uncompromised understanding about human aggressiveness advanced by Sigmund Freud in his *Civilization and Its Discontents.* We recall that what bothers Freud is the widespread, traditional religious belief in universal love, a belief that is epitomized in the Judeo-Christian ideal, "Thou shalt love thy neighbour as thyself" (*Leviticus* 19:18). Against this moralist pinnacle of human civilization, Freud argues that there is a basic antagonism, a fundamental destructiveness, within human beings that will always show up such an ideal as a mere piety and a mass delusion rather than a reachable destination. Consequently, civilization must be understood as a permanent struggle by humankind against itself in an attempt to preserve whatever it has accomplished.[5]

If the popular indictments against stereotyping our others are read in the light of Freud's book, they need to be recognized as the contemporary, secularized reenactments of the religious dictum "love thy neighbor as thyself": "Do not deface your neighbor with false representations; do not refer to her by wicked, demeaning names; do not stereotype her." In terms of the arguments about ethnicity in the previous chapter, such indictments of stereotypes should also be seen as arising from the same modernist, universalist claim about ethnicity as a condition equal to all humans, who must therefore be treated with the same degree of respect (or love) around the world.

Jameson's contrary statements about stereotypes, on the other hand, are as unpious and unflattering as Freud's view of human aggressiveness. Like Freud, he does not think that such acts of violence are ever entirely suppressible. Rather, it is incumbent on us to come to terms with their ineluctability:

> Group loathing . . . mobilizes the classic syndromes of purity and danger, and acts out a kind of defense of the boundaries of the primary group against this threat perceived to be inherent in the Other's very existence. Modern racism . . . is one of the most elaborated forms of such group loathing—inflected in the direction of a whole political program; it should lead us on to some reflection of the role of the stereotype in all such group or "cultural" relations, which can virtually, by definition, not do without the stereotypical. For the group as such is necessarily an imaginary entity, in the sense in which no individual mind is able to intuit it concretely. The group must be abstracted, or fantasized, on the basis of discrete individual contacts and experiences which can never be generalized in anything but abusive fashion. *The relations between groups are always stereotypical insofar as they must always involve collective abstractions of the other group, no matter how sanitized, no matter how liberally censored and imbued with respect. . . . The liberal solution to this dilemma—doing away with the stereotypes or*

pretending they don't exist—is not possible, although fortunately we carry on as though it were for most of the time.[6]

In the midst of these statements, perhaps sensing that their absolute nature would no doubt offend the piously minded, Jameson makes a small concession to the "liberal solution" by adding that "what it is politically correct to do under such circumstances is to allow the other group itself to elaborate its own preferential image, and then to work with that henceforth 'official' stereotype."[7] But the qualifying tone of this remark—"what it is politically correct to do"—has the effect rather of further strengthening his predominant argument that stereotypes are virtually indispensable. Should the politically correct solution be adopted single-mindedly, it would only raise more questions: would everything be all right if we simply let our others tell us what stereotypes to use about them? Does this mean that we should simply divide stereotypes into different categories—the good and safe on one side and the bad and incorrect on the other? How do we differentiate between them in the first place?

In other words, the understanding of stereotypes that Jameson has so succinctly delineated—namely, that it is a matter of the outer edge of one group brushing against that of another, that it is *an encounter between surfaces rather than interiors*—cannot really be foreclosed again by the liberalist suggestion that everyone is entitled to her own stereotypes of herself, which others should simply adopt for general use. Once the inevitability of stereotypes—now clarified as relations conducted around exteriors—is understood, the liberalist solution along the lines of cultural entitlement can no longer be a solution. A chasm has irrevocably opened up between the two ends of Jameson's discussion.

As the politically correct go about attacking stereotypes, what is usually repressed is a paradox in the very act of criticizing stereotyping: namely, that in order to criticize stereotypes, one must somehow resort to stereotypical attitudes and presumptions. For instance, in order to repudiate a certain attitude as racist stereotyping, one would, to begin with, need to have already formed certain attitudes toward that attitude, to have *stereotyped* it or marked it as uniformly possessing a distinguishing set of traits. In other words, any charge that others are stereotyping inevitably involves, whether or not one is conscious of it, one's own participation in the same activity. In Mireille Rosello's words, "there is a stereotype of the stereotype: the stereotype is always bad, simplistic, idiotic." When "attacked as a unit of truth, it takes its revenge by forcing speaking into an act of mimesis."[8] This tendency of stereotypes to force even—perhaps especially—their most severe critics to inhabit or become what they are criticizing points to a fundamental discrepancy in representation—between intention and manner, signified and signifier. Insofar as stereotypes are generalizations that seek to encapsulate reality in particular forms, they are not essentially different from the artificial or constructed makeup of all representations. Where stereotypes differ is in the obviousness and exaggeration of their reductive mode—the unabashed nature of their mechanicity and repetitiveness.

Thus, behind the specific disapproval of stereotypes is, in fact, a general anxiety over the purity of language and speech (or representation) and, with that, an age-old demand for conciseness and correctness, qualities that are perpetually in conflict with the way language and speech actually operate. The demand that stereotypes be eliminated is inevitably the demand for a kind of (boundary and thus ethnicity) cleansing. As in the case of all attempts to cleanse speech, this is also a demand for the kind of violence that is censorship. But more disturbing is the fact that such a demand carries within it an implicit acknowledgment of the dangerous potential residing in that which it wants to eliminate. With stereotypes, I would argue that this dangerous potential is not, as is usually assumed, their conventionality and formulaicness but rather their capacity for creativity and originality. To put it more bluntly still, the potential, and hence danger, of stereotypes is that they are able to conflate these two realms of representational truisms—the conventional and the formulaic, on the one hand, and the creative and the original/originating, on the other—when, for obvious reasons of propriety, they ought to be kept separate.

The best instance of such a conflation is the use of stereotypes by political regimes themselves, whether or not they are recognizably repressive. Anyone who has had any experience with the operations of political regimes knows that the use of stereotypes, especially racial stereotypes, is a regular strategy for constructing a mythic other to be relied on for purposes of war, imperialism, national defense, and protectionism. Examples of such mythic others abound in history—the Jew in the Nazi regime, the Jap in U.S. propaganda during the Second World War, the Africans and South Asians who, even though previously colonized by Great Britain, must be barred from "invading" Great Britain, the Hispanic wetbacks who are said to contribute to the economic malaise of the border states in the United States, and the Arab and Turkish guest workers who are being denied basic legal rights in such European countries as France and Germany. The list can go on and on. As Richard Dyer writes, the most important function of the stereotype is

> to maintain sharp boundary definitions, to define clearly where the pale ends and thus who is clearly within and who clearly beyond it. Stereotypes do not only, in concert with social types, map out the boundaries of acceptable and legitimate behaviour, *they also insist on boundaries exactly at those points where in reality there are none.*[9]

When a community, under the leadership of a government, decides to draw a boundary between itself and what is not itself, racial stereotypes are typically deployed as a way to project onto an other all the things that are supposedly alien. In the light of an idealized group identity to be guarded in its purity, such stereotypes (of unwelcome others) are, indeed, demons—bad figures to be exorcised.

At the same time, what the successful use of stereotypes by political regimes has proved is not simply that stereotypes are clichéd, unchanging forms but also—and much more importantly—that stereotypes are capable of engendering realities that do not exist. The fantastic figures of the Jew, the Jap, and the wetback have all produced substantive political consequences, from deportation to incarceration to genocide or ethnic cleansing. Contrary to the charge that they are misrepresentations, therefore, stereotypes have demonstrated themselves to be effective, realistic political weapons capable of generating belief, commitment, and action. His astute insight into the irreducible nature of stereotypy in cultural relations notwithstanding, Jameson has, it seems to me, stopped short of elaborating the issue of power differentials in the very deployment of stereotypes. Such an elaboration would have helped explain how and why stereotypes can be so controversial and explosive under specific circumstances, while under other circumstances the act of stereotyping can pass for acceptable or even conscionable speech. As Dyer puts it, "it is not stereotypes . . . that are wrong, but who controls and defines them, what interests they serve" (12). For instance, in the United States, there is a much higher intolerance of anti-Jewish than of anti-Islamic representations, to the extent that Bill Clinton could, in his public statements as the U.S. president, repeatedly refer to an Islamic head of state such as Saddam Hussein by his first name without raising eyebrows. (To understand the absurdity of this situation, we need only to imagine what it would be like were Clinton himself to be repeatedly referred to as "Bill" in public speeches made by other government leaders. What is disturbing, nevertheless, is not simply his irreverent use of "Saddam" but also its apparent acceptance by the American public.)[10] Similarly, as Rosemary J. Coombe writes,

> It is . . . inconceivable that a vehicle could be marketed as "a wandering Jew," but North Americans rarely bat an eyelash when a Jeep Cherokee© passes them on the road or an advertisement for a Pontiac© flashes across their television screens. More people may know Oneida© as a brand of silverware than as the name of a people and a nation.

A third instance: The racist rejection of black people is equally common among Asians both in Asia and within the United States, but often it is only white people's stereotypes of blacks that receive media attention. Could this be because it is not only the stereotypes themselves but also the power behind their use that accounts for their perceived atrocity, that really counts as it were—so that the question of who is being stereotyped becomes—in this instance, at least—subordinate to that of who is doing the stereotyping and who is accepting/endorsing it? If this is the case, then doesn't it mean that the phenomenon of stereotyping is far more tricky than hitherto thought, because the perception or awareness of stereotypes—that is, at those times when we happen critically to *notice* such representations—may itself already be following a certain stereotypical pattern, the pattern of focusing predominantly on the powers that be? . . .

- "Stereotypes are indespensable"
- "they are generalizations that seek to encapsulate reality in particular forms" pg 51

- Diminating stereotypes is stopping the flow of creativity . . . expressu and censorship.

- use of them by political regimes
  ↳ Japs in WWII
  ↳ wetbacks → mexicans in America

- are seens to be a realistic political weapon,

- stereotypes are not dangerous but the power behind their use that counts

5

The Politics of Admittance

FEMALE SEXUAL AGENCY, MISCEGENATION, AND THE FORMATION
OF COMMUNITY IN FRANTZ FANON

A leading feature that connects the many studies of the black psychiatrist Frantz Fanon since the first publication of his work in the 1950s is undoubtedly the politics of identification. As Henry Louis Gates, Jr. writes, "Fanon's current fascination for us has something do with the convergence of the problematic of colonialism with that of subject-formation."[4] Beginning with Jean-Paul Sartre, critics have, when examining Fanon's texts, focused their attention on the psychic vicissitudes of the black man's identity. While Sartre, writing in the heyday of a leftist existentialism, draws attention to those vicissitudes in terms of a third-world nationalism in formation, a collective revolt that could be generalized to become the revolt of the world proletariat,[5] contemporary critics, geared with lessons in poststructuralism, have alternately reformulated those vicissitudes by way of Derridean deconstruction, Lacanian psychoanalysis, and gender politics involving the representations of white women and the issues of homosexuality.[6] If these critics have rightly foregrounded the tortuous ambiguities that inform the politics of identification in the contexts of colonization and postcolonization, their discussions tend nonetheless to slight a fundamental issue—the issue of community formation. Once we put the emphasis on community, it would no longer be sufficient simply to continue the elaboration of the psychic mutabilities of the postcolonial subject alone. Rather, it would be necessary to reintroduce the structural problems of community formation that are always implied in the articulations of the subject, even when they are not explicitly stated as such.

As the etymological associations of the word "community" indicate, community is linked to the articulation of commonality and consensus; a community is always based on a kind of collective inclusion. In the twentieth century the paradigm of ideal community formation has been communism, which is the secular version of a holy communion with a larger Being who is always beyond but with whom man nonetheless seeks communication.[7] At the same time, however, there is no community formation without the implicit understanding of who is and who is not to be admitted. As the principle that regulates community formation, admittance operates in several crucial senses.

There is, first, admittance in the most physical sense of letting enter, as when we say we are admitted to a theater, an auditorium, a school, a country, and so forth. The person who is or is not admitted bears on him or her the marks of a group in articulation. This basic, physical sense of admittance, of being allowed to enter certain spaces, governs a range of hierarchically experienced geographical and spatial divisions in the colonial and postcolonial world, from the segregation of black and white spaces in countries such as the United States and South Africa, to the rules forbidding local people to enter "foreign concessions" in their own land during the heyday of the "scramble" for Africa and China, to the contemporary immigration apparatuses in politically stable nations that aim to expel "illegal immigrants" from such nations' borders. Meanwhile, to "let enter" is, as can be surmised from these examples, closely connected with recognition and acknowledgment, which is the second major connotation of admittance. Admittance in this second sense is a permission to enter in the abstract, through the act that we call validation. To be permitted to enter is then to be recognized as having a similar kind of value as that which is possessed by the admitting community. Third, there is admittance in the sense of a confession—such as the admittance of a crime. Insofar as confession is an act of repentance, a surrender of oneself in reconciliation with the rules of society, it is also related to community.

To this extent, I feel that the work in cultural studies that has followed poststructuralist theory's close attention to issues of identification and subjectivity is both an accomplishment and a setback: an accomplishment, because such work—which I shall call "subject work"—enables the subject to be investigated in ever more nuanced manners across the disciplines, holding utopian promise often by concluding that the subject, be it masculine, feminine, gay, postcolonial, or otherwise, is infinitely "unstable" and therefore open-ended; a setback, because nuanced readings of the subject as such also tend to downplay issues of structural control—of law, sovereignty, and prohibition—that underlie the subject's relation with the collective. Much "subject work" has, in other words, too hastily put its emphasis on the "post" of "poststructuralism," (mis)leading us to think that the force of structure itself is a thing of the past. I believe that these neglected other issues, which are the issues of admittance, pertain even more urgently to the kind of conceptualization of community that begins as a revolt against an existing political condition, such as the condition of colonization. In turning to the texts of Fanon, then, the questions I would like to explore are not questions about the colonized or postcolonized subject per se, but rather: how is community articulated in relation to race and to sexuality? What kinds of admittance do these articulations entail, with what implications?

RACE AND THE PROBLEM OF ADMITTANCE

Fanon's discussions of the existential dilemmas facing the black man, which he interprets with the explicit purpose of liberating the black man from himself, are well known.[8] From the feelings of "lust" and "envy" that accompany the historically inevitable violence toward the white man in *The Wretched of the Earth,* we move to the picture of an "infernal circle" of shame and longing-for-recognition in *Black Skin, White Masks:*

> I am overdetermined from without, I am the slave not of the "idea" that others have of me but of my own appearance. . . .
>
> Shame. Shame and self-contempt. Nausea. When people like me, they tell me it is in spite of my color. When they dislike me, they point out that it is not because of my color. Either way, I am locked into the infernal circle.[9]
>
> Man is human only to the extent to which he tries to impose his existence on another man in order to be recognized by him. As long as he has not been effectively recognized by the other, that other will remain the theme of his actions. It is on that other being, on recognition by that other being, that his own human worth and reality depend. It is that other being in whom the meaning of his life is condensed. (217)

These compelling passages indicate that for the black man, selfhood and communal relations are entirely intertwined with skin color and race. If the forced coexistence with the white man is impossible as a basis for community, it is because the white man, with his attitudes of racist superiority, does not *admit* the black man as an equal. Significantly, admittance here operates in the first two senses I mentioned: first, in the sense of letting enter; second, in the sense of validation and acknowledgment. The physical sense of admittance connotes in a vivid manner the process of acceptance by permission, and hence the process of identification as the successful or failed acquisition of a particular kind of entry permit. And yet, being "admitted" is never simply a matter of possessing the right permit, for validation and acknowledgment must also be present for admittance to be complete. The existential burden that weighs on the black man is that he never has admittance in these first two, intimately related senses of the word: his skin color and race mean that even if he has acquired all the rightful permits of entry into the white world—by education, for instance—he does not feel that he is acknowledged as an equal.

For Fanon, the conceptualization of a community alternative to the colony is thus inseparable from a heightened awareness of race as a limit of admittance. If the black man is not admitted by the white man because of his skin color, then this very skin color would now become the basis of a new community—the basis of entry into and recognition by the postcolonial nation. But how does race operate as a new type of admittance ticket, a new communal bond? On close reading, it would seem that race, in spite of the fact that it is imagined at the revolutionary moment as the utopian communion among people who suffer the same discrimination, nonetheless does not escape the problems structural to all processes of admittance. The issue of admittance—of legitimate entry and validation—becomes especially acute when we introduce sexual difference—when we read the different manners in which Fanon describes the black man and the black woman.

Fanon's analyses of the woman of color are found in a chapter of *Black Skin, White Masks*, the chapter entitled "The Woman of Color and the White Man." The title signals, already, that identification for the woman of color is a matter of exchange relations, a matter of how the woman of color is socially *paired off* or *contracted*. Unlike the black man, who is considered a (wronged) sovereign subject, the woman of color is first of all an object with exchange value. Fanon's views are based in part on his reading of fiction—such as the stories *Je suis Martiniquaise*, by Mayotte Capecia, and *Nini*, by Abdoulaye Sadji—even though it is clear that his reading is intended beyond the "fictional" contexts. Fanon describes the woman of color in terms of her aspiration toward "lactification" and summarizes her "living reactions" to the European in this manner:

> First of all, there are two such women: the Negress and the mulatto. The first has only one possibility and one concern: to turn white. The second wants not only to turn white but also to avoid slipping back. What indeed could be more illogical than a mulatto woman's acceptance of a Negro husband? For it must be understood once and for all that it is a question of saving the race. (54–55)
>
> For, in a word, the race must be whitened; *every woman* in Martinique knows this, says it, repeats it. Whiten the race, save the race, but not in the sense that one might think: not "preserve the uniqueness of that part of the world in which they grew up," but make sure that it will be white. Every time I have made up my mind to analyze certain kinds of behavior, I have been unable to avoid the consideration of certain nauseating phenomena. The number of sayings, proverbs, petty rules of conduct that govern the choice of a lover in the Antilles is astounding. It is always essential to avoid falling back into the pit of nigger-hood, and *every woman* in the Antilles, whether in a casual flirtation or in a serious affair, is determined to select the least black of the men. Sometimes, in order to justify a bad investment, she is compelled to resort to such arguments as this: "X is black, but misery is blacker." I know a great number of girls from Martinique, students in France, who admitted to me with complete candor—completely white candor—that they would find it impossible to marry black men. (47–48; my emphases)

In the light of these extended remarks, Fanon's later remark regarding the woman of color, "I know nothing about her" (180), can be taken only as a disclaimer of definitive views that he has, in fact, already pronounced. To this extent, critics who, despite their critical sensitivity, accept Fanon's "I know nothing about her" at face value are simply sidestepping a problem that would interfere with the coherence of their own interpretations. This is the problem of the sexuality of the woman of color, the legitimation and delegitimation of which is crucial to the concept of a postcolonial national community.[10] The predominant impression given by the passages just quoted is that women of color are *all alike:* in spite of the differences in pigmentation between the Negress and the mulatto, for instance, they share a common, "nauseating" trait—the desire to become white—that can be generalized in the form of "every woman." In an account of black subjecthood that is premised on the irreducible (racial) difference between black and white people, thus, Fanon's descriptions of the women of color are paradoxically marked by their non-differentiation, their projection (onto femininity) of qualities of indistinguishability and universality.[11] Before we examine Fanon's descriptions of the sexuality of women more specifically, however, I would like to dwell for a moment on the theoretical linkage between community formation and sexual difference by turning to a classic text about community formation—Sigmund Freud's *Totem and Taboo.*

COMMUNITY FORMATION AND SEXUAL DIFFERENCE: A DOUBLE THEORETICAL DISCOURSE

In *Totem and Taboo*, Freud offers a theory of community formation that is drawn from anthropological, sociological, and religious studies of "primitive" societies. As is well known, Freud, instead of contradicting the findings of early studies, supports them by focusing on two interrelated aspects of community formation.[12] First, participation in a common bond is achieved through the murder and sacrifice of the primal father, who is afterward venerated and raised to the status of a god, a totem. Second, this bond is secured through the institution of a particular law, the law against incest:

> Thus the brothers had no alternative, if they were to live together, but—not, perhaps, until they had passed through many dangerous crises—to institute the law against incest, by which they all alike renounced the women whom they desired and who had been their chief motive for dispatching their father. In this way they rescued the organization which had made them strong—and which may have been based on homosexual feelings and acts. (144)

The two principles at work in community formation are thus the incorporation of kin (the primal father is being eaten and internalized as law) and the exportation of sex (the women are being banned and transported outside). Freud's model is thought provoking because it signals the crisis-laden nature of the relationship between community and sexual difference. Here is an area, his text suggests, where things are likely to be explosive. If the potential destruction of the group is likely to result from heterosexual relations within the group, then precisely those relations must be tabooed—hence the prohibition of incest.

But what is dangerous about incest? In his explication of taboos, Freud emphasizes that touching or physical contact plays a major role in taboo restrictions because touching is "the first step toward obtaining any sort of control over, or attempting to make use of, a person or object" (33–34). In other words, the taboo has as its power the force of contagion—the force of passing from object to person and then from person to person—through physical contact. If a taboo is not only a thing or an act, but also the person who has violated the taboo, then the person who *embodies* "touching" and "physical contact" must be looked upon as the taboo as well. Women, because they have the capability of embodying physical contact—of giving material form to "touching," to the transgression of bodily boundaries—in the form of reproduction, are always potentially dangerous; and incest, which could result in such reproduction within the same tribe, is thus danger raised to the second degree and the cultural taboo par excellence. Even though Freud's account leaves many questions unanswered, what stands out from his text is the unmistakable recognition of female sexuality as a form of physical power. It is this physical power, this potentiality of transmission, confusion, and reproduction through actual bodies, that could break down all boundaries and thus disrupt social order in the most fundamental fashion. Because of this, female sexuality itself must be barred from entering a community except in the most non-transgressive, least contagious form.

The implications of Freud's theory are eventually extended, among others, by Claude Lévi-Strauss, who argues that the incest taboo is the origin of human culture because it ensures the practice of exogamy and thus the social relations among different groups of men. Following Marcel Mauss's theory of gift-giving as what sustains the equilibrium of power in tribal society, Lévi-Strauss reads women as the gifts in the kinship system: women are exchanged between families so that kinship as an elaborate network can function.[13] But even though they facilitate *communication* and thus *community relations*, women themselves are not considered as initiators of communication or active partners in community formation. As Gayle Rubin comments in her classic essay, "The Traffic in Women":

> If it is women who are being transacted, then it is the men who give and take them who are linked, the woman being a conduit of a relationship rather than a partner to it. . . .
> If women are the gifts, then it is men who are the exchange partners. And it is the

partners, not the presents, upon whom reciprocal exchange confers its quasi-mystical power of social linkage . . . it is men who are the beneficiaries of the product of such exchanges—social organization.[14]

Moreover, one could argue that this exchange of women as gifts—this "admittance" that in fact preempts women from having the same rights as men—operates not only as the content but also as the structure of Lévi-Strauss's theorizing. For, once the problem of female sexuality is displaced onto the regulation of kinship structures, it is kinship structures that become the primary focus, while the potential significance of female sexuality as a transgressive force becomes subordinated and thus minimized. By barring female sexuality from entering their writings as a disruptive force, Freud's followers such as Lévi-Strauss thus uncannily repeat, with their acts of theorizing, the story of *Totem and Taboo*: even though these male theorists have, following Freud, identified the handling of sexual difference as what makes a community work,[15] seldom do they bother to elaborate sexual difference itself beyond the point that it serves to support the community formation that is, in the final analysis, a veneration of the father. The continual incorporation/internalization of the voice/narrative of the father (in this case, Freud) and the exportation of the "touch" of sexual difference represented by women mean that the paradigm of community building doubles on itself even as it is being enunciated as theory: we have, in the (psychoanalytic, anthropological, sociological) writings about community formation, a metacommunity building that can be named the solidarity of "male homosocial readings." We must note that in this metacommunity building, this solidarity forming through interpretation, women are never being erased but always given a specific, corollary place: while not exactly admitted, neither are they exactly refused admission. To interrupt this metacommunity building, it would therefore not be enough simply to take sexual difference into consideration; what is more crucial is moving sexual difference beyond the status of "corollary" or "support" that Freud and his followers allow it. Instead of the incorporation of the father and the community among men, then, we need to look at what is "exported," the taboo that is female sexuality itself.

Another problem with *Totem and Taboo* is that, as is characteristic of many of Freud's writings, it is most suggestive in its explanation of the mechanics—the displacements, negations, and emotional ambivalences—*within* a group. And yet if this text is eminently useful as a reminder of the linkage between community formation and sexual difference, it is inevitably inadequate in a situation where more than one community is involved. The postcolonized situation, in which a formerly colonized group seeks to establish its new status as a national community that is alternative to the one in preindependent times, necessarily complicates Freud's binarist, interiorist model. The most outstanding feature in the postcolonized

63

situation is not one group of men and women (and the problem of sexuality within their community), but the conflictual relations between the colonized subject, his own ethnic/racial community, and the lingering effects of the colonizer. The presence of what are at the very least two groups—colonizer and colonized—rather than one, as well as the persistent hierarchical injustices brought about by the domination of one over the other, means that any consideration of community formation in the postcolonial aftermath must exceed the model of the *in-house* totemism and taboo as suggested by Freud.

It is, thus, with a twin focus on female sexuality and on the *double* theoretical discourse of admittance and nonadmittance regarding female sexuality that I return to the problem of community formation in Fanon. The question here is not whether Fanon gives us more or less satisfying answers, but how, precisely because Fanon's texts are explicitly political and aimed at revolutionizing thinking about the social bases of identification—from the stage of colonization to national culture, from white imperialist domination to the reclamation of black personhood and agency—they offer a demonstration of the problems that are inherent in all masculinist conceptions of community formation more starkly and thus more disturbingly than most. My aim, in other words, is not to belittle the epochal messages of a seminal political thinker. Rather it is to argue, first, the ineluctability of considering female sexuality and sexual difference as *primary* issues in a discussion of community formation; and second, how, once introduced, female sexuality and sexual difference at both the empirical and theoretical levels interrupt community formation with powerful fissures. Ultimately, my question is: could female sexuality and sexual difference ever be reconciled with community? Are these mutually exclusive events? To begin to answer these questions, we will now examine the specific kinds of analyses Fanon gives of female sexuality.

WHAT DOES THE WOMAN OF COLOR WANT?

Unlike his analyses of the black man, with their intent of foregrounding the existential ambivalences of the black male psyche, Fanon's depictions of women of color are, as we see in the passages quoted earlier, direct and with little doubt: the women of color *want* to have sexual relations with white men because it is their means of upward social mobility, their way of so-called "saving the race." If Fanon's manner of dealing with what the woman of color wants sounds somewhat familiar in its confident tone, it is because it reminds us of the manner in which Freud describes the little girl's acquisition of sexual identity. As feminists have often pointed out, Freud's portrayals of the psychic labor spent by the little girl and little boy in acquiring their respective sexual identities are remarkably different. While the little boy's psyche is full of the complexity of belated or retroactive consciousness—he does not understand the meaning of the female genitalia and hence sexual difference until he is threatened with the possibility of castration—the little girl, by contrast, "behaves differently. She makes her judgment and her decision in a flash. She has seen it and knows that she is without it and wants to have it."[16] As portrayed by Freud, the little boy is an *innocent victim* of his cultural environment, whereas the little girl is an *active agent* in her grasp of the politics of sexuality. Similarly, in Fanon's portrayals, we sense that the black man is viewed as a helpless victim of his cultural environment, whereas the woman of color is viewed as a knowledge-able, calculating perpetrator of interracial sexual intercourses. If the black man's desire to elevate himself to whiteness is a plea for what Fanon affirms as "active understanding,"[17] the similar desire on the part of the woman of color is not given as complex a treatment. To paraphrase Freud, the woman of color simply "has seen it and knows that she is without it and wants to have it."

By refusing the woman of color any of the kind of emotional ambivalence that is copiously endowed upon the psyche of the black man, what Fanon accomplishes is a representation—representation both in the sense of portraying and in the sense of speaking for[18]—of the woman of color as potentially if not always a whore, a sell-out, and hence a traitor to her own ethnic community. Women of color are, in other words, shameless people who forsake their own origins ("the uniqueness of that part of the world in which they grew up") for something more "universally" desirable and profitable—association with the white world. Rather than living and working alongside her black kinsmen and sharing their ordeals, the woman of color jumps at any opportunity for getting out of her ghetto. While the black man is sympatheti-cally and empathetically portrayed as filled with existentialist angst, as subjected to a state of psychic castratedness that is nonetheless a sign of his honor, his integrity as a cultural hero, the choices and actions of the woman of color are rather associated with efficiency, with determination, with confidence, even with "candor"—qualities which, however, become signs of her dishonor, her natural degeneracy. And it is as if, because of these qualities, the woman of color is unworthy of the careful *analytic* attention that is so painstakingly bestowed on her male counterpart.

In contrast to the view that the woman of color has been made to disappear or is deprived of her agency, therefore, I would argue that Fanon in fact gives her a very specific kind of appearance and agency. To confront the issue of female sexuality in Fanon, what is required is not exactly an attempt to "restore" the woman of color by giving her a voice, a self, a subjectivity; rather we need to examine *how* the woman of color has *already* been given agency—by examining the form which this attributed agency assumes. To use the terms of our ongoing discussion, this is, once again, a question about admittance. What kind of admittance does Fanon extend to the woman of color—what kind of entry permit and what kind of acknowledgment?

Fanon describes the woman of color in terms of her conscious wishes and her unconscious desires. This distinction does not in the end amount to a real difference because, as we shall see, whether conscious or unconscious, the woman of color is headed toward the same fate.

We will begin with her conscious wish, her supposed desire for the white man. Since the white man is the oppressor of black people, is this colored female agency, this desire for the white sexual partner, a masochistic act? Viewed as a way to climb up the social ladder in a world where white is superior, it would, at first, not seem so: the woman of color is in fact benefiting rather than bringing pain to herself from such an act. Unlike her black brother, Fanon suggests, she has everything to gain from her association with the white world. But the matter of masochism is not so clear once we juxtapose Fanon's description of the woman of color with yet another counterpart—this time the white woman. This juxtaposition reveals a much more disturbing perspective on the so-called "unconscious" of women *in general*.

In a manner paralleling his description of the woman of color, Fanon's description of the white woman fixes her with a determined sexual agency. The white woman, too, "wants it": she desires to have sex with the Negro in her fantasy. Moreover, this time what the woman "wants" is definitely a part of her masochism—her wanting to be raped:

> First the little girl sees a sibling rival beaten by the father, a libidinal aggressive. At this
> stage (between the ages of five and nine), the father, who is now the pole of her libido,
> refuses in a way to take up the aggression that the little girl's unconscious demands
> of him. At this point, lacking support, this free-floating aggression requires an invest-
> ment. Since the girl is at the age in which the child begins to enter the folklore and
> the culture along roads that we know, the Negro becomes the predestined depository
> of this aggression. If we go farther into the labyrinth, we discover that when a woman
> lives the fantasy of rape by a Negro, it is in some way the fulfillment of a private dream,
> of an inner wish. Accomplishing the phenomenon of turning against self, *it is the*
> *woman who rapes herself.* (179; my emphasis)

From this analysis of the white woman Fanon shifts to a speculation about women in general:

> We can find clear proof of this in the fact that *it is commonplace for women, during the*
> *sexual act, to cry to their partners:* "*Hurt me!*" They are merely expressing this idea: Hurt
> me as I would hurt me if I were in your place. *The fantasy of rape by a Negro is a variation*
> *of this emotion:* "I wish the Negro would rip me open as I would have ripped a woman
> open." (179; my emphases)

66

[handwritten annotation: white women fantasy to be raped by black man.]

This passage indicates that all women fantasize being hurt in the sexual act and that this fantasy, which women project onto their sexual partners, is ultimately a fantasy of women *themselves hurting themselves*. ("It is the woman who rapes herself.") Accordingly, there is no such thing as a man hurting a woman; there is no such thing as rape. The implicit assumption that women are fundamentally unrapable is perhaps the reason, as critics have pointed out, in spite of his sensitivity to interracial sexual violence, Fanon has not attempted/bothered to deal with the prominent issue of the rape of women of color by white men.[19] Instead, women's essential unrapability means that the rape of women must be inverted to become women's desire and that the violence committed against women must be inverted to become the women's violence against themselves. And, since such violence is a condition characteristic of *all* women, the white woman's desire for her racial other, the black man, is merely "a variation of this emotion," to which (the emotion) skin color is but an accident.[20]

[handwritten annotation: 67]

The above description of white female sexuality is then followed by the line in which Fanon claims his lack of knowledge about the woman of color. Revealingly, even as he makes this disclaimer, he adds an observation that in effect shows not exactly his lack of knowledge but (in accordance with the logic of his immediately preceding discussion) his understanding that black and white women are universally alike. If his preceding discussion shows the white woman to "want" rape by a Negro (since all women "want" rape), he now shows that black women, too, "want" the Negro who is socially inferior to them:

> Those who grant our conclusions on the psychosexuality of the white woman may ask what we have to say about the woman of color. I know nothing about her. What I can offer, at the very least, is that *for many women in the Antilles—the type that I shall call the all-but-whites—the aggressor* is *symbolized by the Senegalese type, or in any event by an inferior (who is so considered).*[21]

In an account that ultimately minimizes if not effaces the racial and ethnic differences between black and white women, Fanon portrays women's sexuality in the main as characterized by an active sadomasochistic desire—to be raped, to rape herself, to rip herself open. Furthermore, as in the case of the women in the Antilles who fantasize sex with Senegalese men, this sadomasochistic desire is implicated in class, as it is enacted through fantasies of relations with a socially inferior male. Not only is sex with a woman always a kind of rape generated by herself, but her essential femininity/depravity is proven by her desire for a man of the lower class.

We have by this point two seemingly contradictory descriptions of the woman of color: on the one hand, she wants the white man because he is socially *superior;* on the other hand, she wants certain types of black men because they are socially *inferior*. The first description pertains to the greed for upward social mobility; the second pertains to the realization of lewd sexual fantasies. However, from the perspective of the woman of color, the effect produced by both types of descriptions is the same. This is the effect of the construction of a female sexual agency that is entirely predictable and already understood, conscious or unconscious. Most crucially, this construction, because it admits women *as* sexuality and nothing more, leaves no room for the woman of color to retain her membership among her own racial/ethnic community. In terms of the community formation that is based on race, the admittance that Fanon gives the woman of color is solely based on sex.[22] Fanon's reading means that the woman of color is either a *black traitor* (when she chooses the white man) or a *white woman* (when she chooses a black man).[23] Fanon's admittance of the sexual agency of the woman of color signifies her inevitable expulsion from her community. Between her conscious actions and her unconscious desires, between her wish for "lactification" and her fantasy of being raped "by a Negro," the woman of color is thus, literally, *ex-communicated* even as she is being acknowledged, attacked and assaulted even as she is being "admitted."

In contrast to the agency given to the woman of color, the black man is, as I mentioned, portrayed much more sympathetically as a victim of multiple forces—of colonialism, of his own tormenting emotional responses to history, and ultimately of the infidelity and "whiteness" of "his" women. Instead of a concrete agency, conscious or unconscious, the black man is throughout enhanced with what I will call *the privilege of ambivalence,* a reaction that is defined as the impossible choice between whiteness and blackness. If ambivalence is a privilege, it is because it exempts the black man from the harsh requirements imposed upon the woman of color. Whereas the women of color are required to stay completely within boundaries, the black man is allowed to waver between psychic states and ethnic communities, to be "borderline." The black man is allowed to go in and out of his community—to mate with white women, for instance—without having his fidelity questioned.[24] If unconditional admittance to his ethnic community is what distinguishes the black man from the woman of color, it is because, in the texts of Fanon at least, the black man alone holds "ambivalence" as his entry and exit permit.

THE FORCE OF MISCEGENATION

Clearly, Fanon's descriptions of women do not depart significantly from the traditional masculinist view that equates women with sex. In contrast to men, who are defined by violence and ambivalence, Fanon's construction of womanhood is a

construction through notions of sexual chastity, purity, fidelity, depravity, and per-
version. Such notions of female sexuality are then welded onto the conceptualiza-
tions of the colonized subject and thus inevitably of the prospective communities to
come after colonization. But why is the sexual agency of women such a prohibitive
concern in the aftermath of colonization?

As can be glimpsed already in Freud's text, any conceptualization of community is
by implication a theory about reproduction, both biological and social. Female sexuality, insofar as it is the embodiment of the "touching," the physical intimacy that leads
to such reproduction, is therefore always a locus of potential danger—of dangerous
possibilities. If the creation of a postcolonial national community is at least in part
about the empowerment of the formerly colonized through the systematic preservation of their racial and ethnic specificities, then such an empowerment could easily
be imagined to be threatened by miscegenation, the sexual intermixing among the
races. Such sexual intermixing leads to a kind of reproduction that is racially impure,
and thus to a hybridization of the elements of the community concerned.

Miscegenation leading to the mixing of races and cultures, the threat of impurity, the danger of bastardization—this much is common knowledge. Is this the
reason why women's sexual agency is tabooed and excommunicated—since, as
Fanon portrays it, women are consciously or unconsciously prone to miscegenation?[25] What dangers does a *female* tendency toward miscegenation hold for a theory
of community formation in the aftermath of colonialism?

This is the juncture where two readings of Fanon's texts are, I think, possible.
The first is that Fanon is just like any other man—that he is simply a patriarch who
cannot tolerate differences and impurities. Instead of letting in Fanon's concerns
as specifically the concerns of a person of color, such a reading would read him
exclusively by way of his sexuality. The second reading, which is the one I would
follow, is less straightforward and perhaps more contradictory, because it tries to
admit the implications of Fanon's race as well as sexuality. This reading would show
that what makes the women's conscious or unconscious desires for miscegenation
such a traumatic event in Fanon's theory is that such *"sexual"* desires in fact share
with the male intellectual's *race*-conscious, anti-colonialist message a common
goal—the goal of ending the compartmentalized, Manichean division of the world
into colonizer and colonized, us and them, that is colonialism's chief ideological
legacy. In place of a pure grouping, racial sexual intermixing is the very force—the
force of biological procreation and of social connotation—that gives rise to alternative groups of people whose origins are all bastardized and whose *communal bond*
can henceforth not be based on the purity of their status as black or white. These
groups would be the actual externalizations, the actual embodiments, of the psychical ambivalences, the split between being white and being black, that torment the
black man as Fanon describes it. What such groups would have in common—what

would make them a community—is paradoxically what they do *not* absolutely have in common in terms of blood, skin color, or ethnicity.

This other, alternative kind of community, a community in which the immanence and specificity of corporeality would coexist with a democratic, open-ended notion of collectivity, is the foreseeable consequence of a kind of sexual agency that disrupts the existing boundaries that mark different racial groups apart. It is also, theoretically speaking, the utopian transformative vision that underlies the clear pronouncements made by Fanon against the domineering racist practices of European imperialism. But the difficulty for Fanon is precisely the difficulty inherent to all events of community formation: admittance (into a group) by necessity implies exclusion. What and who must be excluded and why? This fundamental law about community formation is further exacerbated by the postcolonial situation, in which utopian vision and political reality do not exactly correspond. Even though the passionate imagining of a national culture must, in theory, oppose the segregational assumptions inherent in colonialism, the practical implementation of the postcolonial nation as such cannot but mark new boundaries and reinforce new exclusions. The (female) force of miscegenation, with its seemingly opportunistic oblivion to the injustices of a racist history, must be barred from entering the new realm of political necessity.

For Fanon at the postcolonized moment of nation formation, female sexuality is a traumatic event because it poses the danger of a double transgression. What disturbs him is that the women of color, instead of staying put in their traditional position as "gifts," as the conduits and vehicles that facilitate social relations and enable group identity, actually *give themselves*. By giving themselves, such women enter social relationships as active partners in the production of meanings rather than simply as the bearers of those meanings. And, if such sexual giving constitutes a significant form of transgression, this transgression is made doubly transgressive when women of color give themselves *to white men*. In the latter case, the crossing of patriarchal sexual boundaries crosses another crossing, the crossing of racial boundaries. The women of color are, accordingly, the site of *supplementary* danger— of the dangerous supplement (Jacques Derrida's term)—par excellence, adding to the injustice of race the revolt of sex (and vice versa), and substituting/transforming the meaning of both at once.

In the typical dilemma facing nationalist discourse once nationalist discourse encounters gender, thus, Fanon's discourse is beset with the contested issues of identity, agency, and sovereignty. Deniz Kandiyoti comments on this dilemma succinctly:

> A feature of nationalist discourse that has generated considerable consensus is its
> Janus-faced quality. It presents itself both as a modern project that melts and trans-

forms traditional attachments in favour of new identities and as a reaffirmation of authentic cultural values culled from the depths of a presumed communal past. It therefore opens up a highly fluid and ambivalent field of meanings which can be reactivated, reinterpreted and often reinvented at critical junctures of the histories of nation-states. These meanings are not given, but fought over and contested by political actors whose definitions of *who* and *what* constitutes the nation have a crucial bearing on notions of national unity and alternative claims to sovereignty as well as on the sorts of gender relations that should inform the nationalist project.[26]

If the woman of color can be of value to her ethnic community only as a gift and a defenseless victim, then her assumption of any agency would in effect invalidate her and deprive her of admittance. The ultimate danger posed by the Negress and the mulatto is hence not their sexual behavior per se, but the fact that their sexual agency carries with it a powerful (re)conceptualization of community—of community as based on difference, heterogeneity, creolization; of community as the "illegitimate" mixings and crossings of color, pigmentation, physiognomy—that threateningly *vies with the male intellectual's*. The fact that the women are equal, indeed avant garde, partners in the production of a future community—is this not *the* confusion, the most contagious of forces, that is the most difficult to *admit*, to permit to enter, to acknowledge, and to confess? The ultimate taboo, it would seem, is once again the "taboo against the sameness of men and women," the "division of labor by sex."[27]

The woman of color, by virtue of being both female and colored, having entrance points into and out of the community through sex and through ethnicity, becomes extremely suspect in a situation when supposedly only the black man has such privilege of "ambivalence" and when supposedly only "race" as the black man experiences it matters in the articulation of community consciousness. Once we put our focus on this "tabooed" area of female sexuality, we see that female sexuality is what interrupts the unidirectional force of existential violence that is otherwise justified in Fanon's theory of postcolonial nation-building.[28] At this point, the three senses of admittance I mentioned earlier come together. The strategies of simplification and reduction Fanon adopts toward the woman of color (in the many forms of "she wants it") are, in this light, not exactly attempts to refuse her *entry* but rather signs of an implicit, though reluctant, *acknowledgment* of her claim (equal to his) to being the progenitor of the community to come. At the same time, if this acknowledgment could also be seen as a kind of *confession,* it is nonetheless only a confession that reconciles (the male intellectual) with the community of color *and* with male sexuality but not with the women of color; a confession that surrenders to the demands of race and to the distinctions of sex but not to the supplementary transgression of colored female agency.

Because women are, with their sexual behavior, powerful agents in the generation of a different type of community, the male intellectual senses that he cannot trust—cannot bond with—them. He cannot trust them because he cannot control the potentiality that ensues from their acts of miscegenation. But how is the future community to be conceived without women? Fanon, like all revolutionary male thinkers, would bond instead with "the people," which is the figure that empowers him in this *competition between the sexes* for the *birthing* of a new community. Community formation thus takes on, at the theoretical level, the import of a sexual struggle—a seizing of the power to reproduce and procreate. It is in this sense that the "native"—etymologically linked to "nation" and also to "birth"—becomes the progeny of the male postcolonial critic. The exclusive bond with this progeny allows for the fantasy of undoing and outdoing woman.

Interestingly, then, the "native" and the "people" in Fanon's texts are, like the black man, signs that waver with ambivalence. The people waver between complete deprivation—having nothing and thus nothing to lose—and an essential "resistance" toward colonialism.[29] The descriptions of the native/people as possessing nothing and something at once raises fundamental questions. On the one hand, if colonialism is an all-encompassing environment, leaving the native with utterly nothing, where does the native get his readiness to attack, to fight back? This could only mean either that there is an essential something (nature, history) that allows the native to resist, in which case the native is not "nothing"; or that there are gaps and fissures within the colonial system itself that allow the native some room to resist, in which case colonialism as a system of domination is less than airtight.[30]

By portraying the "native" and the "people" in this ambivalent light—now totally deprived, now possessed of resistive energy; now entirely at the mercy of colonial domination, now definitely the source of rebellion against the colonizer—Fanon retains them as empty, mobile figures, figures of convenience onto which he, like other revolutionary male thinkers, can write his own script.[31] Because the "native" and the "people" are fundamentally empty, they accommodate the revolutionary intellectual with a rhetorical frame in which to hang his utopian vision, whereas women, because they are understood to possess a potent sexual agency, stand as an obstinate stumbling block in the path of revolutionary thought. As a result, while the "native" / the "people" continue to be exonerated in the imagined community of the new nation, women are admitted only with reservation—and only as "sex."

COMMUNITY BUILDING AMONG THEORISTS OF POSTCOLONIALITY

Once introduced, female sexuality, because it foregrounds the difference in the kinds of admittance extended to men and women, complicates the entire question of how a new community is conceptualized in the postcolonial aftermath. If, in terms of the inequality of race, Fanon correctly identifies the "infernal circle" of shame and longing-for-recognition as the condition that traps the black man, who is not exactly refused entry yet not exactly given his due recognition by the white world, he also uncannily inflicts a similarly "infernal" circle on the woman of color. If the black man's "skin color" is the place where he can never be sure of his admittance into the world of the "other" men, the white men, then for the woman of color, sexuality as much as skin color is what renders admittance by all communities, *especially that of her own "race,"* problematic.[32]

As in the case of Freud, the politics of admittance works not only at the level of the content and structure of Fanon's articulations, but also at the level of his works' reception. In choosing not to discuss the obviously fraught issues of sexuality in Fanon, in choosing to pass over this significant part of his texts with silence, many postcolonial critics are themselves implicitly building a type of discursive community that repeats the ambivalences and neuroses of Fanon's articulations.[33] This kind of silence is often justified by way of "the more important" issues of racism and colonialism, and by way of the implicit assumption that any discussion of sexuality as such is, like the sexual behavior of Fanon's woman of color, a suspect move toward "lactification." In the collective incorporation of the rhetorical violences of the sexually troubled male intellectual, we see something of the "longing for the father" that Freud describes as the foundation of totem formulation. Totemism in the context of postcolonial theory is a revolutionary male narcissism writ large, instigating the male revolutionary figure as the "primal father" who bestows meaning on the postcolonial horde,[34] while the sexuality of women, in particular the women who "belong" to the father—the women of color, the women of the tribe—continue to have their agency prohibited, exiled, and deferred—this time by postcolonial critics.

On the other hand, what I specify as female sexual agency in this essay is a name for that which is *equivalent* in potentiality to male intellectual agency, and which the latter must therefore ward off with *ambivalence*, as primitive peoples ward off particular powers through specially instituted taboos. Since female sexual agency is a taboo—a prohibited area of potential contagion, miscegenation, and danger—its admittance would always be at a major cost. Admitting female sexual agency would mean that a more purist notion of community cannot but dissolve.

Ultimately, Fanon's opinions about female sexual agency could also be read as a parable about the *inadmissible* position occupied by the "intellectual of color" in the postcolonial situation. Here I can merely allude to the many anxieties and displeasures expressed about such intellectuals' "selling out" to the West in oblivion of the "real" historical tasks at hand. The much criticized use of "Western theory," for instance, could, in the light of this parable, be rewritten as a licentious mixing with the white folks, an *intellectual miscegenation* shall we say, that is, for many, not unlike the depraved sexual behavior of Fanon's woman of color. "The most painful sting of patriarchy," writes one feminist critic, is "the solidarity *against* the other."[35] The fear and accusation of "compradore" mentalities, of intellectual whoredom, and of the lethal infidelities of *others* would thus always remain part and parcel of the patriarchal gestures of community building, and a discursive community—in the academy in particular—is no exception.[36] As we have seen with Fanon, however, such fears and accusations contain an implicit acknowledgment of the alternative agency that the "women of color"—the black whores—possess with their condemned behavior. Perhaps, as in the case of Fanon's reading, what cannot be admitted in the community of postcolonial theorists is that such depraved behavior of intellectual miscegenation, too, shares with those who condemn it similar emancipatory goals. This argument, obviously, will need to be elaborated on a separate occasion.[37]

Reverse orientalism → Japs man ocidental ⎫ he desire her → fantasy
French woman orient ⎭
→ French woman's need to go to Japan
to relive (Jap man) her lover/German.

And For frenchwoman, Jap man the event
is sub for her lost lover → the scene
where she was with
him as a escape of Hiroshima
if it even bombing and
happend

(Not about morals but internal struggle
of the french woman forgetting/moving on) memory in

dialectical
rather than
forgetting

Juxtaposition → film with a film ⇒ she is making
a film abt Peace.

documentary sort of. v/3 val images

- manifestation of
human psychology.

Misogynist-

reconstruction of past ——→ actuality
what is truth
and what isn't.

forgetting

Post structuralism → they believe that the
"self" as a seperate
entity is a fictional construct"

self: eg. race
gender
class
profession

Schema of language

S/2 → what is said
→ what it means

(S) She says I saw
everything
(2) means
something
else

therefore to understand text,
one must understand how
it relates to his or her own
personal concept of self.

feminist literacy critizism — concerned with the
politics of women
authorship and to
representation of
women's condition
in literature.

East - body of collective
concerns/means
West - suggestive individuality
the self
at the end he becomes
Hiroshima and she
becomes Never, France

goal to increase
awareness of the
sexual politics of
language and
style why the
male point of
view.

Hiroshima — does not simply belong to Japanese
people rather everyone because it
was so huge.
- The world's issue and collective
memory of that.
- Taking from individual experiences to
suffering

connect w/ larger
events
an international /world
∧

IS "WOMAN" A WOMAN, A MAN, OR WHAT? THE UNSTABLE STATUS OF WOMAN IN CONTEMPORARY CULTURAL CRITICISM

Since the introduction of poststructuralist theory into the English-speaking academic world, a point of tension between feminists sympathetic toward poststructuralism and feminists hostile toward it has been the controversy over none other than the status of "woman" in representational politics. Whereas, for Anglo-American feminist critics, the individual woman, woman author, or woman critic continues to be understood in terms of the agency derived from the philosophical foundation of individualism, of the gendered person as an ultimate reality, the pivot of French poststructuralism has been precisely to put such foundationalist thinking into question through theories of language, text, signification, and subject, so that what is hitherto considered as an irrefutable certainty, including the individual self, now becomes known more often as a referent, a point in signification that is always *en procès*—that is, constantly disrupted, deferred, dislocated, postponed, if not altogether dissolved. This bifurcation between "Anglo-American" and "French" forms the basis of Toril Moi's 1985 bestseller *Sexual/Textual Politics*.[1] Moi, whose critical sympathies lie with the French, presents Anglo-American feminist critical practice in terms of an unconscious adherence to a Lukácsian realism and humanism that remain securely inscribed within patriarchal ideology (4–7). Her conclusion about American feminist literary critics such as Elaine Showalter, Kate Millet, Myra Jehlen, Susan Gubar, Sandra Gilbert, Annette Kolodny, and others is devastating. To be sure, Moi argues, these critics are politicizing texts through readings of sexuality—but theirs is a naïve politics that leaves patriarchal aesthetics entirely intact (69). In other words, while she gives Anglo-American feminist criticism ample credit for its overt political stance, Moi charges that this sexual politics is far from being political enough:

> The radically new impact of feminist criticism is to be found not at the level of theory or methodology, but at the level of politics. Feminists have *politicized* existing critical methods and approaches. If feminist criticism has subverted established critical judgements it is because of its radically new emphasis on *sexual politics*. . . .
>
> . . . The central paradox of Anglo-American feminist criticism is thus that despite its often strong, explicit political engagement, it is *in the end* not quite political enough; not in the sense that it fails to go *far* enough along the political spectrum, but in the sense that its radical analysis of sexual politics still remains entangled with depoliticizing theoretical paradigms. (87–88; emphases in the original)

Essentialist = generalization stating that certain properties possessed by group are universal, not dependent on context.

For these reasons, Moi has inserted the word "textual" in her book title in order to emphasize the importance of deconstructing linguistic structures alongside a sexual politics. Reading her analyses, one has the impression that textual politics is the more radically political because that is where essentialism, including the essentialism of the term "woman," can be properly confronted and undone. In particular, Moi is taken with the manner in which Julia Kristeva brings attention to the materiality of textual production. From Kristeva, Moi tells us, we learn that the subject position (it is no longer radical enough to talk of the self or the individual) is what indicates revolutionary potential (12).

in review of past events.

In retrospect, Moi's discussion is interesting not least because it is an early example, within the realm of contemporary feminist studies, of an attempt to take note of ethnicity as cultural difference ("Anglo-American," "French," "Norwegian")— indeed, to foreground culture itself as having an undismissable bearing on critical practices. Yet this astute awareness of cultural difference—which in her readings translates into a critique of essentialism and an endorsement of poststructuralist textual politics—does not necessarily save Moi herself from falling into certain kinds of essentialist pitfalls. In this regard, it is necessary to recognize the rhetorical strategies she adopts.

to divide into two parts

deceptive

Chief of these strategies is Moi's attempt to dichotomize politics and textuality. As I will go on to demonstrate in the rest of this chapter, such a dichotomy is a fallacious one. Among other things, it tends to ignore completely the implications of race and ethnicity—in particular, of whiteness as social power—in discourses about sexuality and femininity. In Moi's text, however, this dichotomy serves important tactical purposes. It enables her to give acknowledgment to the accomplishments of Anglo-American feminist critics exclusively in terms of their politics and to argue, by the same gesture, that these critics have not dealt at all with the textuality of their texts. Quickly, then, what looks at first like a straightforward differentiation turns into a specific value judgment. Accordingly, politics, which is what makes Anglo-American feminist critics "Anglo-American," is simple-minded and unsophisticated—*even though it is all they are capable of.* As Deborah E. McDowell points out, this category of "Anglo-American" also includes black and lesbian women: "Lesbian and/or black feminist criticism have presented exactly the same *methodological* and *theoretical* problems as the rest of Anglo-American feminist criticism." "This is not to say that black and lesbian criticism have no . . . importance"; rather, that importance, like that of the rest of Anglo-American feminist criticism, is to be found "not at the level of theory or methodology, but at the level of politics."[2] By contrast, the French theorists are much more supple in the way they deal with texts. But instead of confining them to the "text" half of her divided world (a division she herself proposes), Moi suggests that what they are doing is radically "political" as well, so that the French—and Frenchness—are, strictly speaking, inhabiting both

Anglo-American vs. French women.
→ interested in language and how
it led to hierarchy,
→ more sophisticated

sides of the divided world as women who not only know how to read texts but also
how to do politics. As an account not simply of varied feminist practices but also of
cultural difference, Moi's discussion presents Anglo-American feminists as heavy-
footed country bumpkins who are trapped in their parochial women's worlds (who
just want to find and proclaim "woman" everywhere) and the French as suave and
nimble cosmopolitans because they know how to read. In terms of their respective
performances, the Anglo-Americans are only second-rate even when they do their
best; the French, on the other hand, are already doing revolutionary politics without
necessarily even trying (as they are just paying attention to the marginality and dis-
sidence of texts).

By bifurcating the question of women critics' relationship to texts in this manner, Moi inadvertently introduces a larger problem—what might be called the feminization of culture. Taken in the broadest sense, this phrase may simply refer to a
cultural process in which femininity, together with the figure of woman, becomes
visible and active as an agent and producer of knowledge, yet this is exactly where
the controversy begins. Indeed, the debate that revolves around Ann Douglas's
book of 1977, *The Feminization of American Culture*, takes this issue of the relationship between women and culture as its central focus.[3] Douglas associates feminization with the rise of mass culture and with the conspicuous consumption habits of American society since the early nineteenth century. For her, feminization
means emasculation; a culture feminized is thus a culture in demise, weakened
in comparison with its previous tough—that is, manly—state. The claims made
by the second-wave feminism in the United States in the 1970s and the 1980s (the
feminism whose proponents include many of the authors that Moi criticizes in her
book)[4] were thus explicitly or implicitly aimed at Douglas's unsympathetic view of
women and mass culture.[5] Rather than the demise of culture, the tenet of second-
wave feminism adamantly affirmed an independent women's tradition and genealogy, demonstrating that despite the discrimination they experienced historically in
Western societies, women were creative, imaginative, and as capable of authorship
as men. The feminization of culture, thus, became a feminist revision of culture,
specializing in bringing women from the margins of history to the center of academic attention. Ironically, it is the overtly tough stance taken by feminists during
this period, a stance that was aimed at asserting women's difference from, as well
as equality with, men, that becomes in Moi's reading a sign that these second-wave
feminists are political naïfs mired in patriarchal aesthetics. We thus arrive at a paradox: by focusing on "woman," Anglo-American feminists are, by the criteria of one
account (Douglas), furthering the emasculation of culture; yet, by those of another
(Moi), they are becoming too much like men.

The paradox does not end here. In an essay called "Mass Culture as Woman,"
Andreas Huyssen gives this topic yet another twist by arguing that the very equation

of femininity with lowbrow culture, mediocrity, and leisurely consumption—in other words, precisely what Douglas has called the feminization of culture—is characteristic of high modernism with its interest in promoting "high art."[6] What Douglas characterizes, by way of the twosome man-woman, as the feminization of culture, is hence recast by Huyssen as a socioaesthetic move, in which the debasement of "woman" is part and parcel of a constructed relation between high art and mass culture that is aimed at preserving the interests of high modernism, which nonetheless is dependent on mass culture as its hidden subtext. Moreover, once the use of "woman" is historicized in this manner, Huyssen is able to reveal how high modernist art often derives its authority not so much from radical hedonism (as it would like us to believe) as from a kind of puritanism, one that can be said to be based on the reality principle rather than the pleasure principle:

The autonomy of the modernist art work, after all, is always the result of a resistance, an abstention, and a suppression—resistance to the seductive lure of mass culture, abstention from the pleasure of trying to please a larger audience, suppression of everything that might be threatening to the rigorous demands of being modern and at the edge of time. There seem to be fairly obvious homologies between this modernist insistence on purity and autonomy in art, Freud's privileging of the ego over the id and his insistence on stable, if flexible, ego boundaries, and Marx's privileging of production over consumption. The lure of mass culture, after all, has traditionally been described as the threat of losing oneself in dreams and delusions and of merely consuming rather than producing. Thus, despite its undeniable adversary stance toward bourgeois society, the modernist aesthetic and its rigorous work ethic as described here seem in some fundamental way to be located also on the side of that society's reality principle, rather than on that of the pleasure principle. It is to this fact that we owe some of the greatest works of modernism, but the greatness of these works cannot be separated from the often one-dimensional gender inscriptions inherent in their very constitution as autonomous masterworks of modernity. (55)

In an uncanny manner, Huyssen's reading of man-woman through high modernism-mass culture and vice versa also returns us to Moi's account of the *cultural difference* within feminist criticism of the 1970s and 1980s. Whereas Moi endorses the textual politics of the French poststructuralists with the assumption that it is a more radical and rigorous politics, Huyssen's account shows us that it is precisely this kind of assumption of itself as more modern, more ahead than others, and more at the edge of time that is characteristic of the continual workings of high modernism. By implication of Huyssen's terms, we may say that the reading practices of Anglo-American feminist critics have, in fact, been implicitly equated in Moi's reading with deluded, simple-minded mass culture (woman), while French poststructuralist *écriture feminine* has been equated with the rigor of autonomous high art (man).

This brief account of the divergent, often incompatible or self-contradicting, views of femininity and the feminization of culture is testimony to what I would call the supplementary logic of "woman" in the contemporary West. If the singularity of the name "man" is what is being questioned and challenged by the addition of "woman" as a (minority) category, then, by the same logic, "woman" itself can hardly be expected to remain a stable, unchanging frame of reference. Even in an account that is so apparently unsympathetic toward women as Douglas's, it seems to me that the term "feminization" is much less an attempt to define the essence of woman as such than it is a manner of articulating the historical—that is, mutating—relationships among various parts of culture as they have been socially institutionalized. In the counter move, on the part of the second-wave feminists, to elevate women's status to a respectable separateness from men's, the economic and cultural resonances of Douglas's original argument seem to have been bypassed. What remains takes on the semblance of a project aimed single-mindedly at legitimizing the idea of woman, which then easily lends itself to the pertinent charge of essentialism when poststructuralists such as Moi come along.[7]

Were we, however, to recognize in the epistemologically unstabilizable status of "woman" the supplementary logic of the supplement, a different type of question could be raised. No longer would it be sufficient to think of "woman" simply in relation to "man" (since that addition has already been accomplished); nor would it be sufficient simply to pluralize, to talk of multiple "women" while the assumption of something called "woman" remains intact. Rather, it would be imperative to see how, precisely at the moment "woman" is added to "man," the world can no longer be thought of in terms of the "man-woman" relation alone. This is because "woman" brings with it not only an essential content that can be added on or subtracted at will but also a function of reconceptualizing the status quo itself as fiction, a function whose most radical aspect is its irreversibility and unstoppability. By the time "woman" arrives at man's side, as it were, the coupling of "man-woman" is already obsolete, not so much because its twosomeness is heterosexist as because such a twosomeness itself will have to be recognized as part of something else, something whose configuration—as class or race, for instance—becomes graspable exactly at the moment of the supplement's materialization. This, in part, is the reason it is much more difficult to stabilize "woman" than "man." As we have seen, both the attempts to demote and promote "woman" remain ever unsatisfactory; it is as if, once the term is invoked—once "woman" is made analytically viable—we are already, in spite of our ostensible efforts, moving in and into another realm of cultural relations that can no longer be confined to gender.[8] . . .

81

PART 2

FILMIC VISUALITY AND TRANSCULTURAL POLITICS

Film theory has long suggested a likely a relationship between film and culture and between film and identity. Since the 1970s, feminist film theory has implicated film in producing and reinforcing gendered identities, but not until recently have the relations between ethnic spectatorship and film been explored. Chow takes up these themes in chapter 7, "Film and Cultural Identity," and chapter 8, "Seeing Modern China: Toward a Theory of Ethnic Spectatorship." Here Chow shows that the relations among gender, ethnicity, cultural identity, and film call for a thorough engagement with both contemporary *film* theory as well as with the full range of *cultural* theory. Such an engagement is characteristic of all of Chow's work on film.

Chapter 7, "Film and Cultural Identity," introduces a raft of issues and topics, on which subsequent chapters expand and amplify in various ways. Chapter 8 deals with the fraught process in which the ethnic spectator emerges. This is a process traversed by a complex array of issues—(dis)identification and (mis)recognition, gendering and interpellation, and the like—that are central to the concerns of feminism and postcolonialism. The chapter connects filmic representation with wider issues of orientalism in Western culture at the same time as it identifies and elaborates on an unacknowledged orientalist impulse in poststructuralist feminist thought in order to demonstrate the need to reassess a whole range of bases and biases, both "commonsense" and "radical." A similar intention underpins chapter 9, "The Dream of a Butterfly," which argues (through a reading of David Cronenberg's film *M. Butterfly*, using approaches from Said to Lacan to Baudrillard) that the point at which most analyses of orientalism *end* is actually the point at which they should *begin*. In other words, Chow's analyses exert a forward pressure: a demonstration of limitations and biases, a clarification of their ethical and political consequences, a call for their reassessment, always accompanied by suggestions of how such reassessment and reorientation might proceed.

Although all the chapters in part 2 start with, and focus on, filmic visuality, the last four do so in different ways. In chapter 10, "Film as Ethnography; or, Translation Between Cultures in the Postcolonial World," Chow entangles the implications of feminist film theory's assertion of "the primacy of to-be-looked-at-ness" with both anthropological and poststructuralist linguistic problematics of "cultural origins," "cultural translation," and "cultural resistance."

Similarly, in chapter 11, "A Filmic Staging of Postwar Geotemporal Politics: Akira Kurosawa's *No Regrets for Our Youth*, Sixty Years Later," Chow does not merely reread Kurosawa's film but also explores the political structure of international film studies, revealed by the positions and opinions "allowed" or "sanctioned" in its discourse on particular topics and by the way the discipline reacts to positions that transgress or problematize these limits.

In both chapter 12, an excerpt from *Sentimental Fabulations, Contemporary Chinese Films*, and chapter 13, "The Political Economy of Vision in *Happy Times* and *Not One Less*; or, a Different Type of Migration," Chow looks at the limits, biases, investments, and orientations of film and the discipline devoted to its study, as well as their underexplored and often unexpected relations with other aspects of culture. Both chapters analyze Chinese cinema's cross-cultural and gender-based problematics in ways pertinent to all involved in the study of filmic visuality and transcultural politics.

7

Film and Cultural Identity

A film about how film was first invented in Germany, Wim Wenders's *Die Bröder Skladanowsky* ("The Brothers Skladanowsky" Part I, 1994) offers important clues to the contentious relationship between film and cultural identity. Using the style and the shooting and editing skills of the silent era, and filming with an antique, hand-cranked camera, Wenders and students from the Munich Academy for Television and Film recast this originary moment in cinematic history as the tale of a loved one lost and found.

Disturbed by her Uncle Eugen's imminent departure on a long journey, Max Skladanowsky's 5-year-old daughter implores her father and his other brother, Emil, to bring Eugen back into her life. She gets her wish: as she waves goodbye to Uncle Eugen, the little girl is told that he is still with them, inside the box containing the film they had made of him before he left. Soon she is overjoyed to see, through the "Bioscop" invented by her father, a life-size Uncle Eugen flickering on the screen, making funny expressions and performing acrobatic feats just as when he was still with them. Uncle Eugen has disappeared in person, but has reappeared on film—and he will be there forever.

Elegant and moving, Wenders's film about the beginning of film reminds us of the key features of the medium of signification that was novel in the 1890s.

First, film (and here I intend photography as well as cinema) is, structurally, a story about the relationship between absence and presence, between disappearance and reappearance. Filmic representation reproduces the world with a resemblance unknown to artists before its arrival. Whether what is captured is a human face, a body, an object, or a place, the illusion of presence generated is such that a new kind of realism, one that vies with life itself, aggressively asserts itself. If cultural identity is something that always finds an anchor in specific media of representation, it is easy to see why the modes of illusory presence made possible by film have become such strong contenders in the controversial negotiations for cultural identity. Second, in a manner that summarizes the essence of many early silent films, Wenders's work draws attention to the agile movements of the human body as they are captured by the equipment built by Max Skladanowsky. Because sound and dialogue were not yet available, the filmmaker had to turn the ingredients he had into so many spatial inscriptions on the screen. What could have better conveyed the liveliness of this new illusory world than the exaggerated hieroglyphic movements of the human body, coming across as a series of images-in-motion? The compelling sense of photographic realism in film is thus punctuated with an equally compelling sense of melodrama—of technologically magnified movements that highlight the presences unfolding on the screen as artificial and constructed experiments. Melodrama

here is not so much the result of sentimental narration as it is the effect of a carica-
tured defamiliarization of a familiar form (the human body). Made possible by the
innovative manoeuvres of light and temporality, of exposure and speed, such defamiliarization has a direct bearing on the new modes of seeing and showing.

The coexistence of an unprecedented realism and a novel melodramatization
means that, from the very earliest moments, the modes of identity construction
offered by film were modes of relativity and relations rather than essences and fixi-
ties. Film techniques such as montage, close-ups, panoramic shots, long shots, jump
cuts, slow motion, flashback, and so forth, which result in processes of introjection,
projection, or rejection that take place between the images and narratives shown on
the screen, on the one hand, and audiences' sense of self, place, history, and pleasure,
on the other, confirm the predominance of such modes of relativity and relations.
With film, people's identification of who they are can no longer be regarded as a
mere ontological or phenomenological event. Such identification is now profoundly
enmeshed with technological intervention, which ensures that even (or especially)
when the camera seems the least intrusive, the permeation of the film spectacle by
the apparatus is complete and unquestionable. And it is the completeness of the
effect of illusion that makes the reception of film controversial.

It was the understanding of this fundamentally manipulable constitution of
film—this open-ended relation between spectacle and audience due, paradoxically, to the completeness of technological permeation—that led Walter Benjamin to associate film with revolutionary production and political change.[1] For,
as Benjamin speculated in the 1930s, film's thoroughly mediated nature makes
it a cultural opportunity to be seized for political purposes. Just as for the film
actor performing in front of the camera is a kind of exile from his own body
because it demands the simulation of emotional continuity in what is technically
a disjointed process of production, so for the audience, Benjamin writes, a new
attitude of reception is distraction and manipulation. As opposed to the absorp-
tion and concentration required by the traditional novel, which has to be read
in solitude and in private, film requires a mode of interaction that is public and
collective, and that allows audiences to take control of their situation by adopting
changing, rather than stable, positions. Film, in other words, turns the recipient
potentially into a producer who plays an active rather than passive role in the
shaping of his or her cultural environment.

Whereas Benjamin in his Marxist, Brechtian moments was willing to grant to a
movie audience the significance of an organized mob, later generations of film critics, notably feminist critics with a training in psychoanalysis, would elaborate the
agency of the viewer with much greater complexity by way of processes of subjectivity formation. Such critics would argue that fantasies, memories, and other uncon-

scious experiences, as well as the gender roles imposed by the dominant culture at large, play important roles in mediating the impact of the spectacle. . . .

The crucial theoretical concept informing psychoanalytic interpretations of identity is "suture." In the context of cinema, "suture" refers to the interactions between the enunciation of the filmic apparatus, the spectacle, and the viewing subject—interactions which, by soliciting or "interpellating"[2] the viewing subject in a series of shifting positions, allow it to gain access to coherent meaning.[3] As Kaja Silverman writes, "The operation of suture is successful at the moment that the viewing subject says, 'Yes, that's me,' or 'That's what I see.'"[4] As expressed through suture—literally a "sewing-up" of gaps—cinematic identification is an eminently ideological process: subjectivity is imagined primarily as a lack, which is then exploited, through its desire to know, by the visual field enunciated by the omnipotent filmic apparatus, which withholds more than it reveals. In order to have access to the plenitude that is the basis for identity, the subject must give up something of its own in order to be "hooked up" with the Other, the visual field, which is, none the less, forever beyond its grasp. No matter how successful, therefore, the subject's possession of meaning is by definition compensatory and incomplete. (This process of subject formation through suture is comparable to an individual's attempt to acquire identity in certain social situations. For instance, in order to gain acceptance into a particular social group, an individual must be willing to sacrifice, to part with certain things to which he or she feels personally attached but which are not socially acceptable; such personal sacrifices, however, are not guarantees that the social identity acquired is complete or permanent because, as is often the case, the social group is capricious and arbitrary in its demands.)

Because it foregrounds processes of identification through relations of visuality, cinema is one of the most explicit systems of suturing, the operations of which can be explained effectively through the simple acts of seeing. Meanwhile, cinema also offers a homology with the dominant culture at large, in that the latter, too, may be seen as a repressive system in which individual subjects gain access to their identities only by forsaking parts of themselves, parts that are, moreover, never fully found again.

Using suture, ideology, and other related psychoanalytic concepts, feminist critics concerned with identitarian politics have, since Laura Mulvey's groundbreaking work in 1975,[5] been steadily exposing the masculinism of mainstream cinema as well as of the dominant, heterosexist culture of the West. As a means of countering the repressive effects of dominant modes of visuality and identification, some go on to analyse in detail the ambiguities of the visual representations of women,[6] while others make use of the problematic of spectatorship, notably the spectatorship of women audiences, to theorize alternative ways of seeing, of constructing subjectivities and identities.[7]

Once identity is linked to spectatorship, a new spectrum of theoretical possibilities opens up. For instance, critics who have been influenced by Edward Said's *Orientalism*[8] can now make the connection that orientalism, as the system of signification that represents non-Western cultures to Western recipients in the course of Western imperialism, operates visually as well as narratologically to subject "the Orient" to ideological manipulation. They point out that, much like representations of women in classical narrative cinema, representations of "the Orient" are often fetishized objects manufactured for the satiation of the masculinist gaze of the West. As a means to expose the culturally imperialist assumptions behind European and American cinemas, the spectatorship of non-Western audiences thus also takes on vital significance.[9]

Because it conceptualizes identity non-negotiably as the effect of a repressive but necessary closure, suture has been theoretically pre-emptive. This can be seen in the two major ways in which the relationship between film and identity is usually investigated. For both, an acceptance of the idea of suture is indispensable.

This acceptance may function negatively, when the understanding of suture is used as a way to debunk and criticize certain kinds of identity—as ideologically conditioned by patriarchy and imperialism, for instance. Or, this acceptance may function positively and implicitly, in the counter-critical practice of demonstrating that some types of film may serve as places for the construction of other (usually marginalized) types of identity. It is important to remember, however, that even when critics who are intent on subverting mainstream culture assert that "alternative" cinemas give rise to "alternative" identities, as long as they imagine identities exclusively by way of the classic interpellation of subjectivities, they are not departing theoretically from the fundamental operations of suture. In fact, one may go so far as to say that it is when critics attempt to idealize the "other" identities claimed for "other" cinemas that they tend to run the greatest risk of reinscribing the ideologically coercive processes of identification through suturing.

For these reasons, I would propose that any attempt to theorize film and cultural identity should try to move beyond both the criticism and the implicit reinscription of the effects of suture. In this light, it might be productive to return to aspects of film which may not immediately seem to be concerned with identity as such but which, arguably, offer alternatives to the impasses created by suture.

Let us think more closely about the implications of the modes of visuality opened up by film. To go back to the story of the Skladanowsky brothers, what does it mean for Uncle Eugen to "appear" when he is physically absent? From an anthropocentric perspective, we would probably say that the person Eugen was the "origin," the "reality" that gave rise to the film which then became a document, a record of him. From the perspective of the filmic images, however, this assumption of "origin" is no longer essential, for Eugen is now a movie which has taken on an independent, mechanically reproducible existence of its own. With the passage of time, more and more reprints can be made and every one of them will be the same. The "original" Uncle Eugen will no longer be of relevance.

Film, precisely because it signifies the thorough permeation of reality by the mechanical apparatus and thus the production of a seamless resemblance to reality itself, displaces once and for all the sovereignty of the so-called original, which is now often an imperfect and less permanent copy of itself: Uncle Eugen's image remains long after he is dead. This obvious aspect of filmic reproduction is what underlies Benjamin's argument about the decline of the aura, the term he uses to describe the irreplaceable sense of presence that was unique to traditional works of art when such works of art were rooted in specific times and spaces.[10] What was alarming about the arrival of film (as it was for many poets and artists) was precisely the destruction of the aura, a destruction that is programmed into film's mode of reproduction and is part of film's "nature" as a medium. This essential iconoclasm of filmic reproduction is encapsulated in Wenders's story by the phantasmagorically alive and replayable image of Uncle Eugen in his own absence. This image signifies the end of the aura and the sacredness that used to be attached to the original human figure, to the human figure as the original. It also signifies a change in terms of the agency of seeing: the realist accuracy of the image announces that a mechanical eye, the eye of the camera, has replaced the human eye altogether in its capacity to capture and reproduce the world with precision.[11] As the effects of mechanicity, filmic images carry with them an inhuman quality even as they are filled with human contents. This is the reason why film has been compared to a process of embalming,[12] to fossilization, and to death.

But what film destroys in terms of the aura, it gains in portability and transmissibility. With "death" come new, previously undreamt-of possibilities of experimentation, as the mechanically reproduced images become sites of the elaboration of what Benedict Anderson, in a study of the emergence of nationalism in modern history, calls "imagined communities."[13] We see this, for instance, in the mundane, anonymous sights of the big city that are typical of early silent films such as Walther Ruttmann's *Berlin—Die Sinfonie der Grosstadt* ("Berlin: Symphony of a City," Germany 1927) and Dziga Vertov's *Man with the Movie Camera* (USSR, 1929). Scenes of workers going to work, housewives shopping, schoolchildren assembling for school, passengers travelling by train; scenes of carriages, engines, automobiles, railway stations, typewriters, phones, gutters, street lamps, shop fronts—all such scenes testify to a certain fascination with the potentialities of seeing, of what can be made visible. The mechanically reproduced image has brought about a perception of the world as an infinite collection of objects and people permanently on display in their humdrum existence. At the same time, because film is not only reproducible but also transportable, it can be shown in different places, usually remote from the ones where they are originally made. Coinciding with upheavals of traditional populations bound to the land and with massive migrations from the countryside to metropolitan areas around the world, film ubiquitously assumes the significance of the monumental: the cinema auditorium, as Paul Virilio writes, puts order into visual chaos like a cenotaph. As the activity of movie-going gratifies "the wish of migrant workers for a lasting and even eternal homeland," cinema becomes the site of "a new aboriginality in the midst of demographic anarchy."[14]

The iconoclastic, portable imprints of filmic images and the metropolitan, migratory constitution of their audiences mean that film is always a rich means of exploring cultural crisis—of exploring culture itself as a crisis. We have seen many examples of such uses of film in various cinemas in the period following the Second World War: the suffocating existentialist portrayals of the breakdown of human communication in Italian and French avant-garde films; the sentimental middle-class family melodramas of Hollywood; the aesthetic experiments with vision and narration in Japanese cinema; the self-conscious parodies of fascism in the New German Cinema; the explosive renderings of diaspora and "otherness" in what is called "Third Cinema."[15] By the 1980s and early 1990s, with the films of the mainland Chinese Fifth Generation directors, it becomes clear that film can be used for the exploration of crises, especially in cultures whose experience of modernity is marked, as it were, by conflicts between an indigenous tradition and foreign influences, between the demands of nationalism and the demands of Westernization.

For mainland Chinese directors such as Chen Kaige, Zhang Yimou, Tian Zhuangzhuang, and Zhang Nuanxin, reflecting on "culture" inevitably involves the rethinking of origins—the "pasts" that give rise to the present moment; the narratives, myths, rituals, customs, and practices that account for how a people becomes what it is. Because such rethinking plays on the historical relation between what is absent and what is present, film becomes, for these directors and their counterparts elsewhere in Asia,[16] an ideal medium: its projectional mechanism means that the elaboration of the past as what is bygone, what is behind us, can simultaneously take the form of images moving, in their vivid luminosity, in front of us. The simple dialectical relationship between visual absence and visual presence that was dramatized by film from the very first thus lends itself appropriately to an articulation of the dilemmas and contradictions, the nostalgias and hopes, that characterize struggles towards modernity. In such struggles, as we see in films such as *Yellow Earth* (1984), *Sacrifice Youth* (1985), *Judou* (1990), and *Raise the Red Lantern* (1991), the definitively modernist effort to reconceptualize origins typically attributes to indigenous traditions the significance of a primitive past in all the ambiguous senses of "primitivism." This special intersection between film and primitivism has been described in terms of "primitive passions."[17]

As the viewing of film does not require literacy in the traditional sense of knowing how to read and write, film signals the transformation of word-based cultures into cultures that are increasingly dominated by the visual image, a transformation that may be understood as a special kind of translation in the postmodern, post-colonial world. Intersemiotic in nature, film-as-translation involves histories and populations hitherto excluded by the restricted sense of literacy, and challenges the class hierarchies long established by such literacy in societies, West and East.[18] And, in so far as its images are permanently inscribed, film also functions as an immense visual archive, assimilating literature, popular culture, architecture, fashion, memorabilia, and the contents of junk shops, waiting to be properly inspected for its meanings and uses.[19]

Any attempt to discuss film and cultural identity would therefore need to take into account the multiple significance of filmic visuality in modernity. This is especially so when modernity is part of post-coloniality, as in the case of many non-Western cultures, in which to become "modern" signifies an ongoing revisioning of indigenous cultural traditions alongside the obligatory turns towards the West or "the world at large." In this light, it is worth remembering that film has been, since its inception, a transcultural phenomenon, having as it does the capacity to transcend "culture"—to create modes of fascination which are readily accessible and which engage audiences in ways independent of their linguistic and cultural specificities. Consider, for instance, the greatly popular versions of fairy-tale romance, sex, kitsch, and violence from Hollywood; alternatively, consider the greatly popular slapstick humour and action films of Jackie Chan from Hong Kong. To be sure, such popular films can inevitably be read as so many constructions of national, sexual, cultural identities; as so many impositions of Western, American, or other types of ideology upon the rest of the world. While I would not for a moment deny that to be the case, it seems to me equally noteworthy that the world-wide appeal of many such films has something to do, rather, with their not being bound by well-defined identities, so that it is their specifically filmic, indeed phantasmagoric, significations of masculinism, moral righteousness, love, loyalty, family, and horror that speak to audiences across the globe, regardless of their own languages and cultures. (Hitchcock is reputed to have commented while making *Psycho* (USA, 1960) that he wanted Japanese audiences to scream at the same places as Hollywood audiences.)

The phantasmagoric effects of illusion on the movie screen are reminders once again of the iconoclasm, the fundamental replacement of human perception by the machine that is film's very constitution. This originary iconoclasm, this power of the technologized visual image to communicate beyond verbal language, should perhaps be beheld as a useful enigma, one that serves to unsettle any easy assumption we may have of the processes of identification generated by film as a medium, be such identification in relation to subjectivity or to differing cultural contexts. In a theoretical climate in which identities are usually imagined—far too hastily I think—as being "sutured" with specific times, places, practices, and cultures, thinking through this problematic of film's transcultural appeal should prove to be an instructive exercise.

91

8

Seeing Modern China

TOWARD A THEORY OF ETHNIC SPECTATORSHIP

As contemporary critical discourses become increasingly sensitive to the wide-ranging implications of the term "other," one major problem that surfaces is finding ways to articulate subjectivities that are, in the course of their participation in the dominant culture, "othered" and marginalized. Metaphors and apparatuses of *seeing* become overwhelmingly important ways of talking, simply because "seeing" carries with it the connotation of a demarcation of ontological boundaries between "self" and "other," whether racial, social, or sexual. However, the most difficult questions surrounding the demarcation of boundaries implied by "seeing" have to do not with positivistic taxonomic juxtapositions of self-contained identities and traditions in the manner of "this is you" and "that is us," but rather, who is "seeing" whom, and how? What are the power relationships between the "subject" and "object" of the culturally overdetermined "eye"?

The primacy I accord "seeing" is an instance of the cultural predicament in which the ethnic subject finds herself. The institutionalized apparatuses of "seeing" on which I rely for my analyses—cinema, film theory, and the nexus of attitudes and fantasies that have developed around them—are part and parcel of a dominant "symbolic" whose potent accomplishments are inextricably bound up with its scopophilia. To this extent,

the felicity with which my analyses *can* proceed owes itself to the reversal of history that informs the development of theory in the West. This reversal makes available to those who think and write in the West a spaciousness that is necessary for their conceptual mobility, experimentation, and advancement, and that is nonetheless possible only because many others continue to be excluded from the same spaces. The following discussion should be read in this light.

1

During one of the press interviews inaugurating his film *The Last Emperor* in 1987, Bernardo Bertolucci recalls his experience of going to China:

> I went to China because I was looking for fresh air. . . . For me it was love at first sight. I loved it. I thought the Chinese were fascinating. They have an innocence. They have a mixture of a people *before* consumerism, *before* something that happened in the West. *Yet in the meantime* they are incredibly sophisticated, elegant and subtle, because they are 4,000 years old. For me the mixture was irresistible.[1]

The registers of time in which the European director organizes China's fascination are hardly innocent. His love for this "other" culture is inspired at once by the feeling that it exists "before" or outside his own world, the contemporary world of the consumerist West, and by the feeling that, within its own context, the Chinese culture is highly developed and refined—because, after all, it is "4,000 years old." In this rather casual and touristy response to China lies a paradoxical conceptual structure that is ethnocentric. By ethnocentric, I do not mean an arrogant dismissal of the other culture as inferior (Bertolucci's enthusiasm disputes this), but—in a way that is at once more complex and more disturbing—how positive, respectful, and admiring feelings for the "other" can themselves be rooted in un-self-reflexive, culturally coded perspectives.

The story of Pu Yi, as we know, is that of a boy who became China's last emperor at the age of three, who grew up pampered by a court of corrupt eunuchs at a time when China had already become a republic, who collaborated with Japan's invasion of China during the 1930s by agreeing to be emperor of the puppet state Manchukuo, and who, after nearly ten years of "reeducation" under the Chinese Communist regime in the 1950s, lived the rest of his life as an ordinary citizen in Beijing. For Bertolucci, Pu Yi's story is that of a journey that goes "from darkness to light." Pu Yi is a "great man who becomes little, but also, I think, free." The way in which positive values are assembled in these remarks is interesting. Situated in a culture that is thought to be "before" the West and sophisticated in its own way, the story of Pu Yi is also the story of a man's "liberation." This assemblage makes one ask: In relation to what is Pu Yi "free"? What is darkness and what is light? In the most rudimentary manner, the film's colors contradict this notion of a journey "from darkness to light." If "darkness" refers to Pu Yi's imprisonment in China's imperial past and "light" to his liberation under the Communist regime (those who read Chinese would notice that the wall against which the group activities at the Fushun Detention Center take place is painted with the characters *guangming*, meaning "light"), why is it that the "imperial" scenes were shot with such dazzling arrays of phantasmagoric golds and yellows, while the "Communist" scenes were done in a drab mixture of blues and grays?

Bertolucci's film is an excellent example of a response to modern China that is inscribed at a crossroads of discourses, all of which have to do with "seeing" China as the other. In demonstrating what some of these discourses are, my discussion necessarily leads into more general problems of Chinese modernity, particularly as these pertain to the formulation of a "Chinese" subject.

When he describes the differences among the Japanese and Chinese members of his film crew, Bertolucci makes a revealing comment:

> They are very different. The Chinese, of course, are more ancient. But also, the Japanese have this myth of virility. They are more macho. The Chinese are the opposite, more feminine. A bit passive. But passive, as I say, in the way of people when they are so intelligent and so sophisticated they don't need machismo.

He then goes on to describe how Pu Yi's passivity is a kind of "Oriental dignity" that the West may misunderstand, and so forth. Before we discuss how the equation of the Last Emperor with what is conventionally designated as the "feminine" quality of passivity is enunciated through the cinematic apparatus, let us consider for a moment what this kind of equation means, what its structural intentions are, and why, even if at a certain level it has a subversive potential, it is highly problematic.

A text that would assist us here, because it shares Bertolucci's idealization of China through the category of the feminine, is Julia Kristeva's *About Chinese Women*.[2] Written at a time when the post-Second World War disillusionment with the liberal West was at its peak in European and American intellectual circles, Kristeva's book should first of all be understood in terms of a *critique* of *Western* discourse, a critique that characterizes all of her works. *About Chinese Women* is primarily a book about the epistemological deficiencies of the West rather than about China. However, Kristeva's critique is complicated by the fact that it is sexualized: China is counterposed to the West not only because it is different, but also because it is, in a way that reminds us of Bertolucci's configuration of it, feminine. In the West, as Kristeva's recapitulation of the creation myth of Adam and Eve shows, woman is merely functional—"divided from man, made of that very thing which is missing in him" (17). Even though woman has a body, her corporeality is already a sign of her exclusion from the relationship between man and God. Tracing this "conception" of Western woman through historical as well as mythical sources, Kristeva argues that female sexuality at its most irreducible, that is, physical, level is denied symbolic recognition, and that the sexual difference between man and woman is hence repressed for the more metaphysical fusion between man and God in a monotheistic, patriarchal system. "China," on the other hand, organizes sexual difference differently, by a frank admission of genitality. One example of Kristeva's thesis can be found in the way she interprets the Chinese custom of foot binding. This example reveals in an economical way the problems inherent to the idealist preoccupation with another culture in terms of "femininity." I want therefore to elaborate on it.

Kristeva reminds us of Freud's observation (in the essay "Fetishism," 1927) that foot binding is a symbol of the "castration of woman," which, she adds, "Chinese civilization was unique in admitting" (83). However, Kristeva's appraisal of the Chinese custom goes one step further than Freud's. While the latter sees foot binding as a *variety* of castration, which for him remains the fundamental organizational principle of human civilization, Kristeva emphasizes its specifically feminine significance. Comparing foot binding with circumcision, which she describes as a kind of symbolic castration, she offers the following analysis. Circumcision, which is the equivalent of a prohibitive mark, is made on the body of man. This means that symbolically in the West, it is man who is the recipient of the mark that signifies mutilation, subordination, and hence difference; Western man becomes thus at once man and woman, "a woman to the father" (26), "his father's daughter" (85), so to speak. Western woman, in spite of her physical difference, remains in this way uncounted and superfluous. In foot binding, on the other hand, Kristeva sees Chinese culture's understanding of woman's *equal claim* to the symbolic. The custom is a sign of the anxiety that accompanies that understanding, but more important, it is a sign that is conspicuously displayed on the body of woman, which becomes the conscious symbolic bearer of the permanent struggle between man and woman. The gist of Kristeva's reading of China is utopian. Reading *with* her, we would think that the Chinese practice of maiming women's bodies is Chinese society's recognition, rather than denial, of woman's fundamental claim to social power. Anthropologically, the logic that Kristeva follows may be termed "primitive," with all the ideological underpinnings of the term at work: the act of wounding another's body, instead of being given the derogative meanings attributed to them by a humanistic perspective, is invested with the kind of meaning that one associates with warfare, antagonism, or even cannibalism in tribal society; the "cruelty" involved becomes a sign of the way the opponent's worth is acknowledged and reciprocated—with awe.

Kristeva's insights into the Chinese symbolic belong to the same order that Bertolucci, in the remarks I quote at the beginning, marks with the word "Yet": "Yet in the meantime they are incredibly sophisticated, elegant and subtle, because they are 4,000 years old." These are the insights that situate another culture in an ideal time that is marked off taxonomically from "our" time and that is thus allowed to play with its own sophisticated rhythms. Most important, this ideal time in which China is recognized for its "own" value is much in keeping with the way femininity has been defined in Kristeva's work. First of all, we remember that "Woman can never be defined."[3] To define woman as such is to identify with what Kristeva calls "the time of history"—"time as project, teleology, linear and projective unfolding, time as departure, progression, and arrival."[4] Instead, woman for Kristeva is a "space" that is linked to "repetition" and "eternity." Woman is thus *negative* to the time of history and cannot "be":[5]

> A woman cannot "be"; it is something which does not even belong in the order of *being*. It follows that a feminist practice can only be negative, at odds with what already exists so that we may say "that's not it" and "that's still not it." In "woman" I see something that cannot be represented, something that is not said, something above and beyond nomenclatures and ideologies.[6]

This belief in the "negative" relation occupied by women to the "time of history" helps us comprehend the subversive intent behind *About Chinese Women*. Because the existing symbolic order in the West precludes woman in an a priori manner,

Kristeva's way of subverting it is by following its logic to the hilt, and by dramatizing woman as totally "outside," "negative," "unrepresentable." Her notion of the *chora*,[7] by which she designates the "semiotic," maternal substratum of subjectivity that can be located only negatively, in avant-garde or "poetic" language, or in the nonrational elements of speech such as rhythm, intonation, and gesture, receives here its further extension through her reading of another culture. The result of this reading is precisely to fantasize that other culture in terms of a timeless "before," as we have encountered in Bertolucci's laudatory description of the Chinese as "a people before consumerism, before something that happened in the West." Kristeva's rejoinder to Bertolucci can be found in statements like these: "in China . . . the strangeness persists . . . through a highly developed civilization which enters *without complexes* into the modern world, and yet preserves a logic unique to itself that no exoticism can account for" (12; my emphasis). The attributions of a reality that is "pre-Oedipal" and "pre-psychoanalytic" (58) to China are what in part prompted Gayatri Spivak's criticism of Kristeva's project, which "has been, not to *deconstruct* the origin, but rather to *recuperate*, archeologically and formulaically, what she locates as the potential originary space *before* the sign."[8]

Even though Kristeva sees China in an interesting and, indeed, "sympathetic" way, there is nothing in her arguments as such that cannot be said without "China." What she proposes is not so much learning a lesson from a different culture as a different method of reading from within the West. For, what is claimed to be "unique" to China is simply understood as the "negative" or "repressed" of Western discourse. In thus othering and feminizing China, is Kristeva not repeating the metaphysics she wants to challenge? Especially since she has so carefully explicated the *superfluous* relation that Western woman has to the symbolic, might we not repeat after her, and say that the triangle Kristeva-the West-China in fact operates the same way as the triangle Man-God-Woman, with the last member in each set of relationships occupying the "excluded" position? Isn't the Western critic writing negatively from within her symbolic like Western Man in the "homosexual economy," being reduced to "a woman to the father," "his father's daughter," while China, being "essentially" different, can only be the "woman" whose materiality/corporeality becomes the sign of her repression?

One way out of this metaphysical impasse is, I think, by going against Kristeva's reading of China as an absolute "other." Much as this act of "othering" China is accompanied with modesty and self-deprecation, which Kristeva underscores by emphasizing the speculative, culture-bound nature of her project, perhaps it is precisely these deeply cultivated gestures of humility that are the heart of the matter here. We should ask instead whether the notion that China is absolutely "other" and unknowable is not itself problematic. I will cite three examples of Kristeva's unnecessary attribution of "otherness" to China to illustrate my point.

1. The suggestion that the Chinese language, because it is tonal, preserves an archaic "psychic stratum" that is "pre-Oedipal," "pre-syntactic," "pre-Symbolic" and hence dependent on the "maternal" (55–57). To look at Chinese, and for that matter any language, in this manner is to overlook the uses by its speakers, which are precisely what cannot be written off in such terms as "presyntactic" and "pre-Symbolic." To put this criticism differently, what is the meaning of an "archaic" "psychic stratum" in a culture that Kristeva has herself shown to be "pre-psychoanalytic"? If "archaic" and "pre" are the same, what can China's relevance be other than that of "primitivism"? And, if a *contemporary* culture is valued for its primitivism, doesn't this mean it is "outside" our time, confined to its own immobility?

2. Kristeva's idealization of the "maternal" order in China in terms of an "empty and peaceful center" (159)—in other words, of what she identifies as *chora*. Kaja Silverman's comments in another context apply equally to Kristeva's treatment of Chinese women as they do to her treatment of "China": "By relegating the mother to the interior of the *chora/womb*, Kristeva reduces her to silence."[9] As my analysis of her reading of foot binding shows, her structural understanding of the "primitive" logic behind Chinese society's practice of maiming women's bodies leaves the problem of Chinese women's suffering intact. Instead of seeing women in an active discursive role expressing discontent with this practice, her reading says, "In your suffering, you are the bearers of an archaic truth." Thus negated, women are refused their place as subjects in the symbolic.[10]

3. Ironically, this refusal goes smoothly with Kristeva's affirmation of another strand of "otherness" about China: Taoism. In glorifying the "subversive" and "liberating" impact Taoism has on Chinese society, Kristeva, like many Westerners who turn to the "East" for spiritual guidance, must leave aside the consideration that perhaps it is exactly Taoism's equation of the female principle with "silence" and "negativity" that traditionally allows its coexistence and collaboration with Confucianism's misogyny. In a culture constructed upon the complicity between these master systems, Chinese women not only are oppressed but also would support their own oppression through the feelings of spiritual resignation that are dispersed throughout Chinese society on a mundane basis. Kristeva is told this bitter truth by a Chinese woman whom she interviews, but, intent on her own "materialist" reading of China, she does not want to believe it:

The mother of three children, of whom the eldest is ten, she studied history for four years at the University and has been working at the museum for the past five years. I ask her:

Wang Chong, for you, is a materialist. What is your definition of a materialist? Wasn't it he who fought against the treatises on the body, and certain Taoist rituals as

well? Doesn't the Taoist tradition represent—albeit in mystical form—certain materialist demands against Confucianism?

But my question will remain unanswered, except for her affirmation of "the complicity between Taoism and Confucianism, two aspects of idealism, both of which are
surpassed by Wang Chong." Surpassed? Or suppressed? (177)

So, as Chinese "woman" acquires the meanings of the Kristevian materialism
that is said to exist in a timeless manner, from ancient to Communist China, *About
Chinese Women* repeats, in spite of itself, the historical tradition in which China
has been thought of in terms of an "eternal standstill" since the eighteenth century.[11] By giving that tradition a new reading, Kristeva espouses it again, this time
from a feminized, negativized perspective. The seductiveness of this metaphysics of
feminizing the other (culture) cannot be overstated. Bertolucci's film gives us a text
whose beauty and power depend precisely on such a metaphysics.

99

2

In one of the early scenes in *The Last Emperor,* after the three-year-old Pu Yi has
been installed on the throne, we are shown some of the intimate details of his
daily life. The little boy, surrounded by a group of eunuchs who are eager to please
him, is seen perching over a miniature model of the Forbidden City. His playmate,
one of the eunuchs, takes pains to match the model with "reality," emphasizing
where His Majesty was crowned, where he lives, where he now is, and so forth.
The model therefore functions as an instrument that gives the little boy his "bear-
ings." To use the language of contemporary psychoanalytic criticism, we witness
in this scene a kind of "mirror stage" in which a child learns his "identity" through
a representational structure that coheres the present moment of looking with the
chaotic, tumultuous events that take place around him. While this profound lesson
of self-recognition triggers rings of giggles in little Pu Yi, our attention to it is displaced by another event—the completion of Pu Yi's defecation. Swiftly, one eunuch
puts a woven lid over the imperial chamber pot, and the camera, following his
movements, shows him delivering this precious item to the imperial doctor, who
removes the lid, looks at the feces, smells it, and gives advice on the emperor's diet.
Meanwhile Pu Yi is taking his bath; again surrounded by eunuchs who are at once
servants, entertainers, respondents to questions, and bearers of the little boy's anal-
sadistic tantrums. This series of scenes culminates in the moment when Pu Yi's
wet nurse appears at the door. At the sight of her, Pu Yi abandons his play and runs
toward her, crying, "I want to go home, I want to go home." A eunuch hastens from
behind to cover his small naked body with a cloth. This kind of caring, protective

gesture from a servant would be repeated a few times during the course of the film, always at a moment when Pu Yi feels utterly deserted.

This series of scenes epitomizes one of the several orders of visualism[12] that are crucial to the film's organization. As emperor, Pu Yi *commands* attention no matter where he is. He is thus the "center" of a universe that "belongs" to him. In this respect, "attention" is one of the many embellishments that accompany the emperor's presence. Be they in the form of colors, objects, or human attendants, embellishments as such have no separate existence of their own, but are always part of the emperor's possessions. This "attention" is meanwhile a slanted, not direct, gaze: in the scenes where the emperor is about to approach, people stand aside, turn their heads away, or avert their gaze; the eunuchs dare not contradict what the emperor says; people want to kowtow to him even in 1950, when he is no longer emperor. The emperor's position is thus one of dominance, with all the "phallic" meanings of exclusivity that such a position connotes. As we recall the words of the dying Empress Cixi: no men except the emperor are allowed to stay in the Forbidden City after dark, and "these other men—they are not real men. They are eunuchs." However, intersecting this first order of visualism, in which Pu Yi is seen with imperial power, is another, in which Pu Yi is seen as totally passive. "Commanding" attention becomes indistinguishable from the experience of being watched and followed everywhere. The complexities of this second order of visualism are, as I argue in the following, what constitute the film's "gaze."

As Pu Yi cries "I want to go home, I want to go home," the fascination of the ubiquitous attention he receives as emperor is transformed and superseded by another meaning—one that reveals "from within" Pu Yi's lonely condition as a human being. A doubled gaze, then, is at work; the task that Bertolucci sets his camera is that of portraying the absolutely forlorn *inner* existence of a man whose outer environment bespeaks the most extraordinary visual splendor. How can the camera do this?

In her discussion of Laura Mulvey's classic essay, "Visual Pleasure and Narrative Cinema," Kaja Silverman recalls two representational strategies proposed by Mulvey for neutralizing the anxiety caused by female lack in classical narrative cinema. The first of these strategies "involves an interrogation calculated to establish either the female subject's guilt or her illness, while the second negotiates her erotic overinvestment."[13] If we substitute the words "female subject" with "Pu Yi," this statement becomes a good description of how the space occupied by Pu Yi vis-à-vis the camera is, in fact, a feminized one. What enables this is the portrayal of him primarily as a child who never grew up, and who is aligned metonymically with the ancient and inarticulate (i.e., temporally and linguistically "other") world of his mothers.

Instead of being the straightforward inscription of his imperial power, then, the first order of visualism that shows Pu Yi to be the recipient of ubiquitous attention

already belongs to what Silverman calls "erotic over-investment." Of all the components to this "over-investment," the most obvious are, of course, the visible elements
of a re-created imperial China: the exotic architecture, the abundance of art objects,
the clothes worn by members of the late Manchu court, their peculiar mannerisms,
the camel or two resting on the outskirts of the Forbidden City, and the thousands
of servants at the service of the emperor. The endowment of museum quality on the
filmic images feeds the craving of the eyes. The cinema audience become vicarious
tourists in front of whom "China" is served on a screen. And yet what is interesting
about the erotic overinvestment is perhaps not the sheer visible display of ethnic
imperial plenitude, but the amorous attitude the camera adopts toward such a display. To give one example, in the scene when Pu Yi is practicing calligraphy with his
brother Pu Jie, he notices that the latter is wearing yellow. This greatly displeases
him, because "only the emperor can wear yellow." A verbal confrontation between
the two boys follows, which soon becomes a debate over the question of Pu Yi's
status as emperor. Pu Jie puts down his trump card: "You are not the emperor any
more." Our attention to a detail of the sensuous kind—the color yellow—gives way
to an awareness of ritual proprieties, but the information pertaining to the ethnic
class hierarchy is quickly transformed into the pronouncement of a historical and
political *fait accompli*. This transformation, this movement from one kind of attention to another, indicates that the erotic overinvestment of Pu Yi is negotiated by
a kind of sympathetic understanding, the understanding that he is the victim of a
lavish, elaborate world that is, itself, a historical lie.

Although Pu Yi's perception of the coded meaning of yellow is correct, the environment in which that perception would be of significance has already vanished. At
this point, "erotic over-investment" intersects with the other representational strategy, the "interrogation calculated to establish either the female subject's guilt or
her illness." The "sympathetic understanding" that I am speaking about can thus
be rewritten as a historical interrogation that shows Pu Yi to be "ill" or "deluded";
hence, it follows, we have many suggestions of his entrapment in his dream of
being emperor, and of the guilt that he eventually feels. At the same time, however—and this is what makes the film's "message" highly ambiguous—it is as if
the camera refuses to abandon a certain erotic interest in Pu Yi in spite of such
historical knowledge. Precisely in its "sympathetic" attitude toward him, the camera
takes over the attention bestowed upon the Last Emperor by other filmic characters
and makes it part of *its own trajectory in courting him*. In the scene where Pu Jie
is introduced, which precedes the one we are discussing, this courting is orches-
trated through a combination of memorable image and memorable sound. We first
see a pair of human legs walking toward the prison cell in which Pu Yi is waiting
alone, while faintly but audibly, the beat from the film's theme, which we heard
once already with the opening credits, prepares us for something important. As Pu

101

Jie enters and the two men's eyes meet, the moment of recognition between brothers is amplified by the music, which now comes to the fore and takes us back to the
day when they met each other for the first time as young boys. The forlorn inner
condition of a man whose heart is warmed by the renewed closeness of a kinsman
is thus not merely "displayed," but constructed, interpreted, and interwoven with
richly suggestive "subjective" memory. It is this kind of careful, attentive "courting"
that establishes the second order of visualism and that ultimately accounts for the
film's eroticism.

However, having located the eroticism between Pu Yi the feminine, feminized
object and the aroused, caressing strokes of Bertolucci's camera, we must add that
the latter are figural: they can be felt and heard, but cannot be seen. If Bertolucci's
humanistic sympathy for Pu Yi's predicament belongs to a certain historical "interrogation," that interrogation must remain *invisible* in the film precisely because
it functions as the structuring "gaze." As if by a stroke of fate, this gaze finds in
Chinese history a "stand-in" behind which it can hide—the interrogation of Pu Yi
by the Chinese Communists.

This other, visible interrogation is in fact what introduces the story of the film,
which begins with Pu Yi returning as a prisoner of war from the Soviet Union to
China in 1950. The harshness of this interrogation is made apparent from the very
beginning, when some fellow prisoners of war, on recognizing Pu Yi, come forward
and kowtow to him and are quickly hustled away by others who are wary of the
danger involved in such gestures of loyalty to a national traitor. Pu Yi's (fictional)
attempt to commit suicide fails. As he wakes up at the slapping of the Fushun jail
governor, he asks, "Where am I?" a question that reminds us of the instruction
he received over the miniature model of the Forbidden City decades before. This
time his recognition of "himself" must begin with the loud and cold words, "The
People's Republic of China!" The insensitive and impersonal nature of the interrogation awaiting Pu Yi is obvious. The contrasting lack of sensuality in the scenes
in the Fushun Detention Center goes hand in hand with the interrogators who
are eager for their famous prisoner's confession. The irony of Bertolucci's direction is subtle: Pu Yi's chief interrogator is played by an actor who reminds one of
the young Mao Zedong. There is also the suggestion that the Chinese Communists, apart from coercive terrorizing, understand little about their own history. At
the beginning stage of Pu Yi's confession, we are shown a scene in which the jail
governor, wanting to find out more about his prisoner's life, turns to the pages of
Twilight in the Forbidden City, the book written by Pu Yi's Scottish tutor, Reginald
Johnston (one-time magistrate of the British Leased Territory of Weihaiwei in Shan-
dong Province), after he returned to England. This scene is remarkable because it
shows the elderly Chinese man opening the book in an attempt to know more about
recent Chinese history; what he reads, however, becomes the voice of Johnston

narrating events that take us back to the time when he first arrived in Beijing. It is Johnston's voice, then, that the camera follows, and Johnston's account that shapes the elderly Chinese man's understanding of Pu Yi. As Johnston's entry into Pu Yi's life is placed at the point when Pu Yi loses his wet nurse, he is the symbol of the boy's embarkment on a phase of educational "enlightenment" and his departure from the hallucinatory, decadent, maternal world of breast sucking. In this way, the Chinese Communist interrogation of Pu Yi falls in line with the "Western" educa-tion represented by Johnston. During the interrogation, Johnston's name is invoked at the strategic moment when the jail governor wants Pu Yi to confess to having voluntarily submitted to the Japanese plot to make him emperor of Manchukuo.

The appearance of the Japanese at this point in the film's narrative serves to amplify the utterly passive nature of Pu Yi's political existence. Here, his life as a prisoner—first under the waning Manchu Dynasty, then in the political turmoil of the Chinese Republic, then in Manchukuo, and finally in Communist China—comes together in its multiple layers of "castration," to use once again the language of contemporary psychoanalytic criticism. It is here, therefore, that he appears his most handsome and plays his assigned role as "lack"/the "castrated" to the full. With his eyes staring dreamily into the distance and the flicker of a smile appear-ing on his face, he responds to the moralistic charge of his pro-foreignness with an abandoned, easeful matter-of-factness: "Of course, everything foreign was good . . . especially Wrigley's chewing gum, Bayer aspirin, and cars." But while Pu Yi's defi-ance does not go unnoticed, it serves only to fuel the eroticism that has determined the way we look at him all along. These statements from Silverman's description of the film *Gilda* apply equally well to Pu Yi: "Confession and fetishism do not here work to deflect attention away from female lack to male potency, but to inspire in the viewer (fictional and actual) the desire to have it fully revealed—to have it revealed, moreover, not as a repellent but as a pleasurable sight."[14] Hence, Pu Yi's defiance only leads the interrogators to pressure him for more in what increasingly amounts to their sadistic desire to "have it all" in the name of reform and rehabilitation.

This process of interrogation is conducted over a series of filmic signifiers onto which are displaced the motifs of enlightenment, nationalism, and political pro-gressiveness. As we can see, the interrogative process, like the sensual display of Pu Yi's imperial past, is also directed by a voyeuristic gaze. But with a difference: while the "imperial" display amounts to a museum aesthetics, the "interrogation" comes across with a great sense of domination and oppression. As I have already sug-gested, the most disturbing question is how the Chinese Communist interrogation has been used as a stand-in for the camera's, so that the harshness and cruelty of the act of interrogating can be safely displaced onto the Chinese authorities, while the camera's gaze retains its freedom to roam about the body of the "other" with its "sympathetic" humanism. Silverman's observation that "a gaze within the fiction serves to conceal the controlling gaze outside the fiction" (204) is poignantly relevant in the cross-cultural context of Bertolucci's film. While the Chinese Communist interrogation is shown in an ambivalent light (at best historically necessary, at worst inhumane), the camera is able to sustain its amorous relationship with Pu Yi as a dignified human individual whose truth needs to be protected from the devastation of the interrogators' thirst for facts, thus aesthetically demonstrating what Bertolucci means when he says, "There is a kind of universal meaning in this figure." If my reading of Pu Yi as a figure for China-as-woman is at all tenable, then this interested, protective gesture on the part of the European director can be read as an allegory of what Spivak in a different context refers to as "white men saving brown women from brown men."[15]

The eroticized relationship between the camera's gaze and the last emperor also means that we cannot confront the issue of femininity in terms of the film's women characters. In the private conversations I had with a couple of female American sinologists, I gathered a favorable response to the women characters, especially the empress, who they thought represents a kind of wisdom and courage that they associate with "Chinese" women. I think this kind of reading misses the complexities of the cinematic apparatus because it is content with a straightforward correspondence between "images of women" and "femininity." As a result, femininity as the "space" and "spectacle" that functions in relation to the camera's gaze into another culture, and the politics that are inscribed therewith, are comfortably bypassed. In actuality, because it is Pu Yi and "China" who occupy the feminized space in this cinematic structure of eroticism, the women characters are pushed to what I'd call an astructural outside, the "other" of the other, as it were, that wavers between the ontological statuses of "nature" and "hysteria." The wet nurse, the high consorts of the court, the empress, the Second Consort, and "Eastern Jewel" all appear as either objects of pleasure or addicts to pleasure, strung together through a narrative that remembers them as gratifying female breasts, partners in sex games, perverse lesbians, and opium smokers. Meanwhile, whenever these women characters think and act with "courage" and "wisdom," their thoughts and acts become indistinguishable from excessiveness if not downright insanity. The empress's contempt for Pu Yi's collaboration with the Japanese in Manchukuo is represented through her "crazy" behavior at the inaugurating banquet. The film thus corroborates the commonsense feeling that for a woman to make a sensible point, she must first become a spectacle and show herself to be "out of her mind." As the bearer of truthful political understanding, the empress survives only as an invalid.

That *The Last Emperor* is a perfect example of how another culture can be "produced" as a feminized spectacle is confirmed by its reception in Hollywood. The film was nominated for nine Oscars at the sixtieth Academy Awards ceremony and won all nine. A look at the list reveals more specifically what exactly is rewarded: the *making* of the film. The categories included best motion picture, best director, best screenplay adopted from another medium, best cinematography, best art direction, best film editing, best costume, best sound, and best original score. In spite of his excellent performance, John Lone, who plays Pu Yi, was not even nominated for best actor. The question that arises is of course not whether an Oscar is "genuinely" valuable, but how it is that in a production that seems to be recognized for its excellence in so many respects, the same kind of recognition is not granted its "players." The repeated emphases on the "international" nature of the film's production[16] can hardly disguise the fact that what appear on the screen are mostly what would be identified as "Chinese" faces enacting a "Chinese" story/history. My point is not that Hollywood's neglect of the Chinese actors and actresses is a sign of racial discrimination *tout court;* rather, that in this failure to give equal recognition to the film's acting lies perhaps a confusion of the players with what they play. After all, one of the interesting problems about film acting is that the actor/actress straddles the roles of film *maker* and film *image.* Categorically, therefore, acting contains an ambivalence that distinguishes it from other aspects of film production. In the case of a saga like *The Last Emperor,* this ambivalence can only be more pronounced. In turn, we can say that when an actor/actress is given an award for acting, it is an indication that he/she, the actual individual *outside* the film, has done a good job playing a fictional role. An award for acting can thus be looked upon as the film industry's way of distinguishing an actor/actress from a role and of putting him/her on the side of the film "makers."

On the other hand, I hope my analysis of Pu Yi and *The Last Emperor* as a feminized space in the structure of Bertolucci's commercialized aesthetics has made it clear by now why it is indeed not surprising that the "acting" of this film cannot be recognized as "creative" talent. After all, if this feminized spectacle has grown out of Bertolucci's need for "fresh air" in the first place, it must remain and can only be rewarded as *his* creation, *his* story. (Bertolucci: "I am a storyteller, I am not a historian. . . . To history I prefer mythology. Because history starts with the truth and goes toward lies. While mythology starts from lies and fantasy and goes toward truth.") What at first sight looks like a sensational advertisement announcing the availability of the film on video cassette and laser videodisc offers an accurate summary of Bertolucci's story: "Emperor. Playboy. Prisoner. Man."[17]

3

So far, my reading strategy with regard to *The Last Emperor* has been more or less congruent with the method of dissecting "narrative cinema and visual pleasure" given to us by Laura Mulvey in her essay of the same title. Mulvey argues that, on the basis of vision, there is a fundamental difference in the classical film between the roles it assigns to men and women. The camera's gaze, associated with scopo-philia, is "masculine," while images on the screen, in the state of being looked at and thus eroticized, are "feminine." Silverman comments: "This opposition is entirely in keeping with the dominant cultural roles assigned to men and women, since voyeurism is the active or 'masculine' form of the scopophilic drive, while exhibitionism is the passive or 'feminine' form of the same drive" (223). Accordingly, as they look at cinematic images, the spectators identify with the camera's gaze; identification is thus a "masculinizing" identification that perpetuates the reduction of women to an eroticized image. Although visual pleasure is "threatening in content" (Mulvey, 309) (since, to retrace the logic of Freud's castration complex, it implies male fear and anxiety), it is primarily its function in constructing women as passive and inferior that concerns Mulvey as a feminist.[18]

Mulvey's essay has been controversial since its first publication. Criticisms of her argument converge on what most consider to be its ahistorical theoretical determin-ism. Fairly recently, Mulvey revised and critiqued her own position, notably in an essay called "Changes: Thoughts on Myth, Narrative and Historical Experience."[19] Her self-critique alerts us to the historicity of the *form* in which her original thesis was constructed. Looking at it retrospectively, Mulvey describes the polarization of male and female positions ("active" versus "passive," "spectator" versus "specta-cle," and so on) as a conceptual typology that, despite its relevance to a particular moment in time, may obstruct further theoretical developments:

> It is as though the very invisibility of abstract ideas attracts a material, metaphoric form. The interest lies in whether the forms of this "conceptual typology," as I have called it, might affect the formulation of the ideas themselves and their ultimate des-tiny. Is it possible that the way in which ideas are visualised can, at a certain point, block the process that brings thought into a dialectical relationship with history? . . .
>
> A negative aesthetic can produce an inversion of the meanings and pleasures it confronts, but it risks remaining locked in a dialogue with its adversary. . . .
>
> Apart from inversion, shifts in position are hard to envisage.[20]

While I agree with the historical impetus behind Mulvey's self-critique, I find the metaphors that accompany her efforts to decenter her own original argument disturbing. Two examples: "I feel now that its [her classic essay's] 'conceptual typol-ogy' contributed in some way to blocking *advance*"; "negative aesthetics can act as a motor force in the *early phases* of a movement, initiating and expressing the desire for change" (163, 164; my emphases). These metaphors are metaphors of a teleologi-cal construction of history, which as a rule emphasizes the immaturity, the rash-ness even, of "early" concepts. The rhetorical return to this conventional, almost chronological sense of history is paradoxical in an essay that otherwise offers a very different kind of argument about the historical through the notion of the "pre-Oedipal." Citing as an example the way the image of Our Lady of Guadalupe was used as an emblem for political revolt against Spanish rule in Mexico in the early nineteenth century, Mulvey argues for an understanding of the "pre-Oedipal" that is not in teleological terms: the "pre-Oedipal" is "in *transition* to articulated language" (167); it is not dominant, yet meaningful. Although I would disagree with Mulvey's subscription to the Freudian notion for the same reasons I would with Kristeva's, what is valuable in this part of her argument is not so much the "pre-Oedipal" per se as *where* she tries to locate it. This is not some exotic past or ancient culture, but "the rhetoric of the oppressed"—"a rhetoric that takes on the low side of the polar opposition, in order to turn the world upside down, and stake out *the right to imagine* another" (167; emphasis in the original).

To turn the world upside down, to stake out the right to imagine another: these are the tasks we are still faced with. I think Mulvey's original argument should be read in the light of these statements rather than simply against her later attempt to "historicize'" that argument in a more conventional way. What is most productive about her polarization of male and female positions is a radicalness that is often the only means of effecting change. Only when things are *put in the bold,* so to speak, can a thorough dismantling of the habits of seeing be achieved. The perception of the need to be uncompromisingly thorough is itself historical. It is *this* kind of historical perceptiveness that is behind Mulvey's extremely direct, and only thus effective, statement of her original project: "It is said that analysing pleasure, or beauty, destroys it. That is the intention of this article."[21]

It follows that the most useful aspect of Mulvey's essay lies not so much in the division between masculinity and femininity as "gaze" and "image," as in the conceptual possibilities that inevitably emerge once such a division is so bluntly and crudely crafted. As Mulvey puts it, "A negation or inversion of dominant codes and conventions can fossilise into a dualistic opposition or it can provide a spring-board, a means of testing out the terms of a dialect, an unformed language that can then develop in its own signifying space."[22] This "unformed language" is the language of the oppressed.

In Mulvey's original argument, this language of the oppressed is conceived in visual terms, as part of the state of being-looked-at. This state of being-looked-at is built into the cinematic spectacle itself: "Going far beyond highlighting a woman's to-be-looked-at-ness, cinema builds the way she is to be looked at into the spectacle itself."[23] What this enables is an understanding of the cinematic image not simply as some pure "thing" to be perceived, but as what already contains the gaze (the act of gazing) that cannot be seen itself.

We have seen how, in *The Last Emperor,* it is precisely this invisible gaze that directs our paths of identification and nonidentification. It does so by hiding behind other filmic signifiers such as the Chinese imperial order, which bestows *attention* on the emperor to the finest detail, and the Chinese Communist *interrogation* of Pu Yi. What we see on the screen, then, is already something that has been profoundly worked on. For the camera's gaze does not simply "hide," but negotiates, mediates, and manipulates; it builds on the "gazes" that are visibly available on the screen, turning them into occasions for eroticism or humanistic sympathy and in this way "suturing" the spectators' response.[24]

My use of Mulvey's mode of critique therefore complicates it in two ways. First, I extend the interpretation of image-as-woman to image-as-feminized space, which can be occupied by a man character, Pu Yi, as much as by a woman. Once this is done, "femininity" as a category is freed up to include fictional constructs that may not be "women" but that occupy a passive position in regard to the controlling symbolic. At the same time, this use of "femininity" does not abandon the politics of "to-be-looked-at-ness," which, as Mulvey's argument shows, is most readily clarified through women's assigned role in culture.

The second complication is my use of the elements of this cinematic analysis for a polemics of cross-cultural inquiry. The image-as-feminized space raises disturbing questions as to what is involved in the representation of another culture, especially when that representation is seen by members of that culture. Does it call for the "destruction of visual pleasure" that is the point of Mulvey's critique? Who should destroy it, and how? If not, why not? What are the problems that watching a film like *The Last Emperor* produces for a Chinese audience? If it is a matter of criticizing Bertolucci for using "good drama" to "falsify" Chinese history, one can simply recite historical facts and rechronicle the reality that was not the one of the film.[25] But that precisely is not what matters. What matters is rather how "history" should be reintroduced materially, as a specific way of reading—not reading "reality" as such but cultural artifacts such as film and narratives. The task involves not only the formalist analysis of the *producing* apparatus. It also involves rematerializing such formalist analysis with a pregazing—the "givenness" of subjectivity I indicated in the Preface—that has always already begun.

To rematerialize this pregazing, we need to shift our attention away from the moment of production to the moment of reception. In retrospect, it is the lack of this shift that constitutes the vulnerability in Mulvey's original argument. Given that "visual pleasure" is indeed the "evil" of the scopophilic cinematic apparatus, does it mean that the spectator is affected by it in a uniform way? Indeed, the logic of "Visual Pleasure and Narrative Cinema" would indicate that all spectators are "masculinized" in reception, since they would be identifying with the camera's gaze. The woman whose ontological status is supposedly that of the image on the screen and who nonetheless also sits in the audience hence poses a very special problem. With what does she really identify? Must she simply become schizophrenic?

In her book, *Alice Doesn't: Feminism, Semiotics, Cinema*,[26] Teresa de Lauretis takes up this important question of the female spectator that is left largely unexplored. She does this by supplementing the filmic position of woman as "visual object" with something else—"narrative." De Lauretis argues that the position occupied by "woman" on the screen is not simply a visible "image" but a "narrative image," a term she borrows from Stephen Heath. The "narrative image" of woman refers to "the join of image and story, the interlocking of visual and narrative registers effected by the cinematic of the look."[27] In cinema as much as in conventional narrative, the female position, "produced as the end result of narrativization, is the figure of narrative closure, the narrative image in which the film . . . 'comes together'" (140). By introducing narrative into the understanding of filmic images, de Lauretis is thus able to distinguish *two* sets of identifying relations for the female spectator. The first, well known to classical film theory, consists of "the masculine, active, identification with the gaze (the looks of the camera and of the male characters) and the passive, feminine identification with the image (body, landscape)" (144). The second set of identifying relations is *figural* in nature. It does not consist so much of gazes and looks as it does "the double identification with the figure of narrative movement, the mythical subject, and with the figure of narrative closure, the narrative image" (144). Moreover,

> Were it not for the possibility of this second, figural identification, the woman specta-
> tor would be stranded between two incommensurable entities, the gaze and the image.
> Identification, that is, would be either impossible, split beyond any act of suture, or
> entirely masculine. The figural narrative identification, on the contrary, is double; both
> figures can and in fact must be identified with at once, for they are inherent in nar-
> rativity itself. It is this narrative identification that assures "the hold of the image," the
> anchoring of the subject in the flow of the film's movement. (144)

In thus supplementing the understanding of filmic images with terms other than those of the visual order alone, de Lauretis accomplishes several things at once. First, by reintroducing the processes of narrative, she revises the film theory that relies heavily on the sexual division based on vision, since that division, as all criticisms of Mulvey's original argument indicate, leads to a rigid polarization between man-as-gaze and woman-as-image. Second, in doing so, she enables a critique of the kind of technical analysis involved in a reading strategy such as Mulvey's while at the same time salvaging and reaffirming the valid political import of Mulvey's project, namely, that women, as the oppressed side of the polarization, must also be understood as *subjects*, not objects, in social discourse. Third, this is possible because the political question of female subjectivity is now posed in different terms: not simply that "woman is reduced to the image," but "woman" is a locus of double identification.

It is through a careful discussion of what this "doubleness" signifies that the "female spectator" offers the potential of a new means of sociocultural inquiry.

Put in more mundane terms, the paradigm of gaze-as-male and image-as-female breaks down once we think of women who willingly buy tickets to go to the cinema and derive pleasure from the experience. The rejection of the relevance of this experience would result in the kind of denunciation of mass culture that we associate with Adorno and Horkheimer in their classic piece, "The Culture Industry: Enlightenment as Mass Deception."[28] It is a rejection because, in spite of often attentive analyses of how the mass culture industry works by subjugating the masses, the experience of the masses is not itself considered a problem except insofar as it is assumed to signify, uniformly, "stupefaction." However, if we are to theorize precisely from the perspective of the receiving masses, then the problem is infinitely complicated. As recent studies of popular culture such as Tania Modleski's *Loving with a Vengeance*, Janice Radway's *Reading the Romance*, and Ien Ang's *Watching Dallas* repeatedly indicate, the female viewing/reading subject is elusive, ambivalent, always divided between "conventional" values and expectations on the one hand, and socially disruptive or destructive tendencies on the other. Central to such conflicts in the processes of reception is the issue of identification, and with it, the problem of pleasure.

Because theoretically the female spectator's position offers an example of a division that is "irreparable" and "unsuturable,"[29] film theorists tend to disregard the problem of sexual differentiation in the spectators altogether. This leads to the facile thinking of reception purely in terms of a transcendental or ideal subject, presupposed to be male. Feminist readings such as Mulvey's, also following this thinking but revolting against it, therefore seek to destroy it totally. De Lauretis summarizes this state of affairs with a thoughtful comment about women and pleasure:

> Within the context of the argument, a radical film practice can only constitute itself against the specifications of that cinema, in counterpoint to it, and must set out to destroy the "satisfaction, pleasure and privilege" it affords. The alternative is brutal, especially for women to whom pleasure and satisfaction, in the cinema and elsewhere, are not easily available. (60)

Since the need to destroy visual pleasure stems from the belief that what gives pleasure is pure illusion, de Lauretis goes on to suggest that the word "illusion" be "dislodged from the particular discursive framework of Mulvey's argument" and be interpreted along the associations given to it by E. H. Gombrich, for whom illusion is a process "operating not only in representation, visual and otherwise, but in all sensory perception, and a process in fact crucial to any organism's chances of survival" (61). Readers must turn to de Lauretis's book to realize for themselves the vast implications of this argument based on perception theories. For now, I will limit my discussion to an amplification of "the particular discursive framework of Mulvey's argument" and of how the notion of "illusion" may be mobilized and generalized for a *departure* from that framework.

Briefly, I think the discursive framework of Mulvey's essay takes us back to the formulation of "ideology" advanced by Louis Althusser in his work.[30] Althusser defines ideology in terms of two types of "apparatuses," the "Repressive State Apparatuses" and the "Ideological State Apparatuses." While the former work by brute, militant force, the latter, under which Althusser lists churches, public and private schools, the family, the law, the political system, the trade union, the media, and "cultural" activities such as literature, the arts, and sports (143), work by what we might call "civility." It is such "civil" apparatuses that help reproduce the conditions of capitalist production by "interpellating" individuals into the existing system even as these individuals imagine their actions to be spontaneous and voluntary. Mulvey's essay, I think, draws on this general notion of ideology and localizes it in a specific apparatus, cinema. In this respect, her analysis of the classical narrative film contains two mutually implied equations: first, that between ideology and the masculine gaze; second, that between ideology and falsehood. The critique of cinema as dominated by the masculine gaze is therefore also a critique of ideology as falsehood. And it is, I think, this approach to ideology that de Lauretis means by the "particular discursive framework of Mulvey's argument." The notion of "falsehood" is analogous to that of "illusion" as defined by *The American Heritage Dictionary*: "something, as a fantastic plan or desire, that causes an erroneous belief or perception." Defined this way, "illusion" calls for its own destruction and, by implication, for the restoration of what is nonillusory. For very understandable reasons, much of the work undertaken in feminism partakes of this anti-illusion tendency, resulting in some extreme cases where a profound lack of interest in or a total disregard of anything related to men is heartily applauded.

Althusser's theory, however, indicates another direction in which feminism and the awareness of "ideology" can join forces. For this, we need to ponder anew his way of formulating ideology, as "the *reproduction* of the conditions of production" (127; my emphasis). Or, restating it to the same effect, he says:

Every social formation must reproduce the conditions of its production at the same time as it produces, and in order to be able to produce. It must therefore reproduce:

1. the productive forces,
2. the *existing relations* of production (128; my emphasis)

What else could be the "existing relations" of production but the mental attitudes, wishes, sufferings, and fantasies of the individuals involved in the processes of active production? When he discusses the "reproduction of labor power," Althusser includes not only quantifiable value (wages) but also a "historically variable mini-mum"—"needs." He adds in parentheses that "Marx noted that English workers need beer while French proletarians need wine" (131). Ideology is thus understood by Althusser not really as "something" that "causes" a falsified perception, but more as the experience of consumption and reception, as that store of elusive elements that, *apart from* "wages" and "surplus value," enable people to buy, accept, and enjoy what is available in their culture. This understanding of ideology, then, includes the understanding that any reception of culture—however "passive" and thus "ideo-logical"—always contains a responsive, performative aspect. However neglected by cultural theorists busy with the criticism of ideology-as-falsehood, this aspect of reception is crucial to the notion of "illusion" that de Lauretis would like to dislodge from a deeply ingrained, Platonic tradition of criticism and reinvest with the mean-ing of social survival. As she puts it succinctly:

> The present task of theoretical feminism and of feminist film practice is to articulate the relations of the female subject to representation, meaning, and vision, and in so doing to construct the terms of another frame of reference, another measure of desire. *This cannot be done* by destroying all representational coherence, by denying "the hold" of the image in order to prevent identification and subject reflection, by voiding percep-tion of any given or preconstructed meanings.[31]

In a way that echoes de Lauretis, Silverman points out in her discussion of "suture" the intimate link between suture and "interpellation."[32] Her explana-tion of suture reminds us of Althusser's analysis of the individual's response to the "interpellating" call: "The operation of suture is successful at the moment that the viewing subject says, 'Yes, that's me,' or 'That's what I see'" (205). She mentions also that, as viewing subjects, "we want suture so badly that we'll take it at any price, even with the fullest knowledge of what it entails—passive inser-tions into pre-existing discursive positions (both mythically potent and mythi-cally impotent); threatened losses and false recoveries; and subordination to the castrating gaze of a symbolic Other" (213). These statements serve to empha-size that the task of critiquing processes of ideology, illusion, and suture cannot be performed at the level of pitting reality against falsehood, because in what we think of as "falsehood" often lies the chance of continued survival, some-times the only way to come to terms with an existing oppressive condition. This is especially true in the case of the female spectator, as de Lauretis is at pains to demonstrate.

Instead of seeking to "free" the filmic illusion, de Lauretis restores and redefines its value. She does this by avoiding the tendency in avant-garde film practices to reinscribe materiality *exclusively* in the process of filmmaking. For these practices, by "roughening" and "defamiliarizing" the workings of the apparatus (to borrow terms from the Russian Formalists), often demand of the spectator a cool-headed "detachment" from what they see. Instead, de Lauretis moves toward reinscribing materiality in film watching. Through the writings of Pasolini, she draws attention to the "translinguistic" function of cinema, showing that cinema "exceeds the moment of the inscription, the technical apparatus, to become 'a dynamics of feelings, affects, passions, ideas' in the moment of reception."[33] These words, adds de Lauretis, should not be construed as an emphasis on the purely existential or personal, for they point to "spectatorship as a site of productive relations" (51).

It is by rearguing the relationship between image and spectator and by foregrounding the cultural components that are specific to an *imaged spectatorship* that a film like *The Last Emperor* can be instrumental in an analysis of modern Chinese subjectivity. Here, once again, I would like to extend the feminist basis of de Lauretis's arguments to a cross-cultural context, by asking how the insights she develops around the female spectator could fruitfully become a way of articulating the ethnic—in this case, Chinese—spectator.

Take this statement: "Spectators are not, as it were, either in the film text or simply outside the film text; rather, we might say, they intersect the film as they are intersected by cinema" (44). What happens when a Chinese person sees *The Last Emperor*? Is the process comparable to the one described by de Lauretis with regard to the female spectator, who is caught between the feminine (Chinese) image on the screen and the masculine (non-Chinese) gaze of the camera? How does the double, figural identification—with both narrative movement and narrative closure—work?

I cite my mother's response to the film: "It is remarkable that a foreign devil should be able to make a film like this about China. I'd say, he did a good job!" Instead of being stranded schizophrenically between an identification with Bertolucci's "gaze" and the projection of herself ("Chinese") as image on the screen, my mother's reaction indicates a successful "suturing" in the sense of a cohering of disjointed experiences through "illusion." As an ethnic spectator, she identifies at once with the narrative movement, the invisible subject that "tells" the story about modern China, *and* with the narrative image centering on Pu Yi, signifying "Chinese" history. Even as she highlights the film's non-Chinese making in the phrase "foreign devil," the process of identification appears uninterrupted. In fact, one can say that her identification with the narrative image is most successful when she compliments Bertolucci for doing a good job in spite of being a "foreign devil." For, although "foreign devil" is a mark of the awareness of difference, the "in spite of" attitude points rather to the process in which a seamless interpellative exchange can take place between the spectator and the filmic image. Instead of doubting Bertolucci's version of modern Chinese history, my mother's reaction says, "Still, that's me, that's us, that's our history. I see it in spite of the hand of the foreign devil." This response, coming from someone who, while a young girl, was brutalized and abducted by Japanese soldiers in southwest China during the Second World War, is much more complex and more unsettling than the one suggested to me by some of my academic friends who, not surprisingly, criticize the film as an instance of what Edward Said calls "Orientalism" and thus miss its appeal to many Chinese spectators in Hong Kong, Taiwan, and the People's Republic. I am not applauding the "Orientalism" that is obviously crucial to the film's structure. However, it seems to me equally important to point out how, much like the female spectator, the ethnic spectator occupies an impossible space that almost predetermines its dismissal from a theoretical reading that is intent on exposing the "ideologically suspect" technicalities of production only. In such a reading, my mother's response could only be written off as "unsophisticated," "simplistic," or "manipulated."

If, on the other hand, we are to take de Lauretis's discussion of "illusion" seriously, refusing, that is, to reduce "illusion" to the polarized opposition between "truth" and "illusion," then the position occupied by the ethnic spectator must be reaffirmed in the inquiry of cultural intercourse. To this position belongs, first, "historical" awareness: the knowledge of China's imperialized status vis-à-vis the West for the past century or so, and the memories, more recent and more overwhelming, of the millions of rapes and murders, the massacres, and the "biological experimentations" perpetrated by the Japanese on Chinese soil, in which Pu Yi was undoubtedly chief collaborator in the Northeast. Chinese idioms such as "foreign devil," as part of this historical awareness, emphasize—sentimentally and defensively—Chinese people's "holding their own," implying by that logic an intuitive distrust of any "foreigner's" story of Chinese history. But overlapping with the pain of historical awareness is another, equally intense feeling, describable only partly by phrases like "mesmerization," "nostalgia," and "a desire to be there, *in* the film." All these phrases belong to "illusion" as de Lauretis would understand it, that is, perceptive operations that are, regardless of their so-called falsity, vital to a continual engagement with what is culturally available.

The identification with an ethnic or "national" history, and the pain and pleasure that this involves, cannot be understood simply in terms of "nativism." The spectator is not simply ethnic but *ethnicized*—the recognition of her "Chineseness" is already part of the process of cross-cultural interpellation that is at work in the larger realm of modern history. To use the words of C. T. Hsia with regard to modern Chinese literature, there is, among many Chinese people, an "obsession with China."[34] Why? An answer to this question cannot be given unless we reinsert into the overtones of a collective identity the subjective processes—the desires, fantasies, and sentimentalisms—that are part of a *response* to the solicitous calls, dispersed internationally in multiple ways, to such an identity. In this light, the phrase "imagined communities" in the title of Benedict Anderson's book is especially thought-provoking.[35] In spite of being a specialist in Southeast Asia, however, Anderson's analysis is surprisingly indifferent to the rise of imagined communities in the non-West as a response to European colonialism. His insights into the origins of imagined communities in Europe—origins that encompass capitalism, technology, and the development of languages—are accompanied by a lack of interest in crucial differences in, say, postcolonial Asia. Take, for instance, this matter-of-fact observation: "So, as European imperialism smashed its insouciant way around the globe, other civilizations found themselves traumatically confronted by pluralisms which annihilated their sacred genealogies. The Middle Kingdom's marginalization to the Far East is emblematic of this process."[36] What, we should ask, is the nature of this traumatization and marginalization? The potency of Anderson's two-word phrase—a potency that remains unrealized in his book—lies, I think, not so much in its rapport with the urge in contemporary critical theory to deconstruct centrisms such as "communities" with their rings of monolithic closure, as in the word "imagined" as an index to the involved conceptual movements that may or may not coincide with their imagined content.

The word "imagined" is immensely rich in its suggestions of the process in which the subject is constituted by recognizing, in external objects, that part of herself that has been "dismembered" for cultural and historical reasons. Within contemporary psychoanalytic theories, Lacan's term *"objet petit a"* (object a), generally interpreted to mean the objects in the life of a subject that are neither fully distinguishable from the self nor clearly apprehensible as other, and which receive their value from the subject's representation of them as missing, would be one way of formulating this process.[37] A more concrete, because visually specific, formulation lies with Freud's theory of fetishism.[38] Central to Freud's theory is that a fetish is a substitute for something that is imagined to be lost or losable; in Freud, that something is the penis. But if we should disengage Freud's theory from its masculinist emphasis on the penis as the paradigm signifier, we would see that what is most interesting about fetishism is the process of loss, substitution, and identification that is at play in the formation of a subject. The fetishist is someone who translates the importance of that part of himself which he fears to be lost/losable into "its" lack outside himself, a "lack" that is, moreover, relocalized in another body in multiple ways (e.g., in female hair, feet, breasts, etc.), endowed with a magical power, and thus "fetishized." What should be emphasized is that this "translation" is, in Freud's texts, an imagining process that involves the mutual play between an emotion and a "sight," but more precisely a sight-in-recollection. What *is* seen (the female body) in a first instance (when no neurosis occurs) is remembered in a second instance amid feelings of fear (when the little boy is caught masturbating and threatened to be reported to his father); his "translation" of these feelings into the female body-as-lack is thus the result of a mental sequence. As such, fetishism is the process of a belated consciousness, a consciousness that comes into itself through memory substitution, and representation. Meanwhile, the "original" belief in the mother's "penis" (that is, her complete identification with and indistinguishability from oneself, thus her omnipotence and plenitude) undergoes a twofold change: (1) the knowledge that she does not "have a penis" is disavowed, and (2) the "lack" she signifies is repressed and represented in other forms, forms we call "fetishes." The original belief, in other words, does not disappear but reappears repeatedly as a wish, which is attached to "fetishes" in the form of emotions—the emotions of pleasure and of identification.

Removing these formulations of subjectivity from an exclusively psychoanalytic and metaphysical framework, and placing them in modern Chinese history, we see how the experience of "dismemberment" (or "castration") can be used to describe what we commonly refer to as "Westernization" or "modernization." Typically, as the history of the non-West is divided into the classical/primitive and the "modern" stages, modern non-Western subjects can be said to be constituted primarily through a sense of loss—the loss of an attributed "ancient" history with which one "identifies" but to which one can never return except in the form of fetishism. The "object" with which Chinese people are obsessed—"China" or "Chineseness"—cannot therefore be seen as an emotional simplism, but must rather be seen as the sign of a belated consciousness and a representation, involving mental processes that are not, as Kristeva would have it, "prepsychoanalytic." We might say that a response such as "Yes, that's me, that's Chinese" is a fetishizing imagining of a "China" that never is, but in that response also lies the wish that is the last residue of a protest against that inevitable "dismemberment" brought about by the imperialistic violence of Westernization.

The point must be emphasized, especially from the position of those that are feminized and ethnicized: these identificatory acts are the sites of productive relations that should be reread with the appropriate degree of complexity. This complexity lies not only in the identification with the ethnic culture, but also in the strong sense of complicity with the "dismembering" processes that structure those imaginings in the first place. For instance, the Chinese person obsessed with China emotionally is not necessarily one that would dress and live in a "Chinese" manner, as any superficial acquaintance with "Westernized" Chinese would reveal. Unlike what Oriental things still are to many Europeans and Americans, "Western things" to a Chinese person are never merely dispensable embellishments; their presence has for the past century represented the necessity of fundamental adaptation and acceptance. It is the permanence of imprints left by the contact with the West that should be remembered even in an ethnic culture's obsession with "itself."

4

In the preceding analysis, I demonstrate the problems pertaining to the ethnic spectator through a specific cultural instance, a film about modern China. I argue that the film, as a technical apparatus, provides the means of redistributing that "primitive" history to the ethnic subject as "her own," but it is the ethnic subject's contradictory response—a historical awareness combined with a pleasurable identification with the film's narrative-imagistic effects—that reveals the full complicity of the cross-cultural exchange. The difficulty of the ethnic, and ethnicized, spectator's position can be shown another way, through the currently prevalent academic attitudes revolving around the study of "China."

A few years ago, while attending an Association for Asian Studies meeting, I found myself face-to-face with an American-trained China historian who was lamenting the fact that China was becoming more and more like the West. Among the things that disturbed him the most were the diminishing differences in terms of the technical, cultural, and even linguistic aspects of Chinese life. China's recent development, in other words, makes it more and more impossible to disprove the "convergence" theory advanced by some social scientists about world modernization. Over the years, many versions of the same concern reveal themselves to me in sinological methodology, usually in the form of an eager emphasis on the uniqueness of Chinese history and a defense of "China" studies against the "West." Depending on the interest of the person, "sinocentrism" can either take the theoretical position that China's tradition is adequate to itself, or perform, in practice, elaborate reinscriptions and hermeneutical readings of Chinese history/texts. Often, the sinocentric approach to "China" boils down to an assertion of this kind in the field of literature: if one is studying Chinese texts, one should use "Chinese" methodologies, not "Western" ones. To read "Chinese" texts in terms of "Western" methodologies is to let the latter distort the former.

These encounters, personal or textual, have been instructive for me in that they make me ask myself: Why is it that these China scholars, who argue for the integrity of China studies, have not struck one chord of enthusiasm in me, a Chinese? What is missing in the dialogue between them and me, when in all likelihood I should feel grateful toward them for defending "my" culture? It becomes necessary for me to reflect on the nature of their defense of "Chinese culture," which I would describe as an idealist preoccupation with "authentic" originariness. This kind of preoccupation is, of course, not unique to China studies. But in China studies, it runs into specific difficulties. How to strive for authentic originariness, when the history of China in the nineteenth and twentieth centuries is inundated with disruptive contacts with the West? Where could authentic origins possibly come from? In other words, what is "Chinese"? The concentration on China as "tradition" is an understandable way out, for as an idea, tradition offers the comfort precisely of adequacy, self-sufficiency, and continuity. It is supported, outside academia, by antique collecting, museums, restaurants, tourism, and the pastime of *chinoiserie*, all of which confirm the existence of a Chinese tradition. What is missing from the preoccupation with tradition and authentic originariness as such is the experience of modern Chinese people who have had to live their lives with the knowledge that it is precisely the notion of a still-intact tradition to which they cannot cling—the experience precisely of being impure, "Westernized" Chinese and the bearing of *that* experience on their ways of "seeing" China. Instead of recognizing the reality of this "ethnic spectator," much of China studies prefers, methodologically, taxonomic divisions of China into "premodern" and "modern," "traditional" and "Westernized" periods, and so forth, even as the fragmented, dispersed, ironic developments of Chinese modernity make the clarity of these conceptual divisions useless. Thus, as is often felt though never directly stated, Chinese from the mainland are more "authentic" than those who are from, say, Taiwan or Hong Kong, because the latter have been "Westernized." A preference for the purity of the original ethnic specimen perhaps? But if so, one would have to follow this kind of logic to its extreme, and ask why sinologists should "study" China at all, since studying already implies "othering" and "alienating" it; and to that effect, how even the most sinocentric of sinologists could possibly justify writing about China in any language other than classical Chinese. Doesn't this state of affairs reenact exactly the problematically bifurcated nature of that nineteenth-century Chinese dictum vis-à-vis the West—*zhongxue wei ti, xixue wei yang* (Chinese learning for fundamental structure, Western learning for practical use)? China historians may criticize the conservatism of this dictum for retarding China's progress into the modern world, but aren't those who opt for a "sinocentric" approach to China repeating this conservatism themselves?

This problem becomes especially acute as students of Chinese culture attempt to articulate issues in their field by using the tools of "Western" concepts and theory they have learned. Consider the example of twentieth-century Chinese literature. In his book *Chinese Theories of Literature*, James J. Y. Liu explicitly refrains from discussing this period because it is Westernized:

> I shall not deal with twentieth-century Chinese theories, except those held by purely traditionalist critics, since these have been dominated by one sort of Western influence or another, be it Romanticist, Symbolist, or Marxist, and do not possess the same kind

118

of value and interest as do traditional Chinese theories, which constitute a largely independent source of critical ideas.[39]

The message is loud and clear: twentieth-century Chinese literature is too polluted by the West to merit discussion. On the other hand, however, should one attempt to read modern Chinese literature by means of "Western" theories, one is, to this day, likely to be slapped in the face with a moralistic and nationalistic disapproval of this kind: "Why use Western theory on Chinese literature?"

To this extent, de Lauretis's notion of "imaging"—"the articulation of meaning to image, language, and sound, and the viewer's subjective engagement in that process"[40]—is crucial to an understanding of Chinese modernity from the point of view of the Westernized Chinese subject/reader, who is caught between the sinologist's "gaze" and the "images" of China that are sewn on the screen of international culture. Between the gaze and the image, the Chinese experience of being "spectators" to *representations* of "their" history by various apparatuses is easily erased. China scholars who defend with earnest intent Chinese history's claim to the status of world history help to further the erasure of this spectatorship precisely by their argument for the "adequacy" of the Chinese tradition, for this argument disregards the quotidian truth with which every Chinese person grows up in the twentieth century, the truth that this "adequacy" is not so, for "the world" does not think so. When one has been taught, as a way of survival, the practical necessity of accepting "the West" and of having good French or English, only to be confronted with the charge, from those who are specialists of one's "own" culture, that one's methodology of thinking and reading is "too Westernized," the politics implied in ethnic spectatorship cannot be more stark and bitter. Such a charge demolishes the only premises on which the ethnic spectator can see and speak—premises that are, by necessity, impure and complicitous. The notion that "China" is beautiful and adequate to itself, which arises from an act of sentimental fetishizing on the part of the Chinese, becomes for those who are professionally invested a way to justify fencing off disciplinary territories. For a "Westernized" Chinese spectator/reader, it is impossible to assume an unmediated access to Chinese culture. To use a notion proposed by Yao-chung Li, this spectator/reader is "in exile";[41] to use a notion proposed by Biddy Martin and Chandra Talpade Mohanty, this spectator/reader is "not being home." Exile and homelessness do not mean disappearance. As Martin and Mohanty specify, "'Not being home' is a matter of realizing that home was an illusion of coherence and safety based on the exclusion of specific histories of oppression and resistance, the repression of differences even within oneself."[42] If an ethnicized reader does not simply read by affirming Chinese tradition's continuity and adequacy to itself, how might she read? How might the "Westernized" Chinese spectator be recognized?

In his illuminating study, *Time and the Other: How Anthropology Makes Its Objects*, Johannes Fabian offers many insights that are germane to our discussion. Earlier, I refer to one of them, visualism. Fabian's analysis of "visualism" is situated in a larger analysis of the uses of time in anthropology, which, as he points out, often denies "coevalness" or cotemporality between the subjects and objects of an inquiry. This denial occurs at the moment of writing, when anthropologists are away from the field, where they share an immediate present with their objects. The discrepancy between "field" time and "writing" time is, once again, encapsulated in Bertolucci's remarks that I quote at the beginning, a discrepancy that is between Bertolucci's "Yet in the meantime" and "before." While a coeval engagement with their objects "in the field" may reveal their sophistications, anthropologists slip into what Fabian calls "allochronism" in the process of writing, when shared time is replaced by a more linear, progressive use of time that enables the distinctions between "primitive" and "developed" cultures. Allochronism, the casting of the other in another time, goes hand in hand with "cultural relativism," a process in which other cultures are territorialized in the name of their central values and vital characteristics: "Once other cultures are fenced off as culture gardens or, in the terminology of sociological jargon, as boundary-maintaining systems based on shared values; once each culture is perceived as living its Time, it becomes possible and indeed necessary to elevate the interstices between cultures to a methodological status."[43]

Sinology and China studies, which have significantly structured the ways we "see" China in the West, partake of "cultural relativism" in obvious ways. Typically, "cultural relativism" works by fostering the distinction between "classical" and "modern" China. This is a distinction that shapes the structuring of Kristeva's *About Chinese Women,* in which, "reflecting a broader Western cultural practice, the 'classical' East is studied with primitivistic reverence, even as the 'contemporary' East is treated with realpolitical contempt."[44] The same distinction exists in Bertolucci's "making" of China; in his film the contrast between the sensuous colors of the "imperial" scenes and the drabness of the "Communist" scenes is too sharp not to become emblematic. In different but comparable ways, sinologists who are so much in love with the China of the classical Chinese texts that they refrain from visiting China; who only read the Chinese language silently as pictures but do not speak it; or who, lamenting China's "convergence" with the rest of the world, emphasize the methodological self-sufficiency of Chinese studies in an attempt to preclude readings of Chinese texts with non-Chinese strategies—these sinologists are also reinforcing and perpetuating the "allochronism" to which China has been reduced among world cultures.

Furthermore, in universities where the study of China is often part of "area studies" programs that are made up of political scientists, linguists, anthropologists, geographers, historians, musicologists, as well as literary critics, scholastic territorialization corroborates the bureaucratic. For, once "China" is fenced off in this way, its "fate" is left to the grossly uneven distribution of interests and funding between the humanities and the social sciences. While classical Chinese literature can hold on to a well-established, though isolated, tradition of refined textual study, modern Chinese literature, marginalized against classical hermeneutics but also against the data-yielding "China" of the social scientists, is inevitably deprived of the necessary institutional support that would enable its researchers to experiment with radical theoretical approaches in such a way as to make it accessible and interesting to nonspecialists.

My somewhat personal emphasis on the necessity to change the state of affairs in modern Chinese culture and literature has to do with my feeling that it is in this vastly neglected area that a theory of the ethnic spectator can be most urgently grounded, as Westernized Chinese students come to terms with themselves both as objects and subjects of "seeing" China. Fabian states: "Tradition and modernity are not 'opposed' . . . nor are they in 'conflict.' All this is (bad) metaphorical talk. What are opposed, in conflict, in fact, locked in antagonistic struggle, are not the same societies at different stages of development, but different societies facing each other at the same Time."[45]

Supplementing the terms of Fabian's analysis with those of our ongoing arguments, we can say that the position of the ethnic spectator is the position of "different societies facing each other at the same Time," that is, the position of coevalness.

5

In this chapter I have introduced the problematic of "seeing" modern China from the point of view of the Westernized Chinese spectator. China exists as an "other," feminized space to the West, a space where utopianism and eroticism come into play for various purposes of "critique." Kristeva's book about Chinese women shows us how the alluring tactic of "feminizing" another culture in the attempt to criticize Western discourse actually repeats the mechanisms of that discourse and hence cannot be an alternative to it. "China" becomes the "woman" that is superfluous to the relationship between Kristeva the critic and the metaphysical entity of "the West." Bertolucci's *Last Emperor* seems a timely instance illustrating how the feminizing of another culture can be explained cogently in terms of film theory, which casts the problems in a clear light because of cinema's use of visual images. The writings of Mulvey, Silverman, and de Lauretis make it possible for us to see the initially necessary cooperation between feminism and the critique of ideology as falsehood, while indicating what that combination leaves out—the position of the female spectator, whose interpellation by as well as rejection of the screen images is crucial for an understanding of reception as a mode of performative, not merely passive, practice.

Extending the notion of the female spectator, I ask whether we cannot also begin to theorize the position of the ethnic spectator, who is caught, in a cross-cultural context, between the gaze that represents her and the image that is supposed to be her. I argue that it is by acknowledging the contradictory, complicitous reaction to a film like *The Last Emperor* on the part of some Chinese spectators—a reaction that consists in fascination as well as painful historical awareness—that we can reintroduce the elusive space of the ethnic spectator. In the realm of sinology and China studies, I propose, it is the experience of this space that is often dismissed. Instead, the study of China remains caught in the opposition between "modernity" and "tradition." While Westernization is acknowledged as an idea and a fact in history, its materiality as an indelible, subjective part of modern Chinese people's response to their own "ethnic" identity is consistently disregarded. In thus excluding from its methods of inquiry the position of the ethnic spectator who has never been and will never be purely "Chinese," sinology and China studies partake of what Fabian calls "allochronism," which is central to "a nation-centered theory of culture" (48). It is only through thinking of the "other" as sharing our time and speaking to us at the moment of writing that we can find an alternative to allochronism. The position of the feminized, ethnicized spectator, as image as well as gaze, object of ethnography as well as subject in cultural transformations, is a position for which "coevalness" is inevitable. How might the argument of coevalness affect our reading of China's modernity? What would it mean to include the "other," the object of inquiry, in a cotemporal, dialogic confrontation with the critical gaze? How might we read modern Chinese literature other than as a kind of bastardized appendix to classical Chinese and a mediocre apprentice to Western literature? The following chapters offer a set of responses to these questions.

Background: film vs. playwriter
           ↓ french   ↓ Chinese American

9

The Dream of a Butterfly

M. Butterfly movie

These days we have become complacent about our ability to criticize the racist and sexist blunders inherent in the stereotypical representations of our cultural "others." "Our" here refers to the community of intellectuals, East and West, who have absorbed the wisdom of Edward Said's *Orientalism* and who are on the alert to point out the discriminatory assumptions behind the production of cultural artifacts, in particular those that involve Western representations of the non-West. But Said's work, insofar

as it successfully canonizes the demystification of Western cultural pretensions, is simply pointing to a certain direction in which much work still waits to be done—namely, the direction in which we must examine in detail the multifaceted psychical and philosophical implications of the conflict, confusion, and tragedy arising from "cross-cultural exchange" when that exchange is conditioned by the inequities and injustices of imperialist histories. This work that needs to be done cannot be done simply by repeating the debunking messages that Said has already so clearly delivered in his book. Rather, we need to explore alternative ways of thinking about cross-cultural exchange that exceed the pointed, polemical framework of "antiorientalism"—the lesson from Said's work—by continually problematizing the presumption of stable identities and also by continually asking what else there is to learn beyond destabilized identities themselves. In this chapter, I read the 1993 film *M. Butterfly* (directed by David Cronenberg, screenplay by David Henry Hwang) as an instance of such a badly needed alternative approach to the problematic of Orientalism.[1]

Let me emphasize at the outset that I am not discrediting or deemphasizing the continual need for the criticism of Orientalism. Far from it: I am saying that precisely because Orientalism has many guises—both decadent and progressivist, in the form of sexual adventures and textual devotion, *and also* in the form of political idealization, fascination with subaltern groups and disenfranchised classes, and so forth—what we need to examine ever more urgently is fantasy, a problem which is generally recognized as central to orientalist perceptions and significations.

My task is made all the more challenging because the problem of fantasy, even though it is a predominant consideration of the stage play on which the film was based, is usually dismissed moralistically, in this case also by playwright Hwang. In responding to the real-life story of the French diplomat whose affair with a Chinese male opera singer gave him his inspiration for the play, for instance, Hwang writes confidently: "I . . . concluded that the diplomat must have fallen in love, not with a person, but with a fantasy stereotype."[2] Hwang's interest in this bizarre story is, one might say, primarily didactic, as he expresses it clearly in these remarks:

> M. Butterfly has sometimes been regarded as an anti-American play, a diatribe against the stereotyping of the East by the West, of women by men. Quite to the contrary, I consider it a plea to all sides to cut through our respective layers of cultural and sexual misperception, to deal with one another truthfully for our mutual good, from the common and equal ground we share as human beings.
>
> For the myths of the East, the myths of the West, the myths of men, and the myths of women—these have so saturated our consciousness that truthful contact between nations and lovers can only be the result of heroic effort. Those who prefer to bypass the work involved will remain in a world of surfaces, misperceptions running rampant. (100)

And yet, because the question of fantasy as stated here is already part of a conclusive understanding, of a plea for truthful human contact devoid of "misperception," there is something inherently superfluous about the representation of the story: if these layers of cross-cultural "misperception" are a fact of such crystal clarity, why not simply state it as such? Why, in other words, do we need to have a play in the first place? As a moral fable that was designed to preach a lesson well understood in advance—the lesson about the laughable "fantasy" and ludicrous "false consciousness" of the imperialist Western man—Hwang's play, it would seem, is a gratuitous act. Is the play's overwhelming success in the West due perhaps precisely to this gratuitous, stereotypical, and thus absolutely safe mockery of fantasy and false consciousness? But this success—this approval received by an Asian American playwright in the West for correctly reprimanding Western imperialist fantasies—is it not itself a sign and a warning, not of how the West has finally learned its lessons, but rather once again of the very Orientalism which Hwang intends to criticize, and to which non-Western peoples nonetheless continue to be subjected today?[3]

My interest in the film M. Butterfly begins where Hwang would have us stop. Rather than being my conclusion, fantasy is the beginning of my inquiry, which is framed by two major questions.

[handwritten annotations: "fantasy is also a conscious state when power becomes — distortion of truth cross-cultural comes into play."]

First, if fantasy is not simply a matter of distortion or willful exploitation, but is rather an inherent part of our consciousness, our wakeful state of mind,[4] what are the possibilities and implications of achieving any kind of sexual and racial identification in a "cross-cultural" exchange? Further, if the most important thing about fantasy is not the simple domination of an other but, as Laplanche and Pontalis argue, the variable positionality of the subject, whose reality consists in a constant shifting between modes of dominance and submission,[5] what could be said about the relations between East and West, woman and man, that is perhaps alternative to the ones they are assumed, in antiorientalist discourse, to have?

The second major question that concerns me, after fantasy has been sufficiently understood to be a kind of structuring and setting that is indispensable to any consideration of subjectivity, is how the film *M. Butterfly* also moves *beyond* subjectivity to philosophical issues of phenomenology and ontology. What is of particular interest is the manner in which the film relates the question of "cross-cultural" fantasy not simply to homosexuality, heterosexuality, or race, but also to the larger, open-ended question of the limits of human vision. As I will attempt to demonstrate, the film probes this other question by exploring the phenomenological effects of the image and the gaze.

"EAST IS EAST AND WEST IS WEST, AND NE'ER THE TWAIN SHALL MEET"

[handwritten annotation: "According to the movie → Song portrays an act of weakness however she has influence over white man → submission false."]

For me, what is most remarkable about the *M. Butterfly* story is, to put it in the simplest terms, the fact that it is a stereotype, in which a Western man believes he is romantically involved with an oriental woman. The story goes briefly as follows. It is 1964 in Beijing, China. René Gallimard, an accountant working at the French consulate, has just been to a performance of excerpts from Giacomo Puccini's opera *Madama Butterfly* (1904), staged at one of the foreign embassies. Gallimard finds himself drawn to the Chinese opera singer, Song Liling, who plays the role of Madame Butterfly. When he relates his fascination to his wife, who dismisses the Chinese with the familiar attitude, "East is East and West is West, and never the twain shall meet," he finds that she does not share his enthusiasm. In the rest of the film she is to become less and less significant as he embarks on a clandestine relationship with the opera singer. Song later tells Gallimard she has become pregnant; eventually she shows him a baby boy who is supposedly his son. As the Cultural Revolution progresses, the lovers are separated: Gallimard is sent back to Paris and Song put in a labor camp. Just as he is abandoning all hope, she shows up again unexpectedly in Paris outside his apartment. The lovers are happily reunited until they are arrested for passing secret information of the French government to China. But for Gallimard, the most devastating consequence of this exposure is the revelation by the French government that Song, who has all these years been his "Butterfly," is actually a male spy whose involvement with him has been for the purpose of extracting information for the Chinese government.

Precisely because of its stereotypical structure, the relationship between Gallimard and Song allows us to approach it as a kind of myth. In this myth, Gallimard occupies the role of the supposedly active and dominant white male, and Song, the role of the supposedly passive and submissive oriental female. The superimposition of the racial and sexual elements of this relationship creates the space in which the story unfolds.

In order to heighten the story's mythical quality on film, director Cronenberg dispenses with many of the complexities that characterized both the real-life story and the stage play. For instance, while in the real-life story, the "Chinese woman" that the French diplomat fell for always appeared as a man but told his beloved that he was really a woman, in the film Song always appears as a woman until the final scenes. And, while the stage play contains many farcical moments that present the Frenchman as the obvious object of ridicule, the film trims away such moments, preserving the story instead in an elegant mode, against an often hazy and darkish background, and frequently melancholic music. In thus stripping and reducing the story, Cronenberg makes its macabre structure stand out starkly. In the same vein, the usual elaborate manner in which a leading "feminine" character is fetishized is kept to a minimum. Instead of filling the movie screen with lavish physical, cosmetic, and sartorial details—such as is the case with the film with which *M. Butterfly* is often compared, *Farewell My Concubine*, by Chen Kaige—the portrayal of Song is low-keyed and unglamorous. Her singing and her stage performance, in both Western and Chinese theaters, are presented only briefly and appear to have been rather unremarkable. Some critics, predisposed toward a sensational and extravagantly colorful approach whenever a non-Western culture is represented, are quick to criticize *M. Butterfly* on the basis of *verisimilitude:* they point out disparagingly, for instance, that John Lone, who plays Song, does not look like a woman and that he and Jeremy Irons are unconvincing as lovers, and so forth.[6]

In thus missing the significance of the purposefully restrained design of the film, such critics also miss its status as the uncluttered sculpting of a stereotypical story, the artful experimenting with a familiar myth. What they have utterly failed to grasp is that, as in the case of the Chinese Beijing opera, what we see is not so much realistic props as suggestive ones, which are meant to conjure and signify rather than resemble an entire ambiance.

As the effects of verisimilitude give way to those of simplified plot, sparse detail, and minimalist characterization, the object of the story—fantasy itself—becomes intensified. The film becomes literally the *setting* that typifies fantasy.[7] With little sensational visual detail to distract us, we are compelled to focus on the absurd question: what happens when a man falls in love, not with a woman or even with another man, not with a human being at all but with a thing, a reified form of his own fantasy?[8] In the context of this film, this question is mapped over the question of Orientalism, so that it becomes: what happens when a Western man falls in love with a reification of the orient, with that mysterious thing called the "oriental woman"?

In many ways, we can say that the film teaches the lesson which is summarized in that platitudinous phrase repeated by Mme. Gallimard, "East is East and West is West." The conclusion that "never the twain shall meet" could, obviously, be interpreted in accordance with the argument against Orientalism, with *M. Butterfly* serving as a piece of didacticism. Gallimard, a Frenchman working in the exotic East, harbors the typical Western male fantasy about the East and in particular about submissive oriental women. He is so enamored of this fantasy of his that he cannot tell a fake oriental woman from a real one. This fantastical relation to "the other" could then be said to be symptomatic of a deep-rooted racist, sexist, and homophobic imperialism; and Gallimard could be called a symbol of the West, with a downfall that is well deserved, and so forth.

This kind of moral is, as I already suggested, indeed what the stage play tries to point at explicitly. For Hwang, the significance of fantasy is that of a content that needs to be changed; it needs to be changed because, by using other people as objects and things, fantasy dehumanizes them. Cronenberg, on the other hand, refuses this approach to fantasy and, as in the case of most of his other films, notably *Videodrome*, *The Fly*, *Dead Ringers*, and *Naked Lunch*, explores instead the possibilities and implications of fantasy precisely as a process of dehumanization—of deconstructing the human.[9] Instead of entirely dispensing with the antiorientalist didacticism, however, Cronenberg's film makes it part of its dramatization of the Gallimard-Song relationship. In this dramatization, the film no longer simply offers a diatribe against the stereotyping of the East by the West, or of women by men, but rather raises questions about the fundamental misrecognition inherent to processes of identification, *which the encounter between an oriental woman and a Western man magnifies and thus exemplifies*. The didactic, antiorientalist criticism of the West, then, remains a significant part of the story, but it is no longer its central focus.

Consider, for instance, the scene of the lovers' first encounter, wherein Song, instead of acting flattered, reprimands Gallimard for thinking that the story of Madame Butterfly is a beautiful one. It is only because he is so grossly ignorant of the history of the atrocities committed by Japan in China, Song says, that he could think that a Chinese actress playing a Japanese woman could be convincing. Further, if the races of the roles had been reversed—if it had been a Western woman sacrificing herself for an unattractive Japanese man—the judgment would most likely be that the woman is deranged rather than beautiful:

Song: It's one of your favorite fantasies, isn't it? The submissive Oriental woman and the cruel white man.

Gallimard: Well, I didn't quite mean . . .

Song: Consider it this way: what would you say if a blonde homecoming queen fell in love with a short Japanese businessman? He treats her cruelly, then goes home for three years, during which time she prays to his picture and turns down marriage from a young Kennedy. Then, when she learns he has remarried, she kills herself. Now, I believe you would consider this girl to be a deranged idiot, correct? But because it's an Oriental who kills herself for a Westerner—ah!—you find it beautiful.

While Song's words are undoubtedly historically astute, they also serve to fuel Gallimard's imagination of the "oriental woman" rather than cure it. In other words, the fact that this piece of antiorientalist criticism is inserted in the film as part of the first dialogue between Gallimard and Song means that the film has a relationship to the didactics of antiorientalism that is not direct but mediated. Rather than simply endorsing such a didactics, the film explicitly stages Orientalism as a psychic, interpersonal structure that unfolds with a specific logic. The Western man caught in a fantasy about oriental women is here portrayed as a version of Pavlov's dog: conditioned to respond according to certain artificially induced stimuli, such creatures can, at the mere ringing of a bell or the mere appearance of an oriental woman, be expected to behave in a predictable manner—so predictable, in fact, that their behavior cannot be altered simply by an explicit exposure of the conditions that enable it. These creatures would salivate and come alive *for real* even if the stimulus had nothing "real" behind it. In Gallimard's case, the stimulus is the stereotype of the "inscrutable oriental" in the female form—and the more inscrutable she is, the more charmed he is. Simply by playing "herself," by playing her stereotypical, inscrutable role, the "oriental woman" sets the Western man's mind afire.

There is, however, another twist that makes the film decidedly different from the play. Even though she may be the relentless scheming "woman" working for the Chinese Communist Party, and even though she is fully capable of giving Gallimard lectures about the political incorrectness of his "imperialist" fantasies, Song is, as Lone plays the part, herself attracted to Gallimard. As she tells him at the end of their second encounter before saying good-bye, "sometimes, the fascination could be mutual." Is this a response spoken from her heart? Or is it also part of her role-playing? We have no way of knowing until the very end. What is crucial, nonetheless, is that this suggestion of mutual fascination takes the film beyond the one-sided antiorientalism "message" that Song verbally enunciates. And what is mutuality here if not precisely the problematic of the "meeting" between East and West, and woman and man? As I will go on to argue, mutuality in this film occurs exactly in the form of nonreciprocity, so that together, mutuality and nonreciprocity constitute a symbiotic process of fantasy which, as it draws the lovers together, also ensures that they will never meet.

"THE BEAUTY . . . OF HER DEATH. IT'S A . . . PURE SACRIFICE"

Why is Gallimard so fascinated by the Madame Butterfly character? He explains: he is moved by the beauty of her death. It's a pure sacrifice, he says, for even though the man she loves is unworthy, she sacrifices herself for him. To this Song responds, as I mentioned, by pointing out the imperialist implications of his fascination. But there are other possibilities of understanding this "pure sacrifice" of the "oriental woman."

At the most immediate level, this "pure sacrifice" describes exactly the role that Song plays even as she speaks. In the course of their amorous relationship, Song does, we may say, sacrifice herself for Gallimard, a man who is not worthy of her love, by living up to his fantasy. In this instance, the "pure sacrifice" of the "oriental woman" has the status of what Lacan calls lure—that lack of a coincidence between the eye and the gaze, a lack of coincidence that, however, is often what constitutes love:

> From the outset, we see, in the dialectic of the eye and the gaze, that there is no coincidence, but, on the contrary, a lure. When, in love, I solicit a look, what is profoundly unsatisfying and always missing is that—*You never look at me from the place from which I see you.*
> Conversely, *what I look at is never what I wish to see.*[10]

In this well-known passage, Lacan shows that the essential ingredient in love is misrecognition—a circular pattern of wishing, solicitation, frustration, and desire which stems from the belief that there is something more behind what we see (in the beloved). What Lacan calls lure, Jean Baudrillard calls, in a slightly different manner, seduction. To seduce, Baudrillard writes, is to divert the other from his own truth, from the secret (of himself) that escapes him.[11] In the film, by giving Gallimard the lure, the illusion of the self-sacrificing "oriental woman," Song leads Gallimard astray from his own truth. (I will specify what I think this truth is toward the end of this chapter.) But this process of seduction is, as Song says, mutual: while she successfully lures Gallimard, Song herself is also being seduced by Gallimard in that she has been drawn into his area of *weakness*—his weakness precisely for the beauty of the self-sacrificing Madame Butterfly. As Baudrillard writes, comparing seduction and challenge:

> Challenge and seduction are quite similar. And yet there is a difference. In a challenge one draws the other into one's area of strength, which, in view of the potential

131

for unlimited escalation, is also his or her area of strength. Whereas in a strategy (?) of seduction one draws the other into one's area of weakness, which is also his or her area of weakness. A calculated weakness; an incalculable weakness: one challenges the other to be taken in. . . .

> To seduce is to appear weak. To seduce is to render weak. We seduce with our weakness, never with strong signs or powers. In seduction we enact this weakness, and this is what gives seduction its strength. (83)

If Song seduces Gallimard with the artifice/sacrifice of the submissive "oriental woman," Gallimard seduces Song with his naïveté, his capacity for fascination, and ultimately his gullibility. In spite of her real status as a spy for the Chinese government, therefore, she too seems to have genuinely fallen in love with him.

What seduces, in other words, is not the truth of the other—what he or she really is—but the artifact, the mutual complicity in the weaving of a lure, which works as a snare over the field of encounter, ensuring that the parties meet at the same time that they miss each other, in a kind of rhythmic dance.

Furthermore, because the "pure sacrifice" of the" oriental woman" is the thing that propels and sustains the lure, the act (such as Song's in the earlier scene) of pointing out that it is a *mere* imperialist fantasy does not only not succeed in destroying this lure; it actually enhances it—makes it more alluring. Meanwhile, if the point of the film is not a straightforward antiorientalism, it is not simply homosexual love either: as in the case of the criticism of imperialist fantasy, the lure cannot be destroyed by pointing out that Gallimard is really a bisexual or closeted gay man.

A "homoerotic" reading that is intent on showing what Gallimard's sexual preference really is runs a parallel course with the "antiorientalist" reading in the sense that both readings must rely on the belief in a kind of repressed truth—repressed racism or repressed homosexuality—for their functioning. In both cases, the assumption would be that we need to look beyond the surface structure of the lure in order to locate what is "behind" or "beneath" it. In effect, critics who read this story as the story of a confused sexual identity would be lending themselves to the lure set up by the film itself, in that they would be seduced into going after the real penis, the visible body part, the "fact" of Song being a male; their re-search would be echoing the re-search of the antiorientalist critics, who are seduced into going after the real penis, the visible body part, the "fact" of Gallimard being a white man. Be it through the route of race or the route of sexual preference, such critics would be trapped by their own desire for a secret—the secret of cross-cultural exploitation or the secret of homosexual love, which they might think they are helping to bring to light, when in fact it is they themselves who have been seduced. In each case what seduces (them) is, shall we say, the "purity" of a secret—an indubitable orientalism or an indubitable homoeroticism—the way the indubitable love, the pure sacrifice, of an "oriental woman" seduces Gallimard.[12]

The film *M. Butterfly*, on the other hand, is much more cunning. We can see this, for instance, in the interesting scene in Song's bedroom where she is confronted by a party cadre about her decadent behavior. Dressed in a beautiful traditional Chinese woman's jacket, reclining on her bed by herself, and reading girlie magazines featuring oriental women, Song is surprised by the visit of Comrade Chin, her connection to the party authorities. Comrade Chin contemptuously reprimands Song for indulging in "decadent trash." This scene reveals for the first time that Song is working for the Chinese Communist Party and that her relationship with Gallimard is a means to uncover American military plans in Indochina. Is Song not merely playing a role for the sole purpose of getting information from Gallimard? So why, Comrade Chin demands, is she behaving in such a degraded manner when Gallimard is not even present? Song's response to these moralistic charges is remarkable:

> Song: Comrade, in order to better serve the Great Proletarian State, I practice my deception as often as possible! I despise this costume, yet, for the sake of the Great Helmsman, I will endure it along with all other bourgeois Western perversions!
>
> Comrade Chin: I am not convinced that this will be enough to redeem you in the eyes of the Party.
>
> Song: I am trying my best to become somebody else.

Significantly, deception, as it is described by Song, has shifted from the status of dishonesty to that of honor: the seductive "oriental woman," as we are now given to understand, is not only a romantically but also a politically self-sacrificing figure, who gives up herself—her "real" identity—for the cause of the revolution, so much so that she sacrifices even her private moments in order to immerse herself in this cause entirely, purely. The greatest deception, then, is also the greatest act of loyalty—to the people, to the country, to the "Great Helmsman." Even though, as the audience, we cannot but sense that these words of loyalty are spoken with irony—that Song's loyalty to the party is dubious precisely because she is so eloquent about it—this scene reveals that the myth of the self-sacrificing "oriental woman" far exceeds the "imperialist fantasy" that has been commonly used to decode it, and that in her artificial role, Song is faithfully serving in the intersection of two cultural symbolics—the nationalistic as well as the erotic, the intracultural as well as the intercultural.

Song does not rebel against her intended and prescribed role in either situation; rather she plays it, indeed lives it, with her truest emotions. In the relationship with Gallimard, the disguise, lure, and veil of the "oriental woman" serve the purpose of gaining access to the realm that is his trust, love, and imagination. In Gallimard's words, thus, her love is pure: she performs her artificial role to the hilt and thus sacrifices herself—gives up her "real" identity—for a man who, as he notices in the story of Madame Butterfly, is unworthy of that love. At the same time, with the revelation of Song's relationship with the party, a supplementary dimension of the myth of Madame Butterfly unfolds. In this supplementary dimension, we see for the first time that the Song-Gallimard story, which plays on the stereotype of "imperialist male fantasy," is itself the mere instrument of espionage, a means of gaining access to the forbidden realm of another country's military secrets. Gallimard's words about Madame Butterfly, then, were an unwitting description of Song's role-playing in this *other* political realm as well: for is not the "man unworthy" of her love not only Gallimard, her imperialist aggressor, her foreign enemy, but also her party leader, the Great Helmsman himself?

If, as we already said, the fascination between Gallimard and Song is mutual, we see now how this mutuality is simultaneously structured as a nonreciprocity. While the "oriental woman" remains an erotic object on the side of Gallimard, on the side of Song it is much more complex. For Song, the "oriental woman" is a means to exploit a foreigner as part of her service to the party. Gallimard, then, is not simply an erotic object or subject; rather he has been identified as a political object, a plaything that would unconsciously help Song give the party what it wants.

THE FORCE OF BUTTERFLY; OR, THE "ORIENTAL WOMAN" AS PHALLUS

The foregrounding of this supplementary, political dimension of our Madame Butterfly story enables us to read the Gallimard character in a very different manner from the one originally intended by Hwang and followed by most critics. The fateful encounter between East and West takes place at a critical moment of twentieth-century world politics. For France, it is the end of the imperial empire, when Indochina was recently lost and Algeria has become independent. The emptiness of diplomatic life in Beijing is clear: officials cheat on expense accounts; women have illicit affairs; dinner parties and other gatherings are perfunctory and boring. Like a character from a Kafka novel, Gallimard has an uninspiring, low-ranking job as an accountant, but it is one that he takes seriously, so seriously that his corrupt colleagues become annoyed with him for continually exposing them. The high point of this rationalistic bookkeeping existence is tracking down the documentation from people who try to falsify their expense accounts. While we may say that Gallimard is the perfect example of the disciplined individual whose body and mind have, as Michel Foucault shows us in a work such as *Discipline and Punish*, been produced for the efficient, utilitarian functioning of its society, it is equally important to note that Gallimard is clearly a "flunky" in terms of the unspoken rules of political society. His tireless efforts to track down documentation for dubious expense accounts mean that he is out of tune with the smooth debaucheries that constitute the substance of the bureaucratic world. Precisely because he takes his job of accounting seriously, he reveals himself to be someone who does not know how to play the game. At a dinner gathering, as Gallimard sits down at the same table with his colleagues, they sneer and remind him: "You are nobody. You are worse than nobody: you are an accountant. If you are not careful we'll break all your pencils in half." To this Gallimard responds by leaving the table, clumsily dropping his silverware as he does so.

In terms of his relation to the cultural symbolic that is the world of politics, therefore, Gallimard occupies a place that is not dissimilar to that of Song in that he, too, is a bureaucratic informant, a submissive "woman" to the "man not worthy of her love"—the French government, to which he gives his loyal service. The affinity between Gallimard and Song lies in that both are manipulable and useful instruments of their respective political orders, and both respond to these orders with dedication. Gallimard's political usefulness is soon recognized by the ambassador, who sees in him the qualities of a head servant who is not smart enough to cheat and who can therefore be entrusted with the task of "coordinating a revamped intelligence division," that is, of policing the other employees. But it is obvious that in this world of complex political "intelligence," Gallimard is not at home at all as *a person in command*. As he receives, in the ambassador's office, the surprising news of his own promotion to vice consul, we can see that he does not possess the suave body language to respond appropriately; instead his posture remains awkward and stiff, marking his destiny as someone who will remain marginal and insignificant in French diplomatic culture. When he finally sits in his office as vice consul, he lacks the presence to command the respect of those who are supposedly working for him. Instead of speaking to them with the air of mastery, he reads woodenly from a prewritten script as if he were someone being cross-examined.

It is into this impersonal but overpowering world of bureaucracy, which is echoed by a routine domestic life complete with an uncomprehending wife, classic pajamas, and bedtime tooth-brushing, that "Butterfly" intrudes with an irresistible force. Gallimard, we remember, stumbles upon "Butterfly" unexpectedly. Before the performance of the aria "Un bel di" from Puccini's opera begins, Gallimard tells his neighbor, Frau Baden, with whom he will later have a casual affair, that he has never seen *Madama Butterfly*, even though his lack of culture is unsuspected by most people.[13] In the position of an outsider to his own European culture, then, Gallimard's eyes catch the "oriental woman" on stage, even though the situation—of a contemporary Chinese opera singer performing the role of a fetishized Japanese heroine from an Italian opera—cannot be more bizarre. If the "entrance of Butterfly" (as

printed on the musicians' scores) represents a decisive marking of cultural identity and its concomitant confusion, what it marks first of all is in fact Gallimard's
alienation from his own culture. Rather than simply notice the foreignness, the
exoticness, of the spectacle in front of him, Gallimard finds in "Butterfly" a kind
of anchorage for *himself.* (This is the reason why his behavior takes on a noticeably
greater air of self-assurance from this point on.)

Because it is not fully attainable even as it is consumed through sexual contact, the fantasy of the "oriental woman" keeps the Frenchman *afloat with life* by
inscribing in him an unanswerable lack. Song exists for Gallimard as the phallus
in Lacan's sense of the term—that is, the Other that is always assumed to be more
than it appears and that has the power to give us what we want and also to take it
away. Lacan, we remember, emphasizes that the phallus functions only when it is
veiled and that, once revealed, it becomes shame.[14] Song's tactic, however, includes
precisely this "unveiling" of shame by deliberately calling attention to it in a letter
to Gallimard: "What more do you want?" she writes. "I have already given you my
shame." By feigning loss of dignity, thus, Song preserves her power as phallus,
while the "shame" that has been revealed—the oriental woman's love—continues
to be a sham veiling the male body that is beneath it.

The manner in which the "oriental woman" functions as a phallus is made even
more clear by the fact that Gallimard seems content in love without ever experienc-
ing Song completely naked. (Later in court, responding to the inquiry about this
incredible fact, Song will describe Gallimard as a lover who has been very responsive to his "'ancient oriental ways of love,' all of which I invented myself—just for
him.") The one time Gallimard comes dangerously close to stripping her, Song tells
him at the crucial moment that she is pregnant, thus shifting his sexual desire into
a more paternal frame. Meanwhile, Gallimard can have what he calls an "extra extramarital affair" with Frau Baden without its intruding into his fantasy. In the scene
in which he and Frau Baden are in their hotel room, Gallimard, coming out of the
bathroom in his hygienic-looking undershirt, is shown to be somewhat taken aback
by the sight of Frau Baden sitting casually naked on the edge of the bed. Instead of
the typical sexual excitement one would expect with an illicit affair, the following
matter-of-fact exchange takes place between the would-be copulants:

Gallimard: You look . . . just like I thought you would under your clothes.
Frau Baden: What did you expect? So come and get it!

While Gallimard's remark highlights the complete coincidence between the eye
and the gaze, and therefore the lack precisely of a lure in his relationship with this
other woman, Frau Baden's notion of "getting it" complements his observation by
containing sex entirely within the satiable and short-term realm of physical need.

Sex with her is but a casual meal, in which the physical body, because it is completely available, remains a *mere* body. The force of the phallus—and with it fantasy, the lure, and seduction—does not come into play at all.

"UNDER THE ROBES, BENEATH EVERYTHING, IT WAS ALWAYS ME"

One of the most moving and unforgettable scenes in this film is the one in which, after the costume farce in the French courtroom, Song and Gallimard, both in men's suits, sit face to face alone in the police van taking them to prison. As the two men stare at each other, Song is the first to break the silence: "What do you want from me?" he asks. In psychoanalytic terms, this question is an indication of the fundamental issue in our relationship with an other—demand. However, even though Song has brought up this fundamental issue, he has, nonetheless, posed his question imprecisely, because he still thinks in terms of Gallimard's wanting *something from him.* Instead, as Lacan has taught us, the significance of demand is never simply what can be effectively enunciated by way of what the other can literally give us; rather, it is what remains resistant to articulation, what exceeds the satisfaction provided by the other.[15] To pose the question of demand with precision, therefore, Song would have had to ask: "What do you want, by wanting me? What is your demand, which you express through me?"

Gallimard, on the other hand, responds to (the philosophical implications of) this question precisely: "You are my Butterfly."

With this exchange, what takes place between the former lovers is now a new kind of nonreciprocity. If, in the past, their nonreciprocity was a matter of their playing their respective roles in the game of erotics and politics, a nonreciprocity that enabled them to meet through the lure, the new nonreciprocity has to do rather with Song's attempt to change the very terms of their relationship. Instead of playing "Butterfly" the way he has for Gallimard all these years, Song does something he has never done before: he undresses, challenging Gallimard to see for the first time what he has always wanted but somehow always failed to see. Kneeling completely naked in front of Gallimard, Song pleads for a rekindling of the affection that once existed between them. As he gazes tenderly up at his former lover, Song says, in a manner that reveals that he has indeed loved the Frenchman all along: "Under the robes, beneath everything, it was always me."

If, until this tragic moment, the lure has been kept intact because it is upheld on both sides, Song, by the very gesture of undressing with which he tries to regain Gallimard's love, has destroyed that lure forever. While Song intends by this brave and defiant gesture a new beginning for their relationship—a beginning in which they can face each other honestly as they really are, two men physically and

137

ΛSψɕ

emotionally entangled for years—what he actually accomplishes is the death of that relationship. Song fails to see that what Gallimard "wants" is not him, Song, be he in the definitive form of a woman or a man, but, as Gallimard says, "Butter-fly." Because Gallimard's desire hinges on neither a female nor a male body, but rather on the phallus, the veiled thing that is the "oriental woman," Song's candid disclosure of his physical body can only be lethal. Like Frau Baden, who, having dis-clothed herself, invites Gallimard frankly to "come and get it," Song's gesture of undressing serves not to arouse but extinguish desire.

The naked body destroys the lure once and for all by demonstrating that what lies under the veil all these years is nothing, no thing for fantasy. With the veil lifted, the phallus shows itself shamefully as merely a man, a penis, a pathetic body in all its banal vulnerability, which Gallimard rejects in abhorrence. (As many have pointed out, this moment in *M. Butterfly* is comparable to a similar one in *The Crying Game*, in which the man, in love with a transvestite whom he supposes to be a female, vomits at the sight of his beloved's actual genitalia. What has to be thrown up literally is the repugnant reality of the physical.) Song's naked body must therefore be understood ultimately as the traumatic Real that tears apart the dream of "Butterfly," forcing Gallimard to wake up in the abyss of his own self. In the two men's *parting* conversation, we see how, instead of rescuing Gallimard, Song's sincere love finally brings about the nonreciprocity that is their absolute parting of ways:

> Gallimard: You, who knew me so well—how could you, of all people, have made such a mistake?
>
> Song: What?
>
> Gallimard: You've just shown me your true self—when all I loved was the lie. A perfect lie—it's been destroyed.
>
> Song (genuinely hurt): You never really loved me?
>
> Gallimard: I'm a man who loved a woman created by a man. And anything else—simply falls short.

"IT'S NOT THE STORY; IT'S THE MUSIC"

From Gallimard's perspective, the disappearance of that "lie" he loves, that very thing in which he has found a means of anchoring his identity, means a traumatic self-awakening that is the equivalent of madness. Before examining this awak-ening/madness closely, I think it is necessary to discuss one more aspect of this "thing"—the music from *Madama Butterfly*—which, as much as the fetishized "ori-ental woman," serves as Gallimard's anchorage.

It is possible to think of the operatic music as a kind of big Other, to which the human characters submit in such a manner as to create their "fate." This fate is predicted by a remark made by Song in an early conversation with Gallimard, in regard to his fascination with the Madame Butterfly story: "The point is," she says, "it's not the story; it's the music." Indeed, one could argue that, as much as the "oriental woman," the music is the agent that engenders the plot of the story, so that it is the story which follows the lead of the music rather than the reverse. From the initial performance at the foreign embassy of "Un bel di," which establishes contact between Gallimard and Song, we move through scenes in which the music of *Madama Butterfly* continues to haunt the characters, as if always to recall them to the primal moment of their fateful encounter. For instance, even Gallimard's wife, when she hears about his captivation by Song's performance, bursts into a spontaneous performance complete with hand gestures. In the mirror reflection that follows, we see Gallimard looking bewildered and uneasy at his wife's uncanny mimicry of the "other woman." He goes on to place a special order for the record album of the opera, noticing, upon its arrival, its cover illustration of the "oriental woman" in a submissive posture to her Western lover.

Crucially also, Gallimard's amorous relationship with "Butterfly" takes place at a time when both *Madama Butterfly* and Chinese opera singers are considered to be relics of the past.

In the China of the mid-1960s, not only were imported items such as Western operatic music considered bourgeois and imperialist; even indigenous traditional art forms such as the Beijing opera were deemed feudal and corrupt. The revolution demanded that all such ideologically suspect relics be purged and replaced by new, progressive practices. The second time Gallimard visits the Chinese theater where Song used to perform, a Maoist "model play" is being staged with a different kind of dramatic semiotics and a noticeably different didactic sentience. Such ostensible state intervention in aesthetic forms, together with the massive burning of traditional artifacts, the forced trial and punishment of intellectuals, writers, and artists, and the coerced surrender of personal ideals for the common good, made up the new reality of Chinese political life. In the film, the communist revolution establishes itself in Chinese society as a new big Other with its power to interpellate ordinary citizens with the call to repudiate the past and labor for the future. As Gallimard is finally sent back to France (since, as he is told, his foreign policy predictions about Vietnam and China were all wrong), Song is seen working with other intellectuals in a labor camp, where loudspeakers blare away with "reeducation" messages to cleanse people's souls.

If the loudspeaker of a labor camp is the apparatus for a new type of fantasy—the fantasy of revolutionized subjectivity, of proletarian agency, of nationalist progress—it is shown to compete rather weakly with that other, older and "corrupt"

139

apparatus of interpellation, the operatic music of *Madama Butterfly*. As Song looks up strained and exhausted from her labor, she seems to hear another voice from afar, which gradually takes over the audible space hitherto occupied by the loud-speaker. As this voice becomes louder, we recognize it to be the familiar music from *Madama Butterfly*, and the grayish backdrop of the labor camp changes into Paris, 1968, when Gallimard is watching a performance of *Madama Butterfly*, with tears slowly trickling down his face, at the Paris Opera. Song and Gallimard are thus, we might say, reunited through this persistent "corrupt" big Other of "Butterfly," which was what brought them together in the first place.

This dream of a Butterfly, of an unforgettable erotic and emotional experience, inserts itself in a Paris that, as Gallimard's acquaintance in a bar tells him, is looking more like Beijing, with students shouting Maoist slogans and rioting in the streets. The juxtaposition at this point of the erotic and the political, the "personal" and the "historical," raises a question that *M. Butterfly* merely hints at but that nonetheless is crucial to any consideration of fantasy: is "revolution" itself, the film seems to say, not simply another type of "fantasy stereotype"—the fantasy stereotype that exploits in the name of the collective, the people? If we mobilize, as we must, criticism against Western "orientalist" and "imperialist" fantasies about the East, then should the cru-elties committed by way of this *other* fantasy stereotype not also be under attack? The pro-Chinese communist fervor in France of the 1960s—is it an awakening from Western imperialism and Orientalism, or is it not simply the other side of that dream called Butterfly, which fetishizes the East this time not in the form of an erotic object but in the form of a political object, not in the form of the beautiful "oriental woman" but in the form of the virile oriental man, the Great Helmsman, Mao Zedong?

In his indifference to the political revolution, Gallimard will listen again to the music from *Madama Butterfly* in his own private space, away from the clamor of the streets. An evening alone in his minimalist, orientalist apartment, where a meal consists of mere bread and broth, he sits forlornly accompanied by the "Humming Chorus" played on his MCA record. As if by miracle, "Butterfly" again enters: in the midst of the melancholic music, Song has mysteriously reappeared.

MADAME BUTTERFLY, C'EST MOI

After this scene of reunion, the music from *Madama Butterfly* will be heard one final time—as an accompaniment to Gallimard's performance in jail. Played on a cassette, the music has by this time become a portable object, very much like the other things that Gallimard consciously displays *on himself* in this scene. How then are we to bring together the music, the "pure sacrifice" of the "oriental woman," and Gallimard's gory suicide?

In this final one-man show, which progresses as Song is meanwhile released and sent back to China, Gallimard begins by commenting on his own "celebrity" and then proceeds to tell the story that led up to it. Gradually but steadily, as he describes his vision of the slender "oriental women" in "cheongsams and kimonos, who die for the love of unworthy foreign devils," Gallimard performs a transformation into Madame Butterfly herself. The camera shows him putting on the sash for his kimono, followed by white foundation across his face, eyelining, shiny red lip gloss, and finally a wig. As his transformation becomes complete, the transvestite pronounces: "At last, in a prison far from China, I have found her. . . . My name is René Gallimard! Also known—as Madame Butterfly!" [14]

This scene of dramatic transformation offers, I think, one of the most compelling and complex moments in cinematic history. Because of this I must emphasize that the readings I provide below are much more experimental explorations than exact renderings of its significance.

First, what is effected in these last moments of the film seems to be a merging of two separate identities. This merging returns us, once again, to the theme of the self-sacrificing "oriental woman" discussed above, with a new twist. If Gallimard is Madame Butterfly, then this performance of his transformed identity should perhaps be described as a retroactive enactment, a slow-motion replay, of a story whose meaning has become visible only now—for the first time. In this story, Gallimard the "oriental woman" has been sacrificing himself (herself) for a man (Song) who, as Gallimard points out, is not worthy of his (her) love. This merging and swapping of identities, through which Gallimard turns into "Butterfly," is what Hwang intends as the basic "arc" of his play: "the Frenchman fantasizes that he is Pinkerton and his lover is Butterfly. By the end of the piece, he realizes that it is he who has been Butterfly, in that the Frenchman has been duped by love; the Chinese spy, who exploited that love, is therefore the real Pinkerton."[16] To return to the point of seduction I made earlier, we may add, paradoxically, that in seducing Gallimard, Song in fact led him temporarily away from his own truth—the truth of a fantasy that is not a fantasy of the other but rather *of himself as the suicidal "oriental woman."* In desiring Song, Gallimard was desiring not exactly to have her but to be her, to be the "Butterfly" that she was playing. While being the setting and structuring of fantasy, therefore, the encounter with Song served in effect to displace and postpone the fulfillment of Gallimard's wish for his own immolation. The "Butterfly" that was Song, in other words, shielded Gallimard from the "Butterfly" that is himself.

But if the relationship with Song has been a screen against the Real by giving Gallimard a conventional anchorage—a relation with a physical other and within the acceptable symbolic of heterosexual sociality—the revelation of Song's banal maleness means that this screen, which protected him but also prevented him from seeing, has evaporated. With the screen also disappear the fixed positions that are usually ascribed to man and woman, occident and orient. In a manner similar to Laplanche and Pontalis's argument about fantasy, what Gallimard's fantasy of "Butterfly" accomplishes in this final scene of monstrous transformation is ultimately a belated staging of a field of relations with multiple entry points, a field where positions of dominance and submission, of male and female, of aggressor and victim, are infinitely substitutable and interchangeable. Gallimard's transformation continues, in tandem, the series of vertiginous transvestist masquerades that began with Song.

Second, while this interpretive narrative of interchangeable racial and sexual subjectivities that I have just offered is perhaps the one most likely to be favored by critics who are invested in the utopian potential of destabilized identities, there are other elements in this transformation that far exceed such a narrative. For one thing, the conclusion that Gallimard finally discovers himself to be Madame Butterfly does not explain the power of the *visual* play of this last series of shots. How, in other words, might we understand his transformation in terms of the dynamics, the power structure of vision—of the relations between the image and the gaze? What does the interplay between Gallimard the Frenchman, Gallimard the performer, and Gallimard the Madame Butterfly signify *in terms of visuality*? For my own aid, I turn at this point to Lacan's reading of a story which has much genealogical affinity with ours.

I am referring to Lacan's consideration of the Chinese philosopher Zhuang Zi's well-known butterfly dream. Zhuang Zi wrote that one day, he dreamt that he was a butterfly happily flitting and fluttering around. He did not know he was Zhuang Zi. On waking up, he was, of course, once again solidly and unmistakably himself, but he did not know if he was Zhuang Zi who had dreamt that he was a butterfly, or a butterfly dreaming he was Zhuang Zi.[17] Lacan's analysis, which foregrounds the relations of visuality, goes as follows:

> In a dream, he is a butterfly. What does this mean? It means that he sees the butterfly in his reality as gaze. What are so many figures, so many shapes, so many colours, if not this gratuitous *showing*, in which is marked for us the primal nature of the essence of the gaze. . . . In fact, it is when he was the butterfly that he apprehended one of the roots of his identity—that he was, and is, in his essence, that butterfly who paints himself with his own colours—and it is because of this that, in the last resort, he is Choang-tsu [Zhuang Zi].[18]

What fascinates Lacan, I think, is that the dream, in which the "I"/eye of Zhuang Zi becomes this Other, the butterfly, returns Zhuang Zi for a moment to a state of nondifferentiation in which the Other exists as pure gaze.[19] In this state of nondifferentiation, one is not conscious of oneself as consciousness, as thought. This dream is so powerful that even when he wakes up, Zhuang Zi is not sure whether "he" is not simply (a lost object) dreamt by the butterfly. For Lacan, Zhuang Zi's butterfly dream is a glimpse into the truth: "it is when he was the butterfly that he apprehended one of the roots of his identity—that he was, and is, in his essence, that butterfly who paints himself with his own colours—and that it is because of this that . . . he is Choang-tsu." The conscious identity of Zhuang Zi, the "I"/eye of waking life, in other words, is the result of the butterfly's "causing" him to exist or marking him with the grid of desire.[20] Waking from this dream back into consciousness is therefore an unsettling awakening into the fact that in one life's as *cogito*, one is a captive butterfly, captivated by nothing but the inescapable law and structure of human cognition.

Lacan's reading of Zhuang Zi's dream brings us one step closer to unraveling the visual dynamics of Gallimard' s transformation. Accordingly, we could see Gallimard's transformation as an equivalent to Zhuang Zi's dream, in which he, Gallimard, becomes a "Butterfly." The very image of the "oriental woman" in her strange shape and figure, in her bright colors, is then the gratuitous *showing* that Lacan mentions as the primal nature of the essence of the gaze. This gaze returns Gallimard to the roots of his identity by showing, by giving to the eye, (the knowledge) that "Butterfly" is what causes him to exist by marking him with desire. As in Zhuang Zi's story, therefore, the question implicit in Gallimard's performance is: how do "I," Gallimard, know that I, with my fantasy, my longing for the "oriental woman," am not merely an object dreamt by "Butterfly," the gaze that I (mis)took for an image? Instead of being Gallimard dreaming of a "Butterfly," might I not myself be the dream of a "Butterfly"?

Third, just as Lacan writes that Zhuang Zi is, in his essence, "the butterfly who paints himself with his own colours," so Gallimard, strictly speaking, does not simply perform but rather *paints* himself into Madame Butterfly—or more precisely, paints himself with her colors. Once this emphasis is introduced, we are able for the first time to view this scene of transformation as about a process of painting, with philosophical implications to be deduced from the relationships between the act of painting, the painted image, and the gaze.

Lacan, contrary to conventional thinking and following philosophers such as René Caillois and Maurice Merleau-Ponty, writes that painting is not really mimicry or imitation in the sense of creating a secondary, derivative form on the basis of a pre-existing one. Rather, if it is indeed mimicry or imitation in the sense of producing an image, this image is part of a process in which the painter enters a specific relation with the gaze—a relation in which the gaze (especially as embodied by the spectator) is tamed:

> To imitate is no doubt to reproduce an image. But at bottom, it is, for the subject, to be inserted in a function whose exercise grasps it. . . .

The function of the picture—in relation to the person to whom the painter, literally, offers his picture to be seen—has a relation with the gaze. This relation is not, as it might at first seem, that of being a trap for the gaze. It might be thought that, like the actor, the painter wishes to be looked at. I do not think so. I think there is a relation with the gaze of the spectator, but that it is more complex. The painter gives something to the person who must stand in front of his painting which, in part, at least, of the painting, might be summed up thus—*You want to see? Well, take a look at this!* He gives something for the eye to feed on, but he invites the person to whom this picture is presented to lay down his gaze there as one lays down one's weapons. This is the pacifying, Apollonian effect of painting. Something is given not so much to the gaze as to the eye, something that involves abandonment, the *laying down* of the gaze.[21]

These passages indicate that painting can be described as a process of disarming the Other, of warding off the menace that comes from the Other. The means of disarming the Other is the painted image, which may thus be described as a second-order gaze, an artificial eye, a fetish in the sense of an amulet or talisman that may ward off evil. However, in using this understanding of painting as a way to read Gallimard's transformation, we are immediately confronted by the fact that Gallimard is not only the painter, nor only both painter and image, but painter, image, and spectator, all three at once. This fact considerably complicates the combative relation between the painter and the gaze that Lacan sets forth. By painting himself as Madame Butterfly, is Gallimard simply making an image to fend off the gaze (in which case he would remain in the subjectivity of the painter)? Is he not also the painted image, and is he not, as he looks at himself in the mirror, also the spectator, the one to be tamed? As "Butterfly," Gallimard appears also as a clown—but is the clown mocking us or is she the object of our mockery, and for what reason? All in all, how are we to describe this ultimate act of Gallimard's *passion*, his *passage* from painter to image to spectator?[22]

This passion/passage that is painting, we might say, is a process of making visible that which could otherwise never be directly seen. Significantly, therefore, painting here rejoins the etymological meaning of the word "fantasy," which means, precisely, "to make visible."[23] But "making visible" at the end of *M. Butterfly* is no longer simply a making visible of the multiple positions available to the subject. Rather, it is a process of throwing off the colors that make up the "self," a process of stripping and denuding that is comparable with processes of change in the natural world: "If a bird were to paint," Lacan writes suggestively, "would it not be by letting fall its feathers? a snake by casting off its scales, a tree by letting fall its leaves?"[24]

As Gallimard looks at the "Butterfly" in the mirror, he is transformed into the spectator who is invited to lay down his own gaze. This laying down of the gaze is the laying down of the weapon, the protective shield that separates us from the

Other. What Gallimard finally meets, in the painted picture of himself as Madame Butterfly, is that thing which, in its muteness and absoluteness, renders him—the man Gallimard—obsolete, inoperant, excluded.[25] If the gaze is that which is always somehow eluded in our relation to the world,[26] then what Gallimard meets, in his own Butterfly image, in a manner that can no longer be eluded, is the gaze as it has all along looked at him.

If this scene of transformation could indeed be seen as a performing of enlightenment—of Gallimard's discovery that Madame Butterfly is none other than he himself—it is also enlightenment-as-self-deconstruction. From the perspective of the man with desire, this enlightenment is not progress but a regression, a passage into inertia, into the thing he loves. With this passage and passion, which we call death, the illusory independence that one achieves through the primary narcissism of the "mirror stage," which shows one as "other" but gives one the illusion of a unified "I," disappears. Significantly, therefore, the instrument of death in the film is not simply the *seppuku* dagger in the opera *Madama Butterfly* or the knife in the play *M. Butterfly*, but a mirror—a mirror, moreover, which has lost its reflective function. Being no longer the usual means with which one says, "This is me, myself," the mirror now returns to its material being as a shard of glass with which to terminate life and pass into the inorganic. Gallimard's suicide completes and fulfills the fateful plot of *Madama Butterfly*, but instead of him performing "Butterfly," it is, strictly speaking, "Butterfly" which has been performing him. As the Frenchman "sacrifices" himself and passes into his beloved spectacle, the "Butterfly" that is the character, the story, and the music—in short, the gaze—lives on.[27]

CODA: NEW QUESTIONS FOR CULTURAL DIFFERENCE AND IDENTITY

What I have attempted to show through a more or less Lacanian reading is the ineluctability of a serious consideration of fantasy—and with it, questions of cognition—in a story of exchange that is overtly "cross-cultural." What this reading makes explicit, I hope, is that fantasy is not something that can be simply dismissed as willful deception, as "false consciousness" to be remedied by explicit didactics. Once fantasy is understood as a problem structural to human cognition, all the "cross-cultural" analyses of ideology, misogyny, and racism that are rooted in a denigration of fantasy will need to be thoroughly reexamined.

If, in this fantasy, the orient is associated with femininity itself, then the problem of coming to terms with the orient is very much similar, structurally speaking, to the problem of coming to terms with woman in psychoanalysis—in that both the orient and woman have been functioning as the support for the white man's fantasy, as the representation of the white man's *jouissance*. However, what distinguishes Cronenberg's film from many examples of such representation—one thinks, for instance, of Bernardo Bertolucci's *The Last Emperor, The Sheltering Sky,* and *The Little Buddha*—is precisely the manner in which the lavish, visible painting of fantasy finally takes place not on the female, feminized body of the other but on the white male body, so that enlightenment coincides with suicide, while the woman, the other, escapes.[28]

What remains unknown, then, is the "supplementary" *jouissance* of woman (and, by implication, of the orient) as spoken of by Lacan, who, in an aptly deconstructionist manner, puts his emphasis on the word "supplementary."[29] What does woman want, and what does the orient want? At no moment in the film *M. Butterfly* does Song's subjectivity and desire become lucid to us—we never know whether she is "genuine" or masquerading, whether her emotions are "for real" or part of her superb playacting—until in the "showdown" scene in the police van. In that scene, we see for the first time that what she "wants" is a complete overturning of the laws of desire which have structured her relationship with Gallimard. In other words, in spite of her love for the Frenchman, what the "oriental woman" wants is nothing less than the liquidation of his entire sexual ontological being—his death.

Even though Song does not get what she wants directly, her wish is vindicated by the ending of the film. Gallimard's transformation into Madame Butterfly indicates that femininity and the "oriental woman" are the very truth of Western Man himself, and, because he is traditionally identified with power, he is so far removed from this truth that his self-awakening must be tragic. Gallimard's death shows that Western Man is himself no-thing more than a French penis dreaming of (being) an oriental butterfly.

By definition, the death of the white man signals the dawn of a fundamentally different way of coming to terms with the East. The film closes with "Butterfly" flying back to China. This "oriental woman" that existed as the white man's symptom—what will happen to her now that the white man is dead? That is the ultimate question with which we are left.

10

Film as Ethnography; or, Translation Between Cultures in the Postcolonial World

HOW CAN ONE WRITE/THINK/TALK THE
NON-WEST IN THE ACADEMY WITHOUT IN
SOME SENSE ANTHROPOLOGISING IT?
Dipesh Chakrabarty, "Marx After Marxism"[1]

ANTHROPOLOGICAL "SCIENTIFIC
METHOD" IS THE DECAY OF DIALOGUE,
THE SUSTAINED, CULTIVATED, AND EPIS-
TEMOLOGICALLY ENFORCED ATROPHY OF
DIALOGUE. . . . AS PSYCHIATRY HAS BEEN
THE MODERN WEST'S MONOLOGUE ABOUT
MADNESS AND UNREASON, SO ANTHRO-
POLOGY HAS BEEN THE MODERN WEST'S
MONOLOGUE ABOUT "ALIEN CULTURES."
Bernard McGrane, *Beyond Anthropology*[2]

ETHNOGRAPHY IS STILL VERY MUCH A
ONE-WAY STREET.
James Clifford, introduction to *Writing Culture*[3]

FOR IF THE SENTENCE IS THE WALL
BEFORE THE LANGUAGE OF THE ORIGI-
NAL, LITERALNESS IS THE ARCADE. [DENN
DER SATZ IST DER MAUER VOR DER
SPRACHE DES ORIGINALS, WÖRTLICHKEIT
DIE ARKADE.]
Walter Benjamin, "The Task of the Translator"[4]

A NOVEL ANTHROPOLOGY NOT OF THE
THIRD AND OTHER WORLDS, BUT OF THE
WEST ITSELF AS MIRRORED IN THE EYES
AND HANDIWORK OF ITS OTHERS.
Michael Taussig, *Mimesis and Alterity*[5]

Throughout this book I have been using the term *ethnography* to describe some of the outstanding features of contemporary Chinese cinema, but a more systematic theoretical articulation of what I mean by "ethnography" is still in order, in particular of how this new ethnography may be conceived through visuality. Already, in discussing Zhang Yimou, we see the surfacing of a major problem of cross-cultural politics—the problem of the "foreign devil." The critics who accuse the Chinese directors of pandering to a "foreign" audience rather than to a "Chinese" audience—are they not prioritizing some "original essence" of the Chinese culture? Some readers will object: But wait, do such "nativist" critics not in fact alert us to the ongoing reality of Western cultural imperialism? Is their distrust of the "foreign" (meaning the West) not after all a justifiable reaction to the long history of Western hegemony, in which "exchange" between East and West has always meant the demand on non-Western peoples to conform to Western standards and models but not vice versa? As Kwai-cheung Lo writes in a different context, "When the concept of modernity still implies 'progress' and 'westernization,' any translation or introduction of modern texts is by no means free from cultural imperialism."[6] The incensed reaction of nativist critics, the same readers might continue, only demonstrates the point Mary Louise Pratt makes about the artistic activities of "autoethnography" in metropolitan areas—that such activities are bound to be very differently received by metropolitan audiences and by the literate sectors of the artists' own social groups.[7] As Jane Ying Zha writes: "All my American friends love Zhang's movies, all my Chinese friends hate them. . . . Why? What offended the Chinese in these movies? . . . It could be summed up in one thing: selling oriental exoticism to a western audience."[8]

What these observations about cross-cultural "exchange" indicate is what may be called the deadlock of the anthropological situation as created by Western imperialism and colonialism of the past few centuries. We can describe this deadlock by going back to the most basic anthropological scenario—that of the Western anthropologist traveling abroad to study the "primitive" cultures around the world. In order to perform his task, the Western anthropologist must insert himself and his social practices (such as "scientific" observation and recording) into these "primitive" contexts. In spite of the grandiose salvational motives of his profession, the very presence of the Western anthropologist means, effectively, that these "other" cultures are changed and displaced forever from their "origins." Subsequently, in order to find out authoritatively about their cultures, members of such culture often have to look up Western source books. In many cases, the methods and practices of anthropology and ethnography have simply served to reinforce and empower colonial administration, and thus to bring about the systematic destruction of these "other" cultures.[9]

The deadlock of the anthropological situation in the postcolonial world is summarized in the epigraphs by Chakrabarty, McGrane, and Clifford that appear at the beginning of this section of the book: we cannot write/think/talk the non-West in the academy without in some sense anthropologizing it, and yet anthropology and ethnography, atrophied in their epistemological foundations, remain "very much still a one-way street." By their remarks, Chakrabarty, McGrane, and Clifford refer to the inequality inherent to the binary structure of observer/observed that is classical anthropology's operating premise and that has become *the* way we approach the West's "others." For non-Western peoples, the most obvious consequence of this classical operating premise is the continual privileging of Western models of language, philosophy, and historiography as "standard knowledge," and the continual marginalization of the equivalents from the non-West.[10] Because of such fundamental disparity in the classical anthropological and ethnographic situation, any process of cultural translation between West and East will, as Talal Asad writes, likely continue to be marked by an asymmetry of privileges:

> The process of "cultural translation" is inevitably enmeshed in conditions of power— professional, national, international. And among these conditions is the authority of ethnographers to uncover the implicit meanings of subordinate societies. Given that that is so, the interesting question for enquiry is . . . how power enters into the process of "cultural translation," seen both as a discursive and as a non-discursive practice.[11]

Anthropology is . . . rooted in an unequal power encounter between the West and Third World which goes back to the emergence of bourgeois Europe, an encounter in which colonialism is merely one historical moment. It is this encounter that gives the West access to cultural and historical information about the societies it has progressively dominated, and thus not only generates a kind of universal understanding, but also re-enforces the inequalities in capacity between the European and the non-European worlds (and derivatively, between the Europeanized elites and the "traditional" masses in the Third World). We are today becoming increasingly aware of the fact that information and understanding produced by bourgeois disciplines like anthropology are acquired and used most readily by those with the greatest capacity for exploitation.[12]

To put it crudely: because the languages of Third World societies—including, of course, the societies that social anthropologists have traditionally studied—are "weaker" in relation to Western languages (and today, especially to English), they are more likely to submit to forcible transformation in the translation process than the other way around. The reason for this is, first, that in their political-economic relations with Third World Countries, Western nations have the greater ability to manipulate the latter. And, second, Western languages produce and deploy *desired* knowledge more readily than Third World languages do.[13]

Understandably, therefore, it is in response to this fundamentally unequal and unfair situation of knowledge organization and distribution in the postcolonial world that criticisms of contemporary Chinese films' "betrayal" of "China" have been made. The moral question behind such criticisms is this: because the exoticizing of the East is part of the agenda of Western imperialism, how could we support directors such as Zhang, who make images that seemingly further this agenda? As I argued in the previous chapter, however, charges of "betrayal" or "infidelity" are themselves far from being innocent; they are part of a defensive nativism that, in the case of Chinese film, is itself deeply rooted in the hierarchical criteria of traditional aesthetics. What such zealous charges accomplish is not exactly the preservation of the ethnic culture as such but often an unwitting complicity in perpetuating the deadlock of the anthropological situation. The Euro-American homogenization of the world is then steadily polarized against an equally overwhelming attempt on the part of some "natives" and nativists to hold on to "tradition" even as tradition is disintegrating. Instead of enabling alternatives to the deadlock, nativist demands of cultural "fidelity" have great potential of becoming prohibitive deterrents *against* cultural translation altogether.

To intervene in this deadlock, I will in the following pages argue for a redefinition of ethnography by explicitly linking ethnography with translation. Before doing that, I will explain how a focus on visuality as such is really the first step toward a dismantling of the classic epistemological foundations of anthropology and ethnography.

THE PRIMACY OF TO-BE-LOOKED-AT-NESS

In an essay on representation and anthropological knowledge, Kirsten Hastrup writes: "For the non-anthropologist, all films dealing with exotic cultures may look equally anthropological, while to professional anthropologists it is much more a question of method and theory than of subject-matter."[14]

Contrary to Hastrup's suggestion, the increasingly blurred distinction between "theory and method" on the one hand and "subject matter" on the other is, I think, precisely the new object of ethnographic work in the postcolonial world. Rethought rigorously, ethnography can no longer be the "science" that its practitioners once imagined it to be, nor is it simply a "documentation" of "other" ways of life. Despite its traditional claims to objectivity, ethnography is a kind of representation with subjective origins. But how do we come to terms with such subjective origins? *Whose* subjective origins should concern us? Instead of simply arguing for the necessity of discursive self-reflexivity on the part of *Western* practitioners, with the politically correct admonition that we must watch what we say more carefully,[15] I think it is by focusing on visuality that we can come to terms with the subjective origins of ethnography most productively. In other words, I do not think that an ethnography alternative to the one we have been criticizing can materialize simply through a call for "self-consciousness—let's look at ourselves, our language, and our assumptions more carefully"—since such a call only confirms, once again, what was long ago established by Hegel as the distinguishing trait of Western Man, his capacity for being aware of himself. Rather, I believe that *a new ethnography is possible only when we turn our attention to the subjective origins of ethnography as it is practiced by those who were previously ethnographized and who have, in the postcolonial age, taken up the active task of ethnographizing their own cultures.*

This, however, does not mean exploring subjectivity in the verbal realm only. How are the "subjective origins" of the previously ethnographized communicated in *visual* terms? They are, I think, communicated not so much through the act of looking as through what may be called "to-be-looked-at-ness"—the visuality that once defined the *"object"* status of the ethnographized culture and that now becomes a predominant aspect of that culture's self-representation. We remember that in her famous article "Visual Pleasure and Narrative Cinema," Laura Mulvey alerts us to "to-be-looked-at-ness" as what constitutes not only the spectacle but the very way vision is organized; the state of being looked at, she argues, is built into the way we *look*. Because in our culture, looking and being looked at are commonly assigned respectively to men and women, vision bears the origins of gender inequality.[16] Supplementing Mulvey's argument with the anthropological situation, we may argue, in parallel, that vision bears the origins of ethnographic inequality. But we must go one step further: the state of being looked at not only is built into the way non-Western cultures are viewed by Western ones; more significantly it is part of the *active* manner in which such cultures represent—ethnographize—themselves.

What this means is that in the vision of the formerly ethnographized, the subjective origins of ethnography are displayed in amplified form but at the same time significantly redefined: what are "subjective" origins now include a memory of past *objecthood*—the experience of being looked at—which lives on in the subjective act of ethnographizing like an other, an optical unconscious.[17] If ethnography is indeed autoethnography—ethnography of the self and the subject—then the perspective of the formerly ethnographized supplements it irrevocably with the understanding that being-looked-at-ness, rather than the act of looking, constitutes the primary event in cross-cultural representation.

With visuality as its focus, this reformulation of ethnography destroys the operational premises—of a world divided in the form of us and them, of viewing subject and viewed object—of classical anthropology. "Us" and "them" are no longer safely distinguishable; "viewed object" is now looking at "viewing subject" looking. Moreover, through the reading of films that are not documentary and hence not ethnographic in the conventional sense, this reformulated ethnography challenges as well the factualism that typifies anthropology's hold on representation. These lines from Dai Vaughan on the documentary may be used as a critique of such factualism—if we substitute the words *ethnographers* and *ethnography* for *documentarists* and *documentary:* "Documentarists . . . like to believe that documentary is the 'natural' form of cinema. But fiction film, like painting and literature, rests no special claims upon the provenance of its linguistic elements. It must surely be clear that it is documentary which is the paradoxical, even aberrant form."[18] In studying contemporary Chinese films as ethnography and autoethnography, I am thus advocating nothing less than a radical deprofessionalization of anthropology and ethnography as "intellectual disciplines." Once these disciplines are deprofessionalized—their boundaries between "us" and "them" destabilized; their claims to documentary objectivity deconstructed—how do we begin to reconceive the massive cultural information that has for so long been collected under their rubric? It is at this juncture that I think our discussion about ethnography must be supplemented by a theory of translation.

A similar observation is made by Thomas Elsaesser in his study of the New German cinema of the 1970s. Concluding that German cinema was the consequence of "a vast transcription process," Elsaesser introduces the notion of translation as a way to understand it:

[The New German cinema] was an attempt to gather, record and report the images, sounds and stories—including those that the cinema itself produced—which make up the memory of a generation, a nation and a culture, and to *translate them from their many perishable supports in people's minds to the one medium that, after all, promises paradoxically to be the most permanent: the cinema.* Literature, popular culture, architecture, fashion, memorabilia and the contents of junk shops have all been enlisted in a vast effort to preserve the traces of lives lived for oblivion. This hastily accumulated visual wealth has not yet been tapped or even properly inspected for its meanings or uses. As *a source of understanding the changes from a culture living mainly by the written text to one dominated by the image,* the New German Cinema still awaits to be discovered.[19]

Contemporary Chinese cinema, insofar as it collects images not only of rural but of modern urban China, not only of ancient emperors and scholars but also of women, children, lower classes, and minority cultures, can, like the New German cinema, be thought of in the sense of a "vast transcription process." But of much greater relevance is Elsaesser's notion of translation. Elsaesser's rich passage suggests, crucially, that there are at least two types of translation at work in cinema. First, translation as inscription: a generation, a nation, and a culture are being translated or permuted into the medium of film; and second, translation as transformation of tradition and change between media: a culture oriented around the written text is in the process of transition and of being translated into one dominated by the image. Elsaesser's words are equally applicable to other "national" cinemas such as the Chinese, because these "national" cinemas are, in themselves, at the crossroads of different types and stages of cultural translation. The bulk of this book, then, has in effect been dealing with the filmic transcriptions of Chinese modernity as processes of cultural translation.

In accordance with the movement of the epigraphs at the beginning of this section of the book, what I will attempt in the remaining pages is a focused discussion of translation in the sense of translation between cultures. Although contemporary Chinese film will serve as a major point of reference, various theories of translation will also be introduced in order to highlight the problems of cross-cultural exchange—especially in regard to the commodified, technologized image—in the postcolonial, postmodern age.

TRANSLATION AND THE PROBLEM OF ORIGINS

Etymologically, the word *translation* is linked, among other things, to "tradition" on the one hand and to "betrayal" on the other.[20] The Italian expression *Traduttore, traditore*—"Translator, traitor"—allows us to grasp the pejorative implication of infidelity that is often associated with the task of translating. Because faithfulness is such a crucial issue here, the analogy between translation and a human convention such as matrimony is, as Barbara Johnson writes, far-reaching: "It might seem . . . that the translator ought, despite or perhaps because of his or her oath of fidelity, to be considered not as a duteous spouse but as a faithful bigamist, with loyalties split between a native language and a foreign tongue."[21] To complicate things further, the matrimony that is translation is seldom established on the basis of the equality of the partners. In the classical thinking about translation, Johnson goes on, it is the signified, not the signifier, that is given priority: "Faithfulness to the text has meant faithfulness to the semantic tenor with as little interference as possible from the constraints of the vehicle. Translation, in other words, has always been the translation of *meaning*" (145; emphasis in the original).

Given these deeply entrenched assumptions about translation, it is hardly surprising that the rendering of "China" into film, even at a time when the literary bases of Chinese society are increasingly being transformed by the new media culture, is bedeviled by suspicion and replete with accusations of betrayal. While these suspicions and accusations may express themselves in myriad forms, they are always implicitly inscribed within the ideology of fidelity. For instance, to return to our main concern in the previous chapter, is not the distrust of "surfaces"—the criticism of Zhang Yimou's lack of depth—a way of saying that surfaces are "traitors" to the historical depth that is "traditional China"? And yet the word *tradition* itself, linked in its roots to translation and betrayal, has to do with handing over. Tradition itself is nothing if it is not a transmission. How is tradition to be transmitted, to be passed on, if not through translation?

The common assumption about translation is that it is a rendering of one language into another language. Even though what is involved is actually the traffic between two languages, we tend to suppress our awareness of this by prioritizing one language over the other, by pretending that the traffic goes in one direction only. How does this happen? Consider the terminology we use, which reveals the epistemological uncertainties involved and hence the ideological need to prioritize: we call one language the "original" and the other the "translation" (meaning "unoriginal" and "derivative"). This terminology suppresses the fact that the "unoriginal" language may well be the "native tongue"—that is, the original language—of the translator, whose translating may involve turning the "original" which is actually *not* her native/original language into her "native"/"original" language. (A simple explanation like this already suffices to illustrate the vertiginous nature of any attempt to theorize translation.)

Precisely because translation is an activity that immediately problematizes the ontological hierarchy of languages—"which is primary and which is secondary?"— it is also the place where the oldest prejudices about origins and derivations come into play most forcefully. For instance, what does it mean to make a translation sound "natural"? Must the translation sound more like the "original," which is not the language into which it is translated—meaning that it is by resemblance to the "original" that it becomes "natural"? Or, must it sound more like the language into which it is translated, in which case sounding "natural" would mean forgetting the "origin"? When we say, derogatorily, "This reads like a translation," what we mean is that even though we understand what the "original" meaning might be, we cannot but notice its translatedness—and yet is that not precisely what a translation is supposed to be—*translated* rather than "original"? As in all bifurcated processes of signification, translation is a process in which the notion of the "original," the relationship between the "original" and its "derivations," and the demand for what is "natural" must be thoroughly reexamined.

Using contemporary Chinese cinema as a case in point, I think the criticism (by some Chinese audiences) that Zhang and his contemporaries "pander to the tastes of the foreign devil" can itself be recast by way of our conventional assumptions about translation. The "original" here is not a language in the strict linguistic sense but rather "China"—"China" as the sum total of the history and culture of a people; "China" as a content, a core meaning that exists "prior to" film. When critics say that Zhang's films lack depth, what they mean is that the language/vehicle in which he renders "China" is a poor translation, a translation that does not give the truth about "China." For such critics, the film medium, precisely because it is so "superficial"—that is, organized around surfaces—mystifies and thus distorts China's authenticity. What is implicitly assumed in their judgment is not simply the untranslatability of the "original" but that translation is a unidirectional, one-way process. It is assumed that translation means a movement from the "original" to the language of "translation" but not vice versa; it is assumed that the value of translation is derived solely from the "original," which is the authenticator of itself and of its subsequent versions. Of the "translation," a tyrannical demand is made: the translation must perform its task of conveying the "original" without leaving its own traces; the "originality of translation" must lie "in self-effacement, a vanishing act."[22]

Our discussion here can be facilitated by turning to the work of Walter Benjamin, not least because Benjamin himself was writing at the crossroads of cultural transformation. Though Benjamin's essay "The Work of Art in the Age of Mechanical Reproduction" may seem most immediately relevant to our topic in that it deals with the transformation of traditional art (which possesses "aura") to mass-produced images such as those of photography and film,[23] I find his essay "The Task of the Translator" to be more useful in helping me think through the problem of translation between cultures.[24] In this latter essay, Benjamin offers a theory of translation that is distinctively different from most theories.

It is often assumed, writes Benjamin, that the point of translation is to impart information or convey the meaning of the original; this is, however, not so. Instead, what needs to be translated is an "intention" ("intentio") in the "original" that Benjamin calls "the great longing for linguistic complementation" (p. 79). His mystical language notwithstanding, Benjamin is arguing for a materialist though elusive fact about translation—that translation is primarily a process of *putting together*. This process demonstrates that the "original," too, is something that has been put together. But this "putting together" is not, as I will go on to argue, simply a deconstructive production of differences.[25] It is *also* a process of "literalness" that *displays* the way the "original" itself was put together—that is, in its violence.

Before elaborating this last point, we need to examine closely the way Benjamin discusses the "putting together" that is linguistic translation. What needs to be translated from the original, he writes, is not a kind of truth or meaning but the way in which "the original" is put together *in the basic elements of human language— words*. Hence it is words—in their wordness, their literality—rather than sentences, that matter the most in translation. A real translation, Benjamin writes, "may be achieved, above all, by a literal rendering of the syntax which proves words rather than sentences to be the primary element of the translator. For if the sentence is the wall before the language of the original, literalness is the arcade" (p. 79).

The German "original" of this passage indicates that where Benjamin's English translator, Harry Zohn, uses the words *literal* and *literalness*, Benjamin has used the word *Wörtlichkeit*. But even though the English translation does not exactly reproduce Benjamin's word, a verbatim translation of which would be something like "word-by-word-ness," it nonetheless supplements Benjamin's text in an unexpected, perhaps fateful, manner. To be "literal" in the English language is to be "verbatim," to follow the word strictly. At the same time, "literal" can also connote a certain *lack*—in the sense of that which is matter-of-fact, without imagination, without metaphor, without depth; that which is superficial, crude, or naive. It is this second notion of literalness—this supplement that exists in the translation but not in the original—that brings out, I think, the precise sense of Benjamin's *Wörtlichkeit:* a real translation is not only that which translates word by word but also that which translates literally, depthlessly, naively.

It is obvious that here I depart significantly from the view of literalness held by deconstructionist critics. For Jacques Derrida and Paul de Man, for instance, *literal* is a problematic word that designates "proper," in a way that is opposed to (their preferred) "metaphoric" or "figural." De Man's reading of Rousseau, for instance, is that Rousseau's language tells the story of "the necessary degradation . . . of metaphor into literal meaning," and that a "literal world" is one "in which appearance and nature coincide" whereas a "figural world" is one "in which this correspondence is no longer a priori posited."[26] For me, however, literalness is not simply "proper," but it is not simply "figural"/"metaphorical," either. Rather, I use the term to refer to a third area that is defined by neither of the two categories—the area we may loosely describe as the obvious, the superficial, and what immediately presents itself in signification. This "literal" area is what lacks and/or exceeds the clear boundary implied by Derrida and de Man between the categories of the "proper" and the "figural"/"metaphorical."

Zohn's translation-cum-supplement, then, makes explicit something that was merely lurking in the original in the form of what Benjamin himself calls the original's "intention." Remarkably, the "original" intention is what can only be grasped as a supplement, as what is added (because translated): "In all language and linguistic creations there remains *in addition to* what can be conveyed something that cannot be communicated; depending on the context in which it appears, it is something that symbolizes or something symbolized" (p. 79; my emphasis). For Benjamin, the task of the translator consists in communicating this additional something that nonetheless could come across as a lack and a deprivation. (I will return to this point once again toward the end.)

The elusiveness of his approach to the "original" makes it seem that Benjamin is saying with "translation" what deconstructionists are saying with "language," namely, that the original is self-différance. Examples of the deconstructionist definition of language include statements such as these: "Language . . . can only exist in the space of its own foreignness to itself," "the original text is always already an impossible translation that renders translation impossible,"[27] and so forth. However, even though a deconstructionist reading of Benjamin is useful and necessary,[28] it is inadequate. In the preceding passage by Benjamin, if we take the word *symbol* to mean not a full and complete representation of something but a sign that stands for something else, then what Benjamin is saying would suggest that the "original" intention is not only a self-différance, but also a process of standing-for-something-else, something other than the "self." For Benjamin, the act of translation is less a confirmation of language's "own" impossibility than it is a *liberation,* in a second language, of the "intention" of standing-for-something-else that is already put together but imprisoned—"symbolized"—in the original; hence "it is the task of the translator to release in his own language that pure language which is under the spell of another, to liberate the language imprisoned in a work in his re-creation of that work" (p. 80).

Because Benjamin's notion of the "original" intention comprises *both* self-différance and the act of symbolizing (standing for an other), it is important to emphasize that his theory is not simply that translation is the original's deconstruction, which is the reading proposed, for instance, by de Man. De Man's reading is a persuasive one, but it does not do justice to Benjamin's theory. In his typical manner, de Man zeroes in on the inherent *negativity* of writing: hence he elaborates on the notion of "failure" inscribed in the German title of Benjamin's piece, proving thus that translation is ultimately a failure—a failure, moreover, that is already present in the "original." Comparing the activity of translation to those of critical philosophy, literary theory, and history, de Man writes that all such *intralingual* activities have in common a disarticulation of the original: "They reveal that their failure, which seems to be due to the fact that they are secondary in relation to the original, reveals an *essential* failure, an *essential* disarticulation which was already there in the original."[29]

Because its rigor is a negative one, de Man's deconstructive reading is eminently useful in desacralizing and decanonizing the original. But deconstruction as such nonetheless does *not* depart from the view that there is some original—even if that should prove to be an illusion—to begin with. By concentrating its efforts on the disarticulated and unstable "essence" of the "original," the deconstructive reading in fact makes it unnecessary for one to move outside or down from the realm of the original. Translation would thus remain one-way in the sense that it is intralingual, with all the differences/misreadings it produces moving back to (deconstruct the self that is) the original. This is demonstrated, best of all, by de Man's own reading, in which he repeatedly shows Benjamin's translators up for missing Benjamin's points. In spite of his sacrilegious intentions, therefore, de Man returns a kind of sacredness—now defined as intralingual instability—to the original that is Benjamin's text. De Man's deconstructive reading does not in the end deviate significantly from the conventional, dogmatic belief in the purity or untranslatability of any original. Were a "translation" of culture to be based on de Man's reading, it would be, as he says, a failure: such a translation would be little more than the vicious circle of a search for a complete freedom from the "origin" that is the past, which nonetheless would keep haunting us like the indelible memory of a nightmare.

For Benjamin, on the other hand, translation is not simply deconstructive but, even more important, a "liberation" that is mutual and reciprocal *between* the "original" and the "translation." In Benjamin's text, the nihilistic rigor of deconstruction is combined with a messianic utopianism, a sense of openness that is absent in de Man. For Benjamin, both "original" and "translation," as languages rendering each other, share the "longing for linguistic complementarity" and gesture together toward something larger: "A translation, instead of resembling the meaning of the original, must lovingly and in detail incorporate the original's mode of signification, thus making both the original and the translation recognizable as fragments of a greater language, just as fragments are part of a vessel" (p. 78).[30] The quotation that Benjamin takes from Rudolf Pannwitz illustrates a similar point of complementarity, mutuality, and letting the foreign affect the self:

Pannwitz writes: "Our translations, even the best ones, proceed into German instead of turning German into Hindi, Greek, English. Our translators have a far greater reverence for the usage of their own language than for the spirit of the foreign works. . . . The basic error of the translator is that he preserves the state in which his own language happens to be instead of allowing his language to be powerfully affected by the foreign tongue. Particularly when translating from a language very remote from his own he must go back to the primal elements of language itself and penetrate to the point where work, image, and tone converge. He must expand and deepen his language by means of the foreign language." (pp. 80–81)

In these preceding passages, the relationship between the "original" and the "translation" is problematized by the fact that the "original" does not only refer to the original language in which something is written but can also refer to the (different) native/original language of the native speaker/translator; similarly, "translation" can mean not only the language into which something is translated but also a language foreign to the translator's mother tongue. But the gist of Benjamin's argument remains the same: most work of translation is done in the wish to make the "foreign" sound more like the "native," with the assumption that the "native" is the "original" point of reference; whereas translation is a process in which the "native" should let the foreign affect, or infect, itself, and vice versa. This radical notion of translation is what leads Jean Laplanche to describe Benjamin's theory as an "anti-ethnocentric" one:

Benjamin participates in the great "anti-ethnocentric" movement . . . or what I call the "anti-auto- or self-centred" movement of translation (*le mouvement anti-autocentrique de la traduction*): a movement that doesn't want translation to be self-enclosed and reduce the other to the terms of that self, but rather a movement out towards the other.[31]

The question then is, How is this "movement out towards the other" to be conceived and theorized?

TRANSLATION AS "CULTURAL RESISTANCE"

In a recent work, *Siting Translation*, Tejaswini Niranjana takes up the formidable task of rethinking translation in the context of postcolonial postmodernity. Basing her arguments on poststructuralist theories of language, signification, and representation, Niranjana deconstructs the humanistic, binary oppositional assumptions underlying traditional notions of translation. Moreover, she proposes that both the theory and the practice of translation must be seen in the context of Western imperialism and colonialism, in which the European/Europeanist notions of knowledge reproduce themselves in Europe's encounter with and "translation" of its "others."[32]

Readers must turn to Niranjana's book to see for themselves the extensive implications of her thoughtful and well-researched arguments. If my critique of her book below is a strong one, it is also offered in full appreciation of the significance of her intervention in a context where "cultural translation" is still by and large dominated by Western discourse. This critique will, I hope, be read as an interaction in alliance with that intervention rather than as its opposition.

If, in the hands of deconstructionists such as de Man, translation is that originary intralingual self-*différance*, in Niranjana's analysis, translation is an *interlingual* practice—the exchange of ideas, beliefs, and information between different languages (and thus cultures). Because Niranjana's goal is to rescue the term *translation* for "cultural resistance" even while she criticizes its use by the culturally dominant, the status of "translation" in her analysis is an ambivalent, empty, and, ultimately idealist one: translation is fundamentally a "philosopheme" (pp. 2, 31). The idealist status of the term is what allows Niranjana implicitly to think of translation by differentiating between the good and the bad.

The bad: this is the European translation of its "others" that is otherwise known as "orientalism." Situating translation in the postcolonial context, Niranjana criticizes such orientalist texts for being imperialist and ethnocentric, for simply reinscribing in the "others" the orientalists' own preferences and prejudices. *The good:* on the other hand, Niranjana also wants to turn translation into something that Europe's colonized peoples can use. Translation is here given many analogies, chief of which is that it is an "act of resistance" when practiced by "natives" doing their own ethnography (pp. 84–85). Translation is, alternately, a "problematic" and a "field" (p. 8), a "transactional reading" (p. 42), a "hybrid" act (p. 46), a kind of citation and rewriting (p. 172). Finally, translation is what must be "put under erasure" (p. 48, n. 4).

These multiple analogies demonstrate the moves typical of a certain kind of poststructuralist discourse, which may be paraphrased as follows: deconstruct the danger and pitfalls of a term in its conventional usage; rescue that term for its inherent "heterogeneity" and "difference"; affirm this "heterogeneity" and "difference" *when it is used by certain groups of people.* By implicitly distinguishing between an incorrect and a correct practice of translation, what this type of poststructuralist rendering accomplishes is a *rationalist* understanding of "translation." This rendering returns "translation" to an *idea* (hence translation is first and foremost a "philosopheme"), debunks the dirty practice of the West, and reinstates the cleaner practice of the West's "others" as the alternative. Apart from idealism, this poststructuralist discourse also tends to invest heavily in the form of attentiveness that is a vigilance to words. Reading the *verbal text* meticulously becomes the fundamental way to "resist" the pitfalls of corrupt translation. In this regard, Niranjana's argument about translation does not add anything to the complex, nuanced arguments of writing, supplementarity, and différance that we already find in Derrida's work.

"History" is here rewritten as a careful reading, with the verbal text as its primary and predominant frame of reference.

The idealism and verbalism of her parameters mean that Niranjana must leave unasked the entire question of translation from verbal language into other sign systems and, more important, of *the translation of ethnic cultures from their previous literary and philosophical bases into the forms of contemporary mass culture,* a translation that is, arguably, European colonialism's foremost legacy in the non-European world. The privileging of verbal texts prevents the poststructuralist critic from coming to terms with significations whose value does not necessarily reside in their linguistic profundity and complexity—that is, their hermeneutic depth. Since "to make complicated" remains poststructuralist textualism's primary strategy of resisting domination, surfaces, simplicities, and transparencies can only be distrusted as false. If Niranjana's point is that we need to bring "history" into "legibility," it is a legibility in the sense of a dense text. The decoding of this dense text, however, could mean exactly a perpetuation of the existing institutional practice of scholarly close reading.

On the other hand, does cross-cultural "translation" not challenge precisely the scholarly mode of privileging the verbal text? If translation is "transactional reading," must the emphasis fall on "reading"? What if the emphasis is to fall on "transaction," and what if the transaction is one between the verbal text and the visual image? It would seem that no consideration of cultural translation can afford to ignore these questions, simply because the translation between cultures is never West translating East or East translating West in terms of verbal languages alone but rather a process that encompasses an entire range of activities, including the change from tradition to modernity, from literature to visuality, from elite scholastic culture to mass culture, from the native to the foreign and back, and so forth.

If de Man's notion of translation ultimately revalorizes the "original" that is the untranslatability of the (original) text, there is a way in which contemporary cultural studies, in the attempt to vindicate the cultures of the West's "others," end up revalorizing the "original" that is the authentic history, culture, and language of such "others." In spite of its politically astute intentions, what a work such as Niranjana's accomplishes in reversing are the asymmetrical, hierarchical power relations between West and East but *not* the asymmetrical, hierarchical power relations between "original" and "translation." In an attempt to do justice to the East, Niranjana, like many antiorientalist critics, deconstruct/destabilize the West by turning the West into an *unfaithful translator/translation* that has, as it were, betrayed, corrupted, and contaminated the "original" that is the East. When this revalorization of the "original" is done through a concentration on the depths and nuances of verbal texts, what continues to be obliterated is the fact that such texts are traditionally the loci of literate and literary culture, the culture through which *class hierarchy is established not only in Western but also in Eastern societies.*

THE "THIRD TERM"

My concerns about cultural translation up to this point can be summarized as follows: First, can we theorize translation between cultures without somehow valorizing some "original"? And second, can we theorize translation between cultures in a manner that does not implicitly turn translation into an *interpretation* toward depth, toward "profound meaning"?

To answer such questions, we would need to move beyond the intralingual and interlingual dimensions of translation that we have seen in de Man and Niranjana, and include within "translation" the notion of intersemiotic practices, of translating from one sign system to another.[33] Specifically, translation would need to encompass the translation, as Elsaesser suggests, of a "culture" into a medium such as film. Such translation, however, is not to be confused with "expression," "articulation," or even "representation," simply because these terms would too easily mislead us back into the comfortable notion that some pure "original" was there to be expressed, articulated, or represented. Instead, the notion of translation highlights the fact that it is an activity, a transportation between two "media," two kinds of already-mediated data, and that the "translation" is often what we must work with because, for one reason or another, the "original" as such is unavailable—lost, cryptic, already heavily mediated, already heavily translated. On the other hand, as I clarify in my discussion of de Man, I do not think that intersemiotic translation is simply "deconstruction," either, because the negative momentum of deconstruction, while effectively demystifying the spontaneism and mimeticism of terms such as expression, articulation, and representation, remains incapable of conveying a sense of the new medium into which the "original" is being transported.

What is useful from deconstruction, as is always the case, is the lesson about the "original"—a lesson I am pushing to the extreme here by asking that even in translation, where it usually goes without saying (even for deconstructionists) that the "original" is valued over the translated, we take absolutely seriously the deconstructionist insistence that the "first" and "original" as such is always already différance—always already translated. There are two possible paths from this lesson: one leads, as in the case of de Man, back to the painstaking study of the "original" as an original failure; the other leads to the work of translations and the values arising from them without privileging the "original" simply because it was there first. The choice of either path constitutes a major political decision.

And it is here, rather than in the opposition between "language" and "history" as Niranjana argues, that Benjamin's essay on translation, together with Benjamin's interest in mass culture, is most useful for a theory of cultural translation.[34]

There are multiple reasons why a consideration of mass culture is crucial to cultural translation, but the predominant one, for me, is precisely that asymmetry of power relations between the "first" and the "third" worlds. Precisely because of the deadlock of the more or less complete Europeanization of the world, which has led not only to the technocratic homogenization of world cultures but also to an organization of these cultures by way of European languages, philosophies, and sciences, the recourse to the archaic, authentic *past* of other cultures, in the assumption that somehow such past is closer to the original essence of humanity than Western culture, is a futile one. Critiquing the great disparity between Europe and the rest of the world means not simply a deconstruction of Europe as origin or simply a restitution of the origin that is Europe's others but a thorough dismantling of *both* the notion of origin and the notion of alterity as we know them today. This dismantling would be possible only if we acknowledge what Johannes Fabian speaks of as the *coevalness* of cultures[35] and consider the intersemiotic transformations that have happened as much to non-Western societies as to Western ones. The mass culture of our media, into which even the most "primitive" societies have been thrown, makes this coevalness ineluctable. The "primitive" is not "of another time" but is our contemporary.

The necessity of accepting the coevalness of cultures is what Laplanche, speaking in the context of translation, refers to as the necessity of "the third term":

> The difference between two terms and three terms seems important to me. Two terms don't allow for an orientation. Two terms—the translated and the translator—are either surrendered to a centring on the translator which we've called somewhat narrowly "ethnocentrism"; or they are surrendered to a centring on what's to be translated, which can in the extreme lead to a refusal to translate. . . . There must be a third term so that translation (and interpretation) exit from [the first two terms'] subjectivity.
>
> Every interpretative trajectory which links two terms is doomed to be arbitrary if it doesn't relate to a third term, and if it doesn't postulate something which is unconscious.[36]

Besides. acknowledging the co-temporality of cultures through our media, the "third term" would also mean acknowledging that the West's "primitive others" are equally caught up in the generalized atmosphere of unequal power distribution and are actively (re)producing *within themselves* the structures of domination and hierarchy that are as typical of non-European cultural histories as they are of European imperialism. As Dipesh Chakrabarty writes in regard to India, the project of "provincializing Europe"—a project that is essential to deconstructing European history's hegemony over other ethnic histories—"cannot be a nationalist, nativist, or atavistic project. . . . One cannot but problematize 'India' at the same time as one dismantles 'Europe.'"[37] In other words, genuine cultural translation is possible only when we move beyond the seemingly infinite but actually reductive permutations of the two terms—East and West, original and translation—and instead see both as full, materialist, and most likely equally corrupt, equally decadent participants in contemporary world culture. This would mean, ultimately, a thorough disassembling of the visualist epistemological bases of disciplines such as anthropology and ethnography as we know them to date.

WEAKNESS, FLUIDITY, AND THE FABLING OF THE WORLD

To elaborate my argument further, I will turn briefly to the work of Gianni Vattimo.[38] Basing his philosophy primarily on readings of Nietzsche and Heidegger, Vattimo's concern is that of figuring out possibilities of survival that are *practically* available in the deadlock of the European domination, homogenization, and standardization of the world. Among the most compelling ideas in Vattimo's writings is that of a weakening Western metaphysics, which he theorizes by drawing upon Nietzsche's idea of the death of God and Heidegger's notions of *Andenken* (recollection) and *Verwindung* (the overcoming that is not a transcendence but an acceptance and that carries with it the meaning of a cure, a convalescence).[39] For Vattimo, weakening—in the sense of a gradual decline, an ability to die—signals not a new, radical beginning but rather a turning and twisting of tradition away from its metaphysical foundations, a movement that makes way for the hybrid cultures of contemporary society.

Reading specifically for a tactics of translation between cultures, I find Vattimo's writings useful in several ways. First, he takes as his point of departure, realistically, the deadlock of the anthropological situation that has resulted from Western hegemony and that has led to the disappearance of alterity. Second, he refuses to think through this deadlock by constructing a brand-new beginning that is typical of the heroic radicalism of modernist narratives. Third, he attempts an alternative way of conceiving of the coevalness of cultures that is neither cynical and negative (in its criticism of the West) nor idealist and idealistic (by valorizing the East). Most important, Vattimo urges that we need to recognize the fact that these "other" cultures, rather than being lost or disappearing, are themselves transforming and translating into the present. He cites from Remo Guidieri:

> Those who have lamented the deaths of cultures have neither known how to see, nor wanted to see, that these same cultures—which are as obsessed as we are with the myth of abundance—have nevertheless produced their own specific way of entering into the Western universe. Although they may be paradoxical, irrational, or even caricatural, these modalities are just as authentic as the ancient ways, tributary as they are to the cultural forms from which they derive their condition of possibility. The non-Western contemporary world is an immense construction site of traces and residues, in conditions which have still to be analysed.[40]

This notion of the other—not as the idealized lost origin to be rediscovered or resurrected but as our contemporary—allows for a context of cultural translation in which these "other" cultures are equally engaged in the contradictions of modernity, such as the primitivization of the underprivileged, the quest for new foundations and new monuments, and so forth, that have been blatantly exhibited by Western nations. The coevalness of cultures, in other words, is not simply a peaceful co-existence among plural societies but the co-temporality of power structures—what Mary Louise Pratt calls the "contact zones"[41]—that mutually support and reinforce the exploitation of underprivileged social groups, nonhuman life forms, and ecological resources *throughout the world*.

Once the coevalness of cultures is acknowledged in this manner, cultural translation can no longer be thought of simply in linguistic terms, as the translation between Western and Eastern verbal languages alone. Instead, cultural translation needs to be rethought as the co-temporal exchange and contention between different social groups deploying different sign systems that may not be synthesizable to one particular model of language or representation. Considerations of the translation of or between cultures would thus have to move beyond verbal and literary languages to include events of the media such as radio, film, television, video, pop music, and so forth, without writing such events off as mere examples of mass indoctrination. Conversely, the media, as the loci of cultural translation, can now be seen as what helps to weaken the (literary, philosophical, and epistemological) foundations of Western domination and what makes the encounter between cultures a fluid and open-ended experience:

> Contrary to what critical sociology has long believed (with good reason, unfortunately), standardization, uniformity, the manipulation of consensus and the errors of totalitarianism *are not* the only possible outcome of the advent of generalized communication, the mass media and reproduction. Alongside these possibilities—which are objects of political choice—there opens an alternative possible outcome. The advent of the media enhances the inconstancy and superficiality of experience. In so doing, it runs counter to the generalization of domination, insofar as it allows a kind of "weakening" of the very notion of reality, and thus a weakening of its persuasive force. The society of the spectacle spoken of by the situationists is not simply a society of appearance manipulated by power: it is also the society in which reality presents itself as softer and more fluid, and in which experience can again acquire the characteristics of oscillation, disorientation and play.[42]

What the fluidity of the co-presence of cultures signifies is not the harmony but—to use a word from Vattimo—the thorough "contamination" of the world, so thorough that it has made the world become "soft" and tender. If the Western domination of the world has been the result of rationalistic progress, a progress that moves the world toward the general transparency that is evidenced by our media, this transparency is also a recovery, a convalescence from rationalistic progress in that it shows the world to be, finally, a fable:

> Instead of moving toward self-transparency, the society of the human sciences and generalized communication has moved towards what could, in general, be called the "fabling of the world." The images of the world we receive from the media and the human sciences, albeit on different levels, are not simply different interpretations of a "reality" that is "given" regardless, but rather constitute the very objectivity of the world. "There are no facts, only interpretations," in the words of Nietzsche, who also wrote that "the true world has in the end become a fable."[43]

167

In the transcultural world market, contemporary Chinese films can be understood by way of this transparency becoming fable. In order to see this, we need to return once again to the problem of translation and to Walter Benjamin's essay.

THE LIGHT OF THE ARCADE

We come to what is perhaps the most difficult point in Benjamin's discussion: besides the "longing for linguistic complementarity," what exactly is that "active force in life" (p. 79) that Benjamin describes as being imprisoned in the original and that the translation should liberate? How is this "active force" related to the "longing for linguistic complementarity"? Much as Benjamin's phrase carries with it a kind of organicist baggage, I propose that we think of it in terms other than organicism. By way of contemporary Chinese film, I would suggest that, *first*, the "active force of life" refers to the cultural violence that is made evident or apparent by the act of translation. In its rendering of the prohibitions, the oppressive customs, and the dehumanizing rituals of feudal China, for instance, the translation that is film enables us to see how a culture is "originally" put together, in all its *cruelty*. This putting together constitutes the violent active force to which the culture's members continue to be subjugated. For anyone whose identity is sutured with this culture, filmic representation thus makes it possible to see (with discomfort) one's "native origins" as foreign bodies.

Second, the "active force of life" refers to the act of transmission. While the callousness and viciousness of "tradition" is clearly visible on the screen, what makes it possible for Chinese audiences to become not simply inheritors of but also foreigners to their "tradition" is the act of transmission—the fact that whatever they experience, they experience as a passing-on. Writing in another context, Benjamin has defined transmission as what distinguishes Franz Kafka's work from that of his contemporaries. A work's transmissibility, Benjamin writes, is in opposition to its "truth":

> The things that want to be caught as they rush by are not meant for anyone's ears. This implies a state of affairs which negatively characterizes Kafka's works with great precision. . . . Kafka's work presents a *sickness of tradition.* . . . [The haggadic] consistency of truth . . . has been lost. Kafka was far from being the first to face this situation. Many had accommodated themselves to it, clinging to truth or whatever they happened to regard as truth and, with a more or less heavy heart, [forsaking] its transmissibility. Kafka's real genius was that he tried something entirely new: he sacrificed truth for the sake of *clinging to its transmissibility,* its haggadic element.[44]

Following Benjamin, we may argue that transmissibility is what *intensifies* in direct proportion to the sickness, the weakening of tradition. Ironically, then, it is indeed "tradition" that is the condition of possibility for transmission, but it is tradition in a debilitated and exhausted state.

Furthermore, in the age of multimedia communication, transmissibility is that aspect of a work which, unlike the weight of philosophical depth and interiority, is literal, transparent, and thus capable of offering itself to a popular or naive *handling.* What is transmissible is that which, *in addition to* having meaning or "sense," is accessible. This last point, incidentally, is quite the opposite of the manner in which we usually think of accessibility, which is typically regarded as a *deprivation,* a *lack* of depth and meaning. For Benjamin, however, transmissibility and accessibility are not pejorative or negligible qualities; instead they are what enable movement—that is, translation—from language to language, from medium to medium. Transmissibility and accessibility are what give a work its afterlife.

Once we see these implications of transmission, the "literalness" or *Wörtlichkeit* in Benjamin's essay that I have already discussed can be further defined as a transmissibility oriented toward a here and now—that is, a simultaneity rather than an alterity in place and time. Rather than a properly anchored "truth," "literalness" signifies mobility, proximity, approximation. Thus "literalness" is, as Benjamin writes, an arcade, a passageway.

Juxtaposing "The Task of the Translator" with Benjamin's interest in mass culture, we can now say that the "literalness" of popular and mass culture is not "simplistic" or "lacking" as is commonly thought. Rather, in its naive, crude, and literal modes, popular and mass culture is a supplement to truth, a tactic of passing something on. In the language of visuality, what is "literal" is what acquires a light *in addition to* the original that is its content; it is this light, this transparency, that allows the original content to be transmitted and translated: "A real translation is transparent; it does not cover the original, does not block its light, but allows the pure language, as though reinforced by its own medium, to shine upon the original all the more fully" (p. 79).

For most interpreters, Benjamin's notion of "light" and "transparency" in this passage corroborates that of "literalness" and "arcade" in the sense of "letting light through." Derrida, for instance, writes that "whereas the wall braces while conceal-ing (it is *in front* of the original), the arcade supports while letting light pass and the original show."[45] John Fletcher, commenting on Laplanche's reading of Benjamin's text, defines "Benjamin's Wörtlichkeit" as "the arcade that gives access and circula-tion rather than blocks out."[46] According to these interpretations, the arcade casts a light on the original in such a way as to make the original shine more brilliantly. *But what about the arcade itself—the "word-for-word-ness," the translation?*

By putting the emphasis on the arcade as a letting-light-through, critics such as Derrida and Fletcher alert us correctly to the "passageway" that is the *conventional* meaning of the arcade. Insofar as it understands the relationship between "original" and "translation" in terms of clarity and obscurity, this is a familiar move, which Derrida himself has described and critiqued in the following terms: "The appeal to the criteria of clarity and obscurity would suffice to confirm . . . [that the] entire philosophical delimitation of metaphor already lends itself to being constructed and worked by 'metaphors.' How could a piece of knowledge or a language be properly clear or obscure?"[47]

We may borrow Derrida's passage to critique the way *translation* is often evalu-ated (even by himself) in terms of clarity and obscurity, light and blockage. "Light" in this common philosophical tradition is assumed to be transparent in the sense of a *nonexisting* medium—and the arcade, which is equated with light, implicitly becomes a *mere* passageway. Since the "arcade" also corresponds in this context to translation, we are back once again in the classical situation in which "translation" is a mere vehicle, disposable once it completes its task.

And yet, does light not have another kind of transparency, the transparency of our media and consumer society? Such transparency moves us, it seems to me, not back to the "original" but rather to the *fabulous constructedness* of the world as spoken of by Nietzsche and Vattimo. Rather than some original text, it is the brilliance of this "fabling of the world" to which Benjamin's "arcade" leads us.

What is forgotten, when critics think of translation only in terms of literary and philosophical texts, is that the arcade, especially in the work of Benjamin, is never simply a linguistic passageway; it is also a commercial passageway, a passageway with shop fronts for the display of merchandise.[48] I would therefore emphasize this *mass culture aspect of the arcade* in order to show that the light and transparency allowed by "translation" is also the light and transparency of commodification. This is a profane, rather than pure and sacred, light, to which non-Western cultures are subjected if they want a place in the contemporary world. In "literal," "superficial" ways, this arcade is furnished with exhibits of modernity's "primitives" such as the women in contemporary Chinese film, who stand like mannequins in the passage-ways between cultures. The fabulous, brilliant forms of these primitives are what we must go through in order to arrive—not at the new destination of the truth of an "other" culture but at the weakened foundations of Western metaphysics as well as the disintegrated bases of Eastern traditions. In the display windows of the world market, such "primitives" are the toys, the fabricated play forms with which the less powerful (cultures) negotiate the imposition of the agenda of the powerful.[49] They are the "fables" that cast light on the "original" that is our world's violence, and they mark the passages that head not toward the "original" that is the West or the East but toward survival in the postcolonial world.[50]

Contemporary Chinese films are cultural "translations" in these multiple senses of the term. By consciously exoticizing China and revealing China's "dirty secrets" to the outside world, contemporary Chinese directors are translators of the violence with which the Chinese culture is "originally" put together. In the dazzling colors of their screen, the primitive that is woman, who at once unveils the corrupt Chi-nese tradition and parodies the orientalism of the West, stands as the naive symbol, the brilliant arcade, through which "China" travels across cultures to unfamiliar audiences. Meanwhile, the "original" that is film, the canonically Western medium, becomes destabilized and permanently infected with the unforgettable "ethnic" (and foreign) images imprinted on it by the Chinese translators. To borrow Michael Taussig's words, contemporary Chinese films constitute that "novel anthropology" in which the "object" recorded is no longer simply the "third world" but "the West itself as mirrored in the eyes and handiwork of its others." This novel anthropology is, we may add, translation in the sense of the "interlinear version" and "plurality of languages" as described by Benjamin (p. 82).

Like Benjamin's collector, the Chinese filmmakers' relation to "China" is that of the heirs to a great collection of treasures, the most distinguished trait of which, writes Benjamin, "will always be its transmissibility."[51] If translation is a form of betrayal, then the translators pay their debt by bringing fame to the ethnic culture, a fame that is evident in recent years from the major awards won by Chinese films at international film festivals in Manila, Tokyo, Nantes, Locarno, London, Honolulu, Montreal, Berlin, Venice, and Cannes.[52] Another name for fame is afterlife. It is in translation's faithlessness that "China" survives and thrives. A faithlessness that gives the beloved life—is that not . . . faithfulness itself?

11

A Filmic Staging of Postwar Geotemporal Politics

ON AKIRA KUROSAWA'S *NO REGRETS FOR OUR YOUTH*, SIXTY YEARS LATER

In the summer of 2005, I was invited to deliver a keynote lecture at an international conference on Japanese cinema jointly hosted by the Kinema Club and the Japan Foundation in Tokyo.[1] Not being a specialist, I chose as my topic Akira Kurosawa's film *No Regrets for Our Youth* (1946), based on the controversy of the dismissal, in 1933, of a Kyoto University law professor, Takigawa Yukitoki, on grounds of his pro-Communist views by the then education minister Ichiro Hatoyama. Despite its mid-twentieth-century Japanese location, the film's narrative mode, I thought, spoke acutely to our own time of global warfare and spiritual fundamentalism—but how? I was not entirely sure, though I was particularly interested in exploring the way Kurosawa's work provided a discursive opening for rethinking political issues such as fascism, imperialism, and militarism with a transnational awareness.

Mainly because of the lack of time, I received only two questions after my speech, both of which were, to my surprise, directed not at the film or my argument but rather critically at Kurosawa's wartime "political position" and the "degeneracy" of his generation of Japanese intelligentsia, the suggestion being that I should have taken him and his work to task on those grounds. As these questions were, unwittingly, pertinent to the reading I was offering, I believe it would be of interest to recapitulate my discussion of the film as part of a more general response to the questions' rhetorical implications.

Kurosawa's *Rashomon* (1950) catapulted "Asian cinema" to international recognition at the Venice Film Festival of 1951. In retrospect, it is remarkable that Kurosawa's experimentation with narrative perspectives—and their lack of a common or unified referent—was one of the first events to give Japanese and Asian cinema a revered place in world cinema. (In contrast to Satyajit Ray's *Pather Panchali* [1955], the other famous film work that gave Asian cinema international acclaim, Kurosawa's success did not stem from a more old-fashioned stylistic realism.) One could attribute this to the prevalence of modernist experimentation with narrative forms, in fiction as in cinema, experimentation that specializes in disrupting the continuous, coherent linearity of storytelling. Coming from a non-Western director not too long after the Second World War, however, this avant-garde interest in using film as a medium to explore the irreconcilable multiplicity of perspectives must have been quite astonishing to the world audience. (Many of the works associated with the French *nouveau roman* and *nouvelle vague* / New Wave Cinema, for instance, by authors and directors such as Alain Robbe-Grillet, Alain Renais, Marguerite Duras, and Jean-Luc Godard, who exerted a lasting influence well beyond Paris, were chronologically subsequent to *Rashomon*.) Indeed, as Mitsuhiro

Yoshimoto discusses in his study, scholars of Kurosawa's work have often presented it contradictorily as both very Westernized—more so than the other canonical Japanese masters such as Kenji Mizoguchi and Yasujiro Ozu—and yet entirely Japanese. Kurosawa causes anxiety in film scholars, Japanese and non-Japanese alike, because, Yoshimoto writes, "his films problematize Japan's self-image and the West's image of Japan."[2] Japanese cinema's emergence on the world stage is, in other words, haunted by the question of cultural identity, an identity that is, moreover, always defined transnationally and in relation to the West.[3] What are some of the implications of Kurosawa's supposedly "Western" and modernist interest—in narrativity, for instance?[4]

Unlike the more radical aesthetics of *Rashomon*, *No Regrets for Our Youth* has a much more straightforward structure of narration, using the woman character, Yagihara Yukie, as its focal point. The daughter of a liberal professor of law at Kyoto Imperial University, Yukie is attracted to two of her father's students, Itokawa, who eventually becomes a public prosecutor, and Ryukichi Noge, a radical leftist involved in an underground movement to prevent a war with the United States. Yukie moves to Tokyo, where she eventually cohabits with Noge until he is arrested by the secret police. Jailed and interrogated as Noge's accomplice, Yukie gradually comes to an understanding of her father's and Noge's political sentiments, and refuses to cooperate with the authorities. As the news of the Japanese naval attack on Pearl Harbor is announced on the radio, she is released and returns to Kyoto with her father. Noge, falsely indicted as a spy ringleader who tried to sabotage the government's war effort, is reported as having died in prison. Yukie, representing herself as his widow, goes to live with his parents as a peasant in the countryside. Working with her mother-in-law in the rice fields despite the villagers' animosity and harassment, Yukie is inspired by the memory of Noge, who had devoted his life to preventing Japan from getting involved in a disastrous war. The war finally ends and, after being back in Kyoto for a while, Yukie returns to Noge's village to work for its democratization, especially for the improvement of women's conditions.[5]

Despite what seems to be its realism, this film raises a fundamental question about narrative *transition*. Although (for American Occupation censorship reasons) there are no explicit representations of the Second World War in the diegesis (except for the announcement, in 1941, of Japan's attack on Pearl Harbor and, eventually, Japan's loss of the war), the transition suggests a significant transformation from a world dominated by the furor over war (both in the form of prowar and antiwar sentiments) to one that affirms the peaceful, down-to-earth practices of agrarian life. Notably, by a kind of modernist convention, this narrative transition is objectified through the woman character. Whereas the male revolutionary, Noge, remains unchanged throughout the story, Yukie undergoes a process of transformation from her former role as a privileged, Westernized professor's daughter to that of a dutiful wife and daughter-in-law, and, most important, a hardworking peasant woman who is determined to vindicate her husband's (misunderstood) patriotism in the eyes of the community. The delicate feminine hands and fingers that once swept along the keys of the piano, producing the tunes of Western music, are now shown to labor steadily in the soil, cultivating rice for the village. It is as though the vigor of this second role were lived as a form of atonement for the earlier sins of bourgeois leisure and idleness.

However, Kurosawa's narrative does not, in my view, simply present the latter part of the film as a logical, rational succession to the first. To put it in a slightly different manner, we can already see in this simple "succession"—that is, a consecutive chronological sequence of happenings in what comes across as a moral fable— the emergence of a certain epistemic uncertainty. (More unsympathetic audiences have been known to criticize the transformation of Yukie's character as extreme and unnatural, and this is not entirely without justification, since the film remains rather vague in accounting for her motivations.)[6] Once we start thinking about *the transition not simply as a natural order of things but as an event in itself*, we need to ask: just what has happened between the early and final parts of the story?

The early part of the story takes place in contemporary, urban Japan, in what might be called a progressive time (the 1930s): all the signs of Westernization, including the activist, antifascist sentiments, may be understood as part of a forward-looking cultural ambience, directed toward a vision of the future in which Japan can become an equal to the West. The latter part of the story (first near and then after the end of the war, in the mid-1940s), on the other hand, returns us to a rural environment, in which the most important activity is the cultivation of rice, the staple of the country. In contrast to the progressive time in the earlier part, we witness here a time that seems backward- and inward-looking, as though the process of national soul-searching in the aftermath of political and military failure must involve a (re)turn, literally, toward roots and a hands-on working-through of those roots. (At one point, Yukie says, "I have found my roots in that village.") The politics of temporality set up in the narrative transition thus evokes the classic opposition between Westernized modernity and native tradition, but the catch is that the seemingly backward and inward (re)turn toward Japan's "roots"—in what I'd call a kind of spiritual fundamentalism—is at the same time presented as a form of advancement (including a protofeminist awareness of women's liberation). That is to say, the rehabilitation of tradition is now given to us as the bona fide way of moving on to the future.[7]

Is the latter part of the story really a straightforward succession to the earlier one, then? Or is it a fantasy, its fantastical nature underscored precisely by the impossible, contradictory logic of its juxtaposition with the earlier narrative? The feminine and protofeminist libidinal qualities that seem to pay off in the redemptive return to the soil—courage, stamina, endurance, self-sacrifice for the wellbeing of the collective—are not these also the libidinal qualities that underlie the masculinist, war-centered upheavals in the earlier part of the story? If the stigmatization and ostracization faced by Noge's family is an allegory of the stigmatization and ostracization faced by Japan in the community of nations at the end of the war, it is through an unconditional, indefatigable *submission* and *dedication* to the goal of collective self-fashioning and refashioning—exactly the kind of affective aggressivity that bolstered both Japan's militarism *and* antimilitarist activism before and during the war—that Noge's family, led by Yukie, now tries to extricate itself from its predicament. Even though a peaceful corrective, the return to the soil is, therefore, resonant with patterns of obsessive mental behavior that were inscribed in Japan's historical catastrophe in the first place. In both cases, it is about the need to (re)gain footing in and recognition by a hostile, unsympathetic external world by asserting and reiterating Japan's exceptional difference, a difference that is typically argued in what came to be known as *Nihonjinron* (the discourse on the Japanese).

The privilege of hindsight reveals how noteworthy it is that the film was made soon after the war, at the beginning of the Cold War period, in which Japan and the rest of Asia would be placed in a new world configuration dominated by the United States and its own version of expansionism and Orientalism vis-à-vis the Pacific. Ironically, this was also the period in which the American Occupation forbid the representation of Occupation forces in Japanese films: "the American censors tried not only to suppress criticism of it [the Occupation], but also to hide the very fact that Japan was being occupied at all and that foreign officials were closely supervising the Japanese media."[8] This active prohibition of reference to a coercive political and military presence—and thus to the "structural link between the Japanese war experiences and the larger historical context of Western imperialism and colonialism"[9]—means that (for a filmmaker such as Kurosawa) the complex historicity of the so-called second chance of the postwar years had to be dealt with by means other than direct representation. To this extent, the strikingly ambivalent, almost enigmatically incongruent, temporalities of Kurosawa's film narrative can be read—irrespective of Kurosawa's personal convictions and intentions—as a kind of silent, anticipatory decoding of the destinies scripted for the Pacific in its postwar transactions with the United States and the rest of the capitalist Western world. (This could be one way of reading Gilles Deleuze's analysis of Kurosawa as a director whose stories are not so much about the search for meaningful actions in response to a given situation, as about the discovery of large, metaphysical *questions* deeply hidden in that situation. Interestingly, Deleuze believes that no flight is possible in Kurosawa's space.)[10]

First among these postwar transactions (between Japan and the West) is the inducement of discipline that takes the form of a rationalistic submission and dedication to work. From the ashes of the war, Japan was to rise to the status of a world economic power through quantifiable capitalist productivity (in the form, for instance, of industry and manufacture). This phenomenon, greatly encouraged and supported by the United States in its attempt to arrest the spread of Communism in East Asia, was to replicate itself in the emergence of the so-called Asian Tigers (Taiwan, South Korea, Singapore, and Hong Kong) in the 1970s and 1980s, and, finally, since the 1990s, in the rise of an ideologically capitulating and complicit People's Republic of China. The ability to work hard under and despite unfavorable conditions has become such a fetish attached to "Asian-ness" that in the United States itself, Asian Americans are considered a "model minority" on account of their reputation for an indomitable efficiency ethic. The fetishization of work and, in particular, the hardworking Asian—especially Asian women with their deft hands and nimble fingers—have, in other words, become key to a way of normativizing social antagonism and conflict, precisely as such antagonism and conflict constitute the historicity of modernity and continue to shape its unevenness across the globe.[11]

Second, even though this magical capacity for work, often attributed to Asians, is an indispensable ingredient in the postindustrial capitalist vision of economic growth, in Kurosawa's film it is nonetheless associated with another kind of time— the time of the peasant, of agriculture, and of country life. (Agrarian reform was one of the most successful Occupation programs.) As has become clearest in the case of contemporary China (which only belatedly consented to the peremptoriness of such economic growth), the relentless demands of capitalism always mean the uprooting of populations from the countryside and massive migrations to urban areas where work opportunities are more abundant. To valorize the work ethic through an affirmation of a return to the soil is thus, as Kurosawa's narrative suggests, to place Japan (and by implication the rest of postwar Asia) in an impossible bind, an impossible transaction: if Japan and Asia are given recognition as participants in the global present through their devotion to work, such devotion is nonetheless understood— or granted intelligibility—only as the attribute of a nonpresent time (that is, of a continuous, albeit oppressive, tradition, an essentialist "Asian-ness," and so forth).[12] And nowhere was such transactional politics of temporality more evident than in the American Occupation's "benevolent" decision to retain the Japanese Emperor and imperial court, a decision that amounted, in actuality, to the preservation in a modern nation of an archaic form of governance and social order whose rituals were entirely directed to winning good fortune for the agricultural community.

The narrative transition in *No Regrets for Our Youth* may thus be viewed as a strong example of a *cinematic theorization*, through the device of narrative juxtaposition, of the predicament of modernity as it is lived in and by non-Western cultures. I would contend that this theorization—this speculative thinking—is not simply dependent on mimetic representation (the Occupation government's censorship,

instituted in September 1945 and not ending until 1952, would have made this difficult) or even on aesthetic allegorization as such, but rather materializes through
the very schematization of the story into two kinds of temporalities. Despite the
seemingly consecutive developments of the events, and despite what might easily come across as an instance of Kurosawa's postwar "humanism" replacing or
compensating for his wartime militarism (that is, a change in his "political positions"), the narrative presents what are, on close reflection, mutually antagonistic
temporal, or what I would call *geotemporal*, perspectives. What is being theorized
and foregrounded in the narrative transition is the incommensurability between
these perspectives—and the problematic nature of an imaginary effort at cultural
recommencement, or cultural reorigination—under the circumstances after the
war. Can the problems of modernity and urbanization be resolved through a return
to agriculture and country life? Can Japan abandon its fascism and militarism, and
simply "start over" again by growing rice? These are among the large, "metaphysical" questions hidden in Kurosawa's narrative transition.

In his work on postwar European (and select examples of Japanese) cinema,
Deleuze advances the notion of the time-image to describe the change from a world
organized and animated by human action to one marked increasingly by human
memory and reflexivity. Rather than a straightforward relation with the external
world through spontaneous movements, the postwar cinematic image is, Deleuze
argues, traversed by the pathologies of human consciousness as lived through time.
In other words, the real "actor" or agent in postwar films is no longer action directed
toward the external world but rather subjectively experienced time—time that, even
in projected, imagistic form, often remains solipsistic, enigmatic, and inaccessible
to the world.[13] Not exactly coinciding with Deleuze's presupposition, in Kurosawa's
film we see the apparent insistence on the possibility of continued, meaningful
action (in the form of agricultural labor, work for democratization, improvement
of women's lives, and so forth). At the same time, this action—what would ideally
propel Japan into the future—is associated with rural rather than urban space, and
thus with a kind of return that is a contradictory, disorienting turn in time (one
that presents/makes present a past as the definitive way to the future). Considered in this manner, the supposedly forward- but slightly awkward-looking image
of Yukie on her final return to the village (as she climbs on the truck with the help
of other villagers) glosses Deleuze's phrase "time-image" with a rather different set
of connotations. As the leader of the democratic culture movement—a symbol of
hopefulness, willpower, and emancipation—her face seems nonetheless out of sync
with the villagers, who represent the future, yet are also, as we have already seen,
perfectly capable of being stuck in bigotry and malice. It is perhaps in this complex
series of significations, shuttling throughout the film among personal, communal,
national, and international levels of intensity, and superimposed on one another

to produce Yukie's face itself as a time-image, that we should come to terms with Kurosawa's statement "this woman I wanted to show as the new Japan."[14]

Johannes Fabian has used the term *allochronism* to critique a prevalent ethnographic practice whereby non-Western cultures are typically placed in a different time from the present of the West, their contemporaneity—or coevalness—with the West being effectively denied.[15] Extending the implications of Fabian's argument, we may think of allochronism—literally, "other time-ism"—as a narrative method by which a hierarchical divide is introduced into the relation between Western and non-Western cultures. In this narrative method, non-Western cultures are granted recognition only in the form of a nonpresent time, embellished with so-called specific cultural characteristics. My point about *No Regret for My Youth* is that it may be seen as a cinematic staging of such a modernist, allochronicist narrative method, wherein the vision for Japan's postwar, postfascist fate—her chances of surviving into the future—is artificially and proleptically cast in a kind of work that is associated with the past (that is, with what capitalism as a global present has steadily outlived). In other words, Japan's contemporaneity in the postwar world is imagined, paradoxically, in terms of its rice-growing ritual, its return to a pure, rustic Japaneseness, miraculously still uncontaminated by contact with the West, yet assuredly moving forward. How does this come about in the first place, and how to respond to the dictates, the givens, of such a geotemporal politics?[16]

CODA

What Kurosawa has accomplished in this film, then, is nothing short of making visible, in a transnational as much as specifically Japanese time frame, the fascist legacies, the lived ideological effects, embedded in the relation between culture and ethnic/national identity formation. In the often readily accepted—because politically correct—discourses that stridently oppose the degeneracy of fascism, imperialism, and militarism, precisely such legacies tend to get elided or become unseen. In contrast, Kurosawa's film engages the issues by dramatizing the close affinities of seemingly irreconcilable political positions, thus opening a discursive space in which we, the audience, are challenged to think. However discomfiting this challenge may be, we cannot afford to risk closing such a discursive space by collapsing the director's work into a matter of "political positions," as it were—as the two questions I received after my speech at the Tokyo conference seemed to suggest. Precisely as it is motivated by a confident political self-righteousness, such closure tends, in the end, to resemble none other than a practice of fascism.

179

12

From Sentimental Fabulations, Contemporary Chinese Films

ATTACHMENT IN THE AGE OF GLOBAL VISIBILITY

Where Is the Movie About Me? In the academic study of cinema, this is one of the most commonly encountered questions in recent years. Versions of it include some of the following: Where in this discipline am I? How come I am not represented? What does it mean for me and my group to be unseen? What does it mean for me and my group to be seen in this manner—what has been left out? These questions of becoming visible pertain, of course, to the prevalence of the politics of identification, to the relation between representational forms and their articulation of subjective histories and locations. It is one reason the study of cinema, like the study of literature and history, has become increasingly caught up in the study of group cultures: every group (be it defined by nationality, class, gender, ethnicity, sexual orientation, religion, or disability), it seems, produces a local variant of the universal that is cinema, requiring critics to engage with the specificities of particular collectivities even as they talk about the generalities of the filmic apparatus. According to one report, for instance, at the Society of Cinema Studies Annual Conference of 1998, "nearly half the over four hundred papers (read from morning to night in nine rooms) treated the politics of representing ethnicity, gender, and sexuality."[1] Western film studies, as Christine Gledhill and Linda Williams write, is currently faced with its own "impending dissolution . . . in . . . transnational theorization."[2] How did this state of affairs arise? How might we approach it not simply empirically, by way of numerical classifications, but also theoretically, by probing visibility as a problematic, to which film, because of its palpably visual modes of signification, may serve as a privileged point of entry?

Transnational theorization was, in fact, already an acute part of the reflections of non-Western authors on film experiences during the 1900s, 1910s and 1920s. When contemplating the effects of the filmic spectacle, for instance, Lu Xun and Tanizaki Junichiro, writing self-consciously as Chinese and Japanese nationals, readily raised questions of what it meant to be—and to be visible as—Chinese and Japanese in the modern world. The visual immediacy of Chinese and Japanese figures and faces, conveyed on the screen as they had never been before, was experienced by these authors not only as scientific advancement but simultaneously as a type of racially marked signification— specifically, as representations in which their own cultures appeared inferior and disadvantaged vis-à-vis a newly global, mediatized gaze.[3]

In light of these early reflections— reflections that are, strictly speaking, part of the history of film but which have hitherto been relegated to the margins of the West—the current preoccupation with group identities in film studies is perhaps only a belated reenactment of a longstanding set of issues pertaining to the fraught relationship between film and cultural identity. This book, which examines some Chinese films from the period of the late 1980s to the early 2000s, will be an approach to some of these issues.

HIGHLIGHTS OF A WESTERN DISCIPLINE

When film captured the critical attention of European theorists in the early twentieth century, it did not do so in terms of what we now call identity politics. Instead, it was film's novelty as a technological invention, capable of reproducing the world with a likeness hitherto unimaginable, that fascinated cultural critics such as Walter Benjamin, Siegfried Kracauer, and Ernst Bloch. Unlike photography, on which film and the early theorization of film depended, cinema brought with it the capacity for replicating motion in the visual spectacle. But as the motion picture ushered in a new kind of realism that substantially expanded on that of still photographic mimesis, it also demanded a thorough reconceptualization of the bases on which representation had worked for centuries. In this regard, few studies could rival Benjamin's oft-cited essay "The Work of Art in the Age of Mechanical Reproduction" (1936) in its grasp of the challenge posed by film to classical Western aesthetics. Along with his work on Charles Baudelaire's lyric poetry, this essay defines that challenge in terms of what Benjamin calls the decline of the aura, the sum of the unique features of works of art that is rooted in the time and place of the works' original creation.[4] For Benjamin, film's thorough permeation by technology, a permeation that led to its modes of apparent visual transparency, meant that a new kind of sociological attitude, one that associates representation more with reproducibility than with irreplaceability, would henceforth shape the expectations about representation: the repeatable copy, rather than the singular original, would now be the key. Benjamin viewed this fundamental iconoclasm (or irreverence toward the sacredness of the original) as a form of emancipation. No longer bound to specific times, places, and histories, the technically reproducible filmic image is now ubiquitously available, secularized, and thus democratized.

In retrospect, it is important to note the kind of emphasis critics such as Benjamin placed on the cinematic spectacle. This is a kind of emphasis we no longer seem to encounter in contemporary cinema studies. For the critics of Benjamin's era, film's faithful yet promiscuous realism—it records everything accurately yet also indiscriminately—announced the triumph of the camera's eye over human vision. The origins of cinema, they understood, are implicated in a kind of inhumanism even as cinema serves the utilitarian end of telling human stories. This inhumanism, rooted in the sophistication, efficiency, and perfection of the machine, was seen in overwhelmingly positive terms in the early twentieth century. By expanding and extending the possibilities of capturing movement, registering color, enlarging, speeding up, or slowing down the transitory moments of life, and rewinding time past, cinema was regarded first and foremost as an advancement, an overcoming of the limitations inherent in human perception. As in the theorizations and practices of early Soviet filmmakers such as Sergei Eisenstein, Dziga Vertov, and Lev Kuleshev, in Benjamin's thinking, the cinematic was a power to transform what is visible—to enhance, multiply, and diversify its dimensions. Cinema was the apparatus that enabled the emergence of what he called the optical unconscious—the surfacing of the optical that had hitherto been unconscious, on the one hand, and the surfacing of the unconscious in optical form, on the other.

183

These relatively early theorizations of the cinematic spectacle had to account in some rudimentary way for spectators' responses. And yet, although early cinema was closely affined with representational realism, it was, as Tom Gunning writes, not necessarily accompanied by the stability of viewer position: "the appearance of animated images, while frequently invoking accuracy and the methods of science, also provoked effects of astonishment and uncanny wonder. Innovations in realist representation did not necessarily anchor viewers in a stable and reassuring situation. Rather, this obsession with animation, with super-lifelike imagery, carries a profound ambivalence and even a sense of disorientation."[5]

Again, it is necessary to remember how such spectatorial ambivalence and disorientation were theorized at the time when cinema was seen, by European theorists at least, predominantly as a type of scientific and technological progress. Even though the audience was in the picture, as it were, its lack of stability (or uniformity) tended to be configured in terms of a general epochal experience rather than by way of specific histories of reception. For this reason, perhaps, Benjamin made ample use of the notion of shock, the high modernist sensibility he identified with montage and traced back to the artistic work of Baudelaire and the analytic work of Sigmund Freud (among others). While other critics saw cinematic shock in more existential-aesthetic terms, as the product of the abruptness, intensity, and ephemerality of fleeting moments,[6] for Benjamin, shock had a determinedly political significance. As is evident in his discussion of Bertolt Brecht's epic theater, in which the equivalent of cinematic montage could be located in the theatrical tableau (the moment in which ongoing gestures and movements are interrupted and suspended by the entry of an outsider in such a way as to become a frozen and thus quotable spectacle), Benjamin relied for some of his most suggestive insights on a capacity for defamiliarization (that is, for unsettling habitual perception) often associated with aesthetic form,[7] a capacity to which he then attributed the purpose of critical reflection. (His notion of the dialectic image in the unfinished *Arcades Project* arguably belongs as well in this repertoire of visual figures for mobilizing historical change.)[8] It was by engaging with film as shock—a quality of the cinematic spectacle that, by extension, he assimilated to the spectators' general response—that Benjamin wrote of film as a forward-looking medium.[9] He was, of course, deeply aware of the political danger that this entailed—by the 1930s film just as easily lent itself to manipulation by the Nazis and the Fascists for propaganda purposes—but his emphasis remained a utopian one, whereby the cinema stood for liberatory and transformative possibilities.

By contrast, André Bazin, writing in France in the 1950s, was not drawn to the elusive and shocking effects of the cinematic spectacle but instead theorized the filmic image in terms of its ontology, its function as a preserve of time: "photography . . . embalms time, rescuing it simply from its proper corruption. . . . [In film,] for the first time, the image of things is likewise the image of their duration, change mummified as it were."[10] If film was in an earlier era associated with time as progress, Bazin's theoretical emphasis was decidedly different. The cinema was by his time no longer a novelty but more a mundane fact of mass culture, and the political potentiality of cinematic shock that energized theorists in the 1930s had given way in Bazin's writings to phenomenologically oriented reflections, which were, paradoxically, also about the arrest and suspension of time. But whereas for Benjamin the filmic image as halted time provided an impetus for historical action, for Bazin it signaled rather retrospection, the act of looking back at something that no longer exists. The hopefulness and futurism of the earlier film theorizations were now superseded by a kind of nostalgia, one that results from the completion of processes. Accordingly, because time has fossilized in the cinematic spectacle, time is also redeemed there.[11]

In spite of his critics, Bazin's understanding of the cinematic image as time past does not mean that his film theory is by necessity politically regressive or conservative. Indeed, his grasp of the filmic image as (always already) implicated in retroaction enabled Bazin to analyze astutely how it was exploited in the Soviet Union for a political purpose different from that of capitalist Hollywood.[12] Describing the propaganda films in which Joseph Stalin always appeared not only as a military genius and an infallible leader but also as an avuncular, neighborly friend, filled with personal warmth and eagerness to help the common people, Bazin observed that the cinematic spectacle had become, in the hands of the Soviet filmmakers, a completed reality—a perfect image against which the real-life Stalin must henceforth measure himself. Although Stalin was still alive, Bazin wrote, it was as though he had already been rendered dead; beside his own glowing image, he could henceforth only live nostalgically, attempting in vain to become like himself over and over again. The real-life Stalin had become a somewhat inferior version of the Stalin image. Interestingly, in this cynical but perceptive account of Soviet propaganda, the theory of the cinematic image offered by Bazin was derived not so much from its effect of shock, potential for change, or hope for the future as from its effect of stability, permanence, and immobilization. The cinematic image here takes on the status of a monumentalized time, which compels one to look retroactively at something better, larger, and more glorious that no longer is. The remarkable lesson offered by Bazin is that, as much as the futurity imputed to the cinematic image, nostalgia, too, can be a profoundly political message; it, too, can inspire action.

These continental European negotiations with temporality as implied in the cinematic image, negotiations that tended, in a classical manner, to concentrate on film's representational relation to the external world it captured, shifted to a different plane as film gained status as an academic subject in Britain and the United States in the 1960s, 1970s, and 1980s. As a field of intellectual inquiry that sought institutional legitimation, film had to elaborate its own set of disciplinary specificities. At one level, it was, of course, possible to continue with the more abstract theorizations of the cinematic spectacle: as semiotics acquired critical purchase, film was accordingly rendered as a type of signification. Christian Metz's works, notably *Language and Cinema* and *Film Language,* led the way for the kind of inquiry that asks if film could indeed be seen as a kind of language in the Saussurean sense and, even if not, what its governing logic might be.[13] The point of Metz's project was to configure the perceptual possibility of a structuration, a network of permutations, that had a materiality all its own, a materiality that meanwhile was not to be confused with the vulgar materiality of the flesh. From Benjamin's and Bazin's adherence to the visual spectacle, then, with Metz and his followers, theorization moved rigorously into film's internal principles for generating and organizing meanings. As such theorization became increasingly idealist and rationalist, film critics, including Metz himself (in *The Imaginary Signifier*),[14] eventually found themselves returning to psychoanalysis as a remedial means of gauging the more intractable but undeniable issues of human fantasy and desire, and with them the politics of sexuality, to compensate for what had been typically left out of the semiotic explication.[15] In retrospect, it is tempting to see semiotics and psychoanalysis as the two inward turns—and disciplining moments—symptomatic of a process in which *the study of film itself was caught up in its own identity formation.* Be it through the labor of the filmic signifier or the labor of subjectivities interpellated around the cinematic apparatus, film studies was seeking its mirroring, so to speak, by the profession at large.

This is the juncture at which the old question of time, at one point debated in terms that were more or less exclusively focused on the cinematic image per se, splintered. Time could no longer be grasped in the abstract, as the future or the past, but demanded to be understood in relation to the mental, cultural, and historical processes by which the seemingly self-evident cinematic image was produced in the first place. Accordingly, the givenness of the cinematic image was increasingly displaced onto the politics of spectatorship. In the Anglo-American studies of film in the 1970s and 1980s, such as those being published in the influential British journal *Screen,* the continental European focus on the cinematic image was steadily supplemented, and supplanted, by modes of inquiry that were concurrently informed by Marxist, structuralist and poststructuralist, and psychoanalytic writings (the master figures being Jacques Lacan and Louis Althusser). But it was feminist film theory, described by Dudley Andrew as "the first and most telling Anglo-American cinema studies initiative,"[16] that brought about a thorough redesign of the European focus.

In her groundbreaking essay of 1975, "Visual Pleasure and Narrative Cinema," Laura Mulvey turned the question of the cinematic image (and its implications of time) into a story, one that, she revealed, was far from being sexually neutral or innocent.[17] Rather than treating the cinematic image as a single entity, Mulvey approached it in a deconstructive move, in which what seems visually obvious and unified is taken apart by the reintroduction of narrative. The part of the narrative that determines how specific images are looked at while remaining itself hidden and invisible, Mulvey called the gaze. Most critically, Mulvey gave the temporal differential between image and gaze the name of patriarchy, so that, in the case of classical Hollywood melodrama at least, she charged, masculinist scopophilia underwrote the imperative of gazing, while women were cast, as a result, as passive, fetishized objects, as beautiful images to be looked at. Mulvey was formidably direct about her goal: "It is said that analysing pleasure, or beauty, destroys it. That is the intention of this article."[18] As Maggie Humm puts it, "Mulvey's essay marked a huge conceptual leap in film theory: a jump from the ungendered and formalistic analyses of semiotics to the understanding that film viewing always involves gendered identities."[19] By arguing that cinema is irreducibly structured by (hetero) sexual difference, Mulvey succeeded in doing something that her fellow male critics were uninterested in doing—prying the filmic image open and away from its hitherto spontaneous, reified status and reinserting in it the drama of the ongoing cultural struggle between men and women, the drama of narrative coercions and ideological interpellations.

In its justifiable distrust of the cinematic image as deceptive and usurpatory and in its courageous effort to forge a politics that would prevent the woman spectator from completely collapsing, at her own peril, into the cinematic image of femininity produced by men, was feminist film theory, in spite of itself, an unwitting ally to an intellectual tradition that is, to borrow a term from Martin Jay's study of modern French theory, iconophobic?[20] I tend to think so, but it is necessary to add that this iconophobia was a theoretically and institutionally productive one.[21] (Among other things, it posed a crucial question within the politics of film production: how could one make a differently narrativized kind of film?) It was precisely its momentum of negativity, manifested in the belief that the cinematic image has somehow repressed something existing beyond it, that became the characteristic force with which the study of film has since then spread—first to English departments, in which film is often accepted as a kind of pop culture; then to foreign language and literature departments, in which film becomes yet another method of learning about other cultures; and finally to the currently fashionable discussions, in social science as well as humanities programs across the university, of so-called global media.

Feminist film theory, in other words, inaugurated the institutional dissemination of cinema studies in the Anglo-American world with something akin to what Michel Foucault, in his work on the history of sexuality in the West, called the repressive hypothesis, whereby the conceptualization of what is repressive—together with its investment in lack and castration—is reinforced simultaneously by the incessant generation and proliferation of discourses about what is supposedly repressed.[22] (It was no mere coincidence that the political weapon on which Mulvey relied for attacking phallocentrism was Freudian psychoanalysis.)[23] But what was unique—and remarkable—in this instance was the articulation of the repressive hypothesis to the visual field, an articulation wherein the visually full (presence and plenitude of the) cinematic image has become itself the very evidence/sign of repression and lack.

IMAGE, TIME, IDENTITY: TRAJECTORIES OF BECOMING VISIBLE

Because it was underwritten with the push of the repressive hypothesis, the paradigm shift within the cinematic visual field toward the study of narrativity and ideology led to consequences that have gone considerably beyond (the Western parameters of) film studies. Such a paradigm shift harked back to the heightened sense of group self-consciousness already felt by non-Western writers such as Lu Xun and Tanizaki about film technology in the early twentieth century and logically made way, in academia, for the study of differences dispersed along multiple lines of inquiry. In the decades since Mulvey's essay was first published,[24] film and cultural critics have been extending the implications of her work (often in simplified terms) by devoting themselves to problematizing the naturalness of the cinematic image. Rather than being on the image itself, its magic, or its tendency toward monumentalization, the focus in theorizing and analyzing film has increasingly been on identifying and critiquing the multiple narrative and ideological processes that go into the image's production. Bill Nichols sums up this general trend succinctly: "The visual is no longer a means of verifying the certainty of facts pertaining to an objective, external world and truths about this world conveyed linguistically. The visual now constitutes the terrain of subjective experience as the locus of knowledge, and power."[25] Whereas feminist critics, following Mulvey, elaborate and refine women-centered

187

modes of interrogating patriarchy, other critics, equipped with other types of social queries, would complicate the differential between gaze and image in terms of class, race, ethnicity, nationality, and sexual preference in order to expose the repressive effects of dominant modes of visuality and identification. (Think, for instance, of the numerous critiques in postcolonial studies of orientalist representations.) Concurrently, they also theorize the ambiguities inherent in various forms of spectatorship and, by implication, in various forms of seeing and subjectivity.[26]

In these collective endeavors to destroy the pleasure of the beautiful image, what has happened to the problematic of time? At one level, time is infinitely diversified and relativized: as every group of spectators comes forward with its demands, interrogations, and political agendas, one can no longer speak of the image as such but must become willing to subject the image to processes of re-viewing, reimaging, and reassembling. This is perhaps one reason there are so many publications on filmmaking and film reception in different cultures (Brazilian, Chinese, French, German, Hong Kong, Indian, Iranian, Israeli, Italian, Japanese, Korean, and Spanish, just to name some commonly encountered examples). At the same time, in this culturally pluralized way of theorizing the filmic image, one cannot help feeling that a certain predictability has set in and that, despite their local differences, the theoretical moves made by different cultural groups vis-à-vis the cinematic image often share a similar kind of critical prerogative. Borrowing again from Nichols, we may describe this prerogative in this manner:

> The rise of distinct cultures to a condition of visibility accompanies a radical shift away from democratic ideals of universalism (equality under the law for all regardless of gender, color, sexual orientation and so on) toward a particularism that insists on equality precisely in relation to differences of gender, color, sexual orientation and the like.[27]

"Differences of gender, color, sexual orientation and the like," it follows, all generate research agendas, competition for institutional space and funding, and self-reproductive mechanisms such as publications and the training and placing of students. The questions of identity politics with which I began this discussion are therefore, arguably, some of the *temporal* outcomes of the proliferating and disseminating mechanisms that characterize the repressive hypothesis as it has been mobilized around the cinematic visual field.

In this light, the ambivalent logics exemplified by feminist film theory from the very beginning may be seen as constitutive, perhaps paradigmatic, of the process of a subordinated group's rise to visibility. When feminist film theory alerted us to the cinematically fetishized status of women, its apparent iconophobia shared important affinities with the moral charge that accompanied Western political activisms of the 1960s and early 1970s, with their demands for an end to imperialism and military violence and for the granting of civil rights to disenfranchised populations. At the same time, like the mass protests so self-consciously staged during that era, feminist film theory was delivering another message. This was the message that the politics of gender and sexuality (together with the politics of race, class, and ethnicity) was, in fact, none other than the politics of commodified media spectacles, a politics constituted by the demonstrative forces of public display.[28] Indeed, the determination with which feminist critics sought to subvert the widespread "false" representations of women—by actively competing for the right to transform, possess, and manage the visual field; to fabricate women's images; to broadcast women's stories—suggested that the dynamics of late capitalist simulacra was assuming center stage. The mechanically and then electronically produced images; the instantly transmitted, spectacular "reality" shows: these were henceforth going to be the actual, ubiquitous political battleground.

The attempt to anchor one's identity definitively in what Mulvey called to-be-looked-at-ness (on the screen as well as off) is, in view of this history, a newly fetishistic practice in an exponentially expanding and accelerating virtual field of global visibility. (This is, I believe, one reason that those who traditionally would have concentrated on the study of prose fiction have been migrating steadily toward the study of film and visual cultures.)[29] Moreover, this fetishistic practice and its countless simulacra—in so many varieties of "Look at me! Look at us!"—are no longer confined to the realm of gender politics but also repeated and reproduced widely across the disciplines, in which the morally impassioned rebuke of images always goes hand in hand with the massive production and circulation of more images—be those images about classes, races, nations, or persons of different sexual orientations.

Pursued in close relation to a controversial visual medium, feminist film theory since Mulvey hence reveals (in a handy manner) something crucial about the condition of visibility in general. In the course of feminist critique, the immediately present, visible object—the image of woman in classical Hollywood narrative cinema—is delimited or bracketed in an intervention that, notably, cannot abandon the visible as such but instead moves it into a different frame (women's world). This move makes it possible to include that which has hitherto remained invisible and thereby to reinvent the very terms of the relation between the visible and the invisible. In this process, however, becoming visible is no longer simply a matter of becoming visible in the visual sense (as an image or object) but also a matter of participating in a discursive politics of (re)configuring the relation between center and margins, a politics in which what is visible may be a key but not the exclusive determinant. *There is, in other words, a visibility of visibility—a visibility that is the condition of possibility for what becomes visible, that may derive a certain intelligibility from the latter but cannot be simply reduced to it.* It is to this other, epistemic sense of

189

visibility—of visibility as the structuration of knowability—that Gilles Deleuze alerts us in his fascinating study of Foucault. As Deleuze writes in different passages, "Visibilities are not to be confused with elements that are visible or more generally perceptible, such as qualities, things, objects, compounds of objects. . . . Visibilities are not forms of objects, nor even forms that would show up under light, but rather forms of luminosity which are created by the light itself and allow a thing or object to exist only as a flash, sparkle or shimmer"; "Visibilities are neither the acts of a seeing subject nor the data of a visual meaning"; "Visibilities are not defined by sight but are complexes of actions and passions, actions and reactions, multisensorial complexes, which emerge into the light of day."[30]

If we follow Deleuze's thinking along these lines, the question of anyone's or any group's rise to the condition of visibility would turn out to be much more complicated than an attainment of quantifiable image time or even of the empirical status of being represented or seen. Instead, such a question would need to involve a consideration of the less immediately or sensorially detectable elements helping to propel, enhance, or obstruct such visibility in the first place and, even where visibility has occurred, a consideration of the often vacillating relations between the visible and the invisible that may well continue at different levels.

Tied as it is to the problematic of becoming visible (understood in these terms), the fetishization of identity as it is currently found in the study of cinematic images thus tends to proceed with a Janus-faced logic. There are those who, mistaking simple visual presence for (the entirety of) visibility, will always insist on investing artificial images with an anthropomorphic realism—the very thing that the iconoclasm of film, as its early theorists observed, fundamentally undid—and moreover to equate such images with the lives and histories of "real" cultural groups. ("National allegory" readings are one good example of this.) This line of thinking has its productive moments, to be sure, but it is ultimately limited in what it can offer. Meanwhile, for those who remember that what is on the screen are not real people but images, a suspension of such insistence on literal, positivistic identifications can mean a turn, more interestingly, to the specific materialities of image, affect, and fantasy, on the one hand, and the fraught complexities of globalized visibility, on the other.

190

With respect to the recent Western European and North American fascination with East Asian cinema,[31] the first question to ask, then, is this: should we try to direct such fascination back at some authentic, continuous Asianness lying beyond the alluring cinematic images, or would it not be more pertinent to see Asianness itself as a commodified and reproducible value, made tantalizingly visible and accessible not only by the filmic genres of the action or martial arts comedy, the love story, and the historical saga but also by an entire network of contemporary media discourses— economic rivalry, exotic cuisine, herbal medicine, spiritual and physical exercise, sex trade, female child adoption, model minority politics, illegal immigration, and so on—that are at once sustained by and contributing to the flows of capital? Part of my goal in this study is to argue that Chinese cinema since the 1980s—a cinema that is often characterized by multinational corporate production and distribution, multinational cast and crew collaboration, international award competition activity, and multicultural, multiethnic reception, as well as being accompanied by a steady stream of English-language publications, written (not infrequently by those who do not speak or read Chinese or consult Chinese-language sources) for an English-reading market—is an inherent part of a contemporary global problematic of becoming visible. As much as belonging in the history of Chinese culture, the films involved should also, I contend, be seen as belonging in the history of Western cinema studies, in the same manner that modern Asia, Africa, and Latin America, properly speaking, belong in the history of modern European studies.[32]

191

DEFINING THE SENTIMENTAL IN RELATION TO CONTEMPORARY CHINESE CINEMA

To the extent that one implicit aim of her criticism of classical Hollywood cinema was to eradicate conventional Western images altogether, Mulvey's early work can be seen as a British rejoinder to the political aspirations of the French *nouvelle vague* filmmakers (such as Jean-Luc Godard) and the theorists associated with the French journal *Tel quel*, who in the 1960s and 1970s mobilized critiques of Western thinking, often by way of looking east, especially to Mao Zedong's China.[33] Just as Mao and his cohort, following a native revolutionary tradition that began with the May Fourth Movement of 1919, sought to radicalize Chinese society by attacking its most basic social unit—the Chinese family[34]—so, too, did Anglo-American feminist film theory of the mid-twentieth century leave some of its most pronounced critical marks on melodrama, the film genre that is, arguably, most intimately linked to the middle-class nuclear family and its demands for female self-sacrifice.[35] But the Chinese connection, if it may be so called, did not stop at the attempt to deconstruct the family, East or West. As the consequences of Chinese communism began to be questioned by organic intellectuals in China—and as the disasters spawned by Mao's political idealism (which reached its frenzied heights during the Cultural Revolution of 1966–76) became a subject of reflective critique by those who had spent their formative youthful years living under the mainland Chinese regime— Chinese cinema became, for the first time, globally visible. In the astonishing films made by mainland Fifth Generation directors such as Chen Kaige, Zhang Yimou, Tian Zhuangzhuang, and their classmates, as well as by their contemporaries in Hong Kong and Taiwan such as Tsui Hark, Hou Hsiao-Hsien, Ann Hui, Ang Lee,

Edward Yang, Stanley Kwan, Clara Law, Wong Kar-wai, and Tsai Ming-liang, Chinese cinema has since the 1980s become an event with which the entire world has to reckon.[36] Appearing first in international film festivals and art house theaters, then gradually in undergraduate curricula across college campuses in the English-speaking world, and finally in mainstream Hollywood productions, China—in the form of films, directors, actors and actresses, cinematographic techniques, and special effects—has helped to revitalize cinematic discourse in the West and made it necessary, once again, for Western intellectuals to come to terms with aspects of what in so many ways still remains an exotic culture.

What does this becoming-visible of contemporary Chinese cinema signify in light of the small history of the discipline of film studies that I eclectically outlined above, including the critical moment of Anglo-American feminist critique? Many things can be said in response to this question,[37] but I'd like to foreground something that is central to my readings in some of the chapters to follow. Whereas contemporary cultural theory in the West, including feminist film theory, has thrived on an inextricable linkage (itself a legacy from Bertolt Brecht) between political consciousness raising, on the one hand, and an aesthetic-cum-theoretical avant-gardism,[38] on the other, the emergence of Chinese cinema renders this particular linkage a historical—and culturally specific—occurrence rather than a universal or absolute necessity. That is to say, although for left-leaning Western intellectuals since the post–Second World War period, "China" has often stood for a set of political aspirations alternative to the right, when China enters the world picture in the form of a contemporary cinema, it does not necessarily comply with such presumptions. Consciousness raising, contemporary Chinese cinema suggests, does not have to take the route of the avant-garde; conversely, aesthetic and theoretical avant-gardism, so valued in certain academic sectors for purposes of intellectual renewal and regeneration, does not necessarily lead to a progressive or democratic politics. In particular, the persistence of a predominant affective mode,[39] a mode I will describe as the sentimental, indicates that contemporary Chinese cinema, even as its contents fully partake of contemporary film and cultural problematics such as explicit sex, women's lives, gay male relationships, extramarital liaisons, immigrant tragedies and comedies, reproduction, and so forth, simultaneously brings with it fundamental challenges to the cornerstones of Western progressivist theoretical thinking. To engage productively with the global visibility of contemporary Chinese cinema, it is therefore important to work conceptually and speculatively, at a level beyond the (obviously invaluable) documenting and inventorying efforts and the geographical and chronological compartmentalization exercises that currently seem to dominate developments in this fledgling field. To put it bluntly, it is important to aim at goals other than information retrieval and canonization, and other than a monumentalizing of film periods (as tradition) and film directors (as individual talents).

What do I mean, then, by the recurrent sentimental in contemporary Chinese films? It would be helpful to begin with a conventional understanding—namely, of the sentimental as an affective orientation/tendency, one that is often characterized by apparent emotional excess, in the form of exaggerated grief or dejection or a propensity toward shedding tears.[40] But when examined closely, such emotional excess is only a clue to a much broader range of issues.

In his famous discussion, in 1795–96, of naive and sentimental poetry, the German-speaking philosopher and writer Friedrich Schiller defined the sentimental as a modern creative attitude marked by a particular self-consciousness of loss. To reiterate Schiller's statements in simple terms: while the poet who writes "naively" is nature, the poet who writes "sentimentally" *seeks* nature; the latter's "feeling for nature is like the feeling of an invalid for health."[41] The sentimental relation to nature (the condition of simple and sensuous wholeness that, because it is lost, will henceforth become a moral ideal) is, in other words, no longer spontaneous but reflexive—suffused with feelings of longing and characterized by the imaginative infiniteness of thought. What remains instructive in this classic European account is its attempt to understand the sentimental not only as an instance of affect but also as a relation of time: as an affective state triggered by a sense of loss, sentimentalism was, for Schiller, the symptom of the apprehension of an irreversible temporal differentiation or the passing of time. As well, this symptom was mediated by and accessible through aesthetic and cultural form: it was poetry (or "the poetic mood"), which Schiller considered "an independent whole in which all distinctions and all shortcomings vanish,"[42] that seemed generically appropriate for conveying the moral rigor pertaining to the naive and sentimental as contrastive but deeply bonded spiritual states.

Although Schiller's writings are typically classified under the rubric of German romanticism—he wrote about the sentimental belatedly, at a time when the term had already become pejorative in connotations; his formulation of the sentimental (as the awareness of the loss of spontaneous feeling) was also quite distinct from the views advanced in previous decades, as for instance in mid-eighteenth century England—his emphasis on the reflexive character of the sentimental—that is, the character whereby the mind does not receive any impressions without simultaneously observing its own activity and reflection—was illustrative of the general tenets of the well-established debates in eighteenth-century European moral philosophy and literature about the sentiments.[43] Conducted in the vocabulary of sensibility, pity, sympathy, compassion, virtue, refined and delicate feeling, and so forth,[44] some of these debates have also evolved around what in retrospect might be called a dialectical relationship between sentimentality and its darker underside, as discourses about the philanthropic function of benevolence were shown to be regularly underpinned by a fascination with monstrosity, cruelty, violence, and the pleasures

of inflicting pain on others. For some scholars, this dialectical relationship constitutes a definition of humanity that is ridden with ambiguity and puts the European
Enlightenment's presumed (arrival at) rationality into serious question.[45]

In Anglo-American literary and cinematic studies, this rich historical backdrop
of intellectual controversies over the unresolved tensions between compassion and
cruelty, between altruism and sadism gave way to a type of articulation about the
sentiments that links them explicitly with the dynamics of social power struggles.
When studied in relation to modern narrative fiction and film melodrama, in particular, the sentimental, which for many still carries derogative meanings such as
effeminacy and sensationalist self-indulgence, often becomes a means to focalize
issues about the politics of identity. From the novels of Samuel Richardson and
Charlotte Brontë to those of Toni Morrison, to the woman-centered narrative films
of Hollywood, and to the media representations of nonwhite peoples, sentimentalism has, beginning with feminist revisionist scholarship of the 1970s and 1980s,
increasingly been analyzed in conjunction with the agency of those (most typically,
white middle-class women confined to domesticity) who occupy a marginalized
social status and read as an alternative form of power attainment based, ironically,
on the emotional cathexes produced by experiences of social deprivation, subordination, and exclusion.[46] In such reversal of social hierarchy, what used to be considered trivial and weak is accordingly reread as dazzle and strength: the seeming
passivity or minoritization of those who are inmates of their environments are thus
reconceptualized as possessing a manipulable potentiality that was previously dismissed or ignored. In this manner, sentimentalism, rather than designating the
passing of time or the melancholy sensitivity of a lone lyric consciousness, becomes
instead a vindicated instrument in (the reinterpretation of) social entanglements,
often providing new clues as to who is actually in control.

Although far from being a unitary or unified concept, the sentimental in modern
Euro-American humanistic studies clearly occupies a place that has as much to do
with *the enduringly fraught ethics of human sociality as mediated by art and fiction,* be
that ethics conceived negatively, in the form of an individual consciousness's satirical
or elegiac longing for an ideal whose attainment is always deferred, or affirmatively,
in the form of (collective) identity empowerment and the fight for social justice.[47]
And even where the sentimental reveals itself to be much more intimately entwined
with sadism and malevolence than the feeble-minded would prefer, its function in
gauging the textures and nuances of a society's moral duplicity seems indisputable.
The pertinent question to be derived from these cross-cultural considerations is not
exactly how to apply them to Chinese film or how such "Western theory" does not
fit "Chinese reality" but rather the question of a particular discursive relation: how
can the symptoms of prominent affective tendencies, as detectable in certain films,
be theorized in relation to the foundations and practices of social interaction? With

this question in the foreground, the sentimental, instead of being equated with the occurrence of affective excess per se, can more fruitfully be rethought as a discursive constellation—one that traverses affect, time, identity, and social mores, and whose contours tend to shift and morph under different cultural circumstances and likely with different genres, forms, and media.[48] To this extent, this book could perhaps be seen as participating in a larger trend in recent film studies of a (re)turn to the historical relationship between medium and ontology, a (re)turn that has been triggered in part by digitization's radical altering and obsoleting of film's materiality and that has led scholars to rethink the medium-specific and oftentimes somatic, as well as imaginary, effects of cinematic signification itself.[49] . . .

Following the lead of Edward Said and other critics of Western imperialism, some contemporary academic authors, whenever they encounter images of another culture, tend readily to be on the qui vive about stereotyping, exploitation, and deceit and make it their mission to correct the falsehood especially of visual representations. In my previous work on contemporary Chinese cinema, I have attempted to critique such knee-jerk antiorientalist reactions with regard to the early films of Zhang Yimou.[1] From a comparative cultural perspective, what continues to concern me is that a certain predictable attitude tends to dominate the agenda these days whenever works inhabiting the East-West divide come under scholarly scrutiny. Instead of enabling the critical potential embedded in such works to come to light, this attitude often ends up blocking and annulling that potential in the name of political rectitude.

In the study of contemporary Chinese cinema, this fashionable—and at times facile—vigilance over orientalism dovetails felicitously with a long-standing bias in modern Chinese literary studies (published in English as well as in Chinese) for realism, whereby the prerequisite of mimetic responsibility remains hegemonic.[2] This intriguing scenario, in which orientalism critique, initiated theoretically in the West, seems to have become smoothly allied with the pursuit of certain non-Western native traditions and their ideological demands on representation; in which the politics and ethics of vision, in particular, cannot be discussed in separation but must be understood as mutually imbricated paradigms—this I would highlight, as the specific, thorny discursive locus for the ongoing relevance of Zhang's work.[3] In an academic climate in which iconophobia—the distrust and rebuke of the image—seems to have become a predominant way of reading cross-culturally (even as visual images proliferate and circulate across borders at unprecedented speeds), Zhang's work challenges us with the following questions: how might one approach *any* representation of the non-West as such without immediately resorting to the (by now) familiar and secure means of attacking orientalism, by nailing down a certain culprit, in the form of "What has he done and how"? Is it at all possible to conceive of a noniconophobic way of handling social and visual relations?

These questions are worth reiterating at a time when vision has become a totally open yet also totally treacherous minefield of negotiations. Precisely because anything can be instantly transformed into electronic virtuality and precisely because so many of our experiences now come to us first in the form of technologically mediated images, the status of the visual as such is likely to become increasingly polysemic, unpredictable, yet unavoidable. What kinds of processes—mechanical, electronic, and digital, as well as cultural and narrative—stand between our "natural" or spontaneous acts of seeing and the object images "out there"? How to deal with the seemingly obvious or literal appeal of the visual while being mindful of the complexities of engaging with vision? Can visuality include the possibility of not having vision or not having a visual exchange in the first place, or must it be defined exclusively within the positivistic realm of the optically available/present?

Insofar as it approaches vision as a social act as well as an objectified event or a mass spectacle and insofar as it presents the lure of the visual in bold and infinitely expandable possibilities (as light, color, sexuality, narrative, experiment, melodrama, and technical dazzle) even as it heeds the communal and nationalistic demands for mimetic responsibility, Zhang's work occupies a unique place among that of directors from the People's Republic of China. Notwithstanding the rather misleading critical consensus that his more recent films depart sharply from the early ones (*Hong gaoliang* [*Red Sorghum*, 1988], *Judou* [1990], and *Da Hong denglong gaogaogua* [*Raise the Red Lantern*, 1991]) that made him internationally famous,[4] Zhang's films of the late 1990s and early 2000s—such as *You hua haohao shu* (*Keep Cool*, 1997) and *Wo de fuqin muqin* (*The Road Home*, 1999) as well as *Yige dou buneng shao* (*Not One Less*, 1999) and *Xingfu shiguang* (*Happy Times*, 2000)—continue to be marked by a shrewd grasp of the materiality of a medium that has traditionally been associated with transparency, clarity, and wisdom but has become, as some of his stories tell us, quite otherwise.

Among Chinese audiences, it is now often suggested that Zhang has more or less abandoned the visually striking style of his early classics, which supposedly pander to the tastes of foreign devils by portraying a mythified, backward China, for a realist cinematic style that depicts simple people's lives in contemporary Chinese society. The well-known cultural critic Zhang Yiwu, for instance, has argued that this stylistic difference, observed in films such as *Qiuju daguansi* (*The Story of Qiuju*, 1993) and the others from the late 1990s and early 2000s, as mentioned above, may be traceable to the changing trends in the mainland Chinese film industry, which has been compelled by the pressures of globalization to produce a more inward-looking approach to the issues of China today.[5] Having allegedly repositioned himself thus, Zhang has, it seems, finally been accepted and endorsed even by the Chinese authorities, once his most hostile critics, who not only consented to having him serve as the director of the unprecedented, internationally collaborative performance of Puccini's opera *Turandot* in Beijing in September 1998 (with Zubin Mehta as the conductor) but also appointed him to film the official documentary showcasing Beijing in China's bid to host the 2008 Olympics. As I write these lines in 2006, Zhang is scheduled to direct the opening and closing ceremonies of the Olympic Games in Beijing, with Steven Spielberg as one of his artistic advisers.

Without question, this saga of how a native son who was first accused of sell-ing out to the West has subsequently been fully embraced by his state censors for purposes that are, strictly speaking, no less orientalist, no less opportunistic, and no less commodification-driven deserves an independent treatment all its own. (The latest episodes in this saga would have to include the phenomenal box office suc-cesses, inside and outside China, of Zhang's still more recent blockbuster films *Yingxiong* [*Hero*, 2002] and *Shimian maifu* [*House of Flying Daggers*, 2004] amid storms of controversy among Chinese audiences, who attack him this time for pan-dering to Chinese state authoritarianism and, once again, to orientalism.)[6] My point in bringing it up is simply to emphasize how the seemingly unending melodrama of alternating vilification and approval that has been following Zhang's career may itself be taken as an example of the power struggles over vision and visibility in postcolonial postmodernity, power struggles on which Zhang's work to date has provided some of the most provocative commentaries.

While the early films such as *Red Sorghum*, *Judou*, and *Raise the Red Lantern* have been frequently accused of orientalist tendencies involving ungrounded fantasies, the more recent realist ones are generally considered as a return to more authen-tic subject matters and down-to-earth, documentarylike shooting methods. As one critic, Shi Wenhong, points out in relation to the film *Not One Less*, however, the subject matter of present-day poverty, too, can be exotic in the eyes of some (West-ern) audiences.[7] (As will become clear in my discussion of the film, such subject matter is increasingly exotic to urban middle-class Chinese viewers as well.) Within the post–Second World War global framework, the valorization of realism as an ethnographically authentic/truthful manner of representation is, arguably, part and parcel of an ideological legacy that has long accompanied the objectification of non-Western peoples. (One need only think of a periodical such as *National Geographic* to see my point.)[8] Indeed, in the institution of postwar U.S. area studies, this bias toward so-called realism has been instrumental to the strategic targeting of non-Western political regimes and their cultures during the cold war period and since, and the representational politics surrounding China and Asia, we should remem-ber, remain as ever in the grip of such targeting. Accordingly, whenever it comes to Chinese authors, even the most imaginative writings and avant-garde artworks have tended to be read for factographic value, for what in the end is empirical informa-tion retrieval. Against the backdrop of this thoroughly politicized history of cross-cultural reading and viewing, the laudatory revaluation of a director such as Zhang in the form of "Ah, he is finally becoming more realist!" is deeply ironic, especially when it comes from native Chinese audiences.

As I will argue in the following analyses of the films *Happy Times* and *Not One Less*, what is noteworthy about Zhang's work is much less its departure from or return to so-called realism than the possibility it offers for a critique of the historical import of the mediatized image—a critique that may have little to do with Zhang's personal intentions but is definitely discernible in the semiotic nuances of his handling of vision. If, in contrast to the mythical stories of his early classics, Zhang has in some of his more recent work chosen seemingly matter-of-fact locales, characters, and happenings,[9] this more recent work nonetheless continues to deliver sharp reflections on the politics of vision and cultural identity and their imbrications with the massively uneven effects of globalization.

Such reflections have to do with Zhang's fundamental conception of vision as a kind of second-order labor—labor not in the sense of physical exertion but rather in the sense of mediated (and mediatized) signification. Hence, strictly speaking, even the early films displaying China's decrepitude are not only about poor peasants struggling against the injustice of life in the countryside but also about a process in which such struggles are transcoded, through the film apparatus, into signs of a cross-cultural encounter—signs that convey an imaginary Chineseness to those watching China from the outside as well as to those watching it from the inside. Constructing these signs, building entertaining stories around them, and rendering them visually appealing are for Zhang seldom a matter of mimetic realism but always a matter of the specificities of filmmaking, of experimenting with color, sound, narrative, and time coordination and control. His critics, on the other hand, have repeatedly ignored the materiality of this filmmaking process and insisted on some other reality lying beyond it.[10] For such critics, unquestioningly, that reality is China and its people; moreover, it is a reality that (a) must direct and dictate how a film should be made; (b) will itself be exempt from any such framing considerations; and (c) must also be used as the ultimate criterion for judging a film's merits.

In the light of such hegemonic demands for realism and reflectionism in the fields of Chinese literary and film studies and in the light of the intransigent moralism of many of his critics, it is interesting to consider some of the tactical adaptations Zhang has made in his evolving work.[11] As a way perhaps to distract and elude these critics' sight, he did, from the mid-1990s to the early 2000s, make a few films that are more obviously documentarylike in their contents and settings. Often, these films are about poor rural folk or *xiaoshimin* (ordinary citizens) in big cities, whose lives are unglamorous and filled with hardships. Like *Red Sorghum, Judou,* and *Raise the Red Lantern,* these films are characterized by Zhang's fascination with human endurance: the female characters in *The Story of Qiuju, The Road Home,* and *Happy Times,* like those in the early films, stubbornly persist in their pursuit of a specific goal, but whereas Jiu'er, Judou, Songlian, and Yan'er (the servant girl in *Raise the Red Lantern*) pay for their strength or character with their lives or their sanity, the more contemporary female characters in the realist films tend to be more or less successful in getting what they want. These young females' struggles against systemic indifference and cruelty end merely ambivalently (rather than tragically) or even happily. And, whereas the early films stand as exhibits of a bygone cultural system, sealed off with an exotic allure, films such as *Happy Times* and *Not One Less* seem to offer some hope.

Is this indeed so?

In the midst of the assaults and the compliments, few, to my knowledge, have ever stopped to consider the consistent perspicacity with which Zhang has been handling the implications of the give-and-take of visuality or the critical statement his work as a whole has been making on this activity, event, object, commodity, and instrument called vision in postcolonial, postmodern times. While the reception of his work lingers over issues of cinematographic spectacularity, historical truthfulness, and state cooptation and at times over a naive celebration of so-called realism, what I would like to pinpoint instead is the refreshingly intelligent ways in which two of his small-budget films explore the political-economic implications of vision and visuality and, in the process, produce nothing short of an aesthetic—indeed, a Brechtian—staging of the tragicomic antagonisms embroiled in social interaction during an era of ostensible national progress and prosperity.[12]

ALTRUISTIC FICTIONS IN CHINA'S *HAPPY TIMES*

The story of *Happy Times* begins as Lao Zhao, a retired factory worker, is proposing to a fat divorced woman who lives with her indolent teenage son and blind stepdaughter. The woman is agreeable but only if he can come up with the 50,000 yuan for the wedding she requires. To make himself seem like a good catch, Lao Zhao has told the fat woman that he owns a hotel, but in reality he and his friend Li simply try to renovate all abandoned bus in an overgrown area with the intention of renting it as a place of assignation—called "Happy Times"—for young lovers with nowhere to go. Soon, as is often the case nowadays with urban development in mainland China, the renovated bus is abruptly removed by the authorities to make space for a commercial project. In order not to lose his bride to-be, however, Lao Zhao must perpetuate his lies, so he offers to hire the blind young girl as a masseuse in his fantastical hotel. In the huge, darkish spaces of the deserted state factory where they used to work, he and his friends put together a makeshift massage room with corrugated metal and carpet remnants and then take turns at playing customers coming for massage sessions, paying the blind girl handsomely with blank, bill-sized pieces of brown paper (for a glimpse into this farcical situation, see, for instance, fig. 1).

Although Lao Zhao and his friends are engaged in an ever more elaborate series of hoaxes to fool a blind person, they are motivated by kindness, and their clumsy, bumpkinish endeavors are often hilariously comical. Knowing that the girl's deepest wish is to be reunited with her father, who has gone south to Shenzhen, the

FIGURE 1

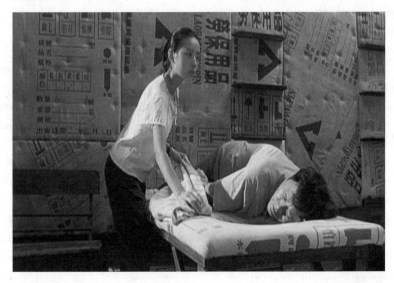

A "CLIENT" FALLING ASLEEP DURING A MASSAGE SESSION AT THE FAKE MASSAGE PARLOR,
XINGFU SHIGUANG / HAPPY TIMES (© GUANGXI FILM STUDIO / XIN HUAMIAN FILM /
ZHUHAI ZHENRONG, 2000)

boomtown near Hong Kong, Lao Zhao writes a fake letter in which the father tells his daughter how much he loves her and promises to find her a cure for her eyes as soon as he has earned enough money. The film ends with Lao Zhao reading this letter aloud, the girl and their friends listening, while the factory grounds on which they have been working together as masseuse and customers—the very stage on which they have been producing their collective performances, so to speak—are being demolished by bulldozers.[13]

Narratively speaking, the girl's sight deprivation provides the impediment around which much of the film's action revolves. The blind person, according to Naomi Schor, is conventionally given a philosophical or critical function in literature: "The blind person as *seer* is the central figure of the literature of blindness, . . . it rests on the double, oscillating meaning of seeing, as both a physical and cognitive act."[14] Although the blind girl in Zhang's film is a sympathetic character, it is important to note that he does not follow this literary convention of turning her into a transcendent seer. Given the fact that he does his work in a visual medium, his alternative approach to sight and blindness is, as I will go on to show, ingenious.

Consider the scene in which Lao Zhao makes his first visit to the fat woman's home. For the first time, we encounter the blind girl, left in the fat woman's care by her previous husband, who has moved on. In order to impress her suitor, the fat woman, who normally treats this stepdaughter with contempt, gives her some ice cream. This gesture of kindness lasts only as long as the duration of Lao Zhao's visit. As soon as he leaves, the fat lady snatches the ice cream from the blind girl and, scolding her as someone not worthy of such a luxury item, puts it back in the freezer.

Although it is possible to draw a moral lesson from this scene (for instance, by viewing it as a commentary on the lamentable condition of human cruelty and hypocrisy), what is far more interesting is the suggestive reading it offers of the semiotics and politics of seeing—indeed, of sightedness itself as a kind of material sign around which specific values are implicitly transacted.

203

The fat woman's opportunistic manner of handling the ice cream indicates that sight, as what renders the world accessible, is not a natural but an artificial phenomenon, one that is, moreover, eminently manipulable. The fat woman consciously performs for Lao Zhao's sight by creating an appearance of generosity, yet as soon as that sight is removed, there is no need for this performance to continue. Sight, in other words, is not a medium of revelation or a means of understanding, as we commonly think; rather, it is a prosthesis, a surveillance mechanism installed on (other) human bodies, which means that one must behave appropriately when someone else is watching but that there is otherwise no intrinsic reason to do so. What Lao Zhao sees—the sight of a kind and fair stepmother—is just that: a sight. It does not, as he assumes it does, have a deeper reality ("a real kind and fair stepmother") attached to it.

The fat woman's behavior is disturbing because, contrary to what most people believe, she has not internalized or naturalized the function of sight in such a way as to make it her own conscience, her automatized self-surveillance. Sight remains for her something of an arbitrary and external function, a kind of mechanical device to be exploited solely for her own benefit. As the film goes on to show, with the events that unfold around the blind girl in the fake hotel, sight can also be a disability, an elaborate network of mendacity devised to deceive others that ends up, ironically, trapping one more and more deeply. Having sight is not necessarily the opposite of being blind but may under some circumstances become an extension of blindness, a kind of handicap that distorts or obstructs reality as much as the physical inability to see.

At the same time, despite convention, Zhang Yimou does not attempt to idealize the *deprivation* of sight by endowing it with the lofty association of philosophical wisdom. In his hands, blindness, like poverty, remains a condition of misfortune of which anyone who is afflicted would want to be free if the means could be found, because, as the simple incident with the ice cream indicates, it is a condition that puts one at the mercy of others. Having thus broken away from the conjoined (philosophical) paths of at once privileging (the accident of most people's natural) sightedness and bestowing an otherworldly value on blindness, Zhang reorganizes sight and blindness as comparable rather than opposed events on the same plane: what those with sight see is not necessarily clarity but often distortion and obstruction, and *sightedness, too, can be a deprived sense.* Through such reorganization, he delivers a radically different way of coming to terms with vision, whereby the ability to see itself does not (as is often the case in a binary opposition) become the privileged term for judging the other term, blindness, but rather stands close to it as a correlate, an approximation.

This subtly reorganized relation between vision and blindness in turn brings into focus the entire problematic of lying, which seems to be the only kind of activity in which Lao Zhao has been engaged from beginning to end. In the scene in which she finally rejects him, the fat woman scorns Lao Zhao as a liar. For those who want to defend him, it can be said that his lying, especially in connection with the blind girl, is justifiable in terms of altruism and that the lies are morally compensated for by his good intentions. But something more is going on in this scene of rejection. Just as her ability to manipulate others' sightedness does not make her a decent person, so, too, does the fat woman's knowledge of the truth (that Lao Zhao lies) stop short of any personal improvement on her part. Indeed, access to the truth simply makes her more viciously self-righteous, as she uses it to attack her suitor and rid herself of him. Like a candid camera in the hands of the wrong people, then, her effortless ability to record and replay—and thus to expose Lao Zhao for the liar that he has been—strangely does not bring about any moral illumination; it simply helps her conveniently to put an end to their relationship now that she has found herself a more lucrative marriage proposition.

As the interplay between sight and blindness, truth and lies, leads toward what becomes increasingly evident as a drama of irresolvable moral confusions, some of the prominent elements of the story paradoxically come together. The awkward marriage proposal at the beginning, the reprehensible conditions in the fat woman's home, the construction first of the fantastical hotel and then of the fantastical massage room with its "clientele," and finally the ubiquitous triumph of big corporate businesses in present-day China: all these narrative details coalesce to highlight the emergence of a political economy in which money and money alone is the agent—and arbiter—of reason and power. Nowhere is this more acutely demonstrated than in the empty factory in which Lao Zhao and his friends put on their absurd acts of altruism. These unemployed factory workers, who at one time probably worked hard day in and day out with their hands and were considered the backbone of the socialist "people's republic," have now turned their abandoned workplace into a surrealist stage on which they become at once the script writers, directors, actors, and audience of a collective fantasy, replete with its (endlessly reproducible, because fake) paper currency, with the sole purpose of cheating a blind person.

When promoting the film in the United States, Zhang Yimou is reported to have commented on this part of the story as follows:

> At the end, when they are building the hotel, it becomes very symbolic. It's like the workers are building a dream in an old abandoned factory. Society has changed a lot in China lately, and everyone dreams of changing their life. Money has become very important, but in the middle of this wave of commercialization, I have started to feel the importance of real sentiments, of the caring among people. Caring is even more important than money.[15]

205

Obviously, such uncontroversial—and, yes, sentimental—remarks should be understood in the context in which they were made—namely, as part of the publicity for the film. As the idiom "Trust the tale, not the teller" reminds us, it seems fair to surmise that, like all gifted artists, Zhang has, perhaps without being consciously aware of it, put his most acute interventions across in silence—that is, within the fictional space opened up by the work itself.

Accordingly, if workers' labor used to be a revered source of national vitality in China's communist ideology, what has become of such labor? In the fantasy acts composed and consumed by Lao Zhao and his friends, such old-fashioned labor has evidently outlived its usefulness and gone to waste. Indeed, human labor itself is no longer regarded as the origin of social relations, which are now increasingly governed by money and by the expedient transactions of exchange values. The only person who still works manually is the blind girl, but her labor, as we know, merely serves a bogus currency (as she is paid with pieces of scrap paper) in a workplace that does not really exist.

This film, in other words, invites one to read it as a kind of national allegory—not necessarily one that represents the familiar, inextricable entanglement between an individual's existential struggle and his nation's political fate but rather one in which the seemingly lighthearted story of fraudulence and debauchery at the trivial, mundane level may be parsed as a story about those in charge of the state and its economic order, engaged conscientiously as they are in the manufacture of altruistic fictions as a strategy of governance even as conditions are moving by leaps and bounds in an opposite direction. The nation, the film suggests, is no more than a bunch of well-meaning, kindhearted people who are collectively *putting on a show* to appease the downtrodden and powerless. China's astonishing feat of a rapid transition to market capitalism on the very site(s) of its former, state-owned national production: isn't *this* the spectacle of a vastly duplicitous operation, in which those who perform physical labor will increasingly be consigned to the margins, their iron rice bowls shattered, their dreams and aspirations bulldozed into the garbage heaps of modernization? Yet who are the culprits? Aren't they, too, often "nice" people—ordinary citizens, local officials, or even party cadres—who are themselves victims of the remorseless forces transforming Chinese society today? Michael Dutton's perceptive comments on urban life in contemporary China may be borrowed for a summary of the volatile situation:

> The market arrives in China in what appears to be an Adornesque moment where everything is rendered "for sale." Yet what one quickly discovers is that salability has chiseled away the certainty of meanings on which party propaganda relied. . . . Our antiheroes [i.e., ordinary people in China] are no pristine harbingers of any future civil society, any more than the despotic state or Communist Party is the single source of their oppression. Our antiheroes are the "collateral damage" suffered in the globalization processes that we [the world's observers] have come to call economic reform.[16]

On the surface, then, Zhang's film offers an apparently straightforward moral tale involving a simple reversal of common sense: in spite of his tendency to tell lies, Lao Zhao ends up impressing us as a more or less benevolent person who, even after his own marriage deal has fallen through, heroically continues to assume the role of a surrogate father to the blind girl. His avuncular kindness brings a modicum of relief in the midst of a desperate environment. This, perhaps, is the story that allows Zhang's audiences to see him as having returned to cinematic realism and humanism and has won him approval even from some of his harshest critics. But the irony that quietly lurks in all the humanistic details, that, in fact, displays such details to be, politically as well as ideologically, thoroughly antagonistic to and irreconcilable with one another, is unmistakable. With the preemptive triumph of artificial vision (the kind of seeing that is not internalized or naturalized as conscience), the ensuing capacity for deception and self-deception, and the efficacious devaluation of human physical labor, what Zhang has produced here (as he has also, as I will argue, in *Not One Less*) is a stark portrayal of a migration—contemporary Chinese society's "advancement" to a new, relentless regime of power.

HOW TO ADD BACK A SUBTRACTED CHILD? THE TRANSMUTATION AND ABJECTION OF HUMAN LABOR IN *NOT ONE LESS*

The story of *Not One Less* can be briefly retold as follows: At the primary school of an impoverished northern Chinese village (Shuiquan Village), a group of pupils are learning under difficult conditions. Their teacher, Mr. Gao, has to go home to tend to his sick mother, and a thirteen-year-old girl from a neighboring village, Wei

Minzhi, is hired as his substitute for one month. Before leaving, Mr. Gao advises Wei that quite a number of the pupils have been dropping out and instructs her to make sure that the remaining twenty-eight stay until he returns—"not one less," he says. For her substitute teaching, Wei has been promised fifty yuan by the mayor, and Mr. Gao reassures her that not only will she get paid but he will himself give her an additional ten yuan if all the students receive proper attention during his absence. As Wei starts teaching, the pupils are not exactly cooperative, and she is confronted with various obstacles, including the relative lack of chalk, which she must use sparingly. One day, a boy named Zhang Huike fails to show up: his mother is ill and in debt and can no longer afford his school fees, so the boy has been sent off to the city to look for work. Wei is determined to bring this pupil back. After a series of failed efforts at locating him, she succeeds in getting the attention of the manager of the city's television station, who arranges for her to make an appeal on a program called *Today in China*. Zhang Huike, who is washing dishes at a restaurant and sees Wei on TV, is moved to tears by Wei's appeal and turns himself in. Teacher and pupil return to the village with a crowd of reporters as well as a large supply of classroom materials and gift donations to the village from audiences who have watched the program.

If (as I mentioned in my discussion of *The Road Home* in chapter 3 [of *Sentimental Fabulations, Contemporary Chinese Films*]) stubbornness, perseverance, and endurance are qualities that frequently recur in Zhang's films, in *Not One Less* they take on the additional significance of being constituents of a humanism vis-à-vis an impersonal and inefficient official system, which is impotent in remedying the disastrous conditions of the village school. Exactly how does this humanism express itself? In contrast to the situation in *Happy Times,* in which humanism appears against a framework of general unemployment (whereupon Lao Zhao and his friends can spend their excess time fabricating lies in order to be kind to the blind girl), humanism expresses itself in *Not One Less* in a vigorous spirit of productionism. A leftover, arguably, from the heyday of official socialist propaganda, such productionism is most evident in the form of quantifiable accumulation. (We recall, for instance, the slogans of the Great Leap Forward period, during which the campaign for national wellbeing was promoted in terms of measurable units of raw materials—so many tons of steel and iron to be manufactured, so many kilos of wheat and vegetables to be harvested, etc.) The clearest example is the elementary method of counting and permutation adopted by Wei and her pupils to collect her bus fare for the city. Moving one brick (in a nearby factory), they discover, will earn them fifteen cents, so, to make fifteen yuan, they should move one hundred bricks. Although this method of making money is based on an exchange principle—X units of labor equals Y units of cash—its anachronism is apparent precisely in the mechanical correspondence established between two different kinds of values involved—concrete muscular/manual labor, on the one hand, and the abstract, general equivalent of money, on the other. Persuaded by the belief that if they contribute their labor they will indeed get the proper remuneration, the girl teacher and her pupils put themselves to work.

Under Zhang Yimou's direction, this simple incident, what appears at first to be a mere narrative detail, turns out to be the manifestation of an entire political-economic rationale. As is demonstrated by the numerical calculations Wei and her pupils perform on the blackboard, this rationale is based not only on manual labor but also on the mathematics of simple addition, subtraction, multiplication, and division. At the heart of this rationale is an attributed continuum, or balance, between the two sides of the equation—a continuum whereby effort logically and proportionally translates into reward.

The tension and, ultimately, incompatibility between this earnest, one-on-one method of accounting, on the one hand, and the increasingly technologized, corporatized, and abstract (that is, Enronesque) method of value generation, on the other, is staged in a series of frustrations encountered by Wei, who is confronted each time with the futility of her own methods of calculation. First, having earned $15 for moving one hundred bricks, she and her pupils discover that the bus fare is actually $20.50 each way. She attempts to solve this problem with her physical body, first by trying to get on the bus illegally and then, reluctantly, by walking. She is finally able to get a ride home with a truck driver. On arriving in the city with $9 (having already spent $6 on two cans of Coca-Cola for her pupils), she has to agree to pay $2.50 to the girl who was last with Zhang Huike before this girl will take her to the train station to look for him. The two girls end up paging him with a loudspeaker announcement around the station—to no avail. Wei spends the remainder of her money, $6.50, on ink, paper, and a brush in order to write out her notices one by one, only to be told by a passerby that such notices are useless and then to have them blown all over by the wind and swept away by the morning street cleaners. By this time, Wei has, at the passerby's suggestion, made her way to the television station. After a long and persistent wait, she finally succeeds in getting the attention of the manager.

Unlike her counterparts in Zhang's early films, women characters who have become immobilized in their rural positions or household status, Wei (much like Qiuju) is the heroine of a migration, one that takes her from the countryside to the city. Even the countryside, however, is not the pure, original, primitive locale it is often imagined to be: the bus fare and the price tag of a can of Coke are but two examples of how a remote poor village, too, is part of the global capitalist circuit premised on commodified exchanges. If there is a residual primitivism here, it is the ideology of accounting that Wei embodies, an ideology that has led her to assume that the expenditure of physical effort will somehow be balanced off by due compensation—and that, if she would try just a little harder, equivalence will some-how occur between the two.

To this extent, the film's title, *Yige dou buneng shao*—literally, "not even one can be allowed to be missing"—foregrounds this ideology of accounting in an unexpected manner: the ostensible goal of bringing back the missing child becomes simultane-ously the epistemic frame over which a familiar kind of passion unfurls—one that is organized around actual, countable bodies, in a political economy in which value is still imagined in terms of successive, iterative units that can be physically sub-tracted and added, saved, stockpiled, expended, or retrieved at will.[17] Wei's migration to the city is thus really a migration to a drastically different mode of value produc-tion in which, instead of the exertions of the physical body, it is the mediatized image that arbitrates, that not only achieves her goal for her but also has the ability to make resources multiply and proliferate beyond her wildest dreams.

Despite her strenuous physical efforts (moving bricks, walking, writing out notices longhand, sleeping on the street, starving, waiting for hours), it is when Wei transforms herself, into an image on metropolitan television (fig. 2) that she finally and *effortlessly* accomplishes her mission. This is what leads Wang Yichuan to

FIGURE 2

THE TEARY IMAGE OF WEI MINZHI ON NATIONAL TELEVISION, *YIGE DOU BUNENG SHAO / NOT ONE LESS* (© GUANGXI FILM STUDIO / BEIJING NEW PICTURE DISTRI-BUTION / COLUMBIA PICTURES FILM PRODUCTION ASIA, 1999).

comment that there are two stories in Zhang's film—one is about human struggle; the other has to do with the importance of money and television and the emergence of the mediatized sign:

> Money has been playing a fundamental role throughout the entire film: it is closely linked to Wei Minzhi's job as a substitute teacher, her attempt to save chalk, the collective moving of bricks, her ride to the city, and her search [for the missing pupil] through television; what's more, money controls it all. On this basis, the film seems emphatically to be narrating or confirming a frequently forgotten "reality," namely, that television and money are playing controlling functions in people's ordinary daily life experiences. My sense is that the narrative structure of the entire film contains two stories: underneath the story about a girl as a substitute teacher lurks another story—the story about the magic of television or money....
>
> When the bumpkin-ish and flustered Wei Minzhi is brought before the TV screen by the program anchor as the interviewee making her appeal to the public, her bumpkin-ness and simplicity are no longer just bumpkin-ness and simplicity but instead turned into a powerful and conquering sign.[18]

Although I concur with Wang's observations, and although it is true that Wei has originally come to Shuiquan Village to work for fifty yuan, I would add that the "magic of . . . money" is only part of the picture here. As the film progresses, what becomes increasingly clear is less the importance of money in and of itself than the transition inscribed *in the very concept of accessing resources*—the fundamentals that drive a system and make it work, the fundamentals of which money is an important but not the exclusive component. Specifically, the film reveals how resources, rather than simply being found, are to be produced and how such production is part of a whole new system of doing things.

The return to Shuiquan Village should therefore be understood as a postmigration event in this sense, whereby the system of value making has been fundamentally revamped and the fatigued, confused, and powerless figure of the girl herself has been repurposed as an image signifying "the rural population." Recall how Wei's appeal is dramatized on television: she is featured on the program *Today in China,* aimed explicitly at educating metropolitan audiences about China's rural areas. As the anchor introduces the objectives of the program, in the background appears a bucolic, bright green lawn with pretty bluish hills in the distance and a clean white tricycle with flowers in front. This landscape fiction, in stark contrast to the landscape of Shuiquan Village we have already seen, conjures the national imaginary by drawing attention to the plight of the countryside as an urgent social problem. Anonymous and unrelated TV consumers are, in this way, interpellated as "the Chinese people": although they have never met the villagers in the flesh or seen how materially impoverished they are, the effect of Wei the image is such that it forges meaningful links among this network of strangers at the speed of virtuality.[19]

Once the rural population has been beamed and disseminated as a televised image, charitable donations pour in, and the return of Wei and Zhang to the village is accompanied by a plenitude of supplies, including especially color chalk of various kinds, which allows the students to practice writing a character each on the blackboard. As well, this return is accompanied by eager reporters with cameras, intent on documenting the village and its inhabitants with a relentless, henceforth infinitely reproducible, gaze. In a public sphere made up of electronically transmitted signals, virtuality transforms exponentially into cash, in ways that would never have been achievable by the earnest logic of physical counting on which Wei and her students once sought to rely. The closing credits offer a glimpse of the positive outcomes of this migration toward the system of the image: Zhang Huike's family debt is paid off, Wei is able to return to her own village, the girl pupil who is a fast runner has gone on to join the county's track meet, and the village is now renamed Shuiquan Village of Hope. Finally, we read this important message: "One million children drop out of school because of poverty in China every year. With financial assistance from various sources, about fifteen percent of them are able to return to school."[20] To use the title of a U.S. primetime television program in the mid-2000s, what we witness in Shuiquan Village is in effect an episode of *Extreme Makeover, Home Edition*.

If what Zhang has provided in his early films is an imaginary ethnographic treatment of China—as a decrepit primitive culture—what he has accomplished in *Not One Less* is, to my mind, a similar kind of ethnographic experiment, albeit within Chinese society itself. What is often criticized as the orientalist gaze in his early films, a gaze that produces China as exotic, erotic, corrupt, patriarchally oppressive, and so forth, for the pleasurable consumption of Western audiences, is here given a thought-provoking twist to become none other than the nationalist gaze. Whereas the object of the orientalist gaze in the early films is arguably an ahistorical China, in *Not One Less,* that object is more specifically China's rural population living in wretched conditions, especially children deprived of education. In the latter case, the similarly fetishistic and exploitative tendency of the media is underwritten not by the discourse of orientalism (read: depraved Western imperialist curiosity) but instead by the oft-repeated and by now clichéd discourse of national self-strengthening and concern for future generations (as in Lu Xun's well-known phrase "Save the children!").[21] These two seemingly opposed discourses are affined, paradoxically, through the magic of the televised image, which not only supersedes older notions of the exchange value of labor but also eradicates the validity of manual labor and production altogether. This image asserts itself now as the indomitable way of creating resources, displacing an obsolete method such as "moving one brick equals fifteen cents" to the invisible peripheries of contemporary Chinese society.

This migration toward the dominance of the mediatized image, which Zhang explores through an apparently realist contemporary story, is therefore (in a manner contrary to his critics' judgment) in tandem with the experimental attitude expressed toward vision in his early films. The humanistic impulses that guide the narrative, leading it toward the telos of collective good, proceed side by side with a firm refusal on Zhang's part to idealize or eulogize the image, including especially that of Wei making her teary plea on the screen. Instead, the latter is consciously presented as a typical media event in the new information economy. The mediatized image works, Zhang's film suggests, by deflating—and subalternizing—the currency of (human) work.

Seen in this light, *Not One Less* rejoins the many explorations of nonurban others in the Chinese films of the 1980s (such as *Huang tudi / Yellow Earth* [Chen Kaige, dir., 1984], *Liechang zhasa / On the Hunting Ground* [Tian Zhuangzhuang, dir., 1985], *Qingchun ji / Sacrificed Youth* [Zhang Nuanxin, dir., 1985], *Dao ma zei / Horse Thief* [Tian Zhuangzhuang, dir., 1986], *Liangjia funü / A Good Woman* [Huang Jianzhong, dir., 1986], *Haizi wang / King of the Children* [Chen Kaige, dir., 1987], to mention just a handful), albeit with a different emphasis. In the 1980s, when cultural introspection took shape in the aftermath of the Cultural Revolution, film offered the Fifth Generation directors and their contemporaries the exciting possibility of experimenting with technological reproducibility and artful defamiliarization. As China's economy took off at astounding rates at the turn of the twenty-first century, the anthropological-ethnographical impulses of the 1980s films have given way to a sociological one. From an investment in, or a fascination with, China's otherness, filmmaking for Zhang—at least insofar as it is evident in a work such as *Not One Less*—has shifted to a seasoned and cautionary approach to vision as social regimentation, discipline, and surveillance but above all as benevolent coercion.

In dramatizing this transmutation of human labor—the labor performed over quantifiable, slowly cumulative time or empirically countable units (bricks, hours, days, dollars, written notices)—into an instantaneous spectacle, *Not One Less* stages a schism between two irreconcilable kinds of philosophical trajectories. There is, on the one hand, the trajectory opened in accordance with a pro-Enlightenment and promodernization telos of a better and brighter future, toward which human willpower and media capability inadvertently join forces. On the other hand, as is demonstrated by the usurpatory nature of the mediatized image and its tendency to cannibalize human labor, we are confronted with an aggressive—and in all likelihood irrevocable—radicalization of the very terms of communication, communal relations, and—increasingly in the case of the People's Republic of China—communism's own founding agenda. The image's limitless potential, in this regard, cannot be seen naively as an ally to human willpower or simply as its latest instrument. Rather, its suave and speedy superficiality announces a new collective reality to which human willpower is likely to find itself increasingly subordinated and to which human beings, especially those struggling against any kind of social inequity, will need to resort just to be seen and recognized. As the ending of the film shows, it is to the mediatized image that people will give their concern and compassion, and it is such images, rather than actual suffering human bodies, that now generate capital and, with it, social influence and political power. Instead of propelling us toward the telos of an improved future, then, this other philosophical trajectory lays bare the expanse and intensity of a new kind of oppression.

This dialectical narrative method, which is as astute in its cynicism (in the etymological sense of skepticism) about mediatized visibility as it is skilled in conveying an eminently warm and sentimental story, remains Zhang's distinctive contribution. In myriad ways, his work has been about the relationship between labor and the image, about the transit from a political economy in which humans can still make the world with their physical bodies to one in which the image has taken over that function, leaving those bodies in an exotic but also abject—because superfluous—condition, a condition in which being "real" simply means being stuck—that is, being unable to undergo transmutation into cash.

As in *Happy Times*, the (positivistic) ability to see, the (positivistic) availability of vision, and the (positivistic) possibility of becoming a spectacle that are made such palpable and topical events in contemporary Chinese life are turned in *Not One Less* into the ingredients of a fable with a certain moral. But the notion of fable is rooted in the process of fabulation, and the moral at stake in Zhang's work is often elsewhere from the place at which his detractors, often driven by their own self-righteous agenda, are determined to see it. However artificial, being and becoming visible is, his recent work says, something no one can afford not to desire; yet, as this work also shows, the ever-expanding capacities for seeing and, with them, the infinite transmigrations and transmutations of cultures—national, ethnic, rural, illiterate—into commodified electronic images are part and parcel of a dominant global regime of value making that is as utterly ruthless as it is utterly creative. With the harsh *and* flexible, inhuman *and* sentimental, materialities of this regime, most critics of Zhang's work have yet, seriously, to come to terms.

213

Notes

EDITOR'S INTRODUCTION

1. Stuart Hall, "Cultural Studies and Its Theoretical Legacies," in *Cultural Studies*, ed. Lawrence Grossberg, Cary Nelson, and Paula Treichler (New York: Routledge, 1992), 285.

2. Ibid.

3. Ibid.

4. Gayatri Spivak uses the term in her Translator's Preface to *Of Grammatology* (Baltimore: Johns Hopkins University Press, 1976), lxxxii. Its meaning is discussed more fully later.

5. See Chantal Mouffe, *On the Political* (London: Routledge, 2005), esp. chap. 2, "Politics and the Political."

6. But there are others. See, for instance, John Mowitt, *Text: The Genealogy of an Antidisciplinary Object* (Durham, N.C.: Duke University Press, 1992); or Paul Bowman, *Post-Marxism Versus Cultural Studies: Theory, Politics and Intervention* (Edinburgh: Edinburgh University Press, 2007).

7. Spivak, Translator's Preface, lxxxii, italics in original.

8. Jacques Derrida, "Resistances," in his *Resistances of Psychoanalysis* (Stanford, Calif.: Stanford University Press, 1998), 35.

9. Hall, "Cultural Studies," 285.

10. Rey Chow, introduction to *Sentimental Fabulations, Contemporary Chinese Films: Attachment in the Age of Global Visibility* (New York: Columbia University Press, 2007), 11. Reproduced here as chap. 12.

11. Chow quotes from Gilles Deleuze, *Foucault*, trans. Sean Hand and foreword by Paul Bové (Minneapolis: University of Minnesota Press, 1988), 52, 58, and 59. See Chow, *Sentimental Fabulations*, 11.

12. Chow, *Sentimental Fabulations*, 11.

13. Jacques Derrida, *Of Grammatology*, trans. Gayatri Spivak (Baltimore: Johns Hopkins University Press, 1976), 63.

14. Ibid.

15. Ibid.

16. For Jacques Rancière, the political moment is a certain "kind of speech situation," which he calls one of "disagreement." It is

> one in which one of the interlocutors at once understands and does not understand what the other is saying. Disagreement is not the conflict between one who says white and another who says black. It is the conflict between one who says white and another who also says white but does not understand the same thing by it. . . .

See Jacques Rancière, *Disagreement: Politics and Philosophy* (Minneapolis: University of Minnesota Press: 1999), x. See also Benjamin Arditi, *Politics on the Edges of Liberalism: Difference, Populism, Revolution, Agitation* (Edinburgh: Edinburgh University Press 2007), 115.

17. Rey Chow, "The Political Economy of Vision in *Happy Times* and *Not One Less;* or, a Different Type of Migration," in her *Sentimental Fabulations: Contemporary Chinese Films: Attachment in the Age of Global Visibility* (New York: Columbia University Press, 2007), 165 and, in this book, chap. 13.

18. Johannes Fabian, *Time and the Other: How Anthropology Makes Its Object* (New York: Columbia University Press, 1983), 106–9.

19. Rey Chow, *Woman and Chinese Modernity: The Politics of Reading Between West and East* (Minneapolis: University of Minnesota Press, 1990), 174, n. 12.

20. Rey Chow, *Writing Diaspora: Tactics of Intervention in Contemporary Cultural Studies* (Bloomington: Indiana University Press, 1993), 1. Reproduced here as chap. 3.

21. Ernesto Laclau and Chantal Mouffe, *Hegemony and Socialist Strategy: Towards a Radical Democratic Politics* (London: Verso, 1985), 144.

22. Rey Chow, *Ethics After Idealism: Theory—Culture—Ethnicity—Reading* (Bloomington: Indiana University Press, 1998), 101.

23. Ibid.

24. Ibid., 101–2.

25. Ibid., 25.

26. Ibid., 115.

27. Ibid., 124.

28. Ibid., 124, italics in original.

29. Chow writes about the ethnic academic subject: "Her only viable option seems to be that of reproducing a specific version of herself—and her ethnicity—that has, somehow, already been endorsed and approved by the specialists of her culture" (*Ethics After Idealism*, 117).

30. Chow, *Ethics After Idealism*, 117.

31. Quoted in Rey Chow, *The Protestant Ethnic and the Spirit of Capitalism* (New York: Columbia University Press, 2002), 95.

32. Chow, *Ethics After Idealism*, 110.

33. Ibid., 117.

34. Ibid.

35. Ibid.

36. Chow, *Writing Diaspora*, 18.

37. Chow, *Ethics After Idealism*, 113.

38. Chow, *Writing Diaspora*, 11.

39. Ibid., 10–11.

40. Ibid., 11.

41. We might ask, what could be clearer to an academic or intellectual than the following act of "undeciding":

> Whatever choice I might make, I cannot say with good conscience that I have made a good choice or that I have assumed my responsibilities. Every time that I hear someone say that "I have taken a decision," or "I have assumed my responsibilities," I am suspicious because if there is responsibility or decision one cannot determine them as such or have certainty or good conscience with regard to them. If I conduct myself particularly well with regard to someone, I know that it is to the detriment of an other; of one nation to the detriment of another nation, of one family to the detriment of another family, of my friends to the detriment of other friends or non-friends, etc.

See Jacques Derrida, "Remarks on Deconstruction and Pragmatism," in *Deconstruction and Pragmatism*, ed. Chantal Mouffe (London: Routledge, 1996), 86.

42. Chow, *Ethics After Idealism*, 8.

43. Ibid.

44. Ibid., 9, italics in original.

45. Ibid., 6.

46. Ibid. For Chow's elaboration of this notion of information target fields, see Rey Chow, *The Age of the World Target: Self-Referentiality in War, Theory, and Comparative Work* (Durham, N.C.: Duke University Press, 2006) and, in this book, chap. 1.

47. Chow, *Ethics After Idealism*, 6–7.

48. Rey Chow, *Primitive Passions: Visuality, Sexuality, Ethnography, and Contemporary Chinese Cinema* (New York: Columbia University Press, 1995), 12–13.

1. THE AGE OF THE WORLD TARGET

1. For an account of the immediate consequences of the dropping of the bombs in Hiroshima, see John Hersey, *Hiroshima* (New York: Alfred A. Knopf, 1946). Hersey's account was first published in *The New Yorker*, August 31, 1946. An excerpt from the account was

reprinted on the 50th anniversary of the end of the war in *The New Yorker* (July 31, 1995), pp. 65–67. For a study of historical events and personal accounts in relation to the dropping of the second bomb, see Frank W. Chinnock, *Nagasaki: The Forgotten Bomb* (New York and Cleveland: The World Publishing Company, 1969). For related interest, see the short account of the sparing of Kyoto in Otis Cary, *Mr. Stimson's "Pet City"—The Sparing of Kyoto, 1945* (Moonlight Series No.3; Kyoto: Amherst House, Doshisha University, 1975).

2. John W. Dower, "The Bombed: Hiroshimas and Nagasakis in Japanese Memory," *Diplomatic History* 19.2 (Spring 1995), pp. 275–95; the quotation is on 281. See also Ian Buruma, *The Wages of Guilt: Memories of War in Germany and Japan* (New York: Farrar, Straus & Giroux, 1994): "To the majority of Japanese, Hiroshima is the supreme symbol of the Pacific War. All the suffering of the Japanese people is encapsulated in that almost sacred word: Hiroshima." Buruma criticizes the manner in which Hiroshima has become the exclusive sacred icon of martyred innocence and visions of apocalypse in Japan, often in total isolation from the rest of the history of the war. In this process of sanctifying Hiroshima, he writes, what has been forgotten is the city's status as a center of military operations during Japan's period of active aggression against other countries such as China. "At the time of the bombing, Hiroshima was the base of the Second General Headquarters of the Imperial Army (the First was in Tokyo)," p. 106. Buruma offers accounts of the Rape of Nanjing and the varied postwar Japanese reactions to Japanese war crimes; see Parts Two and Three of his book.

3. Lisa Yoneyama, *Hiroshima Traces: Time, Space and the Dialectics of Memory* (Berkeley: University of California Press, 1999), p. 3.

4. See Buruma, *The Wages of Guilt,* for comparative accounts of the significance of Hiroshima and Auschwitz. Kentaro Awaya has argued that the stigmatizing of Japan, though different from that of Germany, is widely felt within Japanese circles, including the Diet itself. See Awaya, "Controversies Surrounding the Asia-Pacific War: The Tokyo War Crimes Trials," translated by Barak Kushner, in *America's Wars in Asia: A Cultural Approach to History and Memory,* edited by Philip West, Steven I. Levine, and Jackie Hiltz (Armonk, N.Y.: M. E. Sharpe, 1998), pp. 221–32.

5. For scholarly investigations of the literature, historiography, political debates, and other types of cultural discourses in postwar Japan, see, for instance, John Whittier Treat, *Writing Ground Zero: Japanese Literature and the Atomic Bomb* (Chicago and London: University of Chicago Press, 1995); Yoneyama, *Hiroshima Traces;* Yoshikuni Igarashi, *Bodies of Memory: Narratives of War in Postwar Japanese Culture, 1945–1970* (Princeton: Princeton University Press, 2000). See also the rich and informative discussions in *Living with the Bomb: American and Japanese Cultural Conflicts in the Nuclear Age,* edited by Laura Hein and Mark Selden (Armonk, N.Y.: M. E. Sharpe, 1997). For the early stages of postwar engagement with nuclear culture within the United States, see Paul Boyer, *By the Bomb's Early Light: American Thought and Culture at the Dawn of the Atomic Age* (New York:

Pantheon, 1985); reprinted with a new preface by the author (Chapel Hill and London: University of North Carolina Press, 1994).

6. "The Mushroom Cloud over Art," *The Economist* (February 25,1995), pp. 87–88.

7. The testing of the plutonium bomb on July 16, 1945, at the Trinity site in New Mexico was in the main a concept test: what was tested was the nuclear device but not the precise delivering mechanisms or the blast effects on a real target. "Between Trinity and Hiroshima, the bomb remained [to the scientists] a kind of awesome abstraction, now tested to be sure, but not yet imaginable as a weapon of war." Michael S. Sherry, *The Rise of American Air Power: The Creation of Armageddon* (New Haven and London: Yale University Press, 1987), p. 343. In his notes, Sherry appends information on calculations that were made at Trinity about possible hazards to occupying personnel (nn. 112, 113, on p. 417).

8. For an account of the shift, among U.S. military decision makers, from the older morality of not killing noncombatants to the emerging morality of total war, see Barton J. Bernstein, "The Atomic Bombings Reconsidered," *Foreign Affairs* 74:1 (January/February 1995), pp. 135–52. Murray Sayle writes that the moral line of not bombing civilians was in fact already crossed with the bombing of Dresden in February 1944; see his essay, "Letter from Hiroshima: Did the Bomb End the War?" *The New Yorker* (July 31, 1995), pp. 40–64. For a long and detailed history of the events leading up to the use of the atomic bomb, including the major scientific and political figures involved, see Richard Rhodes, *The Making of the Atomic Bomb* (New York: Simon & Schuster, 1986).

9. The gender politics of the naming of the bombs is noted by Sherry as follows:

> Dominated by men, Western science has aspired to unlock the secrets of the natural world. Often its practitioners have also sought immortality through escape from that world, a world so often associated with women and femininity. By their colloquial language, the men at Los Alamos hinted at such aspirations. . . . Femininity was weakness, masculinity was the power to transcend nature and its mortal reality. If these men entertained a male fantasy of ultimate potency, it was perhaps not coincidence that they gave their bombs masculine names (Fat Man, Little Boy). *(The Rise of American Air Power, pp. 202–3)*

By contrast, crews often gave their own bombers feminine names, since such bombers were regarded as "the symbolic repository of feminine forces of unpredictable nature which men could not control" (*The Rise of American Air Power*, p. 215).

10. For a personal account of these events, see Philip Morrison, "Recollections of a Nuclear War," *Scientific American* 273.2 (August 1995), pp. 42–46. A neutron engineer, Morrison was one of the many physicists enlisted to work on the Manhattan Project in Chicago and Los Alamos.

11. Evan Thomas, "Why We Did It," *Newsweek* (July 24, 1995), p. 28. See also Hersey, *Hiroshima*, pp. 107–8, and Buruma: "There was . . . something . . . which is not often

219

mentioned: the Nagasaki bomb exploded right over the area where outcasts and Christians lived" (*The Wages of Guilt*, p. 100).

12. See Sherry, *The Rise of American Air Power*, especially chapters 8 and 9, pp. 219–300.

13. "According to President Truman, on his part the decision to use the atomic bomb was taken without any second thoughts." Monica Braw, *The Atomic Bomb Suppressed: American Censorship in Occupied Japan* (Armonk and London: M. E. Sharpe, 1991), p. 138. Braw's source is Harry S. Truman, *Year of Decisions*, Vol. I of *Memoirs* (Garden City, N.Y.: Doubleday, 1955), p. 302. Sayle writes that

> No one ever made a positive decision to drop the bomb on Hiroshima, only a negative one: not to interfere with a process that had begun years before, in very different circumstances. Truman later described it as "not any decision that you had to worry about," but a decision implies a choice, and Truman never contemplated, or even heard suggested, any delay, or any alternative to the bomb's use on a Japanese city. ("Letter from Hiroshima," 54)

See also Osborn Elliott, "Eyewitness," *Newsweek* (July 24, 1995):

> Harry Truman . . . buried any qualms he might have had. At a press conference in 1947 he told reporters, "I didn't have any doubts at the time." He said the decision had saved 250,000 American lives. In later years Truman would raise the number of lives saved to half a million or a million. "I'd do it again," Truman said in 1956. In 1965, seven years before he died, he repeated that he "would not hesitate" to drop the A-bomb. (30)

For a detailed account of the decision-making process (by top military personnel and scientists as well as Truman) that led up to the dropping of the bombs, see Bernstein, "The Atomic Bombings Reconsidered."

14. Martin Heidegger, *The Question Concerning Technology and Other Essays*, translated and with an introduction by William Lovitt (New York: Harper Colophon Books, 1977), p. 135. Elsewhere, I have discussed in greater detail the manner in which modern technology, which is aimed at facilitating global "communication" in the broadest sense of the word, has paradoxically led to the increasing intangibility of, and, for some, the disappearance of, the material world. See Chapter VIII, "Media, Matter, Migrants," in my *Writing Diaspora: Tactics of Intervention in Contemporary Cultural Studies* (Bloomington and Indianapolis: Indiana University Press, 1993).

15. Heidegger, "The Thing," *Poetry, Language, Thought*, translated and with an introduction by Albert Hofstadter (New York: Harper Colophon Books, 1975), p. 166.

16. Paul Virilio, *War and Cinema: The Logistics of Perception* (1984), translated by Patrick Camiller (New York and London: Verso, 1989), 20. Virilio's other works, in particular

Pure War (with Sylvère Lotringer), translated by Mark Polizzotti (New York: Semiotext(e), 1983), are also germane to this topic.

17. Virilio, *The Vision Machine* (1988), translated by Julie Rose (Bloomington and Indianapolis: Indiana University Press, 1994), p. 49.

18. Heidegger, *Technology*, pp. 129–30.

19. It should be noted, however, that in the interest of making a philosophical argument about "man" in the singular, Heidegger himself is unwilling to equate the developments of modern science and technology he is describing with the term "Americanism" (see 135). Instead, he defines "Americanism" as that which is "an as-yet-uncomprehended species of the gigantic, the gigantic that is itself still inchoate and does not as yet originate at all out of the complete and gathered metaphysical essence of the modern age" (Appendix 12, 153).

20. Quoted in Virilio, *War and Cinema*, p. 4.

21. On August 10, the day after the Nagasaki bombing, when Truman realized the magnitude of the mass killing and the Japanese offered a conditional surrender requiring continuation of the emperor, the president told his cabinet that he did not want to kill any more women and children. . . . After two atomic bombings, the horror of mass death had forcefully hit the president, and he was willing to return partway to the older morality—civilians might be protected from the A-bombs. But he continued to sanction the heavy conventional bombing of Japan's cities, with the deadly toll that napalm, incendiaries, and other bombs produced. Between August 10 and August 14—the war's last day, on which about 1,000 American planes bombed Japanese cities, some delivering their deadly cargo after Japan announced its surrender—the United States probably killed more than 15,000 Japanese. (Bernstein, "The Atomic Bombings Reconsidered," pp. 147–48)

    In *The Rise of American Air Power*, Sherry argues that the United States' aerial attacks on Japan stemmed from strategic and emotional reasons:

    > The ultimate fury of American aerial devastation came against Japan not because it was more fanatical, but because it was relatively weaker. Germany's strength and tenacity gave the Allies little choice but to resort to invasion because Germany would not surrender without it. It was the relative ease of attacking Japan by air that tempted Americans into the fullest use of air power. As an image, Japan's fanaticism was real enough in the minds of many Americans. But it served mainly to justify, a course of bombing rooted in strategic circumstances and the emotional need for vengeance. (246)

    For records of how ordinary Americans were overwhelmingly in favor of using the bombs against Japan, see Sadao Asada, "The Mushroom Cloud and National Psyches: Japanese and American Perceptions of the Atomic-Bomb Decision, 1945–1995," in Hein and Selden, eds., *Living with the Bomb*, pp. 173–201. According to Asada, a Gallup poll on August 16, 1945 showed 85 percent of respondents in approval; a later, Roper poll showed that 53.5 percent endorsed the bombing of both cities and that an additional 22.7 percent regretted that the United States had not quickly used more atomic bombs before Japan had a chance to surrender (177). See also Boyer, *By the Bomb's Early Light*, for reactions in the United States to the scientific and cultural implications of the arrival of the atomic age.

22. Virilio, *War and Cinema*, p. 6.

23. See Michel Foucault, *The Order of Things: An Archaeology of the Human Sciences*, translated by Alan Sheridan (London: Tavistock Publications, 1970). Foucault means by "episteme" not simply a concept or an idea but a particular relation between "reality" and representation, a relation which produces knowledge (i.e., which exists as a condition for the possibility of knowledge) and which shifts with different historical periods.

24. Ironically, this partnership attests to what Freud, in the famous exchange with Einstein, discusses as the ambivalence of war, which for him advanced as much as threatened civilization. See the section "Why War?" (1932/33) in James Strachey et al., eds., *The Standard Edition of the Complete Psychological Works of Sigmund Freud* (London: Hogarth Press, 1964), Vol. 22, pp. 197–215.

25. Virilio, *War and Cinema*, p. 4.

26. For a series of informative discussions about the United States' cold war military ideology, in particular nuclear ideology, see Hugh Gusterson, *People of the Bomb: Portraits of America's Nuclear Complex* (Minneapolis and London: University of Minnesota Press, 2004).

27. Dower, "The Bombed," p. 2.

28. Dower points out that Japan's conversion to nonmilitary manufacturing activities in the postwar years was greatly facilitated by its previously diverse and sophisticated wartime technology. See the chapter "The Useful War" in his *Japan in War and Peace: Selected Essays* (New York: The New Press, 1993), in particular pp. 14–16.

29. Notably, Japan's rise to supreme economic power in the 1970s and 1980s triggered in the United States a new rhetoric of anxiety and hostility—a rhetoric that is, Dower argues, in fact rooted in the racist attitudes toward Japan in the Second World War. See his discussion of this point in *War Without Mercy: Race and Power in the Pacific War* (New York: Pantheon Books, 1986), pp. 311–17.

30. See Sherry, *The Rise of American Air Power*, pp. 204–18, for an account of the *distance* from the enemy that occurs both because of the nature of air combat and because of the demands of aviation that arise outside of combat. In the history of air war, airmen were conditioned to "see themselves as an elite for whom performance of professional skills—a mastery of technique—was more important than engaging an enemy. Before they went into combat and again when they came out of it, powerful factors of class, education, and policy strengthened their status and their elite image" (p. 213).

31. Tim Weiner, "Pentagon Envisioning a Costly Internet for War," *The New York Times,* November 13, 2004, A1. The phrase "God's-eye view" is reported to be used by Robert J. Stevens, chief executive of the Lockheed Martin Corporation, the United States' biggest military contractor.

32. Karl von Clausewitz, *On War,* edited and translated by Michael Howard and Peter Paret (Princeton: Princeton University Press, 1976), 184. See also Book One, Chapter Three, "On Military Genius" (pp. 100–112) for more extended discussions.

33. Buruma reports that at a United Nations Conference on Disarmament Issues in Hiroshima in July 1992, "an American Harvard professor argued that the Hiroshima bombing 'ended World War II and saved a million Japanese lives.' He also added that the horror of this event had helped to prevent nuclear wars ever since, and thus in effect Hiroshima and Nagasaki saved millions more lives" (*The Wages of Guilt,* 105). See also the account by Mary Palevsky Granados, "The Bomb 50 Years Later: The Tough Question Will Always Remain," *Los Angeles Times Magazine* (June 25, 1995), pp. 10–11, 28–30. Granados was shocked to hear Hans Bethe, the man who was the head of the Los Alamos Lab's Theoretical Physics Division during the time of the war and "who has been called America's most influential advocate of nuclear disarmament, emphatically confirm that "the first use of nuclear armaments was necessary and correct" (p. 28).

34. Richard Nixon visited Hiroshima in 1964, four years before he became president, and Jimmy Carter visited Hiroshima during the late 1980s, on one of his many trips to Japan after he had left office. Neither expressed regret for what was done by the United States during the war. In April 1995, Bill Clinton (consistent with the position taken by Ronald Reagan in August 1985 and by George Bush in a televised interview in December 1991) declared that the United States did not owe Japan an apology for using the atomic bombs and that Truman had made the right decision "based on the facts he had before him." See Robert Jay Lifton and Greg Mitchell, *Hiroshima in America: Fifty Years of Denial* (New York: Grosset/Putnam, 1995), 211–22; Asada, "The Mushroom Cloud and National Psyches," p. 182.

35. It should be pointed out, however, that despite the massive destructions over the decades, attitudes toward the United States in some of these areas remain ambivalent rather than straightforwardly hostile. For instance, in a country that was devastated by U.S. military forces and weapons such as Vietnam, there is, ironically, widespread welcome of the return of American businesses today.

36. See Jacqueline Rose's persuasive discussion of this point in "'Why War?'" the first chapter of *Why War? Psychoanalysis, Politics, and the Return to Melanie Klein* (Oxford and Cambridge, Mass.: Blackwell 1993), pp. 15–40.

37. Dower, *War Without Mercy,* p. 127. Besides Gorer, the notable academics who studied the Japanese national character listed by Dower include Margaret Mead, Gregory Bateson, Ruth Benedict, Clyde Kluckhohn, and Alexander Leighton (p. 119). Of course, these academics did not come to the same conclusions.

38. Dower, *War Without Mercy*, p. 10.

39. Braw, *The Atomic Bomb Suppressed*, p. 142. For details of the censoring of information about the atomic bomb in the aftermath of the Second World War, see in particular chapters 1, 2, 8, 9, 10 of Braw's book.

40. Braw, *The Atomic Bomb Suppressed*, p. 151. Notably, such suppression of information took place *even as Supreme Commander Douglas MacArthur publicly emphasized the virtues of the freedom of the press and freedom of speech.* (MacArthur issued a Directive for the Freedom of Speech and Freedom of the Press in Tokyo on September 10, 1945, and reimposed censorship on the Japanese press on September 18.) From being simply a routine military undertaking that was negative in its function, censorship was transformed into a positive, essential tool, a tool which would assist in the virtuous task of helping Japan emerge from defeat as a democratic, peace-loving nation; see pages 143–56 of Braw's book for an extended discussion. For an account of how the censorship of reports on the human effects of the bombs took place at the same time that U.S. scientists went to Hiroshima and Nagasaki to study the remains of Japanese victims' bodies for the purpose of documenting scientific information, see Gusterson, *People of the Bomb*, pp. 63–72. For an account of the voluntary censorship exercised by Japanese people, in particular the *hibakusha*, the victims of the bombs, after the war, see Braw, "Hiroshima and Nagasaki: The Voluntary Silence," in Hein and Selden, eds., *Living with the Bomb*, pp. 155–72. See also Igarashi, *Bodies of Memory*, Chapter 1 (pp. 19–46), for a revaluation of the myths, historical events, and social discourses that helped produce, in Japan as well as in the United States, the foundational narrative of U.S.-Japan postwar relations.

41. Sherry, *The Rise of American Air Power*, p. 351.

42. Yoneyama, *Hiroshima Traces*, p. 13, p. 15.

43. See for instance, the discussion of the "inhuman face of war" in John Keegan, *The Face of Battle* (London: Jonathan Cape, 1976), pp. 319–34.

44. Sherry, *The Rise of American Air Power*, p. 253.

45. H. D. Harootunian, "Postcoloniality's Unconscious/Area Studies' Desire," in *Learning Places: The After Lives of Area Studies*, edited by Masao Miyoshi and H. D. Harootunian (Durham and London: Duke University Press, 2002), p. 155.

46. Bruce Cumings, "Boundary Displacement: The State, the Foundations, and Area Studies during and after the Cold War," in Miyoshi and Harootunian, eds., *Learning Places*, p. 261. This essay offers an eye-opening account, chock full of details and personalities, of the history of area studies from before the postwar years to the present.

47. Edward W. Said, *Orientalism* (New York: Pantheon Books, 1978), p. 290. As I indicated in the introduction, the teaching of language and literature, too, is (contrary to Said's generalization) a vital part of some area studies programs, though there are, obviously, different practices among the various "areas" being targeted.

48. Cumings, "Boundary Displacement," pp. 264–65.

49. Said, *Orientalism*, p. 301.

50. See my discussions about the pedagogy and politics of Asian studies in American universities in chapters I and VI of *Writing Diaspora*.

51. I am indebted to Richard H. Okada for this suggestion, which he offers in a discussion of the status of Japanese literature in area studies. Following the work of William Epstein, Okada argues that there is a close parallel between the reading habits advocated by New Criticism and cold war strategies—a parallel which finds itself reproduced in postwar Japanologists' tendency to essentialize and aestheticize Japan as an iconic, exclusionary object of study. See Okada, "Areas, Disciplines, and Ethnicity," in: Miyoshi and Harootunian, eds., *Learning Places*, pp. 190–205; the mention of translation and breaking military codes is on p. 197.

52. For a collection of essays that focuses on the predicament of accepted historical representations of the Asia-Pacific War(s) in the mid-twentieth century, see *Perilous Memories: The Asia-Pacific War(s)*, ed. Takeshi Fujitani, Geoffrey M. White, and Lisa Yoneyama (Durham and London: Duke University Press, 2001).

53. Harootunian, "Postcoloniality's Unconscious/Area Studies' Desire," p. 151. Using the study of Japan as his example, Bernard S. Silberman explains it in this manner:

> Area studies begins with notions of fixed substance and cannot provide us with a real understanding of what goes on in the lives of the Japanese. Japan is not a fixed entity of any sort. There is no essential personality nor is there an essential Japaneseness. What is incontrovertibly Japanese is the axis along which the "bargaining" takes place. The axis doesn't require a genealogy, it is there and understood to be the product of a historical but not a substantive *process*. ("The Disappearance of Modern Japan: Japan and Social Science," in Miyoshi and Harootunian, eds. *Learning Places*, p. 317)

54. For an informed discussion of the implications of Anglocentrism in postcolonial studies, see the contributions to the issue on postcolonial studies and comparative literature, *Comparative Studies of South Asia, Africa and the Middle East* 23: 1&2 (2003); in particular Wail S. Hassan and Rebecca Saunders, "Introduction," pp. 18–31.

55. Harootunian, "Postcoloniality's Unconscious/Area Studies' Desire," p. 167.

56. See the exclusive prison interview with the prime suspect, Timothy McVeigh, in David H. Hackworth and Peter Annin, "The Suspect Speaks Out," *Newsweek* (July 3, 1995), pp. 23–26. Eventually found guilty, McVeigh was executed in 2001 for his crime; he remained defiant to the end. His accomplice, Terry Nichols, is serving a life sentence without the possibility of parole.

57. Although this chapter has been substantially revised and lengthened since its first publication, I remain grateful to Beth Bailey, David Farber, James A. Fujii, Peter Gibian, Jackie Hiltz, Austin Meredith, and Susan Neel for their valuable contributions to the initial version.

2. THE POSTCOLONIAL DIFFERENCE

1. In Hong Kong, there have all along been other ethnic groups in addition to the Han Chinese—a fact which I have been obliged to understand since an early age because I happen to come from a Muslim family. Under the circumstances of British hegemony, the non-Chinese ethnic minorities (many of whom had migrated from the Indian sub-continent and Southeast Asia), too, typically identified—and identified with—English-using rather than Chinese-using channels as their means to social success. Obviously, the complex histories of these minorities deserve a much more nuanced examination than I can provide here. However, because those who consider themselves Chinese (including Chinese Muslims, such as members of my family) make up over 97% of Hong Kong's population to this day, I don't think it is entirely erroneous to refer to the implications of knowing Chinese as my primary example of cultural subordination in this brief discussion.

2. For a critique of this general trend of privileging mobile identities, see Pheng Cheah, "Given culture: rethinking cosmopolitical freedom in transnationalism," *boundary 2*, 24(2) Summer 1997, pp. 157–197.

3. Michel Foucault, *The Order of Things: An Archaeology of the Human Sciences*, trans. from the French (London: Tavistock, 1970).

4. For a discussion of the ambiguous status of race in Foucault's work, see Ann Laura Stoler, *Race and the Education of Desire: Foucault's* History of Sexuality *and the Colonial Order of Things* (Durham and London: Duke UP, 1995).

5. Among other works, I have found the essays collected in part two ("Disciplining knowledge") of *Contemporary Postcolonial Theory: A Reader*, ed. Padmini Mongia (London: Edward Arnold, 1996) useful for my thinking about the relation between postcolonial studies and cultural legitimation. In particular, I have learned from the arguments by Biodun Jeyifo, Dipesh Chakrabarty and Paul Gilroy.

3. FROM *WRITING DIASPORA:* INTRODUCTION: LEADING QUESTIONS

1. Stephen Owen, "The Anxiety of Global Influence: What Is World Poetry?" *The New Republic*, November 19, 1990: 28–32. The piece is a review of Bei Dao, *The August Sleepwalker*, trans. Bonnie S. McDougall (London: Anvil Press, 1988; New Directions, 1990).

2. An indictment of contemporary Chinese poetry that is remarkably similar in its racist spirit to Owen's is another review of *The August Sleepwalker*, by W. J. F. Jenner. A few examples from Jenner: "great poetry can no longer, be written in Chinese"; "Bei Dao's lines rarely have the inevitability, the weight, the structure, the authority of real poetry"; "[The modern Chinese poets] Wen Yidou and Xu Zhimo are not up there with Auden and Yeats"; "translations of modern Chinese poetry into English . . . do not lose all that much, because there is not much in the original language to be lost." *The Australian*

Journal of Chinese Affairs, no. 23 (January 1990): 193–95. I am grateful to Gregory B. Lee for this reference.

3. Michelle Yeh, "The Anxiety of Difference—A Rejoinder," p. 8. This essay has been published in Chinese in *Jintian (Today)*, no. 1 (1991), pp. 94–96. The page reference for the English version is taken from Yeh's manuscript.

4. Harry Harding, "From China, with Disdain: New Trends in the Study of China," *Asian Survey* 22.10 (October 1982): 934–58.

5. Colin MacKerras, *Western Images of China* (Hong Kong: Oxford University Press, 1989), p. 3.

6. Rey Chow, "Violence in the Other Country: China as Crisis, Spectacle, and Woman," in *Third World Women and the Politics of Feminism*, ed. Chandra Talpade Mohanty, Lourdes Torres, and Ann Russo (Bloomington: Indiana University Press, 1991), pp. 81–100.

7. Sigmund Freud, "Mourning and Melancholia," *Collected Papers*, vol. iv, trans. Joan Riviere (New York: Basic Books, 1959), pp. 152–70.

8. The mutual implications between "translation" and "betrayal" as indicated in an expression like "*Traduttore, traditore*" and their etymological relations to "tradition" will have to be the subject of a separate study.

9. Naoki Sakai, "Modernity and Its Critique: The Problem of Universalism and Particularism," in *Postmodernism and Japan*, ed. Masao Miyoshi and H. D. Harootunian (Durham: Duke University Press, 1989) (formerly *South Atlantic Quarterly*, 87.3, [Summer 1988]), p. 105; my emphasis.

10. Naoki Sakai, "Modernity and Its Critique," pp. 113–14; emphases in the original.

11. Gayatri Chakravorty Spivak, "Who Claims Alterity?" in *Remaking History*, ed. Barbara Kruger and Phil Marian (Seattle: Bay Press, 1989) p. 281.

12. Tahi Barlow, "'Theorizing Woman': *Funu, Guojia, Jiating* [Chinese Women, Chinese State, Chinese Family]," *Genders* 10 (Spring 1991): 132–60.

13. G. Balandier, "The Colonial Situation: A Theoretical Approach (1951)," translated from the French by Robert A. Wagoner, in Immanuel Wallerstein, *Social Change: The Colonial Situation* (New York: John Wiley & Sons Inc. 1966), pp. 34–61.

14. This paragraph and the next are taken, with modifications, from Rey Chow, "Digging an Old Well: The Labor of Social Fantasy" in *Feminismo y teoría fílmica*, ed. Guilia Colaizzi (Madrid: Ediciones Cátedra, forthcoming). This essay is part of a longer study of contemporary Chinese cinema. I am grateful to Teresa de Lauretis for telling me that I needed to clarify my point about "coloniality."

15. The official position in China today is that nothing of real significance happened in Tiananmen Square in May and June of 1989, and that it is best not to recall the demonstrations and the victims in public. In an interview with Chinese and non-Chinese reporters in early 1991, the Chinese Premier Li Peng responded to questions about the Tiananmen Massacre with the following kind of "rationality": "It has already been two years since the June Fourth incident; there is no need to discuss it any more. . . . Under

the urgent circumstances of the time, had the Chinese government not acted decisively, we would not be able to have the stability and economic prosperity we see in China today." "Zhong wai jizhe zhaodaihua shang Li Peng huida wenti" (Li Peng's responses to questions at the press conference for Chinese and foreign reporters), *Ming Pao Daily News*, Vancouver Edition, April 11, 1991; my translation.

16. Arif Dirlik, "The Predicament of Marxist Revolutionary Consciousness: Mao Zedong, Antonio Gramsci, and the Reformation of Marxist Revolutionary Theory," *Modern China* 9.2 (April 1983): 186.

17. For a historical account of how Maoism inspired antiestablishment intellectuals' thinking in France in the 1960s and 1970s, see Lisa Lowe, *Critical Terrains: French and British Orientalisms* (Ithaca: Cornell University Press, 1991), pp. 136–89.

18. Harding, "From China," p. 939.

19. Nancy Armstrong and Leonard Tennenhouse, "Introduction: Representing Violence, or 'How the West Was Won,'" in *The Violence of Representation: Literature and the History of Violence*, ed. Nancy Armstrong and Leonard Tennenhouse (London: Routledge, 1989), p. 8.

20. Gayatri Chakravorty Spivak, "Three Women's Texts and a Critique of Imperialism," *"Race," Writing, and Difference* (formerly *Critical Inquiry* 12.1, and 13.1), ed. Henry Louis Gates Jr. (Chicago: University of Chicago Press, 1986), p. 267; emphasis in original.

21. Michel de Certeau, *The Practice of Everyday Life*, trans, Steven Rendall (Berkeley: University of California Press, 1984), p. 183; emphases in the original.

22. What Spivak criticizes as the "conflation of the indigenous elite women abroad with the subaltern" is but one prominent aspect of this current trend. "Who Claims Alterity?" p. 273.

23. Armstrong and Tennenhouse, "Introduction," p. 25.

24. Benjamin Disraeli, *Collected Edition of the Novels and Tales by the Right Honorable B. Disraeli, vol. IV—Tancred or The New Crusade* (London: Longmans, Green, 1871), p. 141. I am grateful to Prabhakara Jha for locating this reference for me.

25. Khachig Tölöyan, "The Nation-State and Its Others: In Lieu of a Preface," *Diaspora* 1.1 (Spring 1991): 6.

26. William Safran, "Diasporas in Modern Societies: Myths of Homeland and Return," *Diaspora* 1.1 (Spring 1991): 87.

27. Michel Foucault, "Intellectuals and Power: A Conversation between Michel Foucault and Gilles Deleuze," *Language, Counter-Memory, Practice: Selected Essays and Interviews*, edited and with an introduction by Donald F. Bouchard and Sherry Simon (Ithaca: Cornell University Press, 1977), p. 208.

28. For a discussion of the limits imposed by "field" and "fieldwork," see James Clifford, "Traveling Cultures," *Cultural Studies*, ed. Lawrence Grossberg, Cary Nelson, Paula Treichler (New York: Routledge, 1991), pp. 96–116. In ethnography at least, Clifford advocates cross-cultural studies of travel and travellers as supplements to the more traditional notion of "fieldwork."

29. De Certeau, *Everyday Life*, p. 36.

30. George J. Stigler, *The Intellectual and the Marketplace*, enlarged edition (Cambridge, Mass.: Harvard University Press, 1984), p. 145.

31. De Certeau, *Everyday Life*, p. 37.

32. Even though Derrida points out in *Of Grammatology* that Chinese writing "functioned as a sort of European hallucination" (p. 80), his own project does not go beyond the ethnocentrism of a repeated reference to the other culture purely as a bearer—a sign—of the limits of the West. Gayatri Spivak puts it this way: "There is . . . the shadow of a geographical pattern that falls upon the first part of the book. The relationship between logocentrism and ethnocentrism is indirectly invoked in the very first sentence of the 'Exergue.' Yet, paradoxically, and almost by a reverse ethnocentrism, Derrida insists that logocentrism is a property of the *West*. He does this so frequently that a quotation would be superfluous. Although something of the Chinese prejudice of the West is discussed in Part I, the *East* is never seriously studied or deconstructed in the Derridean text. Why then must it remain, recalling Hegel and Nietzsche in their most cartological humors, as the name of the limits of the text's knowledge?" Translator's Preface, *Of Grammatology* (Baltimore: Johns Hopkins University Press, 1976), p. lxxxii; emphases in the original. By insisting that logocentrism is "Western," Derrida forecloses the possibility that similar problems of the "proper" exist in a deep-rooted ways in the non-West and require a deconstruction that is at least as thorough and sophisticated as the one he performs for "his" tradition.

33. William Hinton, *Fanshen* (New York: Vintage Books, 1966). For an informative account of Western feminism's borrowings from the Chinese Communist Revolution, see Sally Taylor Lieberman, "Visions and Lessons: 'China' in Feminist Theory-Making, 1966–1977," *Michigan Feminist Studies*, no. 6 (Fall 1991), pp. 91–107.

34. For detailed critical discussions on this topic, see Arif Dirlik, *Revolution and History: Origins of Marxist Historiography in China, 1919–1937* (Berkeley: University of California Press, 1978), *The Origins of Chinese Communism* (New York: Oxford University Press, 1989), and *Anarchism in the Chinese Revolution* (Berkeley: University of California Press, 1991).

35. Terry Eagleton, "Defending the Free World," *Socialist Register 1990*, ed. Ralph Miliband, Leo Panitch, John Saville (London: The Merlin Press, 1990), p. 91; my emphasis.

36. Lynn Pan, *Sons of the Yellow Emperor: The Story of the Overseas Chinese* (London: Secker and Warburg, 1990), pp. 363, 373.

37. Dirlik, "Predicament," pp. 203, 184.

38. The danger of a book such as Nien Cheng's *Life and Death in Shanghai* (London: Penguin, 1988) lies precisely in its blindness to what is embraced as a heavenly alternative to Chinese communism—the United States of America.

39. "The non-analysis of fascism is one of the important political facts of the past thirty years. It enables fascism to be used as a floating signifier, whose function is essentially

that of denunciation. The procedures of every form of power are suspected of being fascist, just as the masses are in their desires. There lies beneath the affirmation of the desire of the masses for fascism a historical problem which we have yet to secure the means of resolving." Michel Foucault, "Power and Strategies," in *Power/Knowledge: Selected Interviews and Other Writings 1972–1977*, ed. Colin Gordon, trans. Colin Gordon, Leo Marshall, John Mepham, Kate Soper (New York: Pantheon Books, 1980), p. 139.

40. Foucault, "Power and Strategies," p. 135.

4. BRUSHES WITH THE-OTHER-AS-FACE

1. Theodor W. Adorno has likewise asserted the indispensability of stereotypes *in art*; however, his view about stereotypes in the contemporary media is a negative one. In the latter situation, he writes, dependency on stereotypes is really a result of the stultifying culture industry: "Since stereotypes are an indispensable element of the organization and anticipation of experience, preventing us from falling into mental disorganization and chaos, no art can entirely dispense with them. Again, the functional change is what concerns us. The more stereotypes become reified and rigid in the present set-up of cultural industry, the more people are tempted to cling desperately to clichés which seem to bring some order into the otherwise ununderstandable" ("How to Look at Television," in *Culture Industry: Selected Essays on Mass Culture*, ed. with an intro. By J. M. Bernstein [London: Routledge, 1991], p. 147). This chapter was originally published in *The Quarterly of Film, Radio and Television* 8, no. 3 (1954), pp. 213–35.

2. See Fredric Jameson, "On Cultural Studies," in *The Identity in Question*, ed. John Rajchman (New York: Routledge, 1995), pp. 251–95. In her detailed study, Mireille Rosello also states that she does not believe "it is very useful to argue with stereotypes, to try and confound them, to attack their lack of logic or common sense" (Mireille Rosello, *Declining the Stereotype: Ethnicity and Representation in French Cultures* [Hanover, N.H.: Dartmouth College, University Press of New England, 1998], p. 16). However, the solution she proposes, namely, a way of reading stereotypes that involves the double movement of participation and refusal, of inhabiting while displacing, is fundamentally not different from a deconstructive, and defamiliarizing kind of vigilance that places stereotypes "under constant surveillance" (p. 34). Rosello calls this double movement "declining" (playing on both the conventional and grammatical senses of the word): "Declining a stereotype is a way of depriving it of, its harmful potential by highlighting its very nature" (11). Although I am impressed with Rosello's scholarship, I do not find her solution a theoretically satisfactory one to the issues I am raising.

3. Erving Goffmann, *Stigma: Notes on the Management of Spoiled Identity* (Englewood Cliffs, N.J.: Prentice-Hall, 1963).

4. Jameson, "On Cultural Studies," p. 272.

5. Sigmund Freud, *Civilization and Its Discontents* (1930), in *The Standard Edition of the Complete Psychological Works of Sigmund Freud*, trans. under the general editorship of James Strachey (London: Hogarth, 1961), 21:57–145.

6. Jameson, "On Cultural Studies," p. 274, my emphasis. Jameson's much criticized argument about third world literature as being almost always about "national allegories" can also be understood in the light of these remarks about stereotypes. To that extent, national allegories are stereotypes, and Jameson's reading of third world literature is consistent with his view that stereotypes are inevitable in intercultural relations. See "Third-World Literature in the Era of Multinational Capital," *Social Text* 15 (fall 1986): 65–88. What remains to be debated—and this is the reason so many people have criticized his argument—is, of course, the question of power: who gets to mobilize stereotypes, whose stereotypes matter and become universalized, who becomes invariably stereotyped and ghettoized, and so on. See the next chapter for an extended discussion of national allegories and mimeticism in ethnic self-representation.

7. Jameson, "On Cultural Studies," p. 274. Jane M. Gaines's remark in a different context may be borrowed as a comment on the liberal solution: "Here the rhetorical flaw is in the assumption that the 'positive' image is not itself also a stereotype—that somehow it is exempted from criticism because it is not pejorative (another problem arising from the situation in which 'stereotype' has become synonymous with 'pejorative' even when stereotypes can as easily be laudatory)" (*Fire and Desire: Mixed-Race Movies in the Silent Era* [Chicago: University of Chicago Press, 2000], 261). Gaines's interesting and suggestive discussion of stereotypy in relation to the films made by African Americans in the Silent Era can be found on pages 258–63 and throughout her book.

8. Rosello, *Declining the Stereotype*, p. 32, p. 38.

9. Richard Dyer, *The Matter of Images: Essays on Representations* (New York: Routledge, 1993), 16; emphasis in the original.

10. For a compelling critique of the biases in the Western media that are overwhelmingly in favor of Israel and in discrimination of Palestinians, for instance, see Edward W. Said, "The Ideology of Difference," in *"Race," Writing, and Difference*, ed. Henry Louis Gates (Chicago: University of Chicago Press, 1986), pp. 38–58.

5. THE POLITICS OF ADMITTANCE

1. Gayatri Chakravorty Spivak, "Subaltern Studies: Deconstructing Historiography," *Selected Subaltern Studies*, ed. Ranajit Guha and Gayatri Chakravorty Spivak, foreword by Edward Said (New York: Oxford UP, 1988), p. 28.

2. Deniz Kandiyoti, "Identity and Its Discontents: Women and the Nation," in *Colonial Discourse and Post-Colonial Theory: A Reader*, ed. and intro. Patrick Williams and Laura Chrisman (New York: Columbia UP, 1994), p. 32.

3. Mieke Bal, *Lethal Love: Feminist Literary Readings of Biblical Love Stories* (Bloomington: Indiana UP, 1987), p. 61, emphasis in the original.

4. Henry Louis Gates, Jr., "Critical Fanonism," *Critical Inquiry* 17 (Spring 1991), p. 458.

5. In certain passages of *Orphée Noir*, preface to *Anthologie de la nouvelle poésie nègre et malgache* (Paris: Presses Universitaires de France, 1948), Sartre offers the view that negritude, as a subjective, existential, and ethnic idea, is insufficient as a means of asserting a future society without race discrimination, and that it must by necessity pass into the objective, positive, and exact idea of the proletariat. "Thus," he writes, "negritude is the root of its own destruction, it is a transition and not a conclusion, a means and not an ultimate end." These passages are quoted by Fanon in *Black Skin, White Masks,* trans. Charles Lam Markmann (New York: Grove Weidenfeld, 1967), pp. 132–33. Fanon strongly objects to Sartre's view: "I felt that I had been robbed of my last chance. . . . In terms of consciousness, the black consciousness is held out as an absolute density, as filled with itself, a stage preceding any invasion, any abolition of the ego by desire. Jean-Paul Sartre, in this work, has destroyed black zeal" (pp. 132–34).

6. See for instance Homi Bhabha, "Remembering Fanon: Self, Psyche and the Colonial Condition," in *Colonial Discourse and Post-Colonial Theory: A Reader,* pp. 112–23 (this essay was originally published as the foreword to Frantz Fanon, *Black Skin, White Masks* [London: Pluto, 1986], pp. vii–xxvi); Mary Ann Doane, *Femmes Fatales Feminism, Film Theory, Psychoanalysis* (New York: Routledge, 1991) pp. 215–27; Diana Fuss, "Interior Colonies: Frantz Fanon and the Politics of Identification," *diacritics* 24: 2–3 (Summer-Fall 1994), pp. 20–42 (this essay contains a useful and detailed bibliography of works on Fanon); Gwen Bergner, "Who Is That Masked Woman? or, The Role of Gender in Fanon's *Black Skin, White Masks*," *PMLA* 110: 1 (January 1995), pp. 75–88 (I share many of the observations of Bergner's essay, which was published after this present chapter was first completed and presented as a paper at the conference on Intellectuals and Communities in Sydney, Australia, in early December 1994); *The Fact of Blackness: Frantz Fanon and Visual Representation,* ed. Alan Read (Seattle: Bay, 1996) (I had access to this collection only after the final revisions of this chapter had already been completed). See also the comments on the various readings of Fanon by Edward Said, Abdul JanMohammed, Benita Parry, and Homi Bhabha among others in Gates, "Critical Fanonism." For biographical studies of Fanon, see Peter Geismar, *Fanon* (New York: Dial, 1971) and Irene Gendzier, *Frantz Fanon: A Critical Study* (New York: Grove, 1973).

7. For an example of a detailed theoretical reflection on community, see Jean-Luc Nancy, *The Inoperative Community,* edited by Peter Connor, trans. Peter Connor et al., foreword by Christopher Fynsk (Minneapolis: U of Minnesota P, 1991). Nancy deconstructs— de-works—the notion of "community" and argues for "mortal truth" and "limit" as the basis of a community's sharing.

8. I am using the word "race" here not only to signify "racial difference" or "racial identity" in a neutral sense. More importantly, "race" signifies the major historical legacy of

colonialism—namely, the injustices and atrocities committed against so-called "peoples of color" in the name of their racial inferiority. "Race" as such is thus implicated in the history of racism. To that extent I find the following analytic formulation of "race" useful: "Race is not part of an unproblematic continuum alongside discursive categories such as linguistic rupture, syncretism, hybridity and so on. In all kinds of oppositional post-colonialism (within settler countries themselves and without) race was part of a larger struggle for self-respect. The post-colonial is the single most important phenomenon in which it played such a decisive role." Vijay Mishra and Bob Hodge, "What Is Post(-)colonialism?" in *Colonial Discourse and Post-colonial Theory: A Reader*, p. 285. This essay was originally published in *Textual Practice* 5:3 (1991), pp. 399–414.

9. Fanon, *Black Skin*, p. 116.

10. Both Bhabha and Doane, for instance, cite Fanon's line "I know nothing about her" as "proof" of how he actually deals with the woman of color. Bhabha uses the strategy of deferral: "Of the woman of colour he has very little to say. 'I know nothing about her,' he writes in *Black Skin, White Masks*. This crucial issue requires an order of psychoanalytic argument that goes well beyond the scope of my foreword. I have therefore chosen to note the importance of the problem rather than to elide it in a facile charge of 'sexism'" ("Remembering Fanon," p. 123). For more detailed criticisms of Bhabha, see Bergner, "Who Is That Masked Woman?" pp. 84–85. Doane, focusing on the white woman as the pivotal point of a racist representational economy, asserts time and again the "disappearance" of the woman of color from Fanon's analytic schema (see pp. 220–21, 222, 225 of her book). By interpreting Fanon's claim of lack of knowledge at its face value, Bhabha and Doane avoid having to deal with its most important aspect—its self-contradiction—which is a clear indication of Fanon's troubled views about colored female sexuality. By the same gesture, they also avoid having to examine closely the disturbing manner in which Fanon does, in fact, give the woman of color agency.

11. See also Fuss's discussion of what she calls "Fanon's retrieval of an essentialist discourse of black femininity" (Fuss, p. 28) in his reading of the Algerian Revolution in *A Dying Colonialism* (1959), trans. Haakon Chevalier (New York: Grove Weidenfeld, 1965). Fuss is referring to Fanon's notion that the act of mimesis—mimicry and/or masquerade—is *natural* to women.

12. Sigmund Freud, *Totem and Taboo: Some Points of Agreement Between the Mental Lives of Savages and Neurotics*, trans. James Strachey (New York: Norton), p. 146: "Thus psychoanalysis, in contradiction to the more recent views of the totemic system but in agreement with the earlier ones, requires us to assume that totemism and exogamy were intimately connected and had a simultaneous origin."

13. See Claude Levi-Strauss, *Elementary Structures of Kinship* (1949) (English translation, London, 1969); Marcel Mauss, *The Gift: The Form and Reason for Exchange in Archaic Societies* (1950), trans. W. D. Halls, foreword by Mary Douglas (New York: Norton, 1990).

233

14. Gayle Rubin, "The Traffic in Women: Notes on the 'Political Economy' of Sex," in *Toward an Anthropology of Women,* ed. Rayna Reiter (New York: Monthly Review, 1975), p. 174.

15. See for instance René Girard, *Violence and the Sacred,* trans. Patrick Gregory (Baltimore: Johns Hopkins UP, 1977), in particular chapters 8 and 9. For a feminist analysis of the Freudian framework of community formation, see Juliet Mitchell's discussions in *Feminism and Psychoanalysis: Freud, Reich, Laing and Women* (New York: Vintage, 1975), in particular the conclusion.

16. Freud, "Some Psychological Consequences of the Anatomical Distinction Between the Sexes" (1925), in *Sexuality and the Psychology of Love,* edited and introduced by Philip Rieff (New York: Collier, 1963), pp. 187–88.

17. Fanon, *Black Skin,* p, 81.

18. See Gayatri Spivak's explication of these two senses of representation in "Can the Subaltern Speak?" in *Colonial Discourse and Post-Colonial Theory: A Reader,* pp. 66–111. This essay was originally published in *Marxism and the Interpretation of Culture,* ed. Cary Nelson and Larry Grossberg (Basingstoke: Macmillan Education, 1988), pp. 271–313.

19. Doane: "Fanon's analysis situates rape only as the white woman's fantasy and neglects its status as the historical relation between the white male and the black female both in the colonial context and in that of slavery" (p. 222).

20. Whether or not skin color is simply an accident in a more universal scheme of oppressive experience is a point on which Fanon remains ambivalent. For instance, in the chapter "The Man of Color and the White Woman" in *Black Skin, White Masks,* Fanon argues that blackness is, for the black man, but a coincidence that compounds his neurotic condition: "Jean Veneuse, alias René Maran, is neither more nor less a black abandonment-neurotic. And he is put back into his place, his proper place. He is a neurotic who needs to be emancipated from his infantile fantasies. And I contend that Jean Veneuse represents not an example of black-white relations, but a certain mode of behavior in a neurotic who by coincidence is black" (p. 79). And yet, if this passage clearly suggests that the black man has psychic problems *just like any other man,* Fanon is much more emphatic elsewhere about the absolutely determining power of skin color. See, for instance, p. 163 of *Black Skin, White Masks:* "It is in his corporeality that the Negro is attacked." See also the chapter "The Fact of Blackness" (*Black Skin, White Masks,* pp. 109–40) in which Fanon is primarily concerned with race as the determining factor for individual identity.

21. Fanon, *Black Skin,* pp.179–80; my emphasis.

22. "Fanon does not ignore sexual difference altogether, but he explores sexuality's role in constructing race only through rigid categories of gender. In *Black Skin, White Masks,* women are considered as subjects almost exclusively in terms of their sexual relationships with men; feminine desire is thus defined as an overly literal and limited (hetero)sexuality." Bergner, "Who Is That Masked Woman?" p. 77. See also the discussion

in Lola Young, "Missing Persons: Fantasising Black Women in *Black Skin, White Masks*," in *The Fact of Blackness*, pp. 86–101.

23. The black woman's predicament is succinctly summarized in the title of the anthology *All the Women Are White, All the Blacks Are Men, but Some of Us Are Brave* (Old Harbury, NY: Feminist P, 1982), ed. Gloria Hull, Patricia Bell Scott, and Barbara Smith.

24. See the very different analyses of black female agency in, for instance, Hazel V. Carby, *Reconstructing Womanhood: The Emergence of the Afro-American Woman Novelist* (New York: Oxford UP, 1987). Carby alerts us to how the consideration of black womanhood must take into account the sexism of black men. She also offers very different ways of reading the mulatto figure, who stands as a mediator between the races rather than simply as the offspring of black women's desire for upward social mobility (as Fanon describes it).

25. In this regard the biographical details about Fanon—that his mother was of Alsatian descent, that he grew up in Martinique thinking of himself as white and French, that he "became" a black West Indian only when he arrived in Paris, and that, however, he never afterward returned to Negritude and to the West Indies—become an interesting and thought-provoking intertext. See the brief account by Gates in "Critical Fanonism," p. 468. Gates's major source of information is Albert Memmi, review of *Fanon*, by Peter Geismar, and *Frantz Fanon*, by David Caute, *New York Times Book Review*, 14 March, 1971, p. 5.

26. Deniz Kandiyoti, "Identity and Its Discontents: Women and the Nation," p. 378; emphases in the original.

27. Rubin, "The Traffic in Women," p. 178.

28. See for instance the chapter "Concerning Violence" in *The Wretched of the Earth*, preface by Jean-Paul Sartre, trans. Constance Farrington (New York: Grove P, 1968), pp. 35–106. Fanon argues that for the colonized people, the violence of destroying the colonizer "invests their characters with positive and creative qualities. The practice of violence binds them together as a whole" and mobilizes their consciousness toward "a common cause," "a national identity," and "a collective history" (p. 93)

29. See descriptions in Fanon, *The Wretched of the Earth*, pp. 52–53, 60–61, and throughout.

30. This last possibility is the one taken up, for instance, by Homi Bhabha, who emphasizes the "ambivalence" of the imperialist's speech as a way to subvert imperialist discourse. See Bhabha, "Remembering Fanon," p. 116; "Signs Taken for Wonders: Questions of Ambivalence and Authority Under a Tree Outside Delhi, May 1817," in *"Race," Writing, and Difference*, ed. Henry Louis Gates, Jr. (Chicago: U of Chicago P, 1986), pp. 163–84. I have elsewhere critiqued Bhabha's reading of "ambivalence" as a critical gesture that makes it ultimately unnecessary to pay attention to anything other than the imperialist's speech. See the chapter "Where Have All the Natives Gone?" in *Writing Diaspora: Tactics of Intervention in Contemporary Cultural Studies* (Bloomington: Indiana UP, 1993).

31. It is important to note that Fanon conceives of the moment of decolonization as a kind of *tabula rasa:* "we have precisely chosen to speak of that kind of *tabula rasa* which characterizes at the outset all decolonization." *The Wretched of the Earth*, p. 35. Among male revolutionary thinkers, Mao Zedong's attitudes toward "the people" come readily to mind in resonance with Fanon's. For comparison, see Maurice Meisner's incisive analysis of the manner in which Mao Zedong imagined "the people" for his political purposes: "Mao Tse-tung, by declaring the Chinese people 'blank,' was driven by a utopian impulse to escape history and by an iconoclastic desire to wipe the historical-cultural slate clean. Having rejected the traditional Chinese cultural heritage, Mao attempted to fill the emotional void by an even more iconoclastic proclamation of the nonexistence of the past in the present. A new culture, Mao seemed to believe, could be fashioned *ex nihilo* on a fresh canvas, on a 'clean sheet of paper unmarred by historical blemishes.'" Meisner, *Mao's China and After: A History of the People's Republic* (a revised and expanded edition of *Mao's China*, 1977) (New York: Free P, 1986), pp. 316–17. Immanuel Wallerstein has analyzed how, because "peoplehood" is fundamentally ambiguous, it is "an instrument of flexibility" into which political movements—those based on class, for instance—always collapse. See the chapter "The Construction of Peoplehood: Racism, Nationalism, Ethnicity," in Etienne Balibar and Immanuel Wallerstein, *Race, Nation, Class: Ambiguous Identities* (London: Verso, 1991), especially pp. 84–85.

32. See also Bergner's account of what she calls black women's "double oppression or exclusion," p. 78.

33. Fuss: "Fanon's disquieting discussions of not only femininity but homosexuality—inextricably linked in Fanon as they are in Freud—have received little if any attention from his critical commentators. Passages in Fanon's corpus articulating ardent disidentifications from black and white women and from white gay men (for Fanon homosexuality is culturally white) are routinely passed over, dismissed as embarrassing, baffling, unimportant, unenlightened, or perhaps simply politically risky" (p. 30). Kobena Mercer has also pointed out that Fanon's misogyny is linked to his homophobia in a defensive masculinity revolving around castration. Mercer, "Thinking Through Homophobia in Frantz Fanon," a talk delivered at the conference entitled "Blackness and the Mind/Body Split: Discourses, Social Practices, Genders, Sexualities," October 1995, University of California, Irvine. See as well Mercer's related arguments in "Decolonisation and Disappointment: Reading Fanon's Sexual Politics," in *The Fact of Blackness*, pp. 114–25.

34. For a critique of how the study of Fanon has become a fashionable event in postcolonial criticism, see Gates, "Critical Fanonism." Gates describes Fanon as "both totem and text" (p. 457), "a composite figure, indeed, an ethnographic construct" (p. 459) that has been put together by postcolonial critics' collective desire for a global theorist. It would be interesting to juxtapose the worship of Fanon as a theoretical *leader* with the analyses of coercive group psychology as laid out in Freud's *Group Psychology and the Analysis of the Ego*, translated and edited by James Strachey (New York: Norton, 1959); see in particular chapters 7,

"Identification"; 9, "The Herd Instinct"; and 10, "The Group and the Primal Horde." As Freud points out, it is precisely the father's excesses and neuroses which "forced them [the horde], so to speak, into group psychology" (p. 56). In the process, the father becomes the group ideal, which governs the ego in the place of the ego ideal.

35. Mieke Bal, *Lethal Love*, p.36, emphasis in the original. Even though it deals with an entirely different topic, Bal's book offers many useful insights into the formation of intellectual/interpretive as well as mythic and tribal communities, a formation that often takes place at the expense of women. See in particular her chapter on the story of Samson and Delilah, a story which is, among other things, about the conflict between kinship (which is signified by loyalty to the community that is one's tribe) and sexuality (which is signified by relations with the foreigner, the "unfaithful" woman).

36. For a discussion of the problems inherent in the facile indictment of postcolonial intellectuals "selling out" or being worked over by the language of the "first world," see Sangeeta Ray and Henry Schwarz, "Postcolonial Discourse: The Raw and the Cooked," *Ariel: A Review of International English Literature* 26.1 (January 1995): 147–66. See also Victor Li, "Towards Articulation: Postcolonial Theory and Demotic Resistance," for a critique of the pitfalls of polarizing "postcolonial theory" and "demotic resistance" (same issue of *Ariel*, pp. 167–89). For a related discussion of the impasses created by moralistic dismissals of "Westernized" native intellectuals, see my reading of the debates around Zhang Yimou's films in Part II, chapter 4 of *Primitive Passions: Visuality, Sexuality, Ethnography, and Contemporary Chinese Cinema* (New York: Columbia UP, 1995).

37. In her response to the version of this chapter that was first published in *The UTS Review*, 1.1 (July 1995): 5–29, Susan Schwartz points out that Fanon did in fact attribute a revolutionary capacity to women (in the Algerian Revolution, for instance) and acknowledge women's agency in the formation of a utopian new community. (See her article "Fanon's Revolutionary Woman," *The UTS Review* 1.2 [October 1995]: 197–201.) However, insofar as "revolution" was a cause to which the Algerian women revolutionaries had, in Fanon's eyes, submitted themselves *loyally*, their "agency" was strictly confined within that cause (and the community it engendered) and therefore did not constitute a disruptive issue. Just as the father did not ask what his bomb-bearing daughter had done (Fanon, *A Dying Colonialism*), so neither did the fatherly male theorist need to interrogate such revolutionary women: from the perspective of the revolution, their "female agency" remained a gift to patriarchy (in the terms discussed in this chapter) and posed no threat. For a critique of the problematic nature of (white intellectuals' fondness for) attributing "revolutionariness" to "third world" intellectuals, men or women, see chapter 2 of [*Ethics After Idealism*].

6. WHEN WHITENESS FEMINIZES . . .

1. Toril Moi, *Sexual/Textual Politics: Feminist Literary Theory* (London: Methuen, 1985).

2. Moi, *Sexual/Textual Politics*, p. 86, p. 87, emphases in the original, quoted with slight modifications in Deborah E. McDowell, *"The Changing Same": Black Women's Literature, Criticism, and Theory* (Bloomington: Indiana University Press, 1995), p. 161.

3. Ann Douglas, *The Feminization of American Culture* (New York: Avon, 1977).

4. This second-wave feminism is sometimes known as "difference" feminism or "gyno-centric" feminism. All these terms designate the turning point at which Western feminists systematically developed women-specific approaches that generated more complex explanations for the problem of women's oppression than the ones hitherto provided by classical Marxist analyses. For a succinct account that highlights feminists in nonliterary disciplines, see Linda Nicholson, introduction to *The Second Wave: A Reader in Feminist Theory,* ed. Linda Nicholson (New York: Routledge, 1997), pp. 1–5.

5. In opposition to Douglas, Jane Tompkins, for instance, affirms women's sentimental fiction by arguing that literary sensationalism can be a form of political intervention. See her *Sensational Designs: The Cultural Work of American Fiction, 1790–1860* (New York: Oxford University Press, 1985).

6. Andreas Huyssen, "Mass Culture as Woman: Modernism's Other," in *After the Great Divide: Modernism, Mass Culture, Postmodernism* (Bloomington: Indiana University Press, 1986), pp. 44–62.

7. For an exemplary critique of feminist essentialism and its philosophical origins, see Elizabeth V. Spelman, *Inessential Woman: Problems of Exclusion in Feminist Thought* (Boston: Beacon, 1988).

8. The unstable and unstabilizable status of "woman" is, in part, what has provoked some recent debates about the status of women's studies as a field of inquiry. See the essays in the *differences* special issue "Women's Studies on the Edge," edited by Joan Scott, in particular, Kathryn Cook and Renea Henry, with Joan Scott, "The Edge. Interview," *differences: A Journal of Feminist Cultural Studies* 9, no. 3 (fall 1997): pp. 132–55. See also Robyn Wiegman, "Feminism, Institutionalism, and the Idiom of Failure," special issue "America the Feminine," ed. Philip Gould and Leonard Tennenhouse, *differences* 2, no. 3 (fall 1999/2000). pp. 107–36.

7. FILM AND CULTURAL IDENTITY

1. Walter Benjamin, "The Work of Art in the Age of Mechanical Reproduction," in *Illuminations,* ed. Hannah Arendt and trans. Harry Zohn (New York: Schocken Books, 1936/1969); and "The Author as Producer," in *Reflections: Essays, Aphorisms, Autobiographical Writings,* ed. Peter Demetz and trans. Edmund Jephcott (New York: Schocken, 1986).

2. See Louis Althusser, "Ideology and Ideology State Apparatuses (Notes Towards an Investigation)," in *Lenin and Philosophy and Other Essays,* trans. Ben Brewster (New York: Monthly Review Press, 1971).

3. See Stephen Heath, *Questions of Cinema* (Bloomington: Indiana University Press, 1981).

4. Kaja Silverman, *The Subject of Semiotics* (New York: Oxford University Press, 1983), p. 205.

5. Laura Mulvey, "Visual Pleasure and Narrative Cinema," *Screen*, 16/3, 1975: pp. 6–18; reprinted in Constance Penley, ed., *Feminism and Film Theory* (New York: Routledge; London: British Film Institute, 1989).

6. See, for instance, Judith Mayne, *Kino and the Woman Question: Feminism and Soviet Silent Film* (Columbus: Ohio State University Press, 1989); Mary Ann Doane, Patricia Mellencamp and Linda Williams, eds., *Re-Vision: Essays in Feminist Film Criticism* (Frederick, Md.: University Publications of America, 1984); and Penley, *Feminism and Film Theory*.

7. See, for example, Kaja Silverman, *The Acoustic Mirror: The Female Voice in Psychoanalysis and Cinema* (Bloomington: Indiana University Press, 1988); Teresa de Lauretis, *Alice Doesn't: Feminism, Semiotics, Cinema* (Bloomington: Indiana University Press, 1984); and her *Technologies of Gender: Essays on Theory, Film, and Fiction* (Bloomington: Indiana University Press, 1987).

8. Edward Said, *Orientalism* (London: Routledge & Kegan Paul, 1978).

9. See, for example, Rey Chow, *Woman and Chinese Modernity: The Politics of Reading Between East and West* (Minneapolis: University of Minnesota Press, 1991), pp. 3–33.

10. Benjamin, "The Work of Art."

11. See Jean-Louis Comolli, "Machines of the Visible," in Teresa de Lauretis and Stephen Heath, eds., *The Cinematic Apparatus* (London: Macmillan, 1978).

12. André Bazin, *What Is Cinema?* ed. and trans. Hugh Gray (Berkeley and Los Angeles: University of California Press, 1967), pp. 9–16.

13. Benedict Anderson, *Imagined Communities: Reflections on the Origin and Spread of Nationalism* (London: Verso, 1983).

14. Paul Virilio, *War and Cinema: The Logistics of Perception*, trans. Patrick Camiller (London: Verso, 1989), p. 39.

15. See Stuart Hall, "Cultural Identity and Diaspora," in J. Rutherford, ed., *Identity: Community, Culture, Difference* (London: Lawrence & Wishart, 1990); Jim Pines and Paul Willemen, eds., *Questions of Third Cinema* (London: British Film Institute, 1989).

16. See Wimal Dissanayake, ed., *Cinema and Cultural Identity: Reflections on Films from Japan, India, and China* (Lanham, Md.: University Press of America, 1988).

17. Rey Chow, *Primitive Passions: Visuality, Sexuality, Ethnography, and Contemporary Chinese Cinema* (New York: Columbia University Press, 1995).

18. Chow, *Primitive Passions*.

19. Thomas Elsaesser, *New German Cinema: A History* (New Brunswick, N.J.: Rutgers University Press, 1989), pp. 322–23.

239

8. SEEING MODERN CHINA

1. Brian Lambert, "Interview with Bernardo Bertolucci / *The Last Emperor*," *Twin Cities Reader*, Wednesday, December 9, 1987, p. 14; my emphases. Other remarks quoted from Bertolucci are taken from the same interview.

2. Trans. Anita Barrows (New York and London: Marion Boyars, 1977, 1986). Page references are given in parentheses in the text.

3. Kristeva, "Woman Can Never Be Defined," trans. Marilyn A. August, in Elaine Marks and Isabelle de Courtivron, eds., *New French Feminisms* (New York: Schocken Books, 1981), pp. 137–41.

4. Kristeva, "Women's Time," trans. Alice Jardine and Harry Blake, in *Signs: Journal of Women in Culture and Society*, 7, no. 1 (1981), p. 17.

5. Kristeva, "Women's Time," p. 17.

6. Kristeva, "Woman Can Never Be Defined," p. 137.

7. Kristeva takes this word from Plato, who speaks of "a chora . . . , receptacle . . . , unnamable, improbable, hybrid, anterior to naming, to the One, to the father, and consequently, maternally connoted." See "From One Identity to an Other," in her *Desire in Language: A Semiotic Approach to Literature and Art*, trans. Thomas Gora, Alice Jardine, and Leon S. Roudiez (New York: Columbia University Press, 1980), p. 133.

8. Spivak, "French Feminism in an International Frame," in her *In Other Worlds: Essays in Cultural Politics* (New York and London: Methuen, 1987), p. 146; emphases in the original. The attribution of a "before" to the "other" is not unique to Kristeva. On his visit to China, Roland Barthes observed this culture with the same kind of fascination. China becomes an object of his hallucination: "By gently hallucinating China as an object located outside any bright color or any strong flavor, any brutal meaning (all this not without a bearing on the relentless parade of the Phallus), I wanted to bring together in a single movement the infinite *feminine* (maternal?) of the object itself, that extraordinary way China, in my eyes, had of overflowing the boundaries of meaning, peacefully and powerfully, and the right to a special discourse, that of a slight deviation, or again a yearning, an appetite for silence—for "wisdom" perhaps. . . . This *negative* hallucination is not gratuitous: it is an attempt to respond to the way many Westerners have of hallucinating the People's Republic of China—in a dogmatic mode, violently affirmative/negative or falsely liberal." See "Well, and China?" trans. Lee Hildreth, in *Discourse*, 8 (Fall-Winter 1986–87), p. 120; my emphases. Those who are familiar with Barthes's work know that he "hallucinates" Japan in the same way in *Empire of Signs*, trans. Richard Howard (New York: Hill and Wang, 1982).

9. Silverman, *The Acoustic Mirror: The Female Voice in Psychoanalysis and Cinema* (Bloomington and Indianapolis: Indiana University Press, 1988), p. 112.

10. For a critique of the politics involved in Kristeva's conceptions of femininity, see Ann Rosalind Jones, "Julia Kristeva on Femininity: The Limits of a Semiotic Politic," *Feminist Review*, no. 18 (1984), pp. 56–73.

11. For a superb account of the ideologies accompanying the historical depictions of China in the past few hundred years in the West, see Raymond Dawson, *The Chinese Chameleon* (London: Oxford University Press, 1967); Dawson examines the notion of the Chinese as "a people of eternal standstill" thoroughly in chapter 4.

12. I borrow this term from Johannes Fabian, *Time and the Other: How Anthropology Makes Its Object* (New York: Columbia University Press, 1983), pp. 106–9. Fabian defines visualism as a deeply ingrained ideological tendency in anthropology, which relies for its scientific, "observational" objectivity on the use of maps, charts, tables, etc. The recommendations for such visual aids "rest on a corpuscular, atomic theory of knowledge and information. Such a theory in turn encourages quantification and diagrammatic representation so that the ability to 'visualize' a culture or society almost becomes synonymous for understanding it. I shall call this tendency visualism." Visualism "may take different directions— toward the mathematical-geometric or toward the pictorial-aesthetic." I return to Fabian's arguments later on in this chapter.

13. Silverman, *The Subject of Semiotics* (New York: Oxford University Press, 1983), p. 225. A reprint of Mulvey's article, originally published in *Screen*, 16, no. 3 (Autumn 1975), can be found in *Movies and Methods*, vol. 2, ed. Bill Nichols (Berkeley and Los Angeles: University of California Press, 1985), pp. 303–15.

14. Silverman, *Semiotics*, p. 231.

15. Spivak, "Can the Subaltern Speak?" in Larry Grossberg and Cary Nelson, eds., *Marxist Interpretations of Literature and Culture: Limits, Frontiers, Boundaries* (Urbana: University of Illinois Press), pp. 296–97.

16. From the "Production Notes" attached to the film's compact disc soundtrack: "The logistics of the production were staggering. *The Last Emperor* brought together people from six nations. Actors came from America, Great Britain, China, Hong Kong and Japan to play the 60 main characters in the story. 100 technicians from Italy, 20 from Britain and 150 Chinese worked for 6 months of shooting to put the film on the screen and 19,000 extras, including soldiers of the People's liberation Army, appear altogether in the immense crowd scenes. Costume designer James Acheson gathered 9,000 costumers from all over the world."

17. *Video Review*, August 1988, p. 17.

18. Other feminist critics have produced readings of film that share this concern. See, for instance, Claire Johnston, *Notes on Women's Cinema* (London: Society for Education in Film and Television, 1973), pp. 2–4; Johnston, "Towards a Feminist Film Practice: Some Theses," in Nichols, ed., pp. 315–27; Mary Ann Doane, "Misrecognition and Identity," *Cine-Tracts*, 11 (Fall 1980), pp. 28–30; Doane, "Film and the Masquerade: Theorising the Female Spectator, " *Screen*, 23 (September-October 1982), pp. 74–87.

19. Mulvey, *Visual and Other Pleasures* (Bloomington and Indianapolis: Indiana University Press, 1989), pp. 159–76. (This essay was previously published in *Discourse* in 1985 and *History Workshop Journal* in 1987.). Mulvey's revisions of her original argument can also be found in "Afterthoughts on 'Visual Pleasure and Narrative Cinema' inspired by *Duel in the Sun*," *Framework*, 6, nos. 15–17 (1981), rpt. in Constance Penley, ed., *Feminism and Film Theory* (New York: Routledge, Chapman and Hall, 1988), pp. 69–79.

20. Mulvey, "Changes," pp. 163, 164, 168.

21. Mulvey, "Visual Pleasure," p. 306.

22. Mulvey "Changes," pp. 168–69; my emphasis.

23. Mulvey, "Visual Pleasure," p. 314.

24. For discussions of the term "suture" in cinema, see Stephen Heath, "Narrative Space," in *Screen*, 17, no. 3 (1976), pp. 66–112; "Notes on Suture," *Screen*, 18, no. 2 (1977/78), pp. 48–76; Jacques-Alain Miller, "Suture (Elements of the Logic of the Signifier)," *Screen*, 18, no. 4 (1977/78), pp. 24–34. Silverman's discussion in her book (pp. 194–236) demonstrates the theoretical connections between suture and discourse, subjectivity, cinema, ideology, and sexual difference.

25. To this end, the reader can turn to, for instance, John K. Fairbank, "Born Too Late," *New York Review of Books*, February 18, 1988.

26. Teresa de Lauretis, *Alice Doesn't: Feminism, Semiotics, Cinema* (Bloomington: Indiana University Press, 1984).

27. De Lauretis, *Alice Doesn''t*, p. 140.

28. Theodor Adorno and Max Horkheimer, *Dialectic of Enlightenment*, trans. John Cumming (New York: Continuum, 1987), pp. 120–67.

29. De Lauretis, *Alice Doesn't*, p. 143.

30. Louis Althusser, "Ideology and Ideological State Apparatuses (Notes Towards an Investigation)," in his *Lenin and Philosophy and Other Essays*, trans. Ben Brewster (New York and London: Monthly Review Press, 1971).

31. De Lauretis, *Alice Doesn't*, p. 68; my emphasis.

32. Silverman, *Semiotics*, p. 219.

33. De Lauretis, *Alice Doesn't*, p. 51.

34. Hsia, "Obsession with China: The Moral Burden of Modern Chinese Fiction," in his *A History of Modern Chinese Fiction*, 2nd ed. (New Haven: Yale University Press, 1971), pp. 533–34.

35. Benedict Anderson, *Imagined Communities: Reflections on the Origin and Spread of Nationalism* (London: Verso and New Left Books, 1983).

36. Anderson, *Imagined Communities*, p. 68, note 6.

37. See the chapters "Tuché and Automaton" and "From Love to the Libido," in *The Four Fundamental Concepts of Psychoanalysis*, ed. Jacques-Alain Miller, trans. Alan Sheridan (New York and London: Norton, 1981), pp. 53–66; 187–202.

38. See "Fetishism" and "Splitting of the Ego in the Defensive Process," in his *Sexuality and the Psychology of Love*, ed. Philip Rieff (New York: Collier Books, 1963), pp. 214–19; 220–23. The two essays are also in Freud, *The Standard Edition of the Complete Psychological Works*, ed. James Strachey, trans. James Strachey et al. (London: Hogarth Press), vols. 21 and 23. See also the section "Unsuitable Substitutes for the Sexual Object-Fetishism," in *Three Essays on the Theory of Sexuality*, trans. James Strachey (New York: Basic Books, 1975), pp. 19–21; or *Standard Edition*, vol. 7.

39. James J. Y. Liu, *Chinese Theories of Literature* (Chicago and London: University of Chicago Press, 1975), p. 5.

40. De Lauretis, *Alice Doesn't*, p. 46.

41. Yao-chung Li, "Hermeneutics and Criticism," in *Chinese Culture Quarterly*, I, no. 4 (1987), p. 65.

42. Martin and Mohanty, "Feminist Politics: What's Home Got to Do with It?" in Teresa de Lauretis, ed., *Feminist Studies / Critical Studies* (Bloomington: Indiana University Press, 1986), p. 196.

43. Fabian, *Time and the Other*, p. 47.

44. Spivak, "French Feminism," p. 138.

45. Fabian, *Time and the Other*, p. 155.

9. THE DREAM OF A BUTTERFLY

1. I am very grateful to David Cronenberg for providing me with a copy of the shooting script of the film *M. Butterfly*. For related interest, see David Henry Hwang, *M. Butterfly*, with an afterword by the playwright (New York: Plume, 1989). For a discussion of the play in terms of the politics of transvestism, see Marjorie Garber, *Vested Interests: Cross-Dressing and Cultural Anxiety* (New York: Routledge, 1992), pp. 234–51. For a discussion of the play in terms of its criticism of essentialist identity formed through Orientalism and heterosexism, see Dorinne Kondo, "*M. Butterfly*: Orientalism, Gender, and a Critique of Essentialist Identity," *Cultural Critique*, no. 16 (Fall 1990), pp. 5–29. For a discussion of the misogynist implications of Puccini's opera, see Catherine Clément, *Opera, or the Undoing of Women*, trans. Betsy Wing, foreword by Susan McClary (Minneapolis: U of Minnesota P, 1988), pp. 43–47. For a biography of Bernard Boursicot, the Frenchman whose love affair with the Chinese opera singer Shi Peipu gave rise to the *M. Butterfly* story, see Joyce Wadler, *Liaison* (New York: Bantam, 1993). The epigraphs at the beginning of this chapter are taken respectively from Martin Heidegger, *Poetry, Language, Thought*, trans. Albert Hofstadter (New York: Harper Colophon, 1971), p. 176; Roland Barthes, *Camera Lucida: Reflections on Photography*, trans. Richard Howard (New York: Hill and Wang, 1981), p. 117; Jacques Lacan, *Feminine Sexuality: Jacques Lacan and the école freudienne*, ed. Juliet Mitchell and Jacqueline Rose, trans. Jacqueline Rose (New York: Norton, 1985), pp. 146–47.

2.   Hwang, *M. Butterfly*, p. 94.

3.   See Kondo's essay for summaries of the vexed reactions to Hwang's play from some members of the Asian American communities.

4.   See, for instance, Freud's well-known discussion in "Creative Writers and Day-Dreaming," *The Standard Edition of the Complete Psychological Works of Sigmund Freud*, vol. ix, trans. James Strachey (London: Hogarth, 1959), pp. 141–53. For an authoritative, intensive reading of Freud's works on fantasy, see Jean Laplanche and Jean-Bertrand Pontalis, "Fantasy and the Origins of Sexuality" (first published in the *International Journal of Psychoanalysis*, vol. 49, part 1, pp. 1–17; 1968), in *Formations of Fantasy*, edited by Victor Burgin, James Donald, and Cora Kaplan (London: Methuen, 1986), pp. 5–34. Because I am, in this chapter, primarily interested in exploring the social and cross-cultural implications of fantasy, I am not fine-tuning the various modes of conscious and unconscious fantasies as would be necessary in a more strictly clinical analysis. For the same reasons I am also using terms such as "fantasy" and "dream" interchangeably.

5.   See Laplanche and Pontalis, "Fantasy and the Origins of Sexuality." Two discussions of fantasy that I have found very helpful are Cora Kaplan, "*The Thorn Birds:* Fiction, Fantasy, Femininity," *Formations of Fantasy*, pp. 142–66, and Elizabeth Cowie, "Fantasia," *The Woman in Question*, edited by Parveen Adams and Elizabeth Cowie (Cambridge, MA: MIT P, 1990), pp. 149–96.

6.   Examples of these uncomprehendingly dismissive reviews: "Hwang also wrote the misguided movie version of '*M. Butterfly*' for director David Cronenberg, in which Jeremy Irons and an oddly sullen John Lone act out a straightforward love story devoid of heat or plausibility. The problem is not simply that Lone's drag wouldn't fool a baby. In the magnified intimacy of the camera's eye, it's clear Hwang doesn't really know who these unlikely lovers are" (David Ansen, "Much Stranger than Fiction," *Newsweek*, October 18, 1993, p. 84). "The problem with *M. Butterfly*, both play and movie, is that the audience gets the point right away—it's too crude and too facile to miss—and has nothing to do for the rest of the evening except listen to tiresome restatements of it. . . . Cronenberg's treatment of Hwang's material has the effect of exposing it for what it really is: not a pure, incandescent work of art but an extremely ordinary piece of agitprop drama" (Terrence Rafferty, "The Current Cinema: Blind Faith," *The New Yorker* 69: 33 [October 11, 1993], p. 123). If one were indeed to judge the film on the basis of verisimilitude, the obvious thing to criticize, from the perspective of those who know Chinese, is the improbability of a Cantonese-speaking servant in Song's house, while every other Chinese character, including Song, speaks in Mandarin, the language most commonly used in Beijing.

7.   "Fantasy involves, is characterized by, not the achievement of desired objects, but the arranging of, a setting out of, desire; a veritable *mise-en-scène* of desire. . . . The fantasy depends not on particular objects, but on their setting out; and the pleasure of fantasy lies in the setting out, not in the having of the objects. . . . It can be seen, then, that fantasy is not the object of desire, but its setting" (Cowie, "Fantasia," p. 159).

8. In the early scenes of the film, Gallimard's fascination with "Butterfly" extends even to fly swatting and dragonfly gazing. In terms of the genealogy of Cronenberg's films, *M. Butterfly* is similar to its predecessors in that it stages the manner in which a man's imagination infects him like a disease, which gradually consumes and finally destroys him. For extended discussions of this—his favourite—theme, see the director's *Cronenberg on Cronenberg*, ed. Chris Rodley (London: Faber and Faber, 1992). However, two factors make *M. Butterfly* different from the earlier films. First, the restrained, minimalist design of the film is a major departure from the elaborate special effects and shocking images that are the Cronenberg trademark. Second, the biological and science-fiction modes of Cronenberg's usual film language are here complicated by the story of a cross-cultural encounter with all its sexual, racial, and political implications. Because of these factors, I am reading *M. Butterfly* as a unique work in Cronenberg's corpus, even though the conceptual affinities with the other films are definitely present. In particular, as I will go on to argue, the significations of visuality in this film are unprecedentedly mind-boggling.

9. Even though Hwang too has referred to the notion of deconstruction, what he aims at deconstructing is the fantasy, the stereotype, and the cliché, rather than the human per se: "The idea of doing a deconstructivist *Madame Butterfly* immediately appealed to me. This despite the fact that I didn't even know the plot of the opera! I knew Butterfly only as a cultural stereotype; speaking of an Asian woman, we would sometimes say, 'She's pulling a Butterfly,' which meant playing the submissive Oriental number. Yet, I felt convinced that the libretto would include yet another lotus blossom pining away for a cruel Caucasian man, and dying for her love. Such a story has become too much of a cliché not to be included in the archtypal [sic] East-West romance that started it all. Sure enough, when I purchased the record, I discovered it contained a wealth of sexist and racist clichés, reaffirming my faith in Western culture" (Hwang, *M. Butterfly*, p. 95).

10. Lacan, "The Line and Light," *The Four Fundamental Concepts of Psycho-Analysis*, edited by Jacques-Alain Miller, trans. Alan Sheridan (New York: Norton, 1981), pp. 102–103; emphases in the original.

11. See Jean Baudrillard, *Seduction*, trans. Brian Singer (New York: St. Martin's, 1990).

12. On this point—namely, that *M. Butterfly* is not about the conflict of homosexuality and heterosexuality—Hwang is absolutely clear: "To me, this is not a 'gay' subject because the very labels heterosexual or homosexual become meaningless in the context of this story. Yes, of course this was literally a homosexual affair. Yet because Gallimard perceived it or chose to perceive it as a heterosexual liaison, in his mind it was essentially so. Since I am telling the story from the Frenchman's point of view, it is more specifically about 'a man who loved a woman created by a man.' To me, this characterization is infinitely more useful than the clumsy labels 'gay' or 'straight'" (Hwang, personal communication, 30 April 1989, quoted in Kondo, "*M. Butterfly*," p. 21).

13. This is one of the many significant differences between the film and the play. In the play, Gallimard is familiar with the Madame Butterfly story, which he claims to like, but

complains that he has only seen it "played by huge women in so much bad makeup" (Hwang, *M. Butterfly*, p. 16).

14. Lacan, "The Meaning of the Phallus," edited by Juliet Mitchell and Jacqueline Rose, trans. Jacqueline Rose (New York: Norton, 1985), p. 82.

15. See Lacan's discussion in "Feminine Sexuality in Psychoanalytic Doctrine." Responding to Freud's questions in the investigation of feminine sexuality, "What does the little girl want from her mother?" and "what does she demand of her?" Lacan writes: "What does the little girl demand of her mother?" But it's easy! She has no shortage of words for telling us: to dress her, to make her hurt go away, to take her for a walk, to belong to her, or to her alone, in short all sorts of demands, including at times the demand to leave her alone, that is, the demand to take a rest from all demand. If, therefore, Freud's question has any meaning, it must signify something else, that is, not so much "What is she demanding of *her*?" as "What is she *demanding*, what is she really demanding, by demanding of her mother all that?" In other words, Freud's question implies the separating out of demand onto two planes: that of the demands effectively spoken, or enounced, and that of Demand (with a capital D) which subsists within and beyond these very demands, and which, because it remains resistant to articulation, incites the little girl to make those demands at the same time as rendering them futile, both the demands and any reply they might receive (*Feminine Sexuality*, pp. 130–31; emphases in the original).

16. Hwang, *M. Butterfly*, pp. 95–96.

17. I am following Burton Watson's English translation of Zhuang Zi's text, which appears in *Qiwulun* [a treatise on equalizing (with) all things]. See *The Basic Writings of Chuang Tzu*, trans. and ed. Burton Watson (New York: Columbia UP, 1964), p. 45.

18. Lacan, "The Eye and the Gaze," *Four Fundamental Concepts*, p. 76; emphasis in the original.

19. "When dreaming of being the butterfly, . . . he is a captive butterfly, but captured by nothing, for, in the dream, he is a butterfly for nobody" (Lacan, "The Eye and the Gaze," p. 76).

20. "The butterfly may . . . inspire in him the phobic terror of recognizing that the beating of little wings is not so very far from the beating of causation, of the primal stripe marking his being for the first time with the grid of desire" (Lacan, "The Eye and the Gaze," p. 76).

21. Lacan, "The Line and Light," pp. 100–101; emphases in the original.

22. See Garber for an interesting discussion of "passing" in her reading of the play *M. Butterfly*: "'What passes for a woman.' And what passes for a man. Passing is what acting is, and what treason is. Recall that the French diplomat Boursicot was accused of passing information to his Chinese contacts. In espionage, in theater, in 'modern China,' in contemporary culture, embedded in the very phrase 'gender roles,' there is, this play suggests, only passing. Trespassing. Border-crossing and border raids. Gender, here, exists only in representation—or performance" (*Vested Interests*, p. 250). As my reading throughout this chapter indicates, my reading of passing—and hence of crossing, role-playing, representation, and performance—is quite different from Garber's.

23. See Cowie's discussion in "Fantasia," p. 154.

24. Lacan, "What Is a Picture?" *Four Fundamental Concepts*, p. 114.

25. The passage indicated by the previous footnote continues with these lines: "What it amounts to is the first act in the laying down of the gaze. A sovereign act, no doubt, since it passes into something that is materialized and which, from this sovereignty, will render obsolete, excluded, inoperant, whatever, coming from elsewhere, will be presented before this product" (Lacan, "What Is a Picture?" p. 114).

26. "In our relations to things, in so far as this relation is constituted by the way of vision, and ordered in the figures of representation, something slips, passes, is transmitted, from stage to stage, and is always to some degree eluded in it—that is what we call the gaze" (Lacan, "The Eye and the Gaze," p. 73).

27. This ending could also be read along the lines of Cronenberg's fascination with the resemblance of fantasy to disease. For instance, even though the vocabulary he uses is predominantly biological rather than visual, the following lines from the director could well serve as a reading of the ending of *M. Butterfly* once we substitute the word "fantasy" for the words "virus" and "disease": "To understand physical process on earth requires a revision of the theory that we're all God's creatures. . . . It should certainly be extended to encompass disease, viruses and bacteria. Why not? A virus is only doing its job!' It's trying to live its life. The fact that it's destroying you by doing so is not its fault. It's about trying to understand interrelationships among organisms, even those we perceive as disease. To understand it from the disease's point of view, it's just a matter of life. It has nothing to do with disease. I think most diseases would be very shocked to be considered diseases at all. It's a very negative connotation. For them, it's very positive when they take over your body and destroy you. It's a triumph. It's all part of trying to reverse the normal understanding of what goes on physically, psychologically and biologically to [*sic*] us. . . . I identify with [the characters in *Shivers*] after they're infected. I identify with the parasites, basically" (*Cronenberg on Cronenberg*, p. 82).

28. In terms of a man "painting" his fantasy, a comparison could also be made between Cronenberg's film and Hitchcock's *Vertigo*, in which the male character, Scotty, attempts to rejuvenate his fantasy world by artificially remaking—by painting—Judy, his new girlfriend, into Madeleine, his supposedly dead one. Once again, in *Vertigo* it is the female body that serves as the canvas for male enlightenment and that is ultimately sacrificed; while in *M. Butterfly* it is the male body that bears the consequences of this cruel and crude act of painting.

29. Lacan, "God and the *Jouissance* of the Woman," *Feminine Sexuality*, p. 144.

10. FILM AS ETHNOGRAPHY

1. Dipesh Chakrabarty, "Marx After Marxism: Subaltern Histories and the Question of Difference," *Polygraph* 6, no. 7 (1993): 12.

2. Bernard McGrane, *Beyond Anthropology: Society and the Other* (New York: Columbia University Press, 1989), p. 127 (emphasis in the original).

3. James Clifford, introduction to *Writing Culture: The Poetics and Politics of Ethnography*, ed. James Clifford and George E. Marcus (Berkeley and Los Angeles: University of California Press, 1986), p. 22.

4. Walter Benjamin, "The Task of the Translator," in *Illuminations*, ed. and with an intro. by Hannah Arendt, trans. Harry Zohn (New York: Schocken, 1969), p. 79 ("Die Aufgabe des Ubersetzers," in *Illuminationen* [Frankfurt: Suhrkamp Taschenbuch 345, 1977], p. 59; hereafter, page references to the English version will be given in parentheses in the text).

5. Michael Taussig, *Mimesis and Alterity: A Particular History of the Senses* (New York: Routledge, 1993), p. 236.

6. Kwai-cheung Lo, "Crossing Boundaries: A Study of Modern Hong Kong Fiction from the Fifties to the Eighties" (M.Phil. thesis, University of Hong Kong, 1990), p. 162.

7. Mary Louise Pratt, *Imperial Eyes: Travel Writing and Transculturation* (New York: Routledge, 1992), pp. 7–8.

8. Jane Ying Zha, "Excerpts from Lore Segal, Red Lantern, and Exoticism," *Public Culture* 5, no. 2 (Winter 1993): 329. See my extended discussion of these views in the previous chapter.

9. For a discussion of this point, see Talal Asad, "Two European Images of Non-European Rule," in *Anthropology and the Colonial Encounter*, ed. Talal Asad (New York: Humanities Press, 1973), pp. 103–18.

10. Writing about the discipline of history, for instance, Dipesh Chakrabarty argues that while the names and works of Western historians are often taken as universal knowledge and cited as "musts" in studies of non-Western as well as Western histories, non-Western historians, no matter how astute and erudite they are, are often mentioned only in the context of their "specific" cultures. See Chakrabarty, "Postcoloniality and the Artifice of History: Who Speaks for 'Indian' Pasts?" *Representations* 37 (Winter 1992): 1–26.

11. Talal Asad, "The Concept of Cultural Translation in British Social Anthropology," in *Writing Culture*, p. 163. See also Asad's introduction to *Anthropology and the Colonial Encounter*.

12. Asad, intro. to *Anthropology and the Colonial Encounter*, p. 16.

13. Asad, "The Concept of Cultural Translation," pp. 157–58; emphasis in the original.

14. Kirsten Hastrup, "Anthropological Visions: Some Notes on Visual and Textual Authority," in *Film as Ethnography*, ed. Peter Ian Crawford and David Turton (Manchester: Manchester University Press, 1992), p. 17.

15. For such admonition, see Wilton Martinez, "Who Constructs Anthropological Knowledge? Toward a Theory of Ethnographic Film Spectatorship," in Hastrup, *Film as Ethnography*, pp. 131–61. Martinez's conclusion is that the crisis in anthropological representation "requires that we enhance our self-reflexive and self-critical practices in order to

identify the limits of our knowledge claims as well as their potential impact on the social construction of anthropological knowledge" (p. 156). See also Frances E. Mascia-Lees, Patricia Sharpe, and Colleen B. Cohen, "The Postmodernist Turn in Anthropology: Cautions from a Feminist Perspective," *Signs* 15, no. 1 (1989): pp. 7–33. According to these authors, the goal of a new ethnography is to "apprehend and inscribe 'others' in such a way as not to deny or diffuse their claims to subjecthood" (p. 12).

16. See Laura Mulvey, "Visual Pleasure and Narrative Cinema," in *Movies and Methods*, ed. Bill Nichols (Berkeley and Los Angeles: University of California Press, 1985), vol. 2, pp. 303–15; this is a reprint of the article originally published in *Screen* 16, no. 3 (Autumn 1975).

17. Walter Benjamin first used the term *optical unconscious* in the essay "A Small History of Photography" (1931), in *One-Way Street*, trans. Edmund Jephcott and Kingsley Shorter (London: New Left Books, 1979), pp. 240–57; he again refers to "unconscious optics" in "The Work of Art in the Age of Mechanical Reproduction," in *Illuminations*, pp. 217–51.

18. Dai Vaughan, "The Aesthetics of Ambiguity," in *Film as Ethnography*, p. 102. Vaughan's entire essay, with its careful exposition of the documentary's representational ambiguities and its emphasis on the viewer's role in constructing meaning, can be read as a deconstruction of ethnography's fundamental claim to being simply a "record" rather than a language.

19. Thomas Elsaesser, *New German Cinema: A History* (New Brunswick: Rutgers University Press, 1989), pp. 322–23; my emphases.

20. See the comments under the root *do* in Joseph T. Shipley, *The Origins of English Words: A Discursive Dictionary of Indo-European Roots* (Baltimore: Johns Hopkins University Press, 1984), p. 73; also the comments under the root *do* in the "Indo-European Roots Appendix," in *The American Heritage Dictionary if the English Language*, 3d ed. (New York: Houghton Mifflin, 1992), p. 2101.

21. Barbara Johnson, "Taking Fidelity Philosophically," in *Difference in Translation*, ed. Joseph F. Graham (Ithaca, N. Y.: Cornell University Press, 1985), p. 143.

22. See the pertinent discussion by Lawrence Venuti in his intro. to *Rethinking Translation: Discourse, Subjectivity, Ideology* (New York: Routledge, 1992), p. 4.

23. Walter Benjamin, "The Work of Art in the Age of Mechanical Reproduction," in *Illuminations*, pp. 217–51; see my references to this essay in part 2, chap. 2. I have also offered discussions at greater length elsewhere: see, for instance, my "Walter Benjamin's Love Affair with Death," *New German Critique* 48 (Fall 1989): 63–86; and the chapter entitled "Where Have All the Natives Gone?" in *Writing Diaspora: Tactics of Intervention in Contemporary Cultural Studies* (Bloomington: Indiana University Press, 1993).

24. Walter Benjamin, "The Task of the Translator," in *Illuminations*, pp. 69–82.

25. Cf. my discussion of *Yellow Earth* in part 2, chap. 2 [of *Primitive Passions*], in which "composition" or "putting together" can indeed be seen as a deconstructive production of differences.

26. Paul de Man, *Blindness and Insight: Essays in the Rhetoric of Contemporary Criticism* (Minneapolis: University of Minnesota Press, 1983), p. 136, and *Allegories of Reading: Figural Language in Rousseau, Nietzsche, Rilke, and Proust* (New Haven: Yale University Press, 1979), p. 151. For Derrida's discussion, see, e.g., Jacques Derrida, "White Mythology: Metaphor in the Text of Philosophy," in *Margins of Philosophy*, trans. and with additional notes by Alan Bass (Chicago: University of Chicago Press, 1992), pp. 207–71.

27. Johnson, "Taking Fidelity Philosophically," p. 146.

28. For a discussion of such readings, as well as of deconstruction's and poststructuralism's contributions to the reconsideration of translation theory, see Venuti, intro. to *Rethinking Translation: Discourse, Subjectivity, Ideology*, pp. 6–17.

29. Paul de Man, "'Conclusions': Walter Benjamin's 'The Task of the Translator,' "in *The Resistance to Theory*, with a foreword by Wlad Godzich (Minneapolis: University of Minnesota Press, 1986), p. 84; my emphases. De Man is insistent on the disarticulation of the original throughout his essay. For instance, "One of the reasons why [Benjamin] takes the translator rather than the poet [as the exemplary figure] is that the translator, per definition, fails" (p. 80); "The process of translation . . . reveals the death of the original" (p. 85); "This movement of the original is a wandering, an *errance*, a kind of permanent exile if you wish, but it is not really an exile, for there is no homeland, nothing from which one has been exiled" (p. 92; emphasis in the original); and "The translation is a way of reading the original which will reveal those inherent weaknesses in the original . . . in a . . . fundamental way: that the original is not canonical, that the original is a piece of ordinary language" (p. 98).

30. De Man would argue, instead, that "the translation is the fragment of a fragment. . . . There was no vessel in the first place" (ibid., p. 91). He relies for his argument on a firm notion of one correct translation—his own—of Benjamin's text.

31. Jean Laplanche, "The Wall and the Arcade," in *Seduction, Translation, Drives*, a dossier compiled by John Fletcher and Martin Stanton, with trans. by Martin Stanton (London: Institute of Contemporary Arts, 1992), p. 201.

32. Tejaswini Niranjana, *Siting Translation: History, Post-Structuralism, and the Post-Colonial Context* (Berkeley and Los Angeles: University of California Press, 1992). See in particular chap. 2 for an erudite account of the traditions and theories of translation. Hereafter page references to this book will be given in parentheses in the text.

33. Roman Jakobson calls intersemiotic translation *transmutation*, which he differentiates from both intralingual translation (which he terms *rewording*) and interlingual translation (which he terms *translation proper*). See Jakobson, "On Linguistic Aspects of Translation," in *On Translation*, ed. Reuben A. Brower (Cambridge, Mass.: Harvard University Press, 1959), p. 233.

34. The sidestepping of mass culture in Niranjana's reconsideration of translation can be glimpsed in the way she rewrites Benjamin's word *image*. Where Benjamin intends by *image* a concrete means—a constellation—for understanding the activity called reading,

Niranjana elides such implications and rewrites *image* purely as *reading* in the deconstructive sense. In other words, where Benjamin's emphasis is on *image*, Niranjana's is on *reading*. See Niranjana, *Siting Translation*, pp.171–72.

35. Johannes Fabian, *Time and the Other: How Anthropology Makes Its Object* (New York: Columbia University Press, 1983). For a critique of the repression of coevalness in European anthropological discourse, a repression that is accomplished through notions of "the primitive," which are mapped onto "other" societies, see, e.g., Bernard McGrane, *Beyond Anthropology*, in particular chap. 3 and the conclusion, pp. 77–112, 113–29. McGrane's book also contains interesting discussions of the changing nature of the work of anthropology and ethnography in the context of a heightened awareness of cultural difference.

36. Laplanche, "The Wall and the Arcade," pp. 207, 211. In a discussion of Caribbean cinema that is fully resonant with my discussion of Chinese cinema, Stuart Hall also uses the notion of "the third term" to refer to the cultural space of the New World, where creolizations, assimilations, and syncretisms are negotiated: "The New World is the third term—the primal scene—where the fateful/fatal encounter was staged between Africa and the West." See Hall, "Cultural Identity and Diaspora," in *Colonial Discourse and Post-Colonial Theory: A Reader*, ed. and with an intro. by Patrick Williams and Laura Chrisman (New York: Columbia University Press, 1994), pp. 392–403. This essay was originally published in *Identity: Community, Culture, Difference*, ed. J. Rutherford (London: Lawrence and Wishart, 1990, pp. 222–37).

37. Chakrabarty, "Postcoloniality and the Artifice of History," p. 21.

38. My reading here is based on Gianni Vattimo, *The End of Modernity: Nihilism and Hermeneutics in Post-Modern Culture*, trans. and with an intro. by Jon R. Snyder (Cambridge: Polity Press, 1988), and *The Transparent Society*, trans. David Webb (Cambridge: Polity Press, 1992).

39. See Snyder's lucid and helpful introduction in *The End of Modernity*.

40. This quote is from p. 60 in Remo Guidieri, "Les sociétés primitives aujourd'hui," in *Philosopher: les interrogations contemporaines*, ed. Ch. Delacampagne and R. Maggiori (Paris: Fayard, 1980), pp. 51–64. See Vattimo, "Hermeneutics and Anthropology," in *The End of Modernity*, p. 158.

41. " 'Contact zone' in my discussion is often synonymous with 'colonial frontier.' . . . A 'contact' perspective . . . treats the relations among colonizers and colonized . . . not in terms of separateness or apartheid, but in terms of copresence, interaction, interlocking understandings and practices, often within radically asymmetrical relations of power." Pratt, *Imperial Eyes*, pp. 6–7.

42. Vattimo, "Art and Oscillation," in *The Transparent Society*, p. 59, emphasis in the original.

43. Vattimo, "The Human Sciences and the Society of Communication," in ibid., pp. 24–25. "How the 'Real World' at Last Became a Myth [Fable]" is a chapter in Nietzsche's *Twilight*

251

of the Idols (1889). See Friedrich Nietzsche, *Twilight of the Idols/The Anti-Christ,* trans. R. J. Hollingdale (Harmondsworth: Penguin Books, 1968), pp. 40–41.

44. Benjamin, "Franz Kafka: On the Tenth Anniversary of His Death," in *Illuminations,* pp. 143–44; my emphases.

45. Jacques Derrida, "Des Tours de Babel," in *Difference in Translation,* pp. 187–88; emphasis in the original. Derrida's discussions of Benjamin's essay on translation, which are centered largely on verbal language, can also be found in *The Ear if the Other: Autobiography Transference Translation,* trans. Peggy Kamuf (Lincoln: University of Nebraska Press, 1988), pp. 93–161.

46. John Fletcher, " 'The Letter in the Unconscious,' The Enigmatic Signifier in the Work of Jean Laplanche," in Laplanche, *Seduction, Translation, Drives,* p. 116.

47. Derrida, "White Mythology," p. 252.

48. I can merely refer to Benjamin's arcades project here. For an authoritative study in English, see Susan Buck-Morss, *The Dialectics of Seeing: Walter Benjamin and the Arcades Project* (Cambridge, Mass.: MIT Press, 1989).

49. I borrow this observation from Jeffrey Mehlman, *Walter Benjamin for Children: An Essay on His Radio Years* (Chicago: University of Chicago Press, 1993). Commenting on one of Benjamin's writings on toys, Mehlman writes: "The toy is thus above all that wherein the child negotiates the imposition of an adult agenda. A precarious coming to terms that is marked by a tearing apart (*Auseinander*setzung), it is shot through with the unmastered 'traces' of the other" (p. 4; emphasis as in Mehlman's text).

50. In the 1990s, even the communist state has to adopt market strategies to promote its ideas. For an informed discussion, see Geremie Barmé, "The Greying of Chinese Culture," in *China Review 1992,* ed. Kuan Hsin-chi and Maurice Brosseau (Hong Kong: Chinese University Press, 1992), sec. 13, pp. 1–52.

51. Benjamin, "Unpacking My Library: A Talk About Book Collecting," *Illuminations,* p. 66.

52. These include Chinese films from Taiwan and Hong Kong as well. In 1992 and 1993 alone, major awards were won by Stanley Kwan's *Ruan Lingyu* (*Center Stage*), Xie Fei's *Xianghun nü* (*Oilmaker's Family*), and Ang Lee's *Xiyan* (*The Wedding Banquet*) at the Berlin Film Festival; Zhang Yimou's *The Story of Qiuju* at the Venice Film Festival; and Chen Kaige's *Bawang bie ji* (*Farewell My Concubine*) at the Cannes Film Festival. Films by Ang Lee, Zhang Yimou, and Chen Kaige have also been nominated for the award of "Best Foreign Language Film" in various years at the Oscars.

11. A FILMIC STAGING OF POSTWAR GEOTEMPORAL POLITICS

1. I wish to thank Harry Harootunian and Masao Miyoshi for their generous and helpful comments on a draft of this essay. All remaining errors are mine.

2. Mitsuhiro Yoshimoto, *Kurosawa: Film Studies and Japanese Cinema* (Durham, N.C.: Duke University Press, 2000), p. 2.

3. It would be impossible to mention all the relevant publications on the problematic of Japanese identity in modernity. For my own education, these are some of the historical and theoretical discussions to which I turn: Masao Miyoshi, *Off Center: Power and Culture Relations Between Japan and the United States* (Cambridge, Mass.: Harvard University Press, 1991); Naoki Sakai, *Translation and Subjectivity: On "Japan" and Cultural Nationalism*, foreword by Meaghan Morris (Minneapolis: University of Minnesota Press, 1997); Harry Harootunian, *Overcome by Modernity: History, Culture, and Community in Interwar Japan* (Princeton, N.J.: Princeton University Press, 2000); and Stefan Tanaka, *New Times in Modern Japan* (Princeton, N.J.: Princeton University Press, 2004). This is, of course, just a minimal list.

4. For an account that places Kurosawa among the modernist literary writers and filmmakers who experiment with narrative, see the chapter "Modernist Narrative and Intertextuality," in James Goodwin, *Akira Kurosawa and Intertextual Cinema* (Baltimore, Md.: Johns Hopkins University Press, 1994), pp. 113–64.

5. For an informative account of the key political events surrounding the making of the film, see Kyoko Hirano, *Mr. Smith Goes to Tokyo: Japanese Cinema Under the American Occupation, 1945–1952* (Washington and London: Smithsonian Institute, 1992), pp. 179–204.

6. See Hirano's discussion in the section "Ideological Vacuousness," in *Mr. Smith Goes to Tokyo*, pp. 197–204. James Goodwin, on the other hand, believes the unsympathetic reactions had something to do with Japanese society's resistance to women's independence. He puts it this way: "By the conclusion, beauty has become redefined for Yukie as a matter of ethics rather than aesthetics. Her discovery of a personal code of action, independent of society's dictates, met with misapprehension and disapproval by Japanese critics. Female self-definition appeared perverse in a social context structured to guarantee male interests" (*Akira Kurosawa and Intertextual Cinema*, p. 48).

7. Although I tend to disagree with Donald Richie's liberal humanistic reading of the film, I believe he has made an insightful point when he writes that Kurosawa's treatment of the peasants—and thus by implication the Left and Communism—is not exactly sentimental:

> He has the courage in this film (and it took courage in 1946, a time when Communism was the new hope, when the proletariat was the new ideal) to tell the truth: that poverty may make brutes of men, but that the men themselves are no less responsible for their own brutishness.
>
> The peasants (her in-laws excepted) are awful: they are mean, malicious, destructive, crafty, petty, perverse—they are the opposite of what Rousseau thought they were, they share nothing with the noble George Sand peasants, they are (and this is heresy to Japanese Marxists) not even worth saving.
>
> Kurosawa's political uninvolvement is nowhere better than in these farm sequences. The military, the heroes of the right, are monsters; the peasants,

heroes of the left, are also monstrous. (Donald Richie, *The Films of Akira Kuro-sawa*, 3rd ed., with additional material by Joan Mellon [Berkeley, Los Angeles, and London: University of California Press, 1996], p. 39

However, whereas for Richie this "unsympathetic" treatment of the peasants simply lends support to his (Richie's) own humanistic analysis of Yukie's quest of her self, to my mind such treatment is, as I will go on to argue, precisely the sign of a geotemporal politics whose contours would become increasingly clear in the postwar years. It should be noted that Richie based his view on what Kurosawa himself had said about this film: "I felt that without the establishment of the self as a positive value there could be no free-dom and no democracy. My first film in the post-war era, *Waga seishun ni kui nashi* (*No Regrets for Our Youth*), takes the problem of the self as its theme" (Kurosawa, *Something Like an Autobiography*, trans. Audie E. Bock [New York: Vintage, 1983], p. 146).

8. Hirano, *Mr. Smith Goes to Tokyo*, p. 54.

9. Yoshimoto, *Kurosawa*, 130. Yoshimoto's extended comments are worth quoting: "the Occupation censorship strictly forbade the Japanese filmmakers to show images of the war, particularly the devastation of Japan by the American forces. The Occupation did not simply suppress the Japanese criticism of the Occupation. Instead, the Occupa-tion forbid the Japanese filmmakers to mention, let alone concretely represent, the fact of occupation even in a positive manner. Thus, when we watch the Japanese films of the Occupation period, on the surface, nothing in them explicitly shows or indi-cates the presence of the Occupation forces. The Occupation also tried to make sure that Japanese militarism was responsible for everything negative, including the war devastation and the dire situation of the immediate postwar years. These directives and the general policies of the Occupation led to the situation in which the Japanese filmmakers were forced to concentrate on the images of the Japanese existing in an imaginary space where the villain is always Japanese militarism or more commonly war, and the Japanese are victims of abstract or natural forces beyond their control" (pp. 129–30).

10. See Gilles Deleuze, *Cinema 1: The Movement-Image*, trans. Hugh Tomlinson and Barbara Habberjam (Minneapolis: University of Minnesota Press, 1986), pp. 188–92; reprinted in *Perspectives on Akira Kurosawa*, ed. James Goodwin (New York: G. K. Hall and Co., 1994), pp. 246–50.

11. Harry Harootunian calls this the "inaugural unevenness" of modernity, a kind of time lag that characterizes the relationship between cosmopolitan spaces and their shadowy peripheries: "the division between the city and countryside constantly reinforced the recognition of unevenness, especially as the vast migrations continued to empty rural regions. This inaugural unevenness, imported into the city by migrants seeking work, prefigured the division between metropole and colony and dramatized the formulation of a putative time lag between the center and its colonial periphery." "Time's Envelope,"

in Harootunian's book in progress, *Borrowed Time: History's Search for Temporality* (forthcoming), p. 15.

12. As a parallel, in Western scholarship on Japanese film, critics are fond of finding essentialist principles (such as the samurai code of honor, the warrior ideal, the Zen sensibility for harmony with nature, etc.) in modern Japanese scenarios in order to argue the continuity of a Japanese cultural heritage. See Yoshimoto, *Kurosawa*, pp. 71–74 and throughout.

13. Gilles Deleuze, *Cinema 2: The Time-Image*, trans. Hugh Tomlinson and Barbara Habberjam (Minneapolis and London: University of Minnesota Press, 1986).

14. Cited in Richie, *The Films of Akira Kurosawa*, p. 40.

15. Johannes Fabian, *Time and the Other: How Anthropology Makes Its Object* (New York: Columbia University Press, 1983).

16. Some critics argue that this noticeable engagement with postwar politics would disintegrate in Kurosawa's later work. For instance, Stephen Prince writes, "In Kurosawa's cinema, we are dealing with twin impulses. The postwar imperative to engage history and remake society will be offset in later films by a contrary inclination to conceive the temporal process as fate and human life as an insubstantial shadow in a world of tears. This latter impulse is in marked contrast to the social optimism of the early films like *No Regrets for Our Youth* and *Stray Dog*." Prince, *The Warrior's Camera: The Cinema of Akira Kurosawa* (Princeton, N.J.: Princeton University Press, 1991), p. 114; reprinted in *Perspectives on Akira Kurosawa*, p. 251. My reading here may be seen as an attempt to complicate—and controvert—this assumption of the so-called social optimism of the early films.

12. FROM *SENTIMENTAL FABULATIONS*

1. Dudley Andrew, "'The 'Three Ages' of Cinema Studies and the Age to Come," *PMLA* 115.3 (2000): p. 348. Andrew offers this information as part of a discussion of the history of cinema studies.

2. Christine Gledhill and Linda Williams, introduction to *Reinventing Film Studies*, ed. Christine Gledhill and Linda Williams (London: Arnold, 2000), p. 1.

3. See my discussion of Lu Xun's famous reactions to a slide show of an execution of a Chinese man (which he happened to watch during 1904–5 in Japan), reactions that led him to abandon medical studies and become a writer, at the beginning of part 1 of *Primitive Passions: Visuality, Sexuality, Ethnography, and Contemporary Chinese Cinema* (New York: Columbia UP, 1995). Tanizaki, for his part, noted how, in contrast to Western faces, Japanese faces appeared hideous and repulsive on film. For in-depth commentaries on as well as translations of some of Tanizaki's film essays and stories (written during the 1910s and 1920s), see Thomas LaMarre, *Shadows on the Screen: Tanizaki Junichiro on Cinema and "Oriental" Aesthetics* (Ann Arbor: Center for Japanese Studies, University

of Michigan, 2005), in particular chaps. 7 and 8. It should be added, however, that Tanizaki's emphases were largely aesthetic—indeed, synesthetic, as LaMarre argues—in orientation, whereas Lu Xun's emphases were motivated by his sense of shock at his countrymen's apathy as bystanders and geared toward the urgency of national reform. For a major historical study of early East Asian cinema that elaborates the sensorial aspects of cinematic modernity, see Zhang Zhen, *An Amorous History of the Silver Screen: Shanghai Cinema, 1896–1937* (Chicago: U of Chicago P, 2005).

4. See Walter Benjamin, "The Work of Art in the Age of Mechanical Reproduction" and "On Some Motifs in Baudelaire," in *Illuminations,* trans. Harry Zohn, ed. Hannah Arendt (New York: Schocken, 1969), 217–51, 155–200. For more recent English translations of the first, widely reprinted essay, see Walter Benjamin, "The Work of Art in the Age of Its Technical Reproducibility: Second Version," in *Walter Benjamin: Selected Writings,* vol. 3, 1935–1938, trans. Edmund Jephcott et al., ed. Howard Eiland and Michael W. Jennings (Cambridge: Harvard UP, 2002), 101–33; and Walter Benjamin, "The Work of Art in the Age of Its Technological Reproducibility: Third Version," in *Walter Benjamin: Selected Writings,* vol. 4, 1938–1940, trans. Edmund Jephcott et al., ed. Howard Eiland and Michael W. Jennings. (Cambridge: Harvard UP, 2003), 251–83. The essay "On Some Motifs in Baudelaire" can also be found, with slight modifications, in *Walter Benjamin: Selected Writings,* vol. 4: 1938–1940, 313–55.

5. Tom Gunning, "'Animated Pictures': Tales of Cinema's Forgotten Future, After 100 Years of Films," in *Reinventing Film Studies,* p. 326.

6. An example is the French filmmaker and film theorist Jean Epstein's notion of *photo-génie,* the essence of film that he defines as beyond verbalization and definition. For an informative discussion, see Leo Charney, "In a Moment: Film and the Philosophy of Modernity," in *Cinema and the Invention of Modern Life,* ed. Leo Charney and Vanessa R. Schwartz (Berkeley: U of California P, 1995), 285–88.

7. See Benjamin, "What Is the Epic Theatre?" *Illuminations,* 147–54; and idem, *Understanding Brecht,* trans. Anna Bostock, intro. Stanley Mitchell (London: New Left, 1973). For a version with slight modifications, see also idem, "What Is the Epic Theater? (II)," in *Walter Benjamin: Selected Writings,* vol. 4, 1938–1940, 302–9. The notion of defamiliarization—intimately linked to the notion of art as a technique or device—can be traced to the Russian formalists, who had strongly influenced Brecht. For the work of the most well-known Russian formalists, see, for instance, *Readings in Russian Poetics: Formalist and Structuralist Views,* ed. Ladislav Matejka and Krystyna Pomorska (Cambridge, Mass.: MIT Press, 1971); and *Russian Formalism: A Collection of Articles and Texts in Translation,* ed. Stephen Bann and John E. Bowlt (New York: Barnes and Noble, 1973). See also the chapter "Russian Formalism and the Bakhtin School," in Robert Stam, *Film Theory: An Introduction* (Malden, Mass.: Blackwell, 2000), 47–54.

8. See Walter Benjamin, *The Arcades Project,* trans. Howard Eiland and Kevin McLaughlin (Cambridge: Harvard UP, 1999).

9. Benjamin's contemporary Ernst Bloch developed this forward-looking potential into a principle of hope, and his utopian argument about film and mass culture significantly influenced subsequent generations of cultural theorists, such as, notably, Fredric Jameson. See Ernst Bloch, *The Principle of Hope*, vol. 1, trans. Neville Plaice, Stephen Plaice, and Paul Knight (Cambridge, Mass.: MIT Press, 1986). See Jane Gaines's discussion of this genealogy in her "Dream/Factory," in *Reinventing Film Studies*, 100–13. For another contemporary of Benjamin's who wrote substantially on film, see Siegfried Kracauer, *Theory of Film: The Redemption of Physical Reality* (Oxford: Oxford UP, 1960). For interesting comparisons with a non-Western author's observations about cinematic shock, see Tanizaki's film writings in LaMarre, *Shadows on the Screen*.

10. André Bazin, *What Is Cinema? Essays Selected and Translated by Hugh Gray*, foreword Jean Renoir (Berkeley: U of California P; 1967), 1:14–15.

11. In this regard, Bazin, like many early film theorists, still conceptualized the cinematic in terms of its affinity with and dependency on photography. For a discussion of this tendency, see Gunning, "Animated Pictures," 322–25.

12. See André Bazin, "The Stalin Myth in Soviet Cinema" (1950), trans. Georgia Gurrieri, intro. Dudley Andrew, in *Movies and Methods*, ed. Bill Nichols (Berkeley: U of California P, 1985), 2:29–40.

13. Christian Metz, *Film Language: A Semiotics of Cinema*, trans. Michael Taylor (New York: Oxford UP, 1974); idem, *Language and Cinema*, trans. Donna Jean Umiker-Sebeok (The Hague: Mouton, 1974).

14. See Christian Metz, *The Imaginary Signifier: Psychoanalysis and the Cinema*, trans. Celia Britton, Annwyl Williams, Ben Brewster, and Alfred Guzzetti (Bloomington: Indiana UP, 1982).

15. For an illuminating historical account of the complicated tensions between semiotics and psychoanalysis within the theorizing of film, see Teresa de Lauretis, *Alice Doesn't: Feminism, Semiotics, Cinema* (Bloomington: Indiana UP, 1984). Drawing on the work of fellow feminist theorists such as Laura Mulvey, de Lauretis highlights the sexual politics inscribed in those tensions, and her own work provides a fine example of how the two models can be made to work together in film analysis. For two exemplary studies in feminist film theory during the 1980s that built on Mulvey's contributions, see Mary Ann Doane, *The Desire to Desire: The Woman's Film of the 1940s* (Bloomington: Indiana UP, 1987); and Kaja Silverman *The Acoustic Mirror: The Female Voice in Psychoanalysis and Cinema* (Bloomington: Indiana UP, 1988).

16. Andrew, "The 'Three Ages' of Cinema Studies," 344.

17. Laura Mulvey, "Visual Pleasure and Narrative Cinema," in *Visual and Other Pleasures* (Bloomington: Indiana UP, 1989), 14–26. Mulvey was not alone in her effort to theorize narrativity in relation to film. Among her fellow travelers were Jean-Louis Baudry, Christian Metz, Stephen Heath, and Paul Willemen, who each did substantive work with film narrative during the same period. See Jean-Louis Baudry, "The Apparatus," in *Narrative*,

Apparatus, Ideology: A Film Theory Reader, ed. Philip Rosen (New York: Columbia UP), 1986, 299–319; Christian Metz, *Film Language* and *Language and Cinema;* Stephen Heath, "Narrative Space," *Screen* 17.3 (1976): 68–112, and *Questions of Cinema* (Bloomington: Indiana UP, 1981); and Paul Willemen, *Looks and Frictions: Essays on Cultural Studies and Film Theory* (Bloomington: Indiana UP, 1994). Mulvey, however, was the one who raised the issue of sexual politics.

18. Mulvey, "Visual Pleasure and Narrative Cinema," 16.

19. Maggie Humm, *Feminism and Film* (Bloomington: Indiana UP, 1997), 17. Humm's book offers a thoughtful account that places Mulvey's essay in its historical context of the United Kingdom in 1960s and 1970s, when the British intellectual left encountered the burgeoning of feminist theory.

20. Martin Jay, *Downcast Eyes: The Denigration of Vision in Modern French Thought* (Berkeley: U of California P,.1993).

21. Many criticisms of Mulvey's polemic piece, including feminist criticisms of the 1980s, revolve around her point about destroying pleasure and, as a counterargument, attempt to recuperate the positive value of pleasure, especially for women spectators. My argument is quite different in that it is about the intellectually and institutionally productive—that is, reproducible—nature of Mulvey's original negative move (of deconstructing the image) and how this is thought-provokingly bound up with the iconophobia of our (image-studded) culture at large.

22. See Michel Foucault, *The History of Sexuality,* vol. 1, trans. Robert Hurley (New York: Pantheon, 1978).

23. Mulvey, "Visual Pleasure and Narrative Cinema," 14.

24. To her credit, Mulvey herself has, with historical hindsight, critiqued the binarism of her earlier polemical argument and revised her observations, See the chapter "Changes: Thoughts on Myth, Narrative and Historical Experience" (first published in 1985), in *Visual and Other Pleasures,* 159–76.

25. Bill Nichols, "Film Theory and the Revolt Against Master Narratives," in *Reinventing Film Studies,* 42.

26. See, for instance, essays in the following collections: *Unthinking Eurocentrism: Multiculturalism and the Media,* ed. Ella Shohat and Robert Stam (New York: Routledge, 1994); *Fugitive Images: From Photography to Video,* ed. Patrice Petro (Bloomington: Indiana UP, 1995); *The Image in Dispute,* ed. Dudley Andrew with Sally Shafto (Austin: Texas UP, 1997); *The Oxford Guide to Film Studies,* ed. John Hill and Pamela Church Gibson (Oxford: Oxford UP, 1998); *Visual Culture: The Reader,* ed. Jessica Evans and Stuart Hall (London: Sage, 1999); and *Popular Film and Cultural Studies,* ed. Matthew Tinkcom and Amy Villarejo (New York: Routledge, 2001).

27. Nichols, "Film Theory and the Revolt Against Master Narratives," 40.

28. As Nancy Armstrong writes: "The sixties saw an important shift in the theater of political activism from the plane of physical action and conflicts that we persist in designating as

real to the plane of discourse, representation, and performance, where conflicts deter-
mine how we imagine our relation to the real" ("Who's Afraid of the Cultural Turn?"
differences 12.1 [Spring 2001]: 42). Her essay offers an interesting discussion of the linkage
between the iconophobic legacy of Victorianism and the so-called cultural turn set off
by the media-oriented activist events of the 1960s in the United States.

29. The field of Chinese film scholarship in English provides perhaps one of the best
instances of such an academic migration. To my (obviously incomplete) knowledge,
with the exception of a few—Chris Berry, Esther C. M. Yau, Emilie Yeh Yueh-yu, Zhang
Zhen—many of those who have published on film since the early 1990s are scholars
who hold doctoral degrees in literature.

30. Gilles Deleuze, *Foucault*, trans. Sean Hand, foreword by Paul Bové (Minneapolis: U of
Minnesota P, 1988), 52, 58, and 59.

31. See, for instance, Charles Tesson, "L'Asie majeure," *Cahiers du cinema* 553 (January 2001):
5; Dave Kehr, "In Theaters Now: The Asian Alternative," *New York Times*, January 14,
2001, 2:1, 30. Apart from being featured at film festivals around the world, at which they
have been receiving major awards, East Asian films, directors, and actors and actresses
have also steadily made their way into mainstream cinematic venues in Western Europe
and North America. For a few examples of interesting book publications on East Asian
cinema in recent years, see *Cinematic Landscapes: Observations on the Visual Arts and
Cinema of China and Japan,* ed. Linda C. Erlich and David Desser (Austin: U of Texas P,
1994); David Bordwell, *Planet Hong Kong: Popular Cinema and the Art of Entertainment*
(Cambridge: Harvard UP, 2000); Mitsuhiro Yoshimoto, *Kurosawa: Film Studies and Japa-
nese Cinema* (Durham, N.C.: Duke UP, 2000); *At Full Speed: The Transnational Cinema of
Hong Kong in a Borderless World,* ed. Esther C. M. Yau (Minneapolis: U of Minnesota P,
2001); Eric Cazdyn, *The Flash of Capital: Film and Geopolitics in Japan* (Durham, N.C.:
Duke UP, 2002); Kyung Hyun Kim: *The Remasculinization of Korean Cinema* (Durham,
N.C.: Duke UP, 2004); and *South Korean Golden Age Melodrama: Gender, Genre, and
National Cinema,* ed. Kathleen McHugh and Nancy Abelmann (Detroit: Wayne State UP,
2005). For informed discussions of Asian cinemas in the discursive contexts among con-
temporary Asian cultures, see some of the essays in the special issue "Chinese Culture in
Inter-Asia," guest ed. Kwai-cheung Lo and Laikwan Pang, *Modern Chinese Literature and
Culture* 17.1 (Spring 2005).

32. For an account of the study of Chinese cinema in the West, see the chapter "The Rise of
Chinese Film Studies in the West," in Yingjin Zhang, *Screening China: Interventions, Cin-
ematic Reconfigurations, and the Transnational Imaginary in Contemporary Chinese Cinema*
(Ann Arbor: U of Michigan P, 2002), 43–113.

33. Notable examples of films include Godard's *La chinoise* (1967), *Le vent d'Est (Wind from
the East)* (1969), and *Tout va bien* (1972), while Chris Marker's *Sunday in Peking* (1956)
was among the first European documentaries to chronicle China under Mao (even
though Marker is not considered a representative of the nouvelle vague). Among the

more well-known publications by members of *Tel quel* on China, see, for instance, Julia Kristeva, *About Chinese Women*, trans. Anita Barrows (New York: Urizen, 1977); and Roland Barthes, *Alors la Chine?* (Paris: C. Bourgois, 1975). Among other well-known European endeavors to engage with China during this period and not too long afterward, see Jacques Derrida, *Of Grammatology*, trans. Gayatri Chakravorty Spivak (Baltimore: Johns Hopkins UP, 1976); the film *Chung Kuo/Cina*, directed by Michelangelo Antonioni (1972); and the film *The Last Emperor*, directed by Bernardo Bertolucci (1987).

34. It should, however, be noted that although the Chinese Communist Party was always eager to emphasize that loyalty to the party and the state must come before the family (in case of contradiction), efforts were often made to ensure that the patriarchal family system and the party could coexist in harmony. In other words, communism in China did not in actuality supplant or eradicate loyalty to the patriarchal family.

35. See, for instance, some of the essays by Mulvey in *Visual and Other Pleasures;* Tania Modleski, *Loving with a Vengeance: Mass-Produced Fantasies for Women* (Hamden, Conn.: Archon, 1982); Ien Ang, *Watching Dallas: Soap Opera and the Melodramatic Imagination*, trans. Della Couling (London: Methuen, 1985); Doane, *The Desire to Desire;* Thomas Elsaesser, "Tales of Sound and, Fury: Observations on the Family Melodrama," in *Movies and Methods*, ed. Bill Nichols (Berkeley: U of California P, 1985), 2: 165–89; Geoffrey Nowell Smith, "Minnelli and Melodrama," in *Movies and Methods*, 2:190–94; and Christine Gledhill, "Genre and Gender: The Case of Soap Opera," in *Representation: Cultural Representations and Signifying Practices*, ed. Stuart Hall (London: Sage in association with the Open University, 2003), 337–85. See also some of the essays in the following collections: *Home Is Where the Heart Is: Studies in Melodrama and the Woman's Film*, ed. Christine Gledhill (London: British Film Institute, 1987); *Melodrama: Stage, Picture, Screen*, ed. Jacky Bratton, Jim Cook, and Christine Gledhill (London: British Film Institute, 1994); and *Feminism and Film*, ed. E. Ann Kaplan (Oxford: Oxford UP, 2000). For an informative account that argues melodrama's close affiliations to genres of action and suspense (in contrast to the standard view that sees it as primarily linked to genres of passion and femininity), see Steve Neale, *Genre and Hollywood* (London: Routledge, 2000), 179–204.

36. Before the 1980s, a large number of Chinese films had been produced during various time periods—for example, the silent films from the late 1890s to the early 1930s; the nation-building patriotic films of the 1930s and beyond; films produced on the mainland during and after the reign of Mao Zedong; films in Cantonese, Chaozhouhua (Chiu Chow), Xiamenhua (Amoy), and Minnanhua (Taiwanese) as well as in Mandarin, produced in Shanghai, Taiwan, Hong Kong, and southeast Asia in the decades of the 1940s to the early 1980s. For discussions of these earlier periods, see Jay Leyda, *Dianying: An Account of Films and the Film Audience in China* (Cambridge, Mass.: MIT Press, 1972); Zhang, *The Amorous History of the Silver Screen;* Laikwan Pang, *Building a New China in Cinema: The Chinese Left-Wing Cinema Movement, 1932–1937* (Lanham, Md.: Rowman and Littlefield, 2002); Hu Jubin, *Projecting a Nation: Chinese Cinema Before 1949* (Hong

Kong: Hong Kong UP, 2003); Paul Clark, *Chinese Cinema: Culture and Politics Since 1949* (Cambridge: Cambridge UP, 1987); Ying Zhu, *Chinese Cinema During the Era of Reform: The Ingenuity of the System* (Westport, Conn.: Praeger, 2003); Poshek Fu, *Between Shanghai and Hong Kong: The Politics of Chinese Cinemas* (Stanford: Stanford UP, 2003); Chris Berry, *Postsocialist Cinema in Post-Mao China: The Cultural Revolution After the Cultural Revolution* (New York: Routledge, 2004); and Yingjin Zhang, *Screening China* and *Chinese National Cinema* (New York: Routledge, 2004). Many of these films were targeted at local audiences, though some, such as the Mandarin films produced in Taiwan and Hong Kong during the post–Second World War period, were typically subtitled in both Chinese and English and had circulations in overseas Chinese-speaking communities, such as those in Southeast Asia and North America. Before the 1980s, it was not uncommon for Chinese films to be shown at regional (especially Asian) film festivals, but few participated in international film festivals involving European and American audiences—some notable exceptions being, for instance, Tang Shuxuan's *Dong furen* (*The Arch*) (produced in 1966–67 but premiering in Hong Kong in 1969), which was invited to the Cannes Film Festival's Directors' Fortnight Section; and King Hu's *Xianü* (*A Touch of Zen*) (1975), which won a prize at the Cannes Film Festival of that year. For discussions of Tang and Hu, see Yau Ching, *Filming Margins: Tang Shu Shuen, a Forgotten Hong Kong Woman Film Director* (Hong Kong: Hong Kong UP, 2004); and, Stephen Teo, *Hong Kong Cinema: The Extra Dimensions* (London: British Film Institute, 1997), in particular 138–40, 87–100. Although this concrete and substantial historical record has begun to attract serious academic research efforts, my point is simply that none of these former periods and film productions received the scope and scale of international attention that Chinese cinema began to command as a phenomenon beginning in the mid-1980s. I believe it is this international attention, rather than the historical record itself, that has made the study of Chinese film in English so popular these days.

37. In the Chinese language, various publications have debated the becoming-visible of Chinese cinema in sophisticated terms, though, understandably, these publications tend not to take into consideration the history of film studies in the English-speaking world in which I am locating my inquiry. See, for instance, some of the essays in *Wenhua piping yu huayu dianying* (*Cultural Criticism and Chinese Cinema*), ed. William Tay, intro. Liao Ping-hui (Taipei: Ryefield, 1995); and *Houzhimin lilun yu wenhua rentong* (*Postcolonial Criticism and Cultural Identity*), ed. Zhang Jingyuan (Taipei: Ryefield, 1995). For some of the essays by the well-known mainland Chinese film scholar Dai Jinhua that have been translated into English, see *Cinema and Desire: Feminist Marxism and Cultural Politics in the Work of Dai Jinhua*, ed. Jing Wang and Tani E. Barlow (London: Verso, 2002). For related interest, see also various discussions in the following publications: *Transnational Chinese Cinemas: Identity, Nationhood, Gender*, ed. Sheldon Hsiao-peng Lu (Honolulu: U of Hawaii P, 1997); David Bordwell, *Planet Hong Kong;* Ni Zhen, *Memoirs of the Beijing Film Academy: The Genesis of China's Fifth Generation*, trans. Chris Berry (Durham, N.C.:

Duke UP, 2002); June Yip, *Envisioning Taiwan: Fiction, Cinema, and the Nation in the Cultural Imaginary* (Durham, N.C.: Duke UP, 2004); Paul Clark, *Reinventing China: A Generation and Its Films* (Hong Kong: Chinese UP, 2005), and Chris Berry and Mary Farquhar, *China on Screen: Nation and Cinema* (New York: Columbia UP, 2005).

38. For an informed reappraisal, based on knowledge of the Chinese language as well as of German and French, of the work of Brecht and the journal *Tel quel* in relation to Chinese art and politics, see Eric Hayot, *Chinese Dreams: Pound, Brecht, Tel Quel* (Ann Arbor: U of Michigan P, 2004), 54–102, 103–75.

39. John Frow, referring to Alastair Fowler's *Kinds of Literature: An Introduction to the Theory of Genres and Modes* (Cambridge: Harvard UP, 1982), has provided a succinct formulation of the term "mode" that I find helpful: "What I would . . . like to suggest is that the term 'mode' be reserved for use in . . . the 'adjectival' sense . . . , in which modes are understood as the extensions of certain genres beyond specific and time-bound formal structures to a broader specification of 'tone'" (*Genre* [London: Routledge, 2006], 65).

40. Sir Leslie Stephen defined the sentimental as "the name of the mood in which we make a luxury of grief" in *English Thought in the Eighteenth Century* (London: Smith, Elder, 1902), 2: 436, quoted in Janet Todd, *Sensibility: An Introduction* (London: Methuen, 1986), 7.

41. Friedrich Schiller, *On Naïve and Sentimental Poetry* (1795–96), trans. Julius A. Elias (slightly modified), excerpted in *The Origins of Modern Critical Thought: German Aesthetic and Literary Criticism from Lessing to Hegel*, ed. David Simpson (Cambridge: Cambridge UP, 1988), 148–73; the quoted statements can be found on pp. 155, 156, 158.

42. Ibid., 170.

43. See Raymond Williams, *Keywords: A Vocabulary of Culture and Society*, rev. ed. (London: Fontana, 1983), 280–83, for a brief account of the evolution of the word "sensibility," including its important relation to the word "sentimental" in the eighteenth and nineteenth centuries. In the English-speaking world, a classic treatise is Adam Smith, *The Theory of Moral Sentiments* (1759), ed. Knud Haakonssen (Cambridge: Cambridge UP, 2002), in which Smith, extending the work of moral-sense philosophers such as, Francis Hutcheson and David Hume, elaborated, the notions of sympathy—an imaginative sharing or agreement of feelings that is not simply benevolence—and of the mental construct of an impartial spectator as bases for his theory of conscience and moral judgment.

44. For an informative study of the controversy of sentimentalism in British writings, see Markman Ellis, *The Politics of Sensibility: Race, Commerce and the Sentimental Novel* (Cambridge: Cambridge UP, 1996).

45. For a comparative study that discusses the English, French, and German literary and philosophical contributions to these debates, see James A. Steintrager, *Cruel Delight: Enlightenment Culture and the Inhuman* (Bloomington: Indiana UP, 2004).

46. [Here Chow offers a list of suggested readings that space does not allow us to reproduce (Paul Bowman).]

47. As Ellis puts it in regard to the sentimental novel: "Paradoxically, . . . by addressing an audience that was disenfranchised and lacking power in political life, the sentimental novel effectively created a new political role for literature" (*The Politics of Sensibility*, p. 3).

48. For comparative interest, see Ben Singer, *Melodrama and Modernity: Early Sensational Cinema and Its Contexts* (New York: Columbia UP, 2001), in particular chap. 2. Singer defines melodrama as a "cluster concept"—"a term whose meaning varies from case to case in relation to different configurations of a range of basic features or constitutive factors" (44). The five basic features Singer elaborates are listed in n. 46, above. Although I have found the melodramatic and the sentimental to intersect on some occasions, I do not consider them to be identical phenomena.

49. This interesting reading was suggested by one of the anonymous reviewers of the manuscript. Obviously, a full-fledged discussion of the (re)turn to medium and ontology will have to be saved for another occasion.

13. THE POLITICAL ECONOMY OF VISION IN *HAPPY TIMES* AND *NOT ONE LESS*

1. See in particular part 2, chapter 4 of *Primitive Passions: Visuality, Sexuality, Ethnography, and Contemporary Chinese Cinema* (New York: Columbia UP, 1995).

2. This point, which necessitates a detailed discussion of the history of modern Chinese literature and its study, is obviously one that I can only mention but not substantiate here.

3. Outside academia, there is the additional problem, perpetrated by international film audiences, including organizers of international film festivals, of viewing films from China categorically as being either antigovernment or representing government propaganda. This was the reason Zhang Yimou withdrew *Not One Less* and *The Road Home* from the Cannes International Film Festival in 1999 (see the brief mention of this in the *New York Times*, April 21, 1999, B8). In his letter to the festival organizers, excerpted in the Chinese-language media during that period, Zhang indicated that *Not One Less* was intended as an expression of his love for children and his concern for the current and future conditions of his people's culture as a whole and that *The Road Home* was meant to be a celebration of pure, innocent love.

4. See, for instance, the discussions of Zhang's evolving work in the group of essays devoted to *Not One Less* under the title *Yige dou buneng shao yingpian gean fenxi*, in *Zhongguo dianying meixue: 1999* (*Aesthetics of Chinese Film: 1999*), ed. Hu Ke et al. (Beijing: Beijing Broadcasting Institute, October 2000); and various discussions of the film in *Dianying yishu* (*Film Art*), no. 5 (September 10, 1999), no. 3 (May, 2000), and no, 1 (January 5, 2001).

5. See Zhang Yiwu, "Zaidu xiangxiang zhongguo: quanqiuhua de tiaozhan yu xin de 'neixianghua'" (Once again imagining China: The challenge of globalization and the new "inward-looking tendency"), *Dianying yishu*, no: 1 (January 5, 2001): 16–21. According to

Zhang Yiwu, films made by the Fifth Generation directors in the 1980s represented a brief period in which the directors reacted against the inward-looking tradition in Chinese cinema (a cinema that concerns itself primarily with Chinese history and society) to create an outward-looking one intent on drawing the attention of the rest of the world. With most of the world in economic recession and the oversells market for Chinese film dwindling in recent years, however, that outward-looking moment, argues Zhang, has passed. Globalization, he suggests, has led paradoxically to a renewal of the tradition of inward-looking cinema, centered on China's internal problems and produced for a predominantly Chinese audience. He writes: "Globalization is not just a background but a problem internal to film" (19; my translation).

6. Zhang himself sums up these reactions in good humor: "I always feel that there are two schools of criticism out there when it comes to my films. They say that I'm trying to kiss either foreigners' asses or the Chinese government's ass. I always jokingly respond that I'm actually kissing my own ass! . . . In the eyes of many, I am an opportunist. They think I sit around all day devising schemes to win the approval of foreigners or the Chinese government. . . . It is a big source of uneasiness for me, but what can I do?" (quoted in Michael Berry, *Speaking in Images: Interviews with Contemporary Chinese Filmmakers* [New York: Columbia UP, 2005], 126). For discussions related to the implications of orientalism in Zhang's work, including Zhang's responses to some of his critics, see, for instance, the interviews with Zhang regarding the making of *Not One Less* in the following: *Zhongguo dianying meixue: 1999*, 29–35; *Jiushi niandaide diwudai* (*The Fifth Generation of Chinese Filmmakers in the 1990s*), ed. Yang Yuanying (Beijing: Beijing Broadcasting Institute, November 2000), 121–27. For general interest, see also *Zhang Yimou: Interviews*, ed. Frances Gateward (Jackson: U of Mississippi P, 2001).

7. See Shi Wenhongi, "Yige dou buneng shao de aichou" (The sadness of *Not One Less*), *Yingpingren jikan* (*Film Critics Quarterly*), no. 6 (2000): 7.

8. For a sustained critique of the periodical's politics of representing non-Western cultures, see Catherine A. Lutz and Jane L. Collins, *Reading National Geographic* (Chicago: U of Chicago P, 1993).

9. The cast of *Not One Less*, for instance, was made up of amateur actors, many of whom were actual villagers from the film's location. Some of these villagers' names were used for characters' names in the film. As Xiaoling Zhang points out, however, "the whole suggestion of reality is entirely artificial: the school was chosen from a few dozen schools in that area, the eighteen pupils were selected from among thousands of pupils, and the girl playing Wei Minzhi was picked from twenty thousand girls, in an auditioning process which lasted more than half a month" ("A Film Director's Criticism of Reform China: A Close Reading of Zhang Yimou's *Not One Less*," *China Information* 25.2 (2001): 138.

10. As Zhang puts it forthrightly:

[The critics] think I have no passion for cinema and everything I do is driven by a certain objective. You can say all I care about is kissing up to foreign audiences or the Chinese government. Fine, I don't care. But saying I have no love for the art of cinema and accusing me of using cinema as a tool to achieve my own personal objective is a fundamental negation of my commitment to the art form. Although I don't like it, I don't bother explaining myself. You can hate my films, but no one can accuse me of not loving the art of film. As a filmmaker that is the greatest insult one can receive. (Berry, *Speaking in Images*, 127)

11.   As one critic, Zeng Guang writes: "Under the current political system, he [Zhang Yimou] feels that the biggest difference between himself and directors from foreign countries, Hong Kong, and Taiwan lies in the fact that 'when I receive a film script, the first thing I think about is not whether there will be an investor for the film, but how I can make the kind of film I want with the approval of the authorities.'" This passage is cited as the epigraph in Sheldon H. Lu, "Understanding Chinese Film Culture at the End of the Twentieth Century: The Case of *Not One Less* by Zhang Yimou," *Journal of Modern Literature in Chinese* 4.2 (January 2001): 123–42.

12.   For an earlier, perhaps even more remarkable example of such a cinematic staging method, see my discussion of Zhang's 1994 film *Huo zhe* (*To Live*) in the chapter "We Endure, Therefore We Are: Survival, Governance, and Zhang Yimou's *To Live*," in *Ethics after Idealism: Theory—Culture—Ethnicity—Reading* (Bloomington: Indiana UP, 1998), 113–32. This chapter is a revised version of an essay initially published in the *South Atlantic Quarterly* 95.4 (Fall 1996): 1039–64. Zhang considers *To Live* as "the film closest to [him]"; see his remarks in Berry, *Speaking in Images*, 127–29.

13.   Zhang also made an alternative ending, in the version of the film officially released outside the People's Republic, that averts attention from the big economic picture by focusing on the personal stories. In this version, after writing the fake letter to the blind girl, Lao Zhao is hit by a truck and goes into a coma. The blind girl, not knowing what has happened, decides to move on so that she will no longer be a burden. She leaves behind a tape on which she thanks Lao Zhao for what he has done for her, explaining that she has known all along about the lies but appreciates the intentions behind them. As Lao Zhao's friends listen to the tape while reading aloud Lao Zhao's fake letter, the final scene shows the blind girl walking down the street alone. In his interview with Michael Berry, Zhang Yimou indicates that he was dissatisfied with both endings and classifies *Happy Times* as "a weaker work," in which "neither the style nor the inner philosophical underpinnings of the film ever really came out" (Berry, *Speaking in Images*, 126).

14.   Naomi Schor, "Blindness as Metaphor," *differences* 11.2 (Summer 1999): 88; emphasis in the original. In this semiautobiographical essay, Schor argues for seeing blindness (and other forms of physical deprivation) as part of a human sensorium in its full range of complexity and not simply as a negative version of a normal, healthy body: "The realm

of the senses must . . . be extended to include all manner of sensual deprivation: lack of vision, lack of hearing, lack of speech, lack of taste, lack of smell, lack of touch" (83).

15. See Dave Kehr, "Beyond Glamour There's Humor," "At the Movies" sec., *New York Times*, July 26, 2002, B11. Since Zhang does not speak English, the quoted remarks are most likely a loose translation of what he actually said in Chinese.

16. Michael Dutton, "Street Scenes of Subalternity: China, Globalization, and Rights," in *Whither China? Intellectual Politics in Contemporary China*, ed. Xudong Zhang (Durham, N.C.: Duke UP, 2001), 355, 358. This essay is based on arguments excerpted from Dutton, *Streetlife China* (Cambridge: Cambridge UP, 1998).

17. Note that although the film was adopted from Shi Xiangsheng's story "Tian shang you ge taiyang" (A sun in the sky), *Feitian*, no. 6 (1997) (as cited in Zhang, "A Film Director's Criticism of Reform China," 136, n. 13), Zhang Yimou changed the title to one that highlights the act of counting (bodies).

18. Wang Yichuan, "Wenming yu wenming de yeman" (Civilization and civilized barbarity), *Zhongguo dianying meixue*, 1999, 67–75; the cited passages are on 71 and 73; the loose translation from the Chinese is mine. Among the readings that were published shortly after the film's release in China in 1999, this is the only one I have come across that pointedly identifies money and the media as what constitute the decisive structural significance of the narrative. For an account of the success of *Not One Less* in the People's Republic and the related issue of television's popularity in China today (including how the television episode in the film was modeled after two popular television programs on CCTV in the 1990s), see Laikwan Pang, "Piracy/Privacy: The Despair of Cinema and Collectivity in China," *boundary* 2 31.3 (Fall 2004): 117–22.

19. As Jacques Derrida has written, "What the accelerated development of teletechnologies, of cyberspace, of the new topology of 'the virtual' is producing is a practical *deconstruction* of the traditional and dominant concepts of the state and citizen (and thus of 'the political') as they are linked to the actuality of a territory" (Jacques Derrida and Bernard Stiegler, *Echographies of Television: Filmed Interviews*, trans. Jennifer Bajorek [Cambridge: Polity, 2002], 36; emphasis in the original).

20. Hu Ke writes that Zhang's narrative method is like an "ad for charity." See his "Jishi yu xugou" (Documentary record and fictional construct), *Zhongguo dianying meixue: 1999*, 41–49; the point about "ad for charity" is on 42. This view is shared by other critics: see, for instance, Wang Ailing, "Tinghua de haizi" (Obedient children), in *1999 Xianggang dianying huigu* (A look back at Hong Kong cinema of 1999) (Hong Kong: Xianggang dianying pinglun xuehui, 2000), 301–302; Valerie Wong, "*Not One Less*," *Cinemaya*, no. 45 (1999): 20–21. This type of reading is not incorrect, but the main problem I have with it is that these critics tend to read Zhang's film as a *completed* realist message rather than as a process and a structure in which a dialectical understanding (of the changes brought to Chinese society by the new media) is being actively and aesthetically produced. While they are undoubtedly right about the explicit propaganda at the end of the film, they tend

to miss the significance of the presence of other propaganda messages (including the moral virtues of frugality and hard work and the rationalistic logic, internalized by poor people, of equating units of physical labor with units of financial reward), a presence that is staged throughout the entire film. For an opposite type of reading that approaches Zhang's film not as propaganda but as a laudable piece of social criticism, See Zhang, "A Film Director's Criticism of Reform China."

21. For a discussion of this point as well as an informative discussion of Zhang's film in relation to recent conditions of film production and reception in mainland China, see Lu; "Understanding Chinese Film Culture at the End of the Twentieth Century."

Index